POLITICS, VIOLENCE, MEMORY

POLITICS, VIOLENCE, MEMORY

The New Social Science of the Holocaust

Edited by Jeffrey S. Kopstein, Jelena Subotić, and Susan Welch

CORNELL UNIVERSITY PRESS   ITHACA AND LONDON

Copyright © 2023 by Cornell University

All rights reserved. Except for brief quotations in a review, this book, or parts thereof, must not be reproduced in any form without permission in writing from the publisher. For information, address Cornell University Press, Sage House, 512 East State Street, Ithaca, New York 14850. Visit our website at cornellpress.cornell.edu.

First published 2023 by Cornell University Press

Library of Congress Cataloging-in-Publication Data

Names: Kopstein, Jeffrey, editor. | Subotić, Jelena, editor. | Welch, Susan, editor.
Title: Politics, violence, memory : the new social science of the Holocaust / edited by Jeffrey S. Kopstein, Jelena Subotić, and Susan Welch.
Description: Ithaca : Cornell University Press, 2023. | Includes bibliographical references and index.
Identifiers: LCCN 2022016908 (print) | LCCN 2022016909 (ebook) | ISBN 9781501766749 (hardback) | ISBN 9781501766756 (paperback) | ISBN 9781501766763 (pdf) | ISBN 9781501766770 (epub)
Subjects: LCSH: Holocaust, Jewish (1939–1945)—Historiography. | Holocaust, Jewish (1939–1945)—Research. | Social sciences and history. | Social sciences—Research. | Interdisciplinary research.
Classification: LCC D804.348 . P64 2023 (print) | LCC D804.348 (ebook) | DDC 940.53/180722—dc23/eng/20220609
LC record available at https://lccn.loc.gov/2022016908
LC ebook record available at https://lccn.loc.gov/2022016909

In memory of Susan Welch

Contents

Preface and Acknowledgments	ix
Introduction: A Response Delayed *Jeffrey S. Kopstein, Jelena Subotić, and Susan Welch*	1
1. Can—or Should—There Be a Political Science of the Holocaust? *Charles King*	21
2. Histories in Motion: The Holocaust, Social Science Research, and the Historian *Jan Burzlaff*	53

Part I SITES OF VIOLENCE

3. Pogrom Violence and Visibility during the Kristallnacht Pogrom *Daniel Solomon*	69
4. Historical Legacies and Jewish Survival Strategies during the Holocaust *Eugene Finkel*	87
5. A Common History of Violence?: The Pogroms of Summer 1941 in Comparative Perspective *Jeffrey S. Kopstein*	104
6. Mass Violence without Mass Politics: Political Culture and the Holocaust in Lithuania *Benjamin Mishkin*	124

PART II NEW USES FOR OLD DATA ON ANTISEMITISM AND THE HOLOCAUST

7. Territorial Loss and Xenophobia in the Weimar Republic: Evidence from Jewish Bogeymen in Children's Stories *Robert Braun*	139

CONTENTS

8. Defeating Typhus in the Warsaw Ghetto: A Scientific Look at Historical Sources — 159
Lewi Stone and Stephan Lehnstaedt

9. Holocaust Survival among Immigrant Jews in the Netherlands: A Life Course Approach — 177
Peter Tammes and Andrew J. Simpkin

10. Normalizing Violence: How Catholic Bishops Facilitated Vichy's Violence against Jews — 196
Aliza Luft

11. Using the Yad Vashem Transport Database to Examine Gender and Selection during the Holocaust — 211
Susan Welch

12. Addressing the Missing Voices in Holocaust Testimony — 226
Rachel L. Einwohner

PART III LEGACIES OF THE HOLOCAUST

13. Remembering Past Atrocities: Good or Bad for Attitudes toward Minorities? — 245
Volha Charnysh

14. Legitimating Myths and the Holocaust in Postsocialist States — 267
Zvi Gitelman

15. The International Relations of Holocaust Memory — 283
Jelena Subotić

Conclusion: From the Micro to the Macro — 297
Daniel Ziblatt

Notes — 307
Notes on Contributors — 319
Index — 325

Preface and Acknowledgments

This book's journey began with two observations. The first was our sense that until recently, social science had largely ignored the Holocaust. We found this puzzling because so many of the concepts and theories in contemporary social science had their origins in the aftermath of the destruction of European Jewry. Even with this broadly acknowledged foundational background to modern social science, it is remarkable how few social scientists devoted their scholarly energies to understanding and explaining the causes and consequences of the event itself. There were, of course, important exceptions, but the relative silence of our own disciplines stands in stark contrast to our colleagues in history departments, whose many years of research on the Holocaust has yielded an outpouring of important scholarship.

Our second observation was that, over the past decade, things have started to change. Social scientists from a broad spectrum of disciplines, especially political science and sociology but also demography, economics, psychology, geography, and public health, have begun to ask new kinds of questions, adduce new evidence, and develop new theories and methods for understanding the sources, processes, and impact of the Holocaust. In doing so, they have not only added new layers of understanding to the mass killing, but also initiated the important work of reintegrating the study of the Holocaust into the mainstream of social science. Our goal in editing this book, therefore, is to showcase some of the more interesting contributions to this new research and to set the stage for further inquiry.

The contributors to this volume bring the distinctive scholarly methods and theories of their fields, but all remain committed to the twin projects of Holocaust research and theoretical advancement. These twin commitments may leave "purists" among historians and social scientists dissatisfied, but both projects enrich each other, and each one, we maintain, would be impoverished without the other.

The chapters were originally presented as papers at a conference, "The Holocaust and Social Science Research," held at the University of California, Irvine on January 21–22, 2020, just before the university moved to fully remote operations in the face of the COVID-19 pandemic. They were substantially revised after several rounds of comments. We thank the contributors to and participants in the conference, especially those who gave important feedback on the papers. We were fortunate not only to have convened just in time, but also to have had the financial assistance of UCI's School of Social Sciences, Center for the Study of Democracy, and Center for Jewish Studies. Beyond UCI, we thank Georgia State University, especially the Center for Human Rights and Democracy, for financial support, and Saad Khan for editorial assistance. The Pennsylvania State University's College of the Liberal Arts, Jewish Studies Program, and Department of Political Science also provided generous support.

We also owe a debt of gratitude to our editors at Cornell University Press, Roger Haydon and Jim Lance, for their patience and for their confidence in this project.

Susan Welch passed away during the production of this book. A force within political science, Susan served for almost three decades as dean of liberal arts at Pennsylvania State University. In her final years she devoted her formidable scholarly energies to a deeper understanding of the Holocaust using the tools of modern social science. It is fitting, therefore, that this book is dedicated to her memory.

Jeffrey S. Kopstein
Jelena Subotić
Susan Welch

POLITICS, VIOLENCE, MEMORY

Introduction

A RESPONSE DELAYED

Jeffrey S. Kopstein, Jelena Subotić, and Susan Welch

We live in a culture profoundly influenced by the legacy of the Holocaust. More than seventy-five years later, the Nazi extermination effort against the world's Jews continues to provide the moral lens through which we judge political action. Debates about humanitarian intervention and foreign policy, democracy and authoritarianism, the politics of race, refugees, migration, and citizenship, and perhaps most importantly, our understanding of political violence have taken shape in the shadow of the destruction of European Jewry. The very categories we deploy to think about these matters—the most famous example being the concept of genocide—were developed in an attempt to understand the magnitude of what had occurred and to prevent anything like it from happening again. The Holocaust therefore functions as a "shadow case" of sorts, a yardstick against which to compare a broad range of contemporary social and political processes. And yet, despite the centrality of the Holocaust to the way social scientists think about today's world, study of the event itself and its aftermath has remained largely peripheral to the social sciences, such as economics, geography, political science, psychology, and sociology.[1]

How can we account for the relative absence of interest among social scientists in what is surely the index case of violence in the modern era? Explaining silence is not easy, but it is perhaps helpful to recall that research on the Holocaust did not commence immediately after 1945. There was a significant delay. Today we tend to think of the Holocaust as the most important aspect of World War II, but this intuition is one of recent vintage.[2] Historians have long pointed to the remarkable public silence on Jewish victimhood and the Holocaust itself in virtually every country in the world until the 1960s, and in many respects until the 1980s. In Europe, the Cold War transformed West Germany into an ally, and Germans, while not directly denying the crimes of Nazi perpetrators, mostly stayed silent on the details of the Holocaust—and were permitted to do so. France and the Netherlands avoided tarnishing their self-conceptions as occupied nations that had resisted with uncomfortable questions about collaboration. Communist Europe chose to assimilate Jewish victimhood into crimes against "peaceful citizens" and abjured the use of the word "Holocaust" altogether. In the United States, where the bulk of the world's Jews lived after the war, until the 1960s Jews remained sufficiently concerned about securing their place within US society not to single themselves out as a motivation for the war. Even Israelis avoided the subject, out of both a sense of shame about the *yishuv* having been able to do so little to save Europe's doomed Jewish population and a determination to "negate" the diasporic image of Jews having gone "like sheep to the slaughter" (Segev 1993).[3]

Perhaps understandably, the early studies of the Nazi regime came not primarily from historians but from German social theorists and philosophers, such as Franz Neumann (1942), Hannah Arendt (1951), and Gerald Reitlinger (1956), who explored how modernity could generate such monstrous outcomes.[4] After a slow and hesitant start, by the 1980s and especially during the 1990s, with the opening of the archives in Eastern Europe, Holocaust historians produced a huge quantity of important books and articles on the subject. They asked broad questions, first about German perpetrators, Nazi decision-making, and the implementation of the Final Solution, before moving to closer studies of collaboration, victims, members of communities where the Holocaust transpired, and the Holocaust itself as a transnational, even global, period of history.[5]

But the social sciences remained remarkably silent. In fact, since the early 1950s, social scientists have largely ignored the Holocaust. In this introduction, we begin by outlining some possible professional, political, and demographic reasons for social scientists' limited attention to the Holocaust. While the family of social sciences is large, our focus is primarily on political science, sociology, and demography.[6] We first discuss the analytic framework that has developed to enable these social scientists to begin to make significant contributions to our understanding of the Holocaust, a framework that complements but does not displace the pathbreaking work of Holocaust historians. We then turn to the importance of social scientific research. Sustained social scientific engagement with the Holocaust, we maintain, will benefit our various disciplines, our understanding of the Holocaust, and the new generation of scholars ready to take up this challenge.

Social science is the systematic study of interpretive beings.[7] It is especially self-reflective about methodology, evidence, and empirical generalization. All of these features combine to make it a particularly "modern" way of knowing. It is precisely because of its use of modern methods and its quest for value neutrality that scholars have repeatedly implicated social science in the Holocaust itself (for example, Bauman 1989). The Nazis deployed the concepts and tools of anthropology, demography, economics, geography, political science, and sociology, along with other scientific fields such as statistics, biology, chemistry, and medicine, in planning and carrying out mass murder (see, for example, Barnes and Minca 2013). The study of Generalplan Ost—the Nazi plan for the colonization of Eastern Europe—makes this abundantly clear (Aly and Heim 2003; Suhr 2012). Even though our book does not focus on the contribution of social scientists to the Holocaust, such complicity must be acknowledged.

But having acknowledged this fact, we must also point out that other ways of knowing are also implicated in the Holocaust, ways of knowing generally seen today—but not at the time—as less scientific, most obviously eugenics and race science, but also other less "modern" epistemic frameworks, such as Christian theology, nationalist historiography, mysticism, and even legal philosophy and *Staatslehre* (political science or theories of the state; see Rosenberg [1937]). Each has its respective place in the history of European anti-Judaism, violent and militarized antisemitism, and the lawless *Unrechtstaat* that carried out the destruction of Europe's Jews. It is inappropriate to implicate any single way of knowing on its own, scientific or otherwise, as being causally responsible for the Holocaust. Moreover, this mass killing required nonscientific power to occur. Nazis eviscerated a huge portion of actual scholarship, and most of what passed for social science in Hitler's Europe does not deserve the name.

In what follows, after establishing the scope of the volume and its theoretical, methodological, and empirical ambitions, we provide its general overview, illuminating the common threads that tie the chapters together, particularly the theoretical and methodological contributions that other fields bring to the study of the Holocaust and the value of Holocaust research to other social science fields. Specifically, we argue that social scientific engagement with the Holocaust is necessary because, without it, we lose the extreme example of so many significant concepts and causal explanations in our disciplines.

Why Haven't Social Scientists Studied the Holocaust?

In the immediate aftermath of World War II, several social scientists wrote groundbreaking volumes on what we now term the Holocaust. Eugene Kogan (1950), trained as a sociologist and economist, published *The Theory and Practice of Hell*, an examination of Nazi concentration camps based on his own six years of imprisonment at Buchenwald. In 1961, Raul Hilberg, an Austrian-born American political scientist who had been stationed in Germany after the war, published *The Destruction of the European Jews*, a pioneering work that focused on the administrative and organizational structures that led to mass murder.[8] Jewish refugees from Germany and Austria led the collaboration that resulted in *The Authoritarian Personality*, the influential work on the formation of antisemitism and individual-level authoritarian orientations that were understood to underpin the Nazi regime (Adorno et al. 1950). That book, by the sociologists and psychologists Theodor Adorno, Else Frenkel-Brunswik, Daniel Levinson, and Nevitt Sanford, has been cited nearly twenty thousand times and remains influential today.

These works joined the canon of Holocaust scholarship in the West. Sometime after 1960, however, social science contributions became scarce. Both global politics and social science changed dramatically. The Federal Republic of Germany became a Western ally and the Soviet Union the new enemy. Interest in the war faded. Some perpetrators assumed important government positions in Germany; others were brought to the US (and the Soviet Union), where some former Nazi scientists were prominent in elite fields, including space and armaments programs. Jewish survivors of the mass murders wrote and spoke little about their experiences, at least publicly. In Israel, many were met with suspicion and disdain. Most of the records of the atrocities that had occurred in Eastern Europe were now behind the Iron Curtain. The Soviets were not interested in highlighting, or even acknowledging, the suffering of the Jews, even when they were not pursuing their own antisemitic policies. In the West, there was little desire to look past the stock tales of resistance and mythology of national heroism to deal with the horrific consequences of widespread collaboration and accommodation.

Social science changed too, as scholars began to explore new questions with new techniques. More social scientists developed expertise in quantitative analyses, moving to sophisticated methodological approaches based on survey research and other larger data sources. Although they could theoretically have deployed these techniques to study the causes and consequences of anti-Jewish violence during the war, very few did.[9] Social scientists appeared to have little interest in studying the mass slaughter of the Jews, and data that might have been used to document that suffering lay in archives untouched, and in many cases unavailable.

In the late 1970s, however, public attention to the Holocaust grew. Interest in the Holocaust, and indeed in the label "Holocaust," was sparked by the 1978 US television miniseries by that name (Friess 2015), watched by nearly half the US population (according to a Gallup poll in April 1978) and by one-third of the German viewing population (McGuinness 2019). The number of popular films focusing on Holocaust themes increased dramatically in the 1980s, including Claude Lanzmann's 1985 film *Shoah,* and the Academy Award–winning films *Sophie's Choice* (1982) and *Schindler's List* (1993). Another miniseries, *War and Remembrance,* engaged American and then global audiences a decade after *Holocaust.*

The collapse of the Soviet empire at the end of the 1980s provided new access to material documenting the actions of perpetrators, victims, and communities. The widespread availability of the internet just a few years later facilitated the public dissemination of information about the Holocaust that had, up to then, been found only in archives and scattered libraries. Thirty years later, survivors, motivated by, among other things, the need to answer a new generation's questions and the urgent sense that their stories needed to be preserved, began to publish diaries and write memoirs of their own experiences in increasingly large numbers.[10]

What explains the reluctance of social scientists to write about the Holocaust during this period? Any answer to this is necessarily speculative, but we can begin with the place of Jews in US society and within the social sciences.

After World War II, Jews took up prominent places in US society, especially within the increasingly prestigious social sciences. Although no disciplinary census existed in either political science or sociology that distinguished Jews as a separate category (indeed, Jews would probably have resisted this), Jewish social scientists have long noted their disproportionate presence at professional meetings and in department rosters—mostly using the "family name" test. One would reasonably expect Holocaust research to have emanated from successive large cohorts of Jewish political scientists, sociologists, anthropologists, and economists, but very little did. One reason may have been professional incentives. In search of integration into the broader society and prestige within their own disciplines, Jewish social scientists—most notably within political science—avoided explicitly "Jewish topics" in their research. Doing so, many felt, risked self-marginalization and missing out on contributing to more high-profile and career-defining debates within their disciplines. Most of those who did write on Jewish topics did so only as part of a broader panoply of interests. The risk of professional isolation was simply too high.

Some scholars trained in the social sciences did work on the Holocaust, but their experience provided a cautionary tale to younger scholars. Raul Hilberg began writing what became his two-volume study as a political science dissertation under the supervision of Franz Neumann at Columbia University (awarded in 1955), but Neumann warned him that such a dissertation would amount to professional suicide. "He knew," wrote Hilberg later, "that at this moment I was separating myself from the mainstream of academic research to tread in territory that had been avoided by the academic world and the public alike" (1996, 66). Hilberg landed a position in political science, but neither political scientists nor historians ever fully embraced his work during his lifetime.

Jan Gross, having made his career in the US within sociology after leaving Poland in 1969, published a series of books on the Soviet and German occupation of Poland during the war before turning to the Holocaust itself. His pathbreaking book *Neighbors* (2002) documented a gruesome massacre carried out by ethnic Poles against their Jewish fellow citizens in Jedwabne, Poland, in 1941, while Germans hovered nearby. Gross followed this study with two further books on the antisemitic aftermath of the Holocaust in Poland (Gross 2007; Gross and Gross 2012). Although respected within sociology, his work over the years was read and discussed primarily by historians, and after the publication of *Neighbors*, Gross migrated into a history department.

The political scientist Daniel Jonah Goldhagen's *Hitler's Willing Executioners* (1997) grew out of his dissertation, which won the American Political Science Association's Gabriel Almond Award in comparative politics. Again, however, his audience and readership in the academy consisted mostly of historians, and they were the ones to respond to his provocative thesis that the roots of the Nazi extermination effort were to be found in an "eliminationist antisemitism" in Germany extending back into modern and even premodern German history. That historians responded more vigorously made sense. Goldhagen could speak in the idiom of social science, but his work took aim elsewhere, at a new generation of historians of Nazi perpetrators who had highlighted bureaucratic command, psychological obedience to authority, or avarice rather than ideology. *Hitler's Willing Executioners* was roundly criticized by historians for its dogged focus on the long history of German antisemitism, but the heated debate barely registered in his own discipline.[11] Kristen Renwick Monroe's engagement of Goldhagen in a critical review of his book (1997) was a significant exception. Her work on rescue (Monroe 1996), and that of sociologist Nechama Tec (1987) also contributed to an important discourse on the correlates of altruism and the political psychology of perpetrators, bystanders, and rescuers within genocide, but scholars in neither discipline took up the challenge of the further research for which both Monroe and Tec had called.

In the early 1960s, the psychologist Stanley Milgram (2009) performed a series of experiments that seemed to show that ordinary people would follow orders to inflict pain on others when directed to by those in authority.[12] Influenced by the Eichmann trial in 1961, his experiments tried to explain why so many Germans participated in the Holocaust. Milgram's Jewish identity was important to him, the son of Jewish Eastern European World War I immigrants and part of the family that welcomed their Holocaust survivor relatives after World War II

(Blass 1988, 49–51). His first article on the topic of obedience became a classic but was also widely criticized for leading subjects to believe they were inflicting pain on others (Milgram 1963). Harvard denied him tenure and the American Psychological Association held up his membership (though years later they gave him a prize for his work on obedience).[13]

Milgram's work directly underpinned innovative scholarship on the Holocaust. In *Ordinary Men*, the historian Christopher Browning examined the reasons why men of Reserve Police Battalion 101 were willing to murder tens of thousands of Polish Jews and round up tens of thousands of others for deportations to the Treblinka death camp (Browning 1992). Based on postwar interviews done in conjunction with war crimes trials, he highlighted the motivations of this group of "ordinary," largely working-class, middle-aged German men of the battalion. Most were neither Nazi Party members nor professional police. Though a significant minority (10 to 20 percent) would not participate in the mass murders, most followed orders and did so. Browning attributed this both to their willingness to obey their superiors, as Milgram had shown, and to group pressure to conform.

These examples notwithstanding, it was not until the study of discrete racial, ethnic, and gender groups became legitimized within the social sciences, especially by way of African American, Latinx, and women's studies, that "Jewish topics" such as the Holocaust slowly found their way into the mainstream. Within the firmament of the North American academy, the current generation of scholars, Jewish and non-Jewish, many of whom have contributed to this book, may have had the professional disincentives to studying the Holocaust reduced by scholars of other ethnic and identity groups. Within political science in particular, perhaps nothing illustrates the delay in taking up the Holocaust as an object of study more poignantly than the fact that the first panel in the history of the annual meeting of the American Political Science Association devoted entirely to the subject appeared in the program only in 2011.

The disincentives to the study of the Holocaust among social scientists, however, ran deeper than the professional insecurities of Jewish scholars and concerned the very nature of modern social science itself, which had become increasingly theoretical and technical and focused on empirical generalization, methodology, and prediction. While area studies flourished in the postwar era as a guide to public (especially foreign) policy, the turn away from area studies in the 1980s and 1990s toward large-case generalization did raise a thorny question for social scientists interested in the Holocaust: "What was the Holocaust a case of?" Between the high social theory of Hannah Arendt, who maintained that it was a "case" of modernity, the single-minded focus of Daniel Goldhagen on antisemitism as its cause, and the hard-nosed empiricism of Raul Hilberg, who saw it as a series of discrete bureaucratic acts, the way forward for the social scientist interested in theoretically oriented contributions to Holocaust research was not obvious. And if all of this were not enough, modern social science has always had a "presentist" bent. No one would deny the importance of the Holocaust as a historical event, but the question was how it mattered for "now." And with each passing year, the Holocaust seemed increasingly part of "history" rather than a matter of the immediate past. Apart from seemingly banal lessons on the importance of preventing state-sanctioned mass murder, how could research on the Nazi extermination effort be a useful guide for public policy?

How Social Scientists Are Addressing the Challenges of the Holocaust's Uniqueness

The obstacles to social scientists who turned their attention to the Holocaust were enormous, owing to the difficulties in placing this research into a compelling intellectual framework. "Genocide" provided the first and most important conceptual pathway for integrating the Holocaust into social scientific research. Raphael Lemkin's (1944) initial definition of genocide, clearly inspired by his own experience as a Polish Jew born in Lwów who had fled Hitler's Europe, may have been slippery and too encompassing, but it explicitly opened the way for comparison with other instances of mass killing. Whatever else it was, the Holocaust was a genocide, an attempt to wipe out an entire people. This on its own invited comparison and theorization. Much later, scholars such as Midlarsky (2005) and Valentino (2005) sought to identify the conditions under which genocides occurred and included the Holocaust within a much larger group of cases of "mass killing." Others, such as Scott Straus (2007) in his study of the Rwandan genocide, a subsequent study that compared Rwanda with other African cases in order to draw generalizable conclusions (2015), and an important volume on genocide prevention (2016), explicitly drew on earlier Holocaust research for the categories used and the causes identified.

Classifying the Holocaust as a genocide undoubtedly facilitated its integration into social science by permitting comparisons along at least one dimension. But the label also had its drawbacks, not only because the number of genocides is thankfully small, which inhibits testing of competing hypotheses, but also because genocide at its very core focused attention on the end point, the mass killing, rather than on the multiple processes that led there. To take but one example, the pogroms of summer 1941 on the eastern front, when local non-Jews massacred their Jewish neighbors with the approval of occupying German forces, although today considered by many as part of the Holocaust, could not have been thought of that way at the time. Neither Germans, locals, nor Jews knew there was going to be a Holocaust in the summer of 1941. In fact, the use of the term "pogrom" (a nineteenth-century term that both Germans and Jews used in the summer of 1941 to describe these events) suggests that what was occurring was more easily understood at the time as related to earlier bouts of anti-Jewish violence than to any "final solution." Thus, the concept of genocide is less relevant to our understanding of why these massacres occurred than are the concepts and theories drawn from studies of ethnic politics and violence in other, nongenocidal contexts (Kopstein and Wittenberg 2018).

The Holocaust was a genocide but it was much more than that.[14] An important obstacle to integrating the findings of Holocaust research into mainstream social science has been its sheer enormity. The events that in retrospect we call the Holocaust unfolded over several years across multiple countries in Europe and beyond. Early research focused, on the one hand, on the impersonal and bureaucratic nature of the tragedy, organized and implemented by German *Schreibtischtäter* (desk murderers). Subsequent research showed this view to be inaccurate, or at least incomplete, because it ignored local collaboration, brutality, and the non-"industrial" and premodern nature of much of the killing. The revised view of the Holocaust zeroed in on the local and the personal, and expanded the purview of research beyond concentration and extermination camps to ghettos, killing fields, churches, farms, and apartment buildings. It situated the Holocaust in specific locations, each with its own backstory. It shifted the scholarly gaze from perpetrators and victims to bystanders and rescuers. Above all, it unsettled all of these categories by showing how some people moved back and forth from perpetrator to rescuer to bystander, sometimes within minutes (Bergen 2009). So much that needed to be explained could be explained best by "splitting" the episodes that collectively made up the Holocaust rather than "lumping" them into a single genocide.

The paradigm shift from seeing the Holocaust as "one big thing" to examining it as a series of events altered the way social scientists studied the Holocaust and, in so doing, inspired a new generation of researchers who sought to integrate their findings back into the mainstream of social science disciplines (King 2012; King, chapter 1 in this volume). By viewing the Holocaust as a series of events, social scientists compare across localities and nations, across time, across administrative structures, population types, historical patterns, and many other conditions. This approach has facilitated an understanding of the factors that exacerbated or mitigated violence and death and has provided a powerful tool in accounting for the variation in the long-term impact of the Holocaust in different communities.

This observation helps us deal with the enormity of the event and invites theoretical innovation on important individual aspects of the Holocaust, such as within-country variation in rates of rescue and deportation (Braun 2016; Tammes 2019) and patterns of resistance (Finkel 2015), while relieving scholars of the enormous burden of explaining the whole. The move away from explaining the Holocaust as a genocide means that each class of events can be fruitfully compared with events that take place in different times and places.

Of course, this analytical frame of examining the Holocaust as an "array of event categories" comes at the cost of reducing the scope of that which is explained. Explaining how it could happen, however, remains as relevant as ever, and it would be a shame if rigor came at the cost of empirical or theoretical ambition and scope. There is the danger that fewer social scientists will ask the big questions if it is professionally advantageous to pose smaller ones, the data, methods, and answers for which are more readily comparable with similar event categories elsewhere. We still need social scientists, some at least, to devote their attention to the Holocaust, *tout court*, rather than just its parts. This is especially true when we consider its impact on contemporary politics and society, as do several of the contributions to this volume. Even so, it may be too much to expect social scientists to provide fully satisfactory answers to the "why" question. Explaining the full dimension of the horror would mean, as Gerrit Dworok (2017, 403) has written, "to comprehend it," and that seems a distant prospect, even at this point.

Opportunities for comparison are opportunities to build theories and test hypotheses. But this, too, is not without its pitfalls. In the mid-1980s, for example, German historians sought to historicize the crimes of the Nazi state through comparison with the violence of other totalitarian regimes (primarily that of the Soviet Union and fascist Italy). As critics maintained, some of this work all too easily slipped into an exercise in relativization and justification: the Nazis were not alone in how they ruled or in their mistreatment of those defined as enemies. This view quickly lost appreciation for what made the Holocaust unique and, in so doing, the critics maintained, let Germany off the hook (Maier 1998). Similar efforts after 1989, by post-Communist governments and historians in Eastern Europe, to equate the crimes of the Nazi and Communist eras quickly devolved into nationalist apologetics designed to deflect attention from local collaboration during the war (Subotić 2019).

Even in the United States, comparing the Holocaust to other phenomena remains as morally fraught as ever. Recent examples abound. The controversy in 2019 surrounding the comparison of the detention centers for migrants on the US southern border with "concentration camps" and the subsequent rejection of the historical analogy by the US Holocaust Memorial Museum, followed by an open letter published in the *New York Review of Books* signed by hundreds of scholars in Jewish and Holocaust Studies defending the legitimacy of analogies as the "very core of Holocaust education," illustrates the moral sensitivities surrounding the question of comparison. In 2021 a new round of debates ensued, especially among the transatlantic community of historians of Germany, on whether the Holocaust can be compared with the earlier German colonial genocide of the Herero in today's Namibia, and whether, in fact, the Holocaust is a continuation of German genocidal colonial policies, and not a unique event untethered to Germany's colonial past.[15]

These disputes raised the delicate question of whether the prelude to the Holocaust, events during the Holocaust, or the Holocaust in its entirety could be compared with other events or event categories. There are no easy answers to these questions, and the temptation in Holocaust scholarship is to avoid historical analogies, an inclination reinforced by periodic inappropriate, insensitive, or outrageous analogies drawn by politicians, public officials, or celebrities.

If we refuse to compare, however—if we maintain that the Holocaust is simply incommensurable with any event that has ever occurred, if it is somehow placed outside of history and made unavailable to social scientists—how will the study of it ever be incorporated into the broader corpus of human knowledge? Historical analogies, as Peter Gordon (2020) has argued, constitute the core of a great deal of scientific inquiry. Without comparison, the Holocaust will most likely remain peripheral to both sociology and political science. For the social scientist interested in the Holocaust, navigating between the twin hazards of relativization and analytical paralysis is unavoidable. This is as true for those interested in the event itself as it is for those who study its aftermath.

Why Social Science Research on the Holocaust Matters

One of the motivations for this book is to demonstrate that social science research on the Holocaust matters to the broader social scientific endeavor. Another, however, is to inform and enrich historical and other humanistic research on the Holocaust. There is no denying that historians sometimes balk at what they see as social scientists' penchant for reducing complexity to "variable-based" accounts. But this disciplinary difference is often more apparent than real, and more a matter of expositional style than intellectual substance. Even so, social scientists do ask different kinds of questions, offer different explanations for behavior and events, and use distinctive kinds of data and argumentation. Our project builds on the growing scholarly interest in approaching the Holocaust within different disciplinary and methodological frameworks.

We view our project as analogous to another major research effort that introduced a fresh new disciplinary lens to the study of the Holocaust: *Geographies of the Holocaust* (Knowles, Cole, and Giordano 2014), which brought entirely new perspectives to our understanding of the Holocaust by illuminating its spatial character. The contributions to that volume demonstrated how forced and voluntary population movements during the Holocaust destroyed and transformed hundreds of places (the shtetls across Eastern Europe, for example) and led to the establishment of hundreds of others: the network of prisons, ghettos, labor camps, and killing sites. Such movements facilitated the murder of millions and the enslavement of additional hundreds of thousands. Moreover, *Geographies of the Holocaust* illuminated how the spatial configurations of such sites were designed for maximum control by the oppressors. Geographic information system (GIS) technology provided ways to map verbal descriptions from official documents and survivor testimonies into compelling and easy-to-grasp visual displays. Historians, of course, had described these movements in the context of the broader narrative arc of the Holocaust, but this new focus on geography raised different questions and arrayed data in new ways to highlight the importance of space and spatial movement, and of places and locations, in the Holocaust.[16]

Political science, sociology, statistics, and studies of public health have already offered other perspectives. It is important to know, for example, how and why Jewish communities differed in their response to persecution. Social science research has now shown that Jews who had lived under Soviet occupation between 1939 and 1941 were more likely to rebel than other Jewish communities (Finkel 2015), and Jewish communities with stronger prewar ties with Gentiles had greater success in coping with the Nazi occupation (Finkel 2017). Sociologists found that revolts were most likely to happen when inhabitants of camps and ghettos accurately perceived the threats to their lives, such as in Warsaw and Sobibor (Einwohner and Maher 2011). When they were uncertain about the threats, as in Łódź, or misunderstood them, as in Vilna, uprisings were much less likely (Einwohner 2003, 2009; Einwohner and Maher 2011). Einwohner (2007) also accounted for participation in the Warsaw Ghetto Uprising by applying sociological concepts of identity, proximity, and availability.

Scholars have found important differences in the treatment of Jews among citizens and governments during the Holocaust. What were the dimensions of these differences and why did they occur? These questions are important not only because of the inherent interest of human behavior *in extremis* and the conditions that promote or hinder intercommunal solidarity, but also because they tie directly back to longstanding questions of Holocaust history. The sociologist

Helen Fein showed that survival rates differed significantly from country to country in somewhat predictable ways based on the extent of German control and prewar antisemitism (Fein 1984; see also Hollander 2017). Social scientists have discovered that communities under Soviet control during the prewar years were more likely to help Jews and less likely to harm them during the war (Dumitru and Johnson, 2011), and Christians were much less likely to engage in pogroms against their Jewish neighbors in the first weeks of the war where political polarization between the two communities remained low in the years before the outbreak of hostilities (Kopstein and Wittenberg 2011). In the Netherlands, Jews were far more likely to receive assistance from local religious minorities than from the dominant group, whether Catholic or Protestant (Braun 2016). Other studies on the fate of Dutch Jews have revealed that communities with larger numbers of collaborationist policemen, lower rates of intermarriage between Christians and Jews, and a smaller fraction of Catholics had higher numbers of deportations (Tammes 2019). Identifying who helped and harmed Jews, and the kinds of communities where they were helped or harmed, can go a long way in telling us why this occurred. As in other spheres of social science research, the "who" and the "where" often reveal something important about the "why."

The Holocaust had not only causes but also profound, long-term consequences in every place it occurred. Social scientists are now pinpointing these effects with ever-greater specificity. They have discovered that communities near Treblinka benefited economically from the death of Jews for decades after the war (Charnysh and Finkel 2017), and that the physical proximity to German concentration camps and to the Treblinka death camp in Poland affects the current social and political attitudes of residents in nearby communities (Charnysh and Finkel 2017; Homola, Pereira, and Tavits 2020). Economists have established that cities across Russia that experienced the most extreme annihilation in the Holocaust have lower incomes and growth rates than other Russian cities (Acemoglu, Hassan, and Robinson, 2011).

Social scientists have sought to understand how the Holocaust affected individual and family lives, even before deportations. Along with historians and political scientists, sociologists have shown how the tremendous stresses on Jewish family life altered gender roles at every stage of the Holocaust (Hedgepeth and Saidel 2010; Weitzman 1999; Weitzman and Ofer 1999; Welch 2020). In doing so, they have provided precision and empirical validation to the depictions of life under German occupation inside and outside ghettos that are staples of contemporaneous diaries, memoir literature, and short stories written during and after the war (Klein 1957; Sierakowiak 1998).

Scholars of international relations have asked questions about the Nazi "New Order" as an imperial system of alliances and control (Barder 2021). The policy of extermination was centrally determined, but how was it carried out on the ground in political entities allied with the Germans? We have learned that sometimes governments and civilians protected their Jewish populations and neighbors in the face of German pressure but other times did not, and social scientists have offered compelling explanations for the difference (Dumitru and Johnson 2011; King 2011). As social science perspectives have begun to prompt new questions and provide more systematic data to examine old questions in new ways, this book aims to systematize this research and provide a coherent agenda for social science research on the Holocaust and its legacy going forward.

The objective of the book, however, is broader. The new research on the Holocaust we present contributes not only to our understanding of the Holocaust itself but also to analyses of other instances of historical and contemporary mass violence. Our findings help deepen our understanding of mechanisms of violence (at the micro, meso, and macro levels); the logic and strategy of pogroms, ethnic riots, and systems of camps; the development and diffusion of racist propaganda; the behavior of victims and survivors; and the politicization of historical memory in contexts much different from the Holocaust. It is our hope that the contributions to this book will help enrich the broader scholarship on political violence and its legacies.

A Look Ahead

Two chapters that frame the broader intellectual debates highlighted in this volume follow ours. Drawing on research subsequent to his groundbreaking 2012 article titled "Can There Be a Political Science of the Holocaust?" Charles King elaborates on his idea that the Holocaust is best seen by social scientists as a series of events, shaped in large part by local actors attuned to their own circumstances and institutions alongside the state strategies of the occupying power. He also highlights the Holocaust as a product of interstate collaboration and competition, the dynamics of which greatly affected outcomes in different nations.

One aim of this book is to initiate a conversation with historians who have informed most of our current understanding of the Holocaust. To that end, the historian Jan Burzlaff argues in his chapter that social scientists are now shedding new light on existing critical debates among historians of the Holocaust. Burzlaff makes a convincing case for historians to engage with this steadily growing body of social science scholarship and to consider how its methodological and theoretical developments can help further advance historical Holocaust research.

Following this important introductory framework, the next section of the book focuses on sites of violence, offering four examples of how viewing the

Holocaust as a set of events that can be compared in time and place provides new perspectives on these events. Based on data collected on prewar synagogues in Germany by the Beth Ashkenaz Synagogue Memorial Project, Daniel Solomon explores factors that differentiate those synagogues attacked during Kristallnacht from those that were not, casting light on community attributes of anti-Jewish violence.

Eugene Finkel uses rich archival material and five hundred survivors' testimonies to explain why some Jews in the three Jewish ghettos—Minsk, Kraków, and Białystok—chose to comply, evade, or resist, and how the community setting affected these choices. His analysis moves the discussion of the Holocaust from large structural questions of Nazi occupation and terror to the micro-questions of individual Jews' agency and choice. Jeffrey Kopstein revisits the causes of the 1941 pogroms in the Soviet borderlands, comparing their sources and mobilization techniques to a medieval pogrom in Valencia, Spain, and a pogrom in classical Alexandria in order to explore the theoretical scope conditions for accounts across different epochs. Turning to the Holocaust in Lithuania, Benjamin Mishkin examines the role of Lithuanian paramilitary forces in mobilizing mass violence against their Jewish neighbors, contrasting the mobilization of Lithuanian violence with communal anti-Jewish violence in Poland.

The third section of the volume illustrates how a variety of data sources, new and old, allow us to illuminate in some detail several important questions. Robert Braun's innovative study of the rise of xenophobia in prewar Germany employs data on children's stories collected by folklorists before and after World War I to highlight the importance of borders in generating xenophobia and antisemitism.

Lewi Stone and Stephan Lehnstaedt use German documents and Jewish chronicles from the Warsaw ghetto to analyze the origins and curtailment of the typhus epidemic there. They spotlight the public health actions that were successful in stemming the epidemic and preserving the lives of the tens of thousands infected. Adducing evidence from administrative sources, Peter Tammes and Andrew J. Simpkin examine whether immigrant Jews in the Netherlands had different experiences of isolation, deportation, and survival and death than Dutch-born Jews. Aliza Luft, using French diocesan and national archives as well as French Jewish community archives, examines why French bishops supported the Vichy regime's persecution of Jews in 1940 but two years later mobilized on behalf of Jews.

In the past twenty years, tremendous progress has been made in digitizing records of survivors and victims and organizing them in a way that is useful to social scientists as well as the public. Among the largest collections are the Yad Vashem "Transports to Extinction" website, connecting victims and survivors with documentation on the transports that carried them to ghettos and camps in the East; the US Holocaust Memorial Museum's victims' and survivors' database, and the "Holocaust by Bullets" website, Yad in Unum, documenting the sites of mass slaughter of Jews throughout Eastern Europe.[17] Survivors' testimonies are available on several sites, including Yad Vashem, the Jewish Historical Institute in Warsaw, Hebrew University's Oral History Division of the Avraham Harmon Institute for Contemporary Jewry, the USC Shoah Foundation's Visual History Archive: Testimonies of Holocaust Survivors and Other Witnesses, the US Holocaust Memorial Museum, and Yale University's Fortunoff Video Archive for Holocaust Testimonies, among others.

Susan Welch uses data from the Yad Vashem "Transports to Extinction" database to analyze the role of gender in transport composition, immediate survival at Auschwitz, and wartime survival rates. Rachel L. Einwohner explores some methodological issues in using survivor testimony from the USC Visual History Archive. In her studies of the Warsaw and Vilna Ghetto Uprisings, she analyzes ways to include the missing voices of those who did not survive as a prerequisite to assessing the validity of survivors' voices as reflections of the entirety of the Holocaust victims' experience.

Seventy-five years on, the Holocaust continues to profoundly shape European political life, both individual attitudes and national culture and policies. In our fourth section, three chapters reflect the diversity of this topic. Volha Charnysh explores the impact of different Holocaust narratives in shaping xenophobic and exclusionist attitudes in contemporary Poland, using methods drawn from experimental psychology.[18] Zvi Gitelman uses Belarus and Ukraine as case studies to examine how postsocialist states have shaped their Holocaust histories to secure the continuing political legitimacy of the ruling elites, while Jelena Subotić provides a broader look at how Holocaust remembrance practices serve various state international reputational needs, drawing on, among other ideas, the concepts of "collective psychology," "ontological security," and other elements from psychoanalysis.

In the concluding section, Daniel Ziblatt, while appreciating the disaggregating approach and emphasis on the local in many of the contributions to this volume, fittingly shifts our attention back to the broader national and especially international forces that determined the course of the Holocaust. Exclusive focus on the local and comparative microhistories, or even the internal features of a country or society, he maintains, misses out on the important external factors that determined the causes and impact of the destruction of European Jewry. When democracy died in a regional hegemonic power, such as Germany in the 1930s, this paved the way for the horrors to follow well beyond its borders through force and emulation. Were democracy to die in a *global* hegemon such as the United States—an ominous possibility after

2016—"the reverberations would be massive." The Holocaust, Ziblatt notes, offers an important warning: the local process of political violence and dehumanization we highlight in this book occurred when democracy died in a powerful nation.

In a world shaped by violence and the memory of violence, it should perhaps come as no surprise that social scientists have finally been drawn to the Holocaust—the index case of violence in the modern world—to help us understand the era in which we live. Taken collectively, these chapters reply with a resounding "yes" to Charles King's question of whether, indeed, there can be a social science of the Holocaust. Our book illustrates that social science can shed light on dynamics and actors in the Holocaust, provide new ways of understanding the mobilization and mechanisms of violence and destruction, illustrate the individual and collective choices that led to death or survival, and illuminate ways that the Holocaust has created a set of legacies that haunt Europe to this day. In sum, this volume demonstrates that the social science of the Holocaust is not only possible. It is necessary.

REFERENCES

Acemoglu, Daron, Tarek A. Hassan, and James A. Robinson. 2011. "Social Structure and Development: A Legacy of the Holocaust in Russia." *Quarterly Journal of Economics* 126 (2): 895–946.

Adorno, Theodor, Else Frenkel-Brunswik, Daniel J. Levinson, and R. Nevitt Sanford. 1950. *The Authoritarian Personality*. New York: Harper and Brothers.

Aly, Götz, and Suzanne Heim. 2003. *Architects of Annihilation: Auschwitz and the Logic of Destruction*. Princeton, NJ: Princeton University Press.

Arendt, Hannah. 1951. *The Origins of Totalitarianism*. New York: Schocken Books.

Barder, Alexander. 2021. *Global Race War: International Hierarchy and Politics, 1800–Present*. Oxford: Oxford University Press.

Barnes, Trevor J., and Claudio Minca. 2013. "Nazi Spatial Theory: The Dark Geographies of Carl Schmitt and Walter Christaller." *Annals of the Association of American Geographers* 103 (3): 669–87.

Bauman, Zygmunt. 1989. *Modernity and the Holocaust*. Cambridge: Polity.

Bergen, Doris L. 2009. *War and Genocide: A Concise History of the Holocaust*. 2nd ed. Lanham, MD: Rowman and Littlefield.

Blass, Thomas. 1988. "The Roots of Stanley Milgram's Obedience Experiments and Their Relevance to the Holocaust." *Analyse and Kritik* 20:46–53.

Braun, Robert. 2016. "Religious Minorities and Resistance to Genocide: The Collective Rescue of Jews in the Netherlands during the Holocaust." *American Political Science Review* 110 (1): 127–47.

Browning, Christopher. 1992. *Ordinary Men: Reserve Battalion 101 and the Final Solution in Poland*. New York: HarperCollins.

Charnysh, Volha, and Evgeny Finkel. 2017. "The Death Camp Eldorado: Political and Economic Effects of Mass Violence." *American Political Science Review* 111 (4): 801–18.

Dumitru, Diana. 2018. *The State, Antisemitism, and Collaboration in the Holocaust: The Borderlands of Romania and the Soviet Union*. New York: Cambridge University Press.

Dumitru, Diana, and Carter Johnson. 2011. "Constructing Interethnic Conflict and Cooperation: Why Some People Harmed Jews and Others Helped Them during the Holocaust in Romania." *World Politics* 63 (1): 1–42.

Dworok, Gerrit. 2017. "Forum: Holocaust Scholarship and Politics in the Public Sphere; Reexamining the Causes, Consequences, and Controversy of the Historikerstreit and the Goldhagen Controversy." *Central European History* 50:375–403.

Einwohner, Rachel L. 2003. "Opportunity, Honor, and Action in the Warsaw Ghetto Uprising of 1943." *American Journal of Sociology* 109 (3): 650–75.

———. 2007. "Availability, Proximity, and Identity in the Warsaw Ghetto Uprising: Adding a Sociological Lens to Studies of Jewish Resistance." In *Sociology Confronts the Holocaust: Memories and Identities in Jewish Diasporas*, edited by Judith M. Gerson and Diane L. Wolf, 277–90. Durham, NC: Duke University Press.

———. 2009. "The Need to Know: Cultured Ignorance and Jewish Resistance in the Ghettos of Warsaw, Vilna, and Łódź." *Sociological Quarterly* 50 (3): 407–30.

Einwohner, Rachel, and Thomas Maher. 2011. "Threat Assessment and Collective-Action Emergence: Death-Camp and Ghetto Resistance during the Holocaust." *Mobilization: An International Quarterly* 16 (2): 127–46.

Fein, Helen. 1984. *Accounting for Genocide: National Responses and Jewish Victimization during the Holocaust*. Chicago: University of Chicago Press.

Finkel, Evgeny. 2015. "The Phoenix Effect of State Repression: Jewish Resistance during the Holocaust." *American Political Science Review* 109 (2): 339–53.

———. 2017. *Ordinary Jews: Choice and Survival during the Holocaust*. Princeton, NJ: Princeton University Press.

Frank, Anne. 1993. *Anne Frank: The Diary of a Young Girl*. Reissue, Old Greenwich, CT: Bantam.

Friess, Steve. 2015. "When 'Holocaust' Became 'the Holocaust': An Etymological Mystery." *New Republic*, May 17, 2015. https://newrepublic.com/article/121807/when-holocaust-became-holocaust.

Gerhardt, Uta. 1993. *Talcott Parsons on National Socialism*. New York: Aldine de Gruyter.

Gerson, Judith M., and Diane L. Wolf. 2007a. "Sociology and Holocaust Study." In *Sociology Confronts the Holocaust: Memories and Identities in Jewish Diasporas*, edited by Judith M. Gerson and Diane L. Wolf, 11–38. Durham, NC: Duke University Press.

———, eds. 2007b. *Sociology Confronts the Holocaust: Memories and Identities in Jewish Diasporas*. Durham, NC: Duke University Press.

Goldhagen, Daniel Jonah. 1997. *Hitler's Willing Executioners: Ordinary Germans and the Holocaust*. New York: Vintage.

Gordon, Peter E. 2020. "Why Historical Analogy Matters." *New York Review of Books*, January 18, 2020. https://www.nybooks.com/daily/2020/01/07/why-historical-analogy-matters/.

Gross, Jan T. 2002. *Neighbors: The Destruction of the Jewish Community in Jedwabne, Poland*. New York: Penguin Books.

———. 2007. *Fear: Anti-Semitism in Poland after Auschwitz*. Reprint, New York: Random House.

Gross, Jan Tomasz, and Irena Grudzinska Gross. 2012. *Golden Harvest: Events at the Periphery of the Holocaust*. New York: Oxford University Press.

Haggbloom, Steven J., Jason E. Warnick, Renee Warnick, Vinessa K. Jones, Gary L. Yarbrough, Tenea M. Russell, Chris M. Borecky, Reagan McGahhey, John L. Powell III, Jamie Beavers, and Emanuelle Monte. 2002. "The 100 Most Eminent Psychologists of the 20th Century." *Review of General Psychology* 6 (2): 139–52.

Hedgepeth, Sonja M., and Rochelle G. Saidel, eds. 2010. *Sexual Violence against Jewish Women during the Holocaust*. Waltham, MA: Brandeis University Press.

Hilberg, Raul. 1961. *The Destruction of the European Jews*. Chicago: Quadrangle Books.

———. 1996. *The Politics of Memory: The Journey of a Holocaust Historian*. Chicago: Ivan R. Dee.

Hollander, Ethan. 2017. *Hegemony and the Holocaust: State Power and Jewish Survival in Occupied Europe*. London: Palgrave Macmillan.

Homola, Jonathan, Miguel M. Pereira, and Margit Tavits. 2020. "Legacies of the Third Reich: Concentration Camps and Out-Group Intolerance." *American Political Science Review* 114 (2): 573–90.

King, Charles. 2011. *Odessa: Genius and Death in a City of Dreams*. New York: W. W. Norton.

———. 2012. "Can There Be a Political Science of the Holocaust?" *Perspectives on Politics* 10 (2): 323–41.

Klein, Gerda Weissmann. 1957. *All but My Life*. New York: Hill and Wang.

Knowles, Anne Kelly, Tim Cole, and Alberto Giordano. 2014. *Geographies of the Holocaust*. Bloomington: Indiana University Press.

Kogan, Eugene. 1950. *The Theory and Practice of Hell*. New York: Farrar, Straus and Cudahy.

Kopstein, Jeffrey S., and Jason Wittenberg. 2011. "Deadly Communities: Local Political Milieus and the Persecution of Jews in Occupied Poland." *Comparative Political Studies* 44 (3): 259–83.

———. 2018. *Intimate Violence: Anti-Jewish Pogroms on the Eve of the Holocaust*. Ithaca, NY: Cornell University Press.

Lemkin, Raphael. 1944. *Axis Rule in Occupied Europe*. Washington, DC: Carnegie Endowment for International Peace.

Lower, Wendy. 2017. "Holocaust Scholarship and Politics in the Public Sphere: Reexamining the Causes, Consequences, and Controversy of the *Historikerstreit* and the Goldhagen Debate; A Forum." *Central European History* 50 (3): 375–403.

Maier, Charles S. 1998. *The Unmasterable Past: History, Holocaust, and German National Identity*. Cambridge, MA: Harvard University Press.

Mason, Timothy. 1995. "Intention and Explanation: A Current Controversy about the Interpretation of National Socialism." In *Nazism, Fascism, and the Working Class*, edited by Jane Caplan. Cambridge: Cambridge University Press.

McGuinness, Damien. 2019. "Holocaust: How a US TV Series Changed Germany." BBC News, January 30, 2019. https://www.bbc.com/news/world-europe-47042244.

Midlarsky, Manus I. 2005. *The Killing Trap: Genocide in the Twentieth Century*. New York: Cambridge University Press.

Milgram, Stanley. 1963. "Behavioral Study of Obedience." *Journal of Abnormal and Social Psychology* 67 (4): 371–78.

———. 2009. *Obedience to Authority: An Experimental View*. Reprint, New York: Harper Perennial Modern Classics.

Monroe, Kristen R. 1997. Review of *Hitler's Willing Executioners: Ordinary Germans and the Holocaust*, by Daniel Jonah Goldhagen. *American Political Science Review* 91 (1): 212–13.

Monroe, Kristen Renwick. 1996. *The Heart of Altruism: Perceptions of a Common Humanity*. Princeton, NJ: Princeton University Press.
Neumann, Franz. 1942. *Behemoth: The Structure and Practice of National Socialism*. New York: Oxford University Press.
Reitlinger, Gerald. 1956. *The Final Solution*. New York: Beechhurst.
Rosenberg, Samuel. 1937. "Three Concepts in Nazi Political Theory." *Science & Society* 1 (2): 221–30.
Segev, Tom. 1993. *The Seventh Million: Israelis and the Holocaust*. New York: Hill and Wang.
Sierakowiak, Dawid. 1998. *The Diary of Dawid Sierakowiak: Five Notebooks from the Lódz Ghetto*. Edited by Alan Adelson. Translated by Kamil Turowski. New York: Oxford University Press.
Straus, Scott. 2007. *The Order of Genocide: Race, Power, and War in Rwanda*. Ithaca, NY: Cornell University Press.
——. 2015. *Making and Unmaking Nations: War, Leadership, and Genocide in Modern Africa*. Ithaca, NY: Cornell University Press.
——. 2016. *Fundamentals of Genocide and Mass Atrocity Prevention*. Washington, DC: United States Holocaust Memorial Museum.
Subotić, Jelena. 2019. *Yellow Star, Red Star: Holocaust Remembrance after Communism*. Ithaca, NY: Cornell University Press.
Suhr, Heiko. 2012. *Der Generalplan Ost—Nationalsozialistische Pläne Zur Kolonisation Ostmitteleuropas*. Berlin: GRIN Verlag.
Tammes, Peter. 2019. "Associating Locality-Level Characteristics with Surviving the Holocaust: A Multilevel Approach to the Odds of Being Deported and to Risk of Death among Jews Living in Dutch Municipalities." *American Journal of Epidemiology* 188 (5): 896–906.
Tec, Nechama. 1987. *When Light Pierced the Darkness: Christian Rescue of Jews in Nazi-Occupied Poland*. New York: Oxford University Press.
Valentino, Benjamin A. 2005. *Final Solutions: Mass Killing and Genocide in the 20th Century*. Ithaca, NY: Cornell University Press.
Voigtländer, Nico, and Hans-Joachim Voth. 2012. "Persecution Perpetuated: The Medieval Origins of Anti-Semitic Violence in Nazi Germany." *Quarterly Journal of Economics* 127 (3): 1339–92.
Waller, James E. 2013. "The Social Sciences." In *The Oxford Handbook of Holocaust Studies*, edited by Peter Hayes and John K. Roth, 667–79. Oxford: Oxford University Press.
Weitzman, Lenore J. 1999. "Living on the Aryan Side in Poland." In *Women in the Holocaust*, edited by Dalia Ofer and Lenore J. Weitzman, 187–222. New Haven, CT: Yale University Press.
Weitzman, Lenore J., and Dalia Ofer. 1999. "The Role of Gender in the Holocaust." In *Women in the Holocaust*, edited by Dalia Ofer and Lenore J. Weitzman, 3–26. New Haven, CT: Yale University Press.
Welch, Susan. 2020. "Gender and Selection in the Holocaust: An Analysis of Transports of Western European Jews." *Journal of Genocide Research* 22 (4): 459–78. https://doi.org/10.1080/14623528.2020.1764743.

1

CAN—OR SHOULD—THERE BE A POLITICAL SCIENCE OF THE HOLOCAUST?

Charles King

It is an odd fact that the twentieth century's most infamous instance of political and social violence—the Holocaust—has remained largely peripheral to political science.[1] Despite an enormous archival fund in many languages, comprising everything from oral testimonies to state-level paper trails, as well as a vast secondary literature in history and the cross-disciplinary field of Holocaust studies, the Holocaust has been, until very recently, outside the normal purview of the discipline.

Four intellectual reasons for this standoffishness suggest themselves. First is the vexed issue of the Holocaust's uniqueness. Historians, theologians, and scholars of Jewish studies continue to debate the nature of the Holocaust experience; explanations for the destruction of European Jewry have included a uniquely German form of antisemitism, antisemitism in general, modernity, and other causes (Matthäus, Shaw, Bartov, Bergen, and Bloxham 2011). The high-stakes nature of these conversations has made political scientists—like the public at large—rightly cautious about treating the Holocaust as just another data-generating event (Bischoping and Kalmin 1999). When they have tackled Holocaust-related themes, until recently the trend among political scientists has been to replay the uniqueness debate using the language of social science rather than asking what this particular episode might reveal about mass killing in general or vice versa. (See, for example, *Annals* [1980, 1996]. A more recent survey is Balcells and Solomon [2020].)

Second is the privileged place of memory in Holocaust discourse, a way of speaking and thinking that still provides a sense of meaning to individual survivors as well as a foundation narrative for a modern state, Israel (see Segev 1993). The sheer scale of Holocaust victimhood, its direct link to the long history of European antisemitism, and the memorialization of both in museums, monuments, and popular culture have given rise to a latticework of public memory that can present a challenge to scholars seeking to analyze events in a new light.

Third is a coding issue. Is the Holocaust a single event or many, and if the latter, how ought these to be translated into meaningful dependent variables? Nazi Germany's policy of the "Final Solution to the Jewish Question," the German-run system of concentration camps and killing centers, the atrocities committed by SS units (*Einsatzgruppen*) during their advance into Poland and the Soviet Union, the actions of Germany's allies such as Romania, Hungary, Vichy France, Italy, and Croatia, and the town- and village-level elimination of Jews and other minorities, sometimes at the hands of their neighbors, are all part of the Holocaust experience. Perhaps more than in other instances of genocide, even bracketing the Holocaust in time depends on how one defines it: 1941–45 if the task is to explain industrial killing as state policy, 1941–42 if the focus is the major informal killing operations of the SS and Wehrmacht, 1933–45 if the theme is the evolution of anti-Jewish policy overall, or at least 1920 forward if the issue is the origins of the Nazis' racist ideology. Political scientists face the daunting challenge of classifying events in ways that accord with contentious and multifaceted historiographies across all of these time periods (Lustick 1996; Lieberman 2010).

This conundrum has tended to reproduce itself in the growing field of genocide studies, of which Holocaust studies might be seen as a special part. By reifying a particular episode as a distinct, self-evident, and bounded event—the Armenian genocide, the Cambodian genocide, the Bosnian genocide—scholars have tended to predetermine the unit of analysis, rather than thinking of macrohistory as a cluster of non-case-specific phenomena more amenable to comparative analysis. Moreover, since the case population in comparative genocide studies normally consists of macrohistorical events identified ex ante as "genocide," discrete acts of mass violence outside of genocidal contexts—such as lynchings or pogroms—have rarely featured in the analysis. For these reasons, genocide studies and the literature on substate violence are at best estranged cousins, especially when it comes to the Second World War (Desch 2004; Finkel and Straus 2012).

Finally, the study of the Holocaust has long been tied to the temporality and geography of the events themselves. For historians a key part of the explanation for the Holocaust is that it happened in a particular place and at a particular time: mainly—in terms of the sites of death of the largest number of victims—the German-occupied borderlands of Poland, Belarus, Lithuania, and Ukraine following the rise of the Nazi Party in Germany. For historians, chronology and space are often privileged avenues of causation. The macrohistorical explanations that flow from them are well known: German and European antisemitism, the perils of modernity in Central Europe, the ruthless efficiency and bungling callousness of Nazi bureaucracy. This disciplinary predisposition also accords with the common-sense view that the Holocaust is in some fundamental sense a German story, from Adolf Hitler to Oskar Schindler.

For political science, however, time and place are variables to be tested rather than starting points for analysis. Whether historical context or geographic location matter at all in explaining a particular phenomenon is itself a subject of inquiry, not an assumption structuring the research design. This scholarly difference means that political science approaches to the Holocaust must begin by reframing some of the basic questions posed by the historical scholarship. It also pushes social scientists in general to regard with skepticism the causal robustness of the work of generations of talented historians. All of this, to say the least, takes chutzpah.

Yet what is the value in revisiting an event whose macrolevel causes seem settled? To frame the problem this way is like asking for a political scientist to explain the Renaissance. The macrohistorical phenomenon is so large and multilayered that a social science of it seems meaningless, or perhaps too meaningful. The Holocaust is thus best seen not as a single "case" but as a macrohistorical matrix of highly variable forms of mass killing, resistance, and survival. Recent work within Holocaust studies and an emerging literature offering social scientific insights on the Holocaust itself have revealed a vast field of variation—from the identity of perpetrators, to the possibility of resistance and survivorship, to the evolution of mass killing as state policy. Just as a theory of revolution ought to reveal something important about 1789 and a theory of democratization ought to illuminate the seeming crisis in democratic governance in the 2020s, so too our theories of how small numbers of people are able to kill a great many others ought to be able to speak to the specific causes of Holocaust-era death.

On the face of things, the Holocaust may well reconfirm some of what we believe about violence in general. The intensely local logics of killing and the relationship between selective violence and territorial control, both stressed in the important work of Stathis Kalyvas, seem to map reasonably well the reciprocal horrors committed by Nazi and Soviet forces during their sequential occupations of Eastern Europe (see Kalyvas 2006). That model is particularly apposite in a context where local grievances interacted with a Kalyvasian "master narrative" par excellence: deeply rooted antisemitism. But other aspects of the Holocaust are likely to challenge the findings drawn from different times and places. Why were the moral and emotional imperatives that pushed *campesinos* in El Salvador to transform themselves into insurgents so remarkably weak among Jewish communities in parts of occupied Eastern Europe (see Wood 2003)? Why were the availability of state-supported thugs or the strategic calculations of wartime belligerents—common causal themes in the literature on massacres and genocide—imperfect predictors of the specific patterns of death across Eastern Europe? (See Valentino 2004a; Mueller 2004; Levene 2005. For the work of historians and others, see Naimark 2002, 2010; Weitz 2005; Chirot and McCauley 2006; Kiernan 2009; Snyder 2010.) If the fear and greed prompted by state breakdown and civil war are such powerful motivators for mass killing, as they seemed to be in Rwanda, why did so many Jews die in conditions that were by comparison stable, secure, and orderly (see Straus 2006; Fujii 2009; McDoom 2021)? And given the ubiquity of racism as an ideology and state strategy in the twentieth century, why did the German variety result in a broad program of violent elimination while the American one produced punctuated violence and entrenched segregation (see Whitman 2017; Churchwell 2018; King 2019; Neiman 2019)?

Indeed, several puzzles at the heart of the study of mass violence appear nowhere in starker relief than in the context of the Holocaust:

- Where, why, and how does military occupation enable mass killing?
- Do genocidal perpetrators teach local collaborators how to kill, or do they learn it from them along the way?
- Under what conditions do allies of genocidal regimes cooperate in a high-cost policy—the mass murder of civilians?
- What are the institutional mechanics behind a state policy of mass death?
- In conditions of large-scale violence, why and how do civilians mobilize against it, either by taking up arms themselves or by engaging in collective action to shield intended victims?

The answers to these questions may appear profoundly overdetermined in the case of the Holocaust. Even in this likeliest of environments, however, death, collaboration, and survivorship took on patterns that were unexpected and confounding.

Drawing on emerging trends within history writing and historically informed social science, the first section below surveys contemporary changes in scholarly agendas and approaches to the Holocaust. The second section identifies some of the major questions in the field and sketches a research program for political science centered on the interaction of state power, local communities, and violent mobilization in five areas: military occupation, repertoires of violence, alliance politics, genocidal policymaking, and resistance. The final section offers five specific preliminary findings that challenge and recast some of what we believe about mass killing, from the role of states as makers of genocide to the determinants of resistance. The concluding section also addresses issues of comparison, morality, and memory—especially the question of the uniqueness of the Holocaust and the ethical imperative to acknowledge human suffering.

Beyond Auschwitz

How one answers questions about the Holocaust has always been a function of when one asks them. After 1945 in the West, the term "holocaust" (with a lowercase *h*) usually referred to the atomic blasts over Hiroshima and Nagasaki or the dire prospect of nuclear war between the superpowers. In the Soviet Union and Communist Europe, Jewish victims were rarely named as such, with monuments erected instead to "peaceful citizens" who had perished at the hands of Nazi invaders.

Despite a string of war crimes trials overseen by Allied and other officials and running from the initial Nuremberg judgments through the Adolf Eichmann affair of 1961 and beyond, public perception of the Holocaust as a single, bounded event grew gradually over time. Anne Frank's diary was published in 1947, translated into English in 1952, and made into a film in 1959. Hannah Arendt's dispatches from the Eichmann trial exposed the mind of a perpetrator to public scrutiny (Arendt [1964] 2006). In 1985, Claude Lanzmann's monumental film *Shoah* portrayed Jewish suffering through the lives of real survivors, witnesses, and killers, all with harrowing testimonies.

Scholarship, too, took time to ramp up, as well as to enshrine certain key themes as central to Holocaust studies. Hugh Trevor-Roper's influential *The Last Days of Hitler* contained only three references to Jews, two of them quoting Hitler himself (Trevor-Roper 1947, 19, 193, 196). William Shirer's bestselling *The Rise and Fall of the Third Reich* did give serious attention to Nazi anti-Jewish policies, although it did not contain the word "Holocaust" (Shirer 1960). Still, Shirer's treatment of the mass killing of civilians was secondary to other concerns, such as diplomatic wrangling, the movement of front lines, and the military turning points at Stalingrad and El Alamein. It was only with the pioneering research of Raul Hilberg's *The Destruction of the European Jews* that the Holocaust began to be seen as a major and essential component of the war (Hilberg [1961] 2003). Earlier historians had painstakingly documented the origins and development of the Final Solution, but Hilberg—a political scientist by training and departmental affiliation—emphasized the bureaucratic dimensions of German policy rather than the machinations of a small group of Nazi sadists. That approach opened up new avenues into the interaction of state and society in Germany, its partner countries, and occupied Europe.

Research expanded rapidly from the 1960s forward. The structure of Nazi decision-making and bureaucracy, the Holocaust's relationship to European modernity, the intricacies of Nazi ideology and racial "science," Germany's colonial plans for the Slavic lands to the east, the nature of everyday life in the Third Reich, and the particular role of women, camp guards, business elites, and cultural figures in Germany and its occupied lands came to feature prominently in a vast field of study. (Orientations are provided by Marrus [1989]; Berenbaum and Peck [1998]; Bartov [2000, 2008]; and Stone [2010].) If the Normandy landings of June 6, 1944, became the popular symbol of the war in the West—however skewed that image might be—the Holocaust now took on an even greater mantle: as the representative experience of the cataclysmic twentieth century.

Precisely because of the rapid growth of Holocaust scholarship over the past half century, it is tempting to believe that the study of it is an overplowed field. Indeed, as early as the 1950s, reviewers of Hilberg's manuscript *The Destruction of the European Jews* were already complaining that it simply remapped well-known territory (Hilberg 1996, 105–19). In the 1990s, however, the opening of archives in the former Communist world presented an unimaginable wealth of new information to scholars. That archival base, coupled with the emergence of a younger generation of historians trained in the relevant regional languages (in addition to German) and predisposed to view history in a comparative and transnational frame, has injected new life into the field. The result is that scholars are now beginning to understand how little was actually known about the Holocaust writ large, beyond the details of German policy formulation, antisemitic legislation, and the horrors of the camp system. Four trends are particularly meaningful to social scientists.

Disaggregating the Holocaust

Rather than one big thing, the Holocaust might now be described as an array of event categories. In Christopher Browning's terms, the Holocaust involved three separate "clusters of genocidal projects": euthanasia and "racial purification" directed against the disabled and Sinti and Roma (at the time referred to collectively as "Gypsies") within the Third Reich; the eradication of Slavic populations living in countries east of Germany; and the Final Solution proper—that is, the attempted mass murder of every Jew residing anywhere within Germany's sphere of influence (Browning 2010, 407). (The list of persecuted categories—people targeted by the Nazis in ways short of genocide—would of course be longer.) Pulling apart the many threads of the Holocaust allows scholars to understand the origins and evolution of policy and practice in ways that thinking of it as a single happening does not.

This trend has entailed decentering the concentration camp as the quintessential experience. The camp system—especially the labor and death facility at Auschwitz but also killing centers such as Chełmno, Treblinka, Sobibor, Majdanek, and Belzec, all in Poland—was a crucial element in the Nazi plan for exterminating Europe's Jews. Because of the horrors of life and death in the Nazi-run facilities, the camp experience has long been central to Holocaust studies and popular memory. The architecture of the United States Holocaust Memorial Museum (USHMM) in Washington, DC, reflects the industrial aesthetic of train depots and detention facilities, in everything from the lobby decor to the interior design of the elevators. The camps are thus representative of the Holocaust in two ways: in the loose sense of standing in for the Holocaust overall in public discourse, and in the more scholarly sense of typifying the way in which most killings occurred.

As Timothy Snyder has pointed out, however, two features of the camp system raise questions about its place at the core of Holocaust studies (Snyder 2010, xii–xv). First, a large proportion of victims did not perish in the archipelago of camps and death facilities. Instead they died through mass executions, typically shootings over tank traps, ravines, and pits as the SS and Wehrmacht pushed eastward after the attack on the Soviet Union on June 22, 1941. In all, nearly half of the roughly six million Jews shot, gassed, or starved during the war died without ever seeing a sealed train, a jackbooted camp guard, or the infamous "Arbeit macht frei" sign at the entrance to Auschwitz. In this sense, the "Holocaust by bullets," as it has been called, represented a major but largely silent dimension of the Final Solution. Documenting life in camps and ghettos has been ongoing since the Second World War and is now the subject of a four-volume work coordinated by the USHMM (2009–22), with other volumes still in process. Yet the systematic collection of microlevel information on killing actions by German and other forces in Poland and the Soviet Union has been, until recently, mainly the project of a single Catholic priest, Father Patrick Desbois (2008).

Second, there is an analytical bias in the evidence related to the camps. We know of the terrible suffering endured inside the major Nazi concentration camps precisely because significant numbers of people survived. The most famous—the writers Primo Levi and Elie Wiesel, the psychiatrist Viktor Frankl—left essential testimonies of the abysmal conditions they endured (Levi 1959; Wiesel 1960; Frankl 1962). Other witnesses—Anne Frank, the Protestant rescuer Corrie Ten Boom—told stories of evasion and resistance in occupied Western Europe that still shape popular images of the Holocaust (Frank 1952; Ten Boom 1971). But the millions of Jews who perished in the death facilities of Poland and the killing fields of the Soviet Union left little record. Several of the mass killing events—usually called "actions," after the contemporary German term *Aktionen*—are well known to specialists: for example, the murder of 23,600 Jews at Kamenets-Podolsky in western Ukraine in August 1941, the killing of more than 33,000 Jews at Babi Yar in Kiev in September 1941, and the beating and shooting of 9,000 Jews in Kovno, Lithuania, in October 1941. Although these atrocities remain unfamiliar outside the Holocaust studies field, such mass killings throughout the eastern reaches of the Nazi empire were the way in which millions of Jews and other victims—as well as their tormentors—experienced the Holocaust.

In fact, the variation in experience across Europe was profound, with Jews being protected in some areas and persecuted in others, sometimes by the same government at the same time. Hungary guarded most of its Jews from deportation until late in the war and then, under German occupation, assisted in placing some 440,000 of its citizens on trains to Auschwitz (see Braham 1994). Local antisemitism seemed to play an important role in some instances—such as the emergence of indigenous fascist parties in Hungary, Romania, and Croatia—while being largely absent in others, such as Bulgaria. Military occupation was the context for mass killing in some cases, such as in the western Soviet Union, yet it was ancillary to the anti-Jewish policies of other governments, such as Italy and Vichy France. Appreciating the multinational and pan-European nature of the Holocaust now opens up a range of questions that were difficult to ask so long as the Holocaust was perceived as a largely German story researchable using mainly German sources.

Over the past two decades, former Communist countries in Eastern Europe have mined their own pasts for evidence of either atrocities or heroic efforts to save Jews on their own soil. To some extent, these have been well-meaning efforts to rewrite histories long obscured by Communist propaganda, but they were also tied to the expansion of the European Union. Being sorry for the Holocaust became one of the desiderata of Europeanness in the 1990s. Countries sometimes competed at being sorrier than their neighbors—at least in the form of public memorials, official expressions of regret, and the issuance of governmental reports that created official narratives of the Holocaust in their territory (Judt 2005, 803; see also Subotić 2019). Even older EU members have reevaluated their role in the war. France now features plaques on schools and other buildings from which Jews were deported by Vichy authorities. Public discussions in the Netherlands have begun to balance the narrative of resistance with tougher treatments of collaboration. "Coming to terms with the past" (*Vergangenheitsbewältigung*) has been transformed from a uniquely German preoccupation to a pan-European, perhaps even essentially European, vocation.

Victims and Perpetrators

More than in other great tragedies, memory of the Holocaust has been dominated by personal testimonies of suffering. While personal stories gave an immediacy to the horror of organized violence, they also made it difficult to think about collectivities of victims and to understand the Holocaust via the identities and locations of those who were silent. At the time Adolf Hitler became German chancellor, there were around half a million local Jews in Germany. By comparison, the Polish city of Warsaw alone had 375,000. The number of Jews deported from Vichy and German-occupied France—around 75,000—was roughly equivalent to the number removed from a single provincial Soviet city, Odessa. Nevertheless, the testimonies and experience of West European victims have long shaped the nature of Holocaust remembrance and research.

The fact that so much of the killing involved non-German Jews in non-German lands with the active participation of non-German murderers has prompted scholars to move away from the German-centered approach to the field, especially as regards perpetrators, victims, and the many categories in between. As Saul Friedländer (2007, xv) wrote in the most influential rethinking of Holocaust scholarship in recent decades, "At each step, in occupied Europe, the execution of German measures depended on the submissiveness of political authorities, the assistance of local police forces or other auxiliaries, and the passivity or support of the populations and mainly of the political and spiritual elites. It also depended on the willingness of the victims to follow orders in the hope of alleviating German strictures or gaining time and somehow escaping the inexorable tightening of the German vise."

The Second World War gave rise to a cascading form of victimhood. Poland was carved up between Germany and the Soviet Union in 1939. Ethnic Ukrainians in occupied Poland killed and drove out ethnic Poles in 1943. Poles in turn killed ethnic Ukrainians and then, in 1947, deported Ukrainian communities en masse. Besides fighting each other, Poles and Ukrainians also killed Jews (Gross 1988; Snyder 1999, 2008). The complexities of war, guerrilla resistance, ethnic cleansing, and mass killing are lost in accounts of the Second World War that concentrate on the tectonic workings of strategy and front lines. Revealing the identities of the many groups and individuals involved—the victims, perpetrators, zealots, bureaucrats, resisters, rescuers, and bystanders—has been one of the most important and unsettling aspects of recent scholarship on the Second World War (Hilberg 1992; Aly 2007).

Jan Gross's widely read book *Neighbors* launched a major debate about the complicity of local Poles in the elimination of nearby Jewish residents (Gross 2001). An archive-based reconstruction of events in the town of Jedwabne, Poland, in July 1941, *Neighbors* challenged not only the centrality of German perpetrators but also the comfortable narrative of Poland and the Poles as mainly victims of Nazi aggression. Similar reevaluations apply farther east as well. After June 1941, many of the anti-Jewish atrocities in the Soviet Union were carried out by one of four *Einsatzgruppen* whose explicit task was to work to the rear of the Wehrmacht and sweep up subversives, spies, insurgents, Communists, and Jews—categories that were considered to be overlapping or coterminous. While the *Einsatzgruppen* were under the operational control of the Waffen-SS, a number of other units were implicated in mass killings. The Hungarian and Romanian armies pushed columns of Jews eastward into German-held territory and at times actively assisted in the roundup and killing of civilians. After the initial Axis push into the Soviet Union, local ethnic Germans, grouped into militias under Nazi supervision, oversaw interned Jews and Gypsies. Local Ukrainians took part in pogroms and also served as guards at internment facilities run by Romania, while some Lithuanian, Latvian, and Estonian police officers pursued their activities with a zeal that shocked German military commanders (Hilberg 1992, 87–102).

In each of these cases, we now know more than ever about the people who were holding the rifles. Christopher Browning's pathbreaking work charted the transformation of the middle-aged men of the German Order Police into efficient killers (Browning 1998). The antisemitic ideology of and murders perpetrated by the Organization of Ukrainian Nationalists—the anti-Soviet armed group active in western Ukraine—has darkened the army's hallowed place in the pantheon of fighters for Ukrainian independence (Berkhoff 2004; Lower 2005b). The Parti Populaire Français and the *milice* in France, the Arrow Cross organization in Hungary, and local police recruits and self-protection detachments organized among Ukrainians, Belarusians, Lithuanians, Latvians, local ethnic Germans, and others all played roles in tormenting or murdering civilians.

Research on these groups has also allowed much more appreciation for the variability of Jewish victimhood and resistance, both over time and over space. Early in the war, Hungary deported Jews who were citizens of other states; some of these people were later massacred by SS units. But the remainder of Hungary's Jewish population, although molested by harsh antisemitic legislation, remained relatively safe until the German occupation of Hungary in 1944. In Romania, Jews who lived in the regions of Wallachia and Moldavia were, with some exceptions, protected by the authoritarian government throughout the war, a government that actively resisted German pressure to deport Jews to camps. Yet in the provinces of Bukovina and Bessarabia, Jews were systematically rounded up and pushed to the east, where they were placed in a Romanian-run string of camps and ghettos (Ioanid 2000; Deletant 2006; Case 2009; Solonari 2010). While antisemitism was everywhere, death was not, and patterns of Jewish resistance—both armed and otherwise—did not match either the brutality or the consistency of persecution.

Shifts in the unit of analysis have also enabled more fine-grained pictures of victimhood and survivorship. Digging down to the city and neighborhood level, scholars are now better able to assess the interplay of ideology, neighborliness, and foreign occupation. The city of Thessaloniki in Greece had been a haven for Jews for centuries, yet a combination of military occupation and local collaboration destroyed its Jewish population (Mazower 2005). The city of Łódź was home to Poland's second-largest Jewish population before the war, but its transformation into a "Jewish-free" model city under Nazi occupation was accomplished with the complicity of leading Jewish citizens (Horwitz 2008). The fate of Jews in the Bosnian city of Sarajevo derived from complex interactions among leaders of Orthodox Christian, Catholic, and Muslim communities, all within the context of German and Croatian occupations (Greble 2011).

The fate of non-Jewish victims has been a subject of research that has widened discussions about mass killing during the Second World War. About three million Soviet prisoners of war were in German hands by the end of 1941, and through mass shootings and starvation they became the single largest unarmed victim group in the early stages of the German-Soviet war (Snyder 2010, 175–82). These deaths had much to do with the victims' status as a particular type of racialized target: an underling destined for elimination in the Nazi drive to create an eastern frontier denuded of Slavs and ready for colonization by sedulous Germans. Similar views of purity and pollution surrounded the Gypsies (Lewy 2000). Nazi demographic engineering targeted a range of categories within the Reich itself, such as homosexuals and the physically disabled, but the execution of Gypsies was a practice that reproduced itself well beyond German-held territories, at times linking up with indigenous prejudices and local plans for ethnic cleansing.

Sources of Data

Before 1989 the territory on which the Holocaust took place was largely coextensive with the territory controlled by Europe's most paranoid regimes. In this era of information scarcity, each scrap of evidence was golden. But with the end of one-party rule and the throwing open of archives across the former Communist world, scholars now have the opportunity to know more about everything from high-level decision-making to grassroots participation. They also have the ability to add multiple perspectives to a literature that, until recently, was dominated by the view from Berlin. For decades, the USHMM, the Yad Vashem Archives in Jerusalem, and the Jewish Historical Institute in Warsaw have collected documents from around the world. To these resources can be added the USHMM's massive Jeff and Toby Herr Oral History Archive and the Steven Spielberg Film and Video Archive, records from war crimes trials across Europe and beyond, and the firsthand testimonies collected by Soviet investigators from the middle of the war forward.[2] While many of these resources have been used by historians for half a century, far fewer social scientists have mined them. For those who have, the result is a remarkably variegated account of killing, resistance, and complicity that mirrors the event datasets more commonly used in other episodes of genocidal violence (Kopstein and Wittenberg 2011, 2018; Finkel 2011, 2017).

Contingency, Causality, and Chronology

It is fully possible to accept the uniqueness of the Holocaust as a world-historical event while also fruitfully comparing each of its myriad components with their cognates elsewhere: the relationship between ideology and purposeful killing, the origins of genocidal state policy, collaboration and denunciation, the politics of military occupation, rescue and resistance, the dehumanization of noncombatants, the political economy of violence, and survivorship and the politics of memory, among many others. If earlier historians had argued for why the Holocaust *had* to happen—given the peculiarities of everything from German culture to the psychology of Adolf Hitler—the newer historiography has begun to address why it actually *did* happen, with careful attention to problems of contingency, causality, and chronology.

Each of these issues is particularly meaningful for social scientists. Consider first the issue of contingency. In very general terms, macrohistorical debates about the Holocaust have involved two camps: the so-called intentionalists, who see the destruction of European Jewry as stemming from the psychopathology of elites and long-term features of European (especially German) antisemitism, militaristic culture, and the legacy of the First World War; and the functionalists, who stress the gradual evolution of state policy and the deadly bureaucratic politics of the Third Reich. But one need not revisit these debates about macrohistory (now more than half a century old and still ongoing) to embrace the contingency of the Holocaust's many microhistories—that is, the patterns of deportation or killing in specific instances. Pogroms happened here and not there, in this year and not that one. Jews survived in this place but not in another. Uniformed soldiers were the perpetrators in this action, while neighbors in flannel trousers and shirtsleeves did the killing in another. At a higher level of resolution, it is possible to observe the patterned variation that is critical to developing any social scientific theory. In turn, this variation must be contingent on discrete factors—structural, ideological, institutional, even environmental—that political scientists are in a good position to identify.

New history writing also allows more careful attention to causality. The great contribution of Raul Hilberg's early work was to show that the extermination of Europe's Jews could be understood as well as mourned. His research involved the diligent amassing of government orders, communications records, train schedules, and other evidence to demonstrate the mechanics of killing by the Nazis and their allies. But Hilberg's barefoot empiricism also helped set Holocaust studies on a bifurcated course of development: on the one hand, scholars pursued ever more detailed studies of camp life, Nazi brutality, and miraculous survival; on the other, they plumbed the depths of psychology and German history to account for the root causes of Nazism and eliminationist antisemitism. These two tracks came together in Daniel Goldhagen's *Hitler's Willing Executioners*, perhaps the most widely read and broadly controversial Holocaust book of the last quarter century (Goldhagen 1996). The "Goldhagen thesis" stressed the long-term and peculiarly German origins of Nazi ideology and behavior, a theme pursued through stories of average killers and accomplices. Yet *Hitler's Willing Executioners* was also in many ways a product of the twin arc of Holocaust scholarship: grounded empiricism tied to wobbly causality. It reconfirmed the idea of the Holocaust as, at base, a German phenomenon and one traceable to the peculiarities of German history, culture, and Judeophobia.

That is not, however, the mainstream view within the new scholarship. Indeed, more recent work has stressed the particularist origins of anti-Jewish policies throughout Europe. Some work has even embedded antisemitism within the Nazis' broader commitment to a biologically pure state, rather than seeing it as the defining aspect of Nazi demographic policy overall (Friedlander 1995; Aly 1999; Kay 2006; Rutherford 2007). Other studies have stressed the mutual influence of Nazi and Stalinist killing policies or the long-term patterns of violence across East-Central Europe (Snyder 2010; Prusin 2010; Dekel-Chan, Gaunt, Meier, and Bartal 2011). Still further work has focused on the microdynamics of mass killing during the Second World War outside the Holocaust frame, examining other forms of localized violence that were pursued with grotesque levels of zeal and completeness (Bergholz 2016). While the German and Nazi contexts were the sine qua non of the broad program of destroying Europe's Jews, saying as much does not get us very far in understanding the myriad differences in how mass killing played out on the ground.

Finally, careful attention to chronology has assumed an ever-greater role in recent historiography. Rather than attributing the Final Solution solely, or even mainly, to the preformed plans of Hitler and his henchmen, more recent research has stressed the time-bound nature of state policy between the Anschluss with Austria in 1938 and the first camp-based gassing of civilians in 1942. The ideological intensification of the war prompted by the struggle with the Soviet Union; the iterated experience of on-the-ground killing in Poland, Ukraine, and Belarus; the failure of blitzkrieg on the eastern front by the autumn of 1941; the entry of the United States into a war that Germany increasingly saw as an all-out struggle for national survival; and the use of anti-Jewish policy as Germany's litmus test for the constancy of its allies all contributed to the formation of a state policy of genocide. As one survey of the literature concludes, "It is difficult to accept any longer the intentionalist premise that the unswerving goal of the Nazis from the outset was the immediate physical destruction of European Jews" (Fritzsche 2008, 595). To use anachronistic language, the war years saw the slide from a massive plan for ethnic cleansing—itself genocidal, according to postwar understandings of that term—toward a mandate for mass killing. Getting the terminology right is not just a matter of labeling. It enables scholars to ask questions in a way that situates the Holocaust in a path-dependent history, embeds the victims and perpetrators in their own (often the same) societies, and understands policy as a product of politics—all of which are orientations that fit naturally into a social science frame.

Politics and Mass Killing in the Holocaust

Pogroms, forced migration, interethnic violence, insurgency, and counterinsurgency were all components of Holocaust suffering. Each of these themes has a substantial body of research in the social sciences, yet there has so far been little connection between these literatures and the many cases contained within the macrohistorical phenomenon of the Holocaust. The project of connecting up these lines of research must begin with several assumptions about the rise of Nazi Germany, the military occupations and alliance politics of Western and Central Europe, the attack on the Soviet Union, and the mass killing of Jews and other targeted groups during the Second World War.

These assumptions are drawn from well-established findings in a now massive research base on genocide, civil war, ethnic conflict, and nontraditional warfare. They weave together important perspectives on state power, local communities, and violent mobilization:

1. Mass killing is variable. Even within a macrohistorical context of widespread violence, population movements, and death, mass killing occurs in some places but not in others, at some times but not at others, with shifting intensity, zeal, and completeness.
2. Mass killing is a social act. It derives from the complex interplay of ideology and power in and among human groups, not solely—perhaps not even mainly—from the individual psychology or megalomaniacal ravings of elites. Although the actual trigger pullers may be few in number, killing a group requires some degree of collective action on the part of some other group.

3. Mass killing is local. Large-scale violence is never the straightforward result of direct orders implemented by unquestioning automatons, although individual killing actions may at times lean in this direction. It depends on a distinct set of relationships between institutions and individuals, commanders and subordinates, perpetrators and victims, enablers and onlookers. Violence takes place on a specific piece of real estate and at the hands of identifiable individuals who are embedded in a web of power and influence with formal and informal institutions.
4. A state policy of mass killing is developed over time. The roots of any governmental action may lie in the distant past, in the childhood of a key leader, or in deep cultural predispositions. But there is no prima facie reason to believe that even the most abhorrent form of public policy—the decision to liquidate an entire category of persons—proceeds in ways appreciably different from its more benign counterparts.

Each of these points is a disciplinary predisposition rather than a hypothesis. As such, they are crucial to developing a social science of the Holocaust and, in turn, to transferring the lessons of Holocaust scholarship to other fields. They allow the elaboration of research directions that are explicitly comparative, theoretically informed, hypothesis generating, and amenable to empirical testing.

The subsections below outline four areas of research in Holocaust studies that proceed from the assumptions above and speak to pressing concerns in political science. Some are already the subject of a growing and high-quality literature in the discipline. Others have barely been addressed. Yet the theoretical possibilities and empirical evidence for investigating them are rich.

The Politics of Occupation

One of the most robust findings in the study of mass violence is the connection between insurgent resistance, occupation, and attacks on civilians (Licklider 1995; Harff 2003; Valentino 2004a; Kalyvas 2006). The overwhelming majority of large-scale civilian deaths occur within the context of internal war and regime instability. In no society do citizens wake up one day and decide to systematically dispense with their neighbors. Doing so requires solving a special collective action problem: getting people to act together in ways that are—at least for non-sociopaths—inherently difficult and gruesome. The Holocaust provides telling examples of the way in which this dynamic played itself out on the ground.

The single largest massacre committed during the Holocaust was, from the perspective of the perpetrators, an act of reprisal. Beginning on September 20, 1941, Soviet partisans detonated a series of bombs that leveled the German military headquarters and other buildings in occupied Kiev, the capital of Soviet

Ukraine. A week later, SS battalions and Ukrainian police rounded up Kiev's Jews, who were thought to be harboring Soviet agents or actively working against the occupation. Over the course of two days, at least 33,771 Jews were shot at Babi Yar, a ravine near the city center (Arad 2009, 173–76). Lesser Babi Yars and the actions that enabled them were a common feature of the Holocaust. The idea of exacting retribution and uncovering subversives played crucial roles in motivating behavior, from shootings by German police battalions in Poland, to roundups by French police in Vichy, to denunciations of neighbors in occupied Ukraine. These local narratives also linked up with one of the principal Nazi metanarratives in the war: that Jewry and Bolshevism were twin existential threats to the German nation. All this is revealed by one astonishing fact: that between June and December 1941, as the Wehrmacht made its initial push against the Red Army, the death toll among Jewish civilians was higher than among Soviet soldiers (Fritzsche 2008, 600).

Until the beginning of mass transport to Nazi killing facilities, most murders took place where most Jews actually lived: in the Polish and Soviet countryside. Stathis Kalyvas (2004) has called attention to the "urban bias" in research on civil wars—that is, the tendency of scholars to privilege written sources over oral ones; to stress the role of elite action, ideology, unchanging identities, and cultural causes; and to draw artificial lines between victims and victimized. The Holocaust offers opportunities for dissecting these issues. Relations between Jews and rural Poles, Ukrainians, Russians, Romanians, and others; the enhanced opportunities for evasion and rescue; and the long-term origins of state evasion in rural contexts all find expression in grassroots behavior during the Holocaust. Rurality is itself part of the explanation. The primary killing fields of Eastern Europe were also inhospitable terrain—the Pripyat marshes, the woodlands of Belarus, the rolling hills and proto-steppe of western Ukraine. As we learn more about Soviet partisan activity in the early stages of the war, environment may turn out to be one part of a causal chain: landscape facilitated evasion; evasion enhanced retribution; retribution required local knowledge; and local knowledge came from indigenous informants. While ideology and zeal undoubtedly played a role, one can construct a convincing—and comparatively robust—explanation for this particular type of Holocaust violence without reference to long-term causes or macrohistory.

More detailed study of the Holocaust can address other central questions about mass killing and counterinsurgency as well. For example, Benjamin Valentino (2004b, 211) found that mass killing "tends to be a policy of desperation, employed only when leaders believe their central interests or survival is at stake, and only after other means have failed." That is certainly true of the Nazis' ramping up the use of death facilities toward the end of the Second World War. But it is not the case for the major informal killing actions of the Holocaust: the SS-led massacres that attended the invasion of the Soviet Union. Most of these occurred during a period when the Nazis clearly believed that they were winning what would amount to a very short war. To some degree, that behavior may be attributed to ideology; after all, Germans were clearing the ground for what Hitler called the new "Garden of Eden"—a vast region west of the Ural Mountains that would be cleansed of undesirable indigenes and readied for German colonization. But the constancy of ideology cannot account for the variable timing, pace, and completeness of mass murder during Germany's most "optimistic" phase of the war on the eastern front.

Each of these features played themselves out in various ways in different non-German contexts. Consider two cases of occupation with different outcomes. Bulgaria tended to shelter its own Jews, but during its occupation of Thrace and Macedonia, Bulgarian soldiers deported thousands of Jews from these territories; most later perished in German death facilities (Todorov 2003; Chary 1972). Italy made important distinctions between "home" Jews and foreign Jews residing temporarily on Italian soil; thousands of Jewish noncitizens were sent to a string of internment facilities in southern Italy. Yet when Italy occupied a sliver of southeastern France in 1940, that territory became a refuge for persecuted Jews from Vichy and occupied France—a rare instance of an occupying power acting more beneficently abroad than at home (Marrus and Paxton 1981, 315–21). The fact that multiple countries behaved differently at home and as occupying powers points toward the powerful effects of territory, foreignness, and counterinsurgency. Simply put, where prejudice and counterinsurgency intersected, Jews were likely to die, regardless of whether Nazis or others were in charge. It was the targeting and thoroughness of the Nazis' behavior—not their tactics as such—that sets this aspect of the Holocaust apart from other instances of military occupation and insurgent war (see Valentino, Huth, and Balch-Lindsay 2004; Edelstein 2010).

Repertoires of Violence and Cooperation

When German soldiers and Nazi administrators swept eastward in June 1941, they were moving into a part of the world that many considered wholly alien. Propaganda had fed the notion that both the armed Slavic enemy and unarmed Jewish civilians were subhuman. There was even a German term for the otherworldly feeling that death, inhumanity, and foreignness could produce: *Ostrausch*, literally "getting high on the east." Killing actions were not uniform, however. The patterned variation suggests that factors were at work beyond the zeal of ideologically motivated SS units and propaganda-fed soldiers.

We know too little about the micropolitics of local killing, denunciation, and collaboration during the Holocaust. This is not because those themes have gone unexplored. Indeed, almost from the moment of liberation, states set about mopping up remnants of Nazi-allied governments, exposing the enablers of the German occupation, and punishing those thought to have collaborated with the enemy. Rather, the real problem has been the paucity of work placing these dynamics in a comparative or longitudinal context. To begin with, especially on the eastern front, German military forces were operating in a region that had already experienced sustained social and political violence before the summer of 1941. The territory on which much of the Holocaust occurred had been the site of anti-Jewish pogroms in the Russian Empire from the 1870s forward. During the Polish-Bolshevik War (1919–21) and the Russian Civil War (1917–23), forced migration and troop movements produced yet further massacres (see Veidlinger 2021). Between September 1939 and June 1941, eastern Poland, eastern Romania, and the Baltic republics were overrun by the Red Army and ruthlessly governed by the Soviets, with the attendant massacres, civilian flight, and retributive attacks one would expect from sudden changes of borders and military control.

This history mattered, but not always in the ways one might expect. Violence was, to a degree, iterative. Victims during one period—Jews but also ethnic Poles and Ukrainians—were frequently targets in another. Yet levels of resistance, insurgent recruitment, and atrocities differed by geography. Why? Consider two hypotheses. First, spaces of violence and relative tranquility may align with previous patterns of education, nationalism, social integration, and governance before the war—although crucially not with ethnic balances or ideology (Darden 2009). In other words, in a region where indigenous antisemitism was nearly universal and violence already a recent experience, the patterning of mass killing seems to have reflected longer-term structures of local society.

Second, the shorter-term experience of prewar politics may have conditioned anti-Jewish behavior during the war, especially if we bracket killing actions organized by state institutions. For example, lands that had been controlled by Romania between the two world wars seem to have experienced more discrete incidents of antisemitic violence (beatings, theft, murder, rape) than did the Soviet territories that Romania came to control during the war. The nature of the prewar regime—"nationalist" Romanian or "socialist" Soviet—affected rates of local participation in anti-Jewish violence: the former tended to increase it, the latter to decrease it. Even though Soviet territories were the site of the major state-led killing operations, it may have been harder to mobilize locals for participation there than in the non-Soviet zones. Soviet norms of interethnic cooperation and the rhetoric of "friendship among peoples" provided a relative buffer against mobilized killing when compared with zones that had experienced nationalistic propaganda before the war (Dumitru and Johnson 2011). Patterns of Jewish rebellion in Polish ghettos, as well as pogroms committed by ethnic Poles, may also align with voting behavior and party politics in interwar Poland: where Jews were most politically mobilized before the war, they were most prone to being attacked but also most prone to take up arms in resistance (Kopstein and Wittenberg 2011, 2018; Finkel 2011, 2017).

In both these lines of argument, place and the past overshadow identity—a finding that accords with what we know about conflict and killing in general. This suggests two further features regarding repertoires of violence and resistance during the Holocaust. First, the unit of analysis is critical. A good deal of research on the Holocaust still takes place within a national frame. Scholars ask how "the Ukrainians" or "the French" treated Jews during the war or puzzle over the exceptional behavior of governments that by and large resisted Nazi pressure, such as Denmark. But thinking of violence, collaboration, rescue, and resistance as "ethnic" or "national" phenomena puts the cart before the horse. It assumes, rather than demonstrates, that the relevant unit of social action was the cultural group. In no case did all members of a distinct ethnic population act in exactly the same way—a fact that suggests that group-level factors beyond ethnicity were the drivers of behavior. Although Jewish victims were clearly defined in ethnic—or "racial"— terms, the entrepreneurs of violence had mixed success in mirroring that definition among the perpetrators. Classifying victims by culture was relatively easy. Mobilizing their tormentors along similar ascriptive lines was much harder.

Second, identity did come into the picture when it intersected with a specific state policy of recruitment or coercion. With enough resources and determination, it was possible for an occupying power to mobilize communities along clearly sectarian lines. The most extreme case is Germany's policy toward ethnic Germans beyond the Reich, the so-called *Volksdeutsche*. Given Nazi racial theory, these communities were meant to be the vanguard of Germany's expansion, the agents of its colonization efforts in the Slavic East, and later the beneficiaries of "repatriation" to Germany, where the state could harness their patriotism and productivity. Especially on the eastern front, these usually rural communities became some of the most favored killers in the Nazis' plan for eliminating local Jews and partisans.

The *Volksdeutsche* were a tiny percentage of the population in Ukraine, for example, and there is no reason to assume that their antisemitic commitment or imagined grievances outstripped those of local Slavs. Yet through a system of recruitment and rewards overseen by the German state, the *Volksdeutsche* emerged as a disproportionately high percentage of activists in the "Holocaust by bullets" (Lumans 1993; Dean 2008; Lower 2005a). Given that all of Germany's allies were engaged in their own nationalizing projects in territories they occupied during the war—Hungary in northwestern Romania and eastern Czechoslovakia, Romania in western Ukraine, Bulgaria in Macedonia and Thrace, Croatia in Bosnia—cognates of Germany's *Volksdeutsche* policy existed for each state. Together they point toward the interplay of state policy, ethnicity, and recruitment for murder.

Alliance Politics

As Mark Mazower (2008, 581–90) has argued, Hitler's "New Order"—the plan for reshaping politics and redrawing boundaries that was meant to accompany a German victory—is best seen as an imperial system. It was an arrangement that bought off peripheral elites by promising a reworked map of Europe in which the territorial aspirations of Nazi-allied states would be fully realized.

Yet Hitler's Germany was also at the center of a complex and shifting network of independent states—an empire in Nazi-occupied areas but an alliance across much of the rest of Europe. The politics of ally maintenance proved crucial to the pace and completeness of anti-Jewish activity (Hollander 2006). Romania's wartime government was an enthusiastic endorser of Hitler's territorial plans yet balked when Nazi officials sought to interfere in Romania's domestic affairs. Successive Hungarian governments welcomed the German-sponsored reapportionment of territory in central Europe, which expanded Hungary's borders back toward their pre–First World War limits. Hungarians had deported Jewish noncitizens already in 1941, an action that led to the deaths of tens of thousands of people who fell into the hands of the SS. Yet it took the German military occupation of Hungary in 1944 to get local officials to acquiesce to the mass expulsion of Hungary's Jews. Germany's alliance partners were in fact oddly patriotic when it came to their own Jews: their own policy decisions were often murderous, but they objected when Berlin tried to step up the pace of the Final Solution inside a partner state (Case 2009).

In this context, center-periphery relations, two-level games, and the inconstancy of strategic friends were probably as important in the elimination of Europe's Jews as in more benign spheres of alliance politics. The pursuit of local aims within the Nazi imperial context reveals two key features of the international relations of mass killing. First, partner governments seemed to be active and enthusiastic participants so long as the alliance leader was capable of delivering alliance benefits. In other words, "burden sharing" in the Holocaust was relatively easy for Germany to achieve in the early stages of the war—roughly from the signing of the Tripartite Pact in September 1940 until the stalling of the German-Soviet war by mid-autumn 1941. From that point forward, partner states evaluated their cooperation in mass killing in terms that were increasingly self-interested and wary.

Second, policymaking priorities evolved in divergent ways in Berlin and other Axis capitals. In the Nazi worldview, eliminating Jews was increasingly part of the state's overall survival strategy (Valentino 2004a). Bogged down on the eastern front, Berlin found that the only part of existing policy that could be pursued in the region was the clearing of territory for future colonization. Once the United States entered the war, the theory that world Jewry was rising to the aid of its own carried even greater weight. Yet for partner governments such as Hungary, Romania, and Italy, the intensification of mass killing practices in the German-administered lands—and enhanced pressure for the alliance members to act similarly at home—increased the price of pooling security. These governments were thinking forward to a possible future in which Germany might lose the war and in which non-German governments would be held responsible for their own actions. Genocide raised the cost of cooperation among governments that might ordinarily have bought into the same policy aims.

Death and Policymaking

For all the power of micropolitical perspectives on mass killing, they cannot get at the two recurring questions at the core of Holocaust scholarship: what were the origins of the German state policy of destroying Europe's Jews, and how did this policy intersect with other Nazi political and strategic aims? In 1998, Christian Gerlach published an article that argued for seeing the Final Solution as an essentially "normal" political decision—that is, one that involved internal policy debate, improvisational adaptation to policy challenges, and finally a definitive decision by a key leader. German policy, in other words, was *made*: it evolved from grand schemes for the forced deportation of Jews (to Madagascar, to Poland, to western Eurasia), became a practice of massacres in place, and ended as an array of permanent brick-and-mortar killing centers whose only purpose was to dispose of as many people as possible.

Gerlach's work was considered radically revisionist at the time, since it seemed to treat the Final Solution as a policy like any other—a grotesque one, to be sure, but nevertheless a policy produced over time by people within institutions. The really surprising case, however, would be a form of public policy conceived in the mind of a leader, bequeathed to a circle of like-minded subordinates, and implemented seamlessly through a vast network of civilian, paramilitary, and military institutions, both at home and in allied states, all of which produced an outcome identical to that envisioned by the originator.

The mere facts of the Final Solution's development suggest policy variation over time. A significant adjustment took place in early December 1941: before that point, Germans and their accomplices killed Jews where they found them; after it, the perpetrators spent massive amounts of time and resources to move Jews thousands of miles to specially created camps and death facilities. The particular context of the Nazi state—totalitarian in aspiration but internally competitive in practice—created an environment in which policymaking flowed from an identifiable ideology as well as from institutional competition and careerist ambitions (Aly and Heim 2002). In the end, principal-agent problems, bureaucratic politics, improvisation, institutional learning, imperfect information, miscalculation, and decision-making blinders are as likely to be present when states make evil as when they build roads and bridges.

Policy implementation was also more likely the product of variable state capacities than of differences in commitment or zeal. In Axis-occupied Ukraine, survival rates among Jews varied depending on the occupying forces in control of territory. Of all the areas of Soviet Ukraine seized by a foreign power during the war, districts administered by Romania were among the places where it was most likely for a Jew to survive (Kruglov 2008, 272–90). The Romanian state was certainly no less committed in theory to removing Jews than were the Nazis. Romanian eugenicists and demographers were fully in line with German (and European) goals concerning national purity and the mobilization of the state to realize them (Bucur 2002; Solonari 2010). In prewar Romania, in fact, antisemitic acts on a per capita basis had been far higher than in prewar Germany (Brustein and King 2004).

The difference had to do, in part, with state efficacy. As survivor testimonies confirm, Romanian occupiers were not necessarily less brutal than German ones, but they could be more easily bribed. Even in one of the most abhorrent moments of the Romanian-organized Holocaust—the brutal emptying of the ghetto in the Soviet city of Odessa between January and April 1942—Romanian officers themselves were worried about the ability of their subordinates to fulfill their tasks. Their solution is still present in the archives: a separate declaration signed by every Romanian soldier confirming his commitment to avoid fraternizing with Jews and to carry out orders (King 2011, 215). Even in cases of mass killing, public policy is only as effective as the commitment and talent of those entrusted with implementing it.

Rescue and Resistance

In a time of widespread violence, how does one explain two persistent forms of variation: places where massive attacks on civilians met with sustained armed resistance and places that managed to avoid violent mobilization altogether? Both outcomes are frequently attributed to heroism. The Bielski brothers sheltered more than a thousand Jews in their forest redoubt in German-occupied eastern Poland (Tec 2008). Protestant pastors secreted thousands of Jewish children in the upland villages of the French Massif Central; other religious minorities seemed to play a special role in the Netherlands (Hallie 1994; Paxson 2019; Braun 2019). Numbers alone point to the fact that resistance, in whatever form, was a deeply unusual response to Axis killing policies. For example, of the more than one thousand ghettos created by the Nazis in Poland and the Soviet Union, Jews took up arms in only thirty of them (Finkel 2017, 213).

Still, the extraordinary actions of individuals in each of these cases are not inconsistent with the basic enabling structures of opportunity, organization, and resources. As Evgeny Finkel has pointed out, Jewish armed resistance in Poland was more likely to occur in those areas that had high levels of prewar political activism and that experienced Soviet occupation from 1939 to 1941, a phase of the war that preceded the massive German invasion of Soviet-held territories and the Soviet Union in the summer of 1941 (Finkel 2017, 8–12). The Soviet occupation provided a kind of school for resistance: since non-Communist organizations were pushed underground by Soviet occupiers, they acquired the habits of conspiracy and secrecy, as well as the technical skill sets of guerrilla fighting, that could later be put to use against the far more lethal threat presented by the Nazis.

Similar arguments seem to hold, *mutatis mutandis*, for other forms of Jewish violent mobilization, such as armed resistance to pogroms in the decade preceding the First World War. The harsh but incomplete repression of Jewish social organizations, especially Zionist groups, sharpened the organizational and military skills of members who became practiced in resisting future attacks (Dekel-Chen, Gaunt, Meier, and Bartal 2011). It is thus possible to explain the comparative rarity of Jewish armed resistance in ways that cast the phenomenon less as a mystery than as an outgrowth of organizational capacity (for a general argument along these lines, see Weinstein 2007).

In this light, the most perplexing feature of the Holocaust experience—why did German practice produce a rolling genocide without provoking a mass rebellion?—looks less extraordinary than it might seem. As work on cases as diverse as the French Revolution and the Indian partition has shown, the mere presence of significant numbers of men with recent military experience is a robust explanation for the magnitude of violence in times of ubiquitous confrontation (McDonald 1951; Jha and Wilkinson 2012). Resistance to violence may be a virtue, but it is also crucially a technology. These arguments point toward the darkest irony of the Holocaust in the borderlands between Germany and the Soviet Union. The areas that experienced the "double occupation" by first Soviet and then German armies were the most likely to see the mass murder of Jewish civilians. Yet they were also the places where—given the unusual combination of skill and opportunity—Jews were more prone to defy their would-be destroyers.

The social memory of mass killing usually begins with—and often returns at regular intervals to—accounts that are deterministic and culture-specific: "Those maniacs have always wanted to get rid of us." But as the personal memories of actual victims are transmogrified by the passage of time, and as historians and social scientists enter the debate, explanations tend to incorporate more sophisticated, comparative, and robust ways of recalling an awful history. Research on the Armenian genocide, for example, is today a world away from the essentialism of the past (Bloxham 2005; Akçam 2006; Suny, Göçek, and Naimark 2011; Suny 2017; but see also Morris and Ze'evi 2019).

Until recently the burden of proof has been on those who claim that the Holocaust bears an important resemblance to other instances of mass killing. Indeed, historians of genocide who have dealt with the Holocaust in a comparative light have normally trodden carefully on this issue. But for social science, the burden of proof is on those who claim that a particular case is sui generis. The emerging political science of the Holocaust helps disaggregate this gigantic and atrocious historical event. It provides social scientists with a route toward understanding the twentieth century's most infamous instance of mass killing, while also pointing toward an entire galaxy of cases rarely examined by researchers interested in broad theories of human behavior.

Five preliminary conclusions emerge from the survey above:

- Military occupation may have facilitated mass killing, but the efficacy, pace, and variable completeness of anti-Jewish atrocities—especially in the second half of 1941—complicate the idea that state strategy is the critical component of genocidal violence. The slaughter that defined the early stages of the Holocaust in the occupied Soviet Union had much more in common with the one-sided, selective violence against civilians often found in civil wars. The Holocaust could thus be the key empirical field connecting the generally estranged literatures on genocide and substate conflict.
- Even in a context where state policy privileged ethnic, racial, and religious categories, patterns of intergroup violence and collaboration rarely ran neatly along ascriptive boundaries. Indeed, the quality of being a perpetrator, victim, or resister may have had longer-term sources, measurable in ways ranging from voting behavior in the 1920s and 1930s to literacy levels at the dawn of nationalist movements in the nineteenth century. While most of us are all good constructivists now—believing in the ephemeral

nature of identities and convinced of their manipulability by states—we still engage in a reflexive "groupism" (Brubaker 2004) when describing the behavior of "the Pashtuns," "the Sunnis," or other categories of people who have come to blows. In a time and place where the basic identity categories—Jew and non-Jew—were imagined as stark and the violence profoundly one-sided, patterns of mass murder still did not perfectly map the communities bequeathed by the master narrative of antisemitism. The Holocaust represented an unusual but not unique form of cooperative behavior among states: the shared effort by allied countries to eliminate all or part of a discrete civilian population, both within the foreign territories they occupied and within their own sovereign lands.

- The Holocaust experience points toward the ways in which even horrific acts of violence repeat, at a broad social level, the dynamics of more pedestrian forms of interstate cooperation. For pro-German governments such as Romania and Hungary, genocidal intentions were balanced against the price of pooling security; as the war wound on and the likelihood of a quick German victory appeared ever dimmer, governments increasingly balked at a policy that had meant more to the alliance leader than to the allies themselves. The Holocaust thus has much to say about the spread of violence across international frontiers. What we routinely label "contagion" more closely resembles the purposive working out of informal alliances among regimes and nonstate killers.

- Despite a sizeable literature on the emergence of selective violence and the genocidal targeting of noncombatants, we still know rather little about how a policy of mass killing works its way through formal and informal institutions. Explanations are often abstracted to the level of governments as unitary, self-interested actors or reduced to the microincentives and psychologies of individual *génocidaires*. Yet the Holocaust provides ample scope for understanding the meso-level actions of civilian bureaucracies, military units, paramilitary formations, transport departments, city councils, communal leaderships, and other state and parastate bodies. Indeed, from Raul Hilberg and Hannah Arendt forward, documenting the "banality of evil" has been central to Holocaust studies. The advantage for the comparative study of large-scale violence is clear: where we have the most data on the Holocaust—the everyday institutions that enable genocide, even within what appears from the outside to be utter state and societal collapse—is precisely where we understand mass killing in other contexts most dimly.

- Resistance to genocidal violence—whether by taking up arms against oppressors or by engaging in acts of rescue—is often heroic, but it is also dependent on discrete social technologies. Fighters need to know how to fight well. Rescuers need to know whom to trust and how to ferry the rescued to safety. Counterinsurgents understand this point implicitly, which is why they invest so much time in monitoring insurgent networks, mapping social terrains, and seeking to understand the capabilities and information flows among their enemies (see Nagl 2005; Kilcullen 2009, 2010). The makers of genocide are often in a similar position. They expend considerable effort to identify their targets, ensure those targets' acquiescence, prevent retaliatory attacks, and cover up their crimes—while sometimes getting all these things wrong. The patterning of violence and resistance in the Holocaust illustrates the power of precisely these mechanisms, as well as the way in which the distinction between genocide and civil war may well turn on the technologies of resistance available to targeted populations.

Further research on Holocaust-era violence can add to these debates and help refine theories of mass violence. But what are the moral limits of this work, if any? If there is a danger in this research program, it lies in its own obviousness. Political scientists should of course incorporate the Holocaust into their models, the logic might go, since there is no necessary distinction between this episode of genocide and any other. That it happened to occur among a European, highly literate, memory-laden, and ultimately state-creating ethnoreligious minority gives the Holocaust a separate status when it comes to the sociology of knowledge, but not when it comes to its place in the universe of cases that scholars of large-scale violence might address.

The problem with this view is that it too easily glides over the ethics of comparison, the morality of "modeling" human suffering, and the ultimate purposes for which scholars willingly delve into awfulness. After all, the comparison of discrete human experiences is never a cavalier exercise, especially in the realm of violence, loss, and death. The systematic and thorough nature of Nazi practice still places the Holocaust in a peculiar moral category. Its scale was gargantuan. It involved the purposeful killing of millions of individuals as well as the extinguishing of an entire civilization—the culture of the East European borderlands rooted in Jewish religiosity and the Yiddish language. It flowed from an ideology that was not just distasteful but fundamentally abhorrent, one that marshaled science and history to condemn an entire human population to elimination—in theory, anywhere its members happened to live on the entire planet. It produced social, political, cultural, and economic consequences that are still unparalleled. The Holocaust can still be a moral category of one even when specific episodes of violence, the tactics of perpetrators and heroism of resisters, and importantly the social scientific patterning within this world-historical event turn out not to be unique. The sum of every massacre, pogrom, shooting, and gassing *within* the Holocaust still does not quite *equal* the Holocaust.

Acknowledging this, however, is a good thing. Distinguishing morality from analysis ought to sharpen both perspectives. Millions of Jewish men, women, and children died from a rifle or pistol shot, near their homes, in plain view of their neighbors. That fact gives the victims an essential kinship with Tutsis, Bosnians, Syrians, Rohingya, and Uyghurs. The aspirational slogan "Never again" makes sense only because the Holocaust's many microhistories were not in fact unique. Nor are the tools that social scientists can wield in trying to explain them.

Doing original research in this field entails delving into archives, watching video testimony, reading the memoirs of perpetrators and victims, examining photographs of bystanders and onlookers, and listening to the dwindling number of survivors. Scholars cannot help but be confronted by the shocking immediacy of social violence—a sense of sympathetic terror and collective human responsibility that is, for better or worse, likely to be especially visceral to the North American and European academics who produce the theories that purport to explain the rest of the world's wickedness. This perspective, and its attendant sense of humility and incomprehension, should never be allowed to disappear inside a scholarly model of mass murder.

REFERENCES

Akçam, Taner. 2006. *A Shameful Act: The Armenian Genocide and the Question of Turkish Responsibility*. New York: Metropolitan.
Aly, Götz. 1999. *"Final Solution": Nazi Population Policy and the Murder of the European Jews*. London: Arnold.
———. 2007. *Hitler's Beneficiaries: Plunder, Race War, and the Nazi Welfare State*. New York: Metropolitan.
Aly, Götz, and Susanne Heim. 2002. *Architects of Annihilation: Auschwitz and the Logic of Destruction*. Princeton, NJ: Princeton University Press.
Annals of the American Academy of Political and Social Science. 1980.450 (July).
Annals of the American Academy of Political and Social Science. 1996.548 (November).
Arad, Yitzhak. 2009. *The Holocaust in the Soviet Union*. Lincoln: University of Nebraska Press; Jerusalem: Yad Vashem.
Arendt, Hannah. (1964) 2006. *Eichmann in Jerusalem: A Report on the Banality of Evil*. New York: Penguin.
Balcells, Laia, and Daniel Solomon. 2020. "Violence, Resistance, and Rescue during the Holocaust." *Comparative Politics* 53 (1): 161–80.
Bartov, Omer, ed. 2000. *The Holocaust: Origins, Implementation, Aftermath*. London: Routledge.
———. 2008. "Eastern Europe as the Site of Genocide." *Journal of Modern History* 80 (3): 557–93.

Berenbaum, Michael, and Abraham J. Peck, eds. 1998. *The Holocaust and History*. Washington, DC: United States Holocaust Memorial Museum; Bloomington: Indiana University Press.

Bergholz, Max. 2016. *Violence as a Generative Force: Identity, Nationalism, and Memory in a Balkan Community*. Ithaca, NY: Cornell University Press.

Berkhoff, Karel C. 2004. *Harvest of Despair: Life and Death in Ukraine under Nazi Rule*. Cambridge, MA: Belknap Press of Harvard University Press.

Bischoping, Katherine, and Andrea Kalmin. 1999. "Public Opinion about Comparisons to the Holocaust." *Public Opinion Quarterly* 63 (4): 485–507.

Bloxham, Donald. 2005. *The Great Game of Genocide: Imperialism, Nationalism, and the Destruction of the Ottoman Armenians*. Oxford: Oxford University Press.

Braham, Randolph L. 1994. *The Politics of Genocide: The Holocaust in Hungary*. Rev. ed. 2 vols. New York: Rosenthal Institute for Holocaust Studies, CUNY; Boulder, CO: Social Science Monographs.

Brandon, Ray, and Wendy Lower, eds. 2008. *The Shoah in Ukraine: History, Testimony, Memorialization*. Bloomington: Indiana University Press.

Braun, Robert. 2019. *Protectors of Pluralism: Minorities and the Rescue of Jews in the Low Countries of the Holocaust*. Cambridge: Cambridge University Press.

Browning, Christopher R. 1998. *Ordinary Men: Reserve Police Battalion 101 and the Final Solution in Poland*. New ed. New York: Harper Perennial.

———. 2004. *The Origins of the Final Solution: The Evolution of Nazi Jewish Policy, September 1939–March 1942*. Lincoln: University of Nebraska Press; Jerusalem: Yad Vashem.

———. 2010. "The Nazi Empire." In *The Oxford Handbook of Genocide Studies*, edited by Donald Bloxham and A. Dirk Moses, 407–25. Oxford: Oxford University Press.

Brubaker, Rogers. 2004. *Ethnicity without Groups*. Cambridge, MA: Harvard University Press.

Brustein, William I., and Ryan D. King. 2004. "Anti-Semitism in Europe before the Holocaust." *International Political Science Review* 25 (1): 35–53.

Bucur, Maria. 2002. *Eugenics and Modernization in Interwar Romania*. Pittsburgh: University of Pittsburgh Press.

Carp, Matatias. 1996. *Cartea Neagră: Suferințele evreilor din România, 1940–1944*. 2nd ed. 3 vols. Bucharest: Editura Diogene.

Case, Holly. 2009. *Between States: The Transylvanian Question and the European Idea during World War II*. Stanford, CA: Stanford University Press.

Chary, Frederick. 1972. *The Bulgarian Jews and the Final Solution, 1940–1944*. Pittsburgh: University of Pittsburgh Press.

Chirot, Daniel, and Clark McCauley. 2006. *Why Not Kill Them All? The Logic and Prevention of Mass Political Murder*. Princeton, NJ: Princeton University Press.

Churchwell, Sarah. 2018. *Behold, America: The Entangled History of "America First" and "the American Dream."* New York: Basic Books.

Darden, Keith A. 2009. "Resisting Occupation: Lessons from a Natural Experiment in Carpathian Ukraine." Keith A. Darden personal website. Accessed January 27, 2012. http://keithdarden.files.wordpress.com/2009/11/darden-natural-experiment.pdf.

Dean, Martin. 2008. "Soviet Ethnic Germans and the Holocaust in the Reich Commissariat Ukraine, 1941–1944." In *The Shoah in Ukraine: History, Testimony, Memorialization*, edited by Ray Brandon and Wendy Lower, 248–71. Bloomington: Indiana University Press.

Dekel-Chen, Jonathan, David Gaunt, Natan M. Meier, and Israel Bartal, eds. 2011. *Anti-Jewish Violence: Rethinking the Pogrom in East European History*. Bloomington: Indiana University Press.

Deletant, Dennis. 2006. *Hitler's Forgotten Ally: Ion Antonescu and His Regime, Romania 1940–1944*. Basingstoke, UK: Palgrave Macmillan.
Desbois, Father Patrick. 2008. *The Holocaust by Bullets: A Priest's Journey to Uncover the Truth behind the Murder of 1.5 Million Jews*. New York: Palgrave Macmillan.
Desch, Michael C. 2004. "A 'Final Solution' to a Recurrent Tragedy?" *Security Studies* 13 (3): 145–59.
Dumitru, Diana, and Carter Johnson. 2011. "Constructing Interethnic Conflict and Cooperation: Why Some People Harmed Jews and Others Helped Them during the Holocaust in Romania." *World Politics* 63 (1): 1–42.
Edelstein, David M. 2010. *Occupational Hazards: Success and Failure in Military Occupation*. Ithaca, NY: Cornell University Press.
Finkel, Evgeny. 2011. "Party Politics in Hell: Explaining Ghetto Uprisings during the Holocaust." Unpublished paper. PDF file.
———. 2017. *Ordinary Jews: Choice and Survival during the Holocaust*. Princeton, NJ: Princeton University Press.
Finkel, Evgeny, and Scott Straus. 2012. "Macro, Meso, and Micro Research on Genocide: Gains, Shortcomings, and Future Areas of Inquiry." *Genocide Studies and Prevention* 7 (1): 56–57.
Fitzpatrick, Sheila. 2005. *Tear Off the Masks! Identity and Imposture in Twentieth-Century Russia*. Princeton, NJ: Princeton University Press.
Fitzpatrick, Sheila, and Robert Gellately, eds. 1997. *Accusatory Practices: Denunciation in Modern European History, 1789–1989*. Chicago: University of Chicago Press.
Frank, Anne. 1952. *Anne Frank: The Diary of a Young Girl*. Garden City, NY: Doubleday.
Frankl, Viktor. 1962. *Man's Search for Meaning*. Boston: Beacon.
Friedlander, Henry. 1995. *The Origins of Nazi Genocide: From Euthanasia to the Final Solution*. Chapel Hill: University of North Carolina Press.
Friedländer, Saul. 2007. *Nazi Germany and the Jews: The Years of Extermination, 1939–1945*. New York: Harper Perennial.
Fritzsche, Peter. 2008. "The Holocaust and the Knowledge of Murder." *Journal of Modern History* 80 (3): 594–613.
Fujii, Lee Ann. 2009. *Killing Neighbors: Webs of Violence in Rwanda*. Ithaca, NY: Cornell University Press.
Gerlach, Christian. 1998. "The Wannsee Conference, the Fate of German Jews, and Hitler's Decision in Principle to Exterminate All European Jews." *Journal of Modern History* 70 (4): 759–812.
———. 2010. *Extremely Violent Societies: Mass Violence in the Twentieth-Century World*. Cambridge: Cambridge University Press.
Goldhagen, Daniel Jonah. 1996. *Hitler's Willing Executioners: Ordinary Germans and the Holocaust*. New York: Knopf.
Greble, Emily. 2011. *Sarajevo, 1941–1945: Muslims, Christians, and Jews in Hitler's Europe*. Ithaca, NY: Cornell University Press.
Gross, Jan T. 1988. *Revolution from Abroad: The Soviet Conquest of Poland's Western Ukraine and Western Belorussia*. Princeton, NJ: Princeton University Press.
———. 2001. *Neighbors: The Destruction of the Jewish Community in Jedwabne, Poland*. Princeton, NJ: Princeton University Press.
Hallie, Philip. 1994. *Lest Innocent Blood Be Shed*. New York: Harper Perennial.
Harff, Barbara. 2003. "No Lessons Learned from the Holocaust? Assessing Risks of Genocide and Political Mass Murder since 1955." *American Political Science Review* 97 (1): 57–73.
Hilberg, Raul. (1961) 2003. *The Destruction of the European Jews*. 3rd ed. 3 vols. New Haven, CT: Yale University Press.

———. 1992. *Perpetrators, Victims, Bystanders*. New York: HarperCollins.
———. 1996. *The Politics of Memory: The Journey of a Holocaust Historian*. Chicago: Ivan R. Dee.
Hollander, Ethan J. 2006. "Implementing and Subverting the Final Solution in Nazi-Occupied Europe." PhD diss., University of California, San Diego.
Horwitz, Gordon J. 2008. *Ghettostadt: Łódź and the Making of a Nazi City*. Cambridge, MA: Belknap Press of Harvard University Press.
Ioanid, Radu. 2000. *The Holocaust in Romania: The Destruction of Jews and Gypsies under the Antonescu Regime, 1940–1944*. Chicago: Ivan R. Dee.
Jha, Saumitra, and Steven Wilkinson. 2012. "Veterans, Organizational Skill and Ethnic Cleansing: Evidence from the Partition of South Asia." Stanford Graduate School of Business Working Paper No. 2092. Social Science Research Network. February 7, 2012. https://ssrn.com/abstract=1998429.
Judt, Tony. 2005. *Postwar: A History of Europe since 1945*. New York: Penguin.
Kalyvas, Stathis N. 2003. "The Ontology of 'Political Violence': Action and Identity in Civil Wars." *Perspectives on Politics* 1 (3): 475–94.
———. 2004. "The Urban Bias in Research on Civil Wars." *Security Studies* 13 (3): 160–90.
———. 2006. *The Logic of Violence in Civil War*. Cambridge: Cambridge University Press.
Kay, Alex, 2006. *Exploitation, Resettlement, Mass Murder: Political and Economic Planning for German Occupation Policy in the Soviet Union, 1940–1941*. New York: Berghahn Books.
Kiernan, Ben. 2009. *Blood and Soil: A World History of Genocide and Extermination from Sparta to Darfur*. New Haven, CT: Yale University Press.
Kilcullen, David. 2009. *The Accidental Guerrilla: Fighting Small Wars in the Midst of a Big One*. Oxford: Oxford University Press.
———. 2010. *Counterinsurgency*. Oxford: Oxford University Press.
King, Charles. 2004. "The Micropolitics of Social Violence." *World Politics* 56 (3): 431–55.
———. 2011. *Odessa: Genius and Death in a City of Dreams*. New York: W. W. Norton.
———. 2019. *Gods of the Upper Air: How a Circle of Renegade Anthropologists Reinvented Race, Sex, and Gender in the Twentieth Century*. New York: Doubleday.
Kopstein, Jeffrey S., and Jason Wittenberg. 2011. "Deadly Communities: Local Political Milieus and the Persecution of Jews in Occupied Poland." *Comparative Political Studies* 44 (3): 259–83.
———. 2018. *Intimate Violence: Anti-Jewish Pogroms on the Eve of the Holocaust*. Ithaca, NY: Cornell University Press.
Kruglov, Alexander. 2008. "Jewish Losses in Ukraine, 1941–1944." In *The Shoah in Ukraine: History, Testimony, Memorialization*, edited by Ray Brandon and Wendy Lower, 272–90. Bloomington: Indiana University Press.
Levene, Mark. 2005. *Genocide in the Age of the Nation State*. 2 vols. London: I. B. Tauris.
Levi, Primo. 1959. *If This Is a Man*. New York: Orion.
Lewy, Guenter. 2000. *The Nazi Persecution of the Gypsies*. Oxford: Oxford University Press.
Licklider, Roy. 1995. "The Consequences of Negotiated Settlements in Civil Wars, 1945–1993." *American Political Science Review* 89 (3): 681–90.
Lieberman, Evan S. 2010. "Bridging the Qualitative-Quantitative Divide: Best Practices in the Development of Historically Oriented Replication Databases." *Annual Review of Political Science* 13 (June): 37–59.

Lower, Wendy. 2005a. "Hitler's 'Garden of Eden' in Ukraine: Nazi Colonialism, *Volksdeutsche*, and the Holocaust, 1941–1944." In *Gray Zones: Ambiguity and Compromise in the Holocaust and Its Aftermath*, edited by Jonathan Petropoulos and John K. Roth, 185–204. New York: Berghahn Books.

———. 2005b. *Nazi Empire-Building and the Holocaust in Ukraine*. Chapel Hill: University of North Carolina Press.

Lumans, Valdis O. 1993. *Himmler's Auxiliaries: The Volksdeutsche Mittelstelle and the German National Minorities of Europe, 1933–1945*. Chapel Hill: University of North Carolina Press.

Lustick, Ian S. 1996. "History, Historiography, and Political Science: Multiple Historical Records and the Problem of Selection Bias." *American Political Science Review* 90 (3): 605–18.

Marrus, Michael R. 1989. *The Holocaust in History*. London: Penguin.

Marrus, Michael R., and Robert O. Paxton. 1981. *Vichy France and the Jews*. Stanford, CA: Stanford University Press.

Matthäus, Jürgen, Martin Shaw, Omer Bartov, Doris Bergen, and Donald Bloxham. 2011. Review forum on *The Final Solution: A Genocide*, by Donald Bloxham. *Journal of Genocide Research* 13 (1–2): 107–52.

Mazower, Mark. 2005. *Salonica, City of Ghosts*. New York: Knopf.

———. 2008. *Hitler's Empire*. New York: Penguin.

McDonald, Forrest. 1951. "The Relation of the French Peasant Veterans of the American Revolution to the Fall of Feudalism in France, 1789–1792." *Agricultural History* 25 (4): 151–61.

McDoom, Omar Shahabudin. 2021. *The Path to Genocide in Rwanda: Security, Opportunity, and Authority in an Ethnocratic State*. Cambridge: Cambridge University Press.

Midlarsky, Manus I. 2005. *The Killing Trap: Genocide in the Twentieth Century*. Cambridge: Cambridge University Press.

Morris, Benny, and Dror Ze'evi. 2019. *The Thirty-Year Genocide: Turkey's Destruction of Its Christian Minorities, 1894–1924*. Cambridge, MA: Harvard University Press, 2019.

Mueller, John E. 2004. *The Remnants of War*. Ithaca, NY: Cornell University Press.

Nagl, John A. 2005. *Learning to Eat Soup with a Knife: Counterinsurgency Lessons from Malaya and Vietnam*. Chicago: University of Chicago Press.

Naimark, Norman M. 2002. *Fires of Hatred: Ethnic Cleansing in Twentieth-Century Europe*. Cambridge, MA: Harvard University Press.

———. 2010. *Stalin's Genocides*. Princeton, NJ: Princeton University Press.

Neiman, Susan. 2019. *Learning from the Germans: Race and the Memory of Evil*. New York: Farrar, Straus and Giroux.

Paxson, Margaret. 2019. *The Plateau*. New York: Riverhead.

Prusin, Alexander. 2010. *The Lands Between: Conflict in the East European Borderlands, 1870–1992*. Oxford: Oxford University Press.

Rutherford, Phillip. 2007. *Prelude to the Final Solution: The Nazi Program for Deporting Ethnic Poles, 1939–1941*. Lawrence: University Press of Kansas.

Sambanis, Nicholas. 2002. "A Review of Recent Advances and Future Directions in the Quantitative Literature on Civil War." *Defence and Peace Economics* 13 (3): 215–43.

———. 2004. "What Is Civil War? Conceptual and Empirical Complexities of an Operational Definition." *Journal of Conflict Resolution* 48 (6): 814–58.

Segev, Tom. 1993. *The Seventh Million: The Israelis and the Holocaust*. New York: Hill and Wang.

Shirer, William L. 1960. *The Rise and Fall of the Third Reich: A History of Nazi Germany*. New York: Simon and Schuster.
Snyder, Timothy. 1999. "'To Resolve the Ukrainian Question Once and for All': The Ethnic Cleansing of Ukrainians in Poland, 1943–1947." *Journal of Cold War Studies* 1 (2): 86–120.
———. 2008. "The Life and Death of Western Volhynian Jewry, 1921–1945." In *The Shoah in Ukraine: History, Testimony, Memorialization*, edited by Ray Brandon and Wendy Lower, 77–113. Bloomington: Indiana University Press.
———. 2010. *Bloodlands: Europe between Hitler and Stalin*. New York: Basic Books.
Solonari, Vladimir. 2010. *Purifying the Nation: Population Exchange and Ethnic Cleansing in Nazi-Allied Romania*. Baltimore: Johns Hopkins University Press; Washington, DC: Woodrow Wilson Center Press.
Stone, Dan. 2010. *Histories of the Holocaust*. Oxford: Oxford University Press.
Straus, Scott. 2006. *The Order of Genocide: Race, Power, and War in Rwanda*. Ithaca, NY: Cornell University Press.
———. 2007. "Second-Generation Comparative Research on Genocide." *World Politics* 59 (3): 476–501.
Subotić, Jelena. 2019. *Yellow Star, Red Star: Holocaust Remembrance after Communism*. Ithaca, NY: Cornell University Press.
Suny, Ronald Grigor. 2017. *"They Can Live in the Desert but Nowhere Else": A History of the Armenian Genocide*. Princeton, NJ: Princeton University Press.
Suny, Ronald Grigor, Fatma Müge Göçek, and Norman M. Naimark, eds. 2011. *A Question of Genocide: Armenians and Turks at the End of the Ottoman Empire*. Oxford: Oxford University Press.
Tarrow, Sidney. 2007. "Inside Insurgencies: Politics and Violence in an Age of Civil War." *Perspectives on Politics* 5 (3): 587–600.
Tec, Nechama. 2008. *Defiance*. Oxford: Oxford University Press.
Ten Boom, Corrie. 1971. *The Hiding Place*. With John and Elizabeth Sherrill. Carmel, NY: Guideposts.
Todorov, Tzvetan. 2003. *The Fragility of Goodness: Why Bulgaria's Jews Survived the Holocaust*. Princeton, NJ: Princeton University Press.
Trevor-Roper, H. R. 1947. *The Last Days of Hitler*. London: Macmillan.
USHMM (United States Holocaust Memorial Museum). 2009–22. *Encyclopedia of Camps and Ghettos, 1933–1945*. 4 vols. Bloomington: Indiana University Press.
Valentino, Benjamin A. 2004a. *Final Solutions: Mass Killing and Genocide in the Twentieth Century*. Ithaca, NY: Cornell University Press.
———. 2004b. "*Final Solutions*, Further Puzzles." *Security Studies* 13 (3): 204–18.
Valentino, Benjamin, Paul Huth, and Dylan Balch-Lindsay. 2004. "'Draining the Sea': Mass Killing and Guerrilla Warfare." *International Organization* 58 (2): 375–407.
Veidlinger, Jeffrey. 2021. *In the Midst of Civilized Europe: The Pogroms of 1918–1921 and the Onset of the Holocaust*. New York: Metropolitan Books.
Weinstein, Jeremy M. 2007. *Inside Rebellion: The Politics of Insurgent Violence*. Cambridge: Cambridge University Press.
Weitz, Eric D. 2005. *A Century of Genocide: Utopias of Race and Nation*. Princeton, NJ: Princeton University Press.
Whitman, James Q. 2017. *Hitler's American Model: The United States and the Making of Nazi Race Law*. Princeton, NJ: Princeton University Press.
Wiesel, Elie. 1960. *Night*. New York: Hill and Wang.
Wood, Elisabeth Jean. 2003. *Insurgent Collective Action and Civil War in El Salvador*. Cambridge: Cambridge University Press.

2

HISTORIES IN MOTION
The Holocaust, Social Science Research, and the Historian

Jan Burzlaff

In the winter of 1977, Emmanuel Le Roy Ladurie (b. 1929) caused an upheaval among English-speaking historians.[1] Acknowledging how much historians owe to social scientists, and following in the footsteps of the Annales school, Le Roy Ladurie critiqued his colleagues' inclination toward "narrative" history. Instead, he provocatively called for "motionless" history, which studies "a practically motorless traditional society." Precisely because he considered rural French society from the end of the Middle Ages to the beginning of the eighteenth century as stable—indeed, almost immobile—Le Roy Ladurie asserted that this type of quantitative history needs to be aligned more closely with the social sciences (Le Roy Ladurie 1977; Elster 2020). With the return of narrative history looming large, the placement of his publication in *Social Science History* was fitting (Abbott 1991; McCants 2016). Unfortunately, the journal, which aims to link history and the social sciences, has performed less well for the Holocaust. Despite its explicit emphasis on historical context and contingency, it has featured just four articles about the Nazi genocide of the Jews, undoubtedly one of the most vibrant areas of inquiry since the late 1980s. This paradox is also visible in the well-established journal *Comparative Studies in Society and History*, which has published only seven essays on this vast topic since 1958, ranging from the behavior of Nazi officials to Holocaust memory and politics. Similarly, a search of the journal *Annales: Histoire, sciences sociales* yields fifteen results (mostly book reviews) when combining "Holocaust" and "Shoah." The edited volume you hold in your hands takes a bold step that is long overdue, paving the way for a new generation of social scientists to tackle the Holocaust and, by extension, the origins, dynamics, and legacies of genocide and mass violence.

Elsewhere in this book, the political scientist Charles King maps out how research on the Holocaust fits into and expands on the social science of mass violence and civil war. King enumerates convincing reasons why social scientists have refrained from more systematic studies of the Nazi genocide. Among those he offers is the issue of the Holocaust's uniqueness, which has given way to scholarly anxieties about treating it as "just another data-generating event" (King 2012). King also points out that the public memory and commemoration of individual histories make it difficult for scholars to examine the events quantitatively. To this list of intellectual restraints, one could easily add the general public's appetite for such stories narrated by historians (rather than social scientists), and the political leeway given to low-ranking perpetrators and collaborators in postwar Europe, on both sides of the solidifying Iron Curtain (Beachler 2011; Fulbrook 2018; Finder and Prusin 2018). Overcoming these inhibitions, King makes a strong case that there are many opportunities for social scientists to study the Holocaust and refine social scientific theories, particularly in terms of military occupation, repertoires of violence and cooperation, alliance politics, genocidal policymaking, and resistance.

In what follows, I will build on King's reflections, inviting historians to join in these debates. I want to call for "histories in motion" that share Le Roy Ladurie's wish for less narrative but differ by focusing on rapid social processes under the Nazi occupation. The histories in motion that emerge from this volume do not rely solely on narration; instead, they also incorporate more consciously quantitative data and reflect better the Holocaust's social dynamics. This chapter argues that these histories in motion arrive at a good time. Such an approach not only requires a more interdisciplinary dialogue but also aligns well with recent evolution in Holocaust studies. To make my argument, I will first review existing encounters between Holocaust historians and social scientists to emphasize more common ground than one generally assumes. Building on the various chapters, I will then highlight two perspectives that further enhance such a dialogue, regarding different scales of analysis and variations across Nazi-occupied Europe.

The enduring obstacles to interdisciplinary interventions can be traced back to long-held paradigms of the academic disciplines involved, and the field of Holocaust research itself. Historians and social scientists usually describe their respective disciplines in opposition to each other. This tradition pertains to the difference in research design and the dichotomy of idiographic and nomothetic approaches. On the whole, historians purport to study events embedded in their specific contexts, instead of seeking the replicability that social scientists do. In other words, historians tend to assume that social scientists discard the role of messiness, irregularities, and human agency (Sewell 2005). In addition, there is the conventional division of tasks between history and social science—the former in charge of the past, the latter of the present. Though historical sociology seemed to have bridged this gap during the 1960s and 1970s, it aims to study social patterns over time, therefore largely disqualifying the Holocaust (Mahoney and Rueschemeyer 2003). Notwithstanding structural continuities during the "racial century" from the mid-nineteenth century to the mid-twentieth (Moses 2002), historians usually proceed via various "vanishing points" (Walser Smith 2008) that ought to explain the next stage of the genocidal process. These transformative thresholds include 1933, 1939, the summer and winter of 1941, and the German defeat at Stalingrad in early 1943—in sum, a short period. Engaging with and transcending such scholarly boundaries, as this volume sets out to do, should be commended as a courageous step forward.

One could also argue that misunderstandings between these academic disciplines occurred because of how the field itself evolved (Michman 2020). Studies on Holocaust historiography now appear more abundantly, and, if one were to judge a field by its degree of self-reflexivity, Holocaust studies has reached maturity (Rittner and Roth 2020; Browning et al. 2015; Luhmann 2005). We now know that, for various reasons, the topic prompted historians—more than other scholars—to examine the events, at least until the late 2000s. Historians have long considered their task what Edward H. Carr (1967) influentially framed as the study of origins. The vision of the Holocaust as a key event of the twentieth century proved particularly well suited for such an undertaking. Concurrently, from the 1980s onward, these efforts to historicize the Holocaust required historians from all periods to confront tricky theoretical questions. For example, the issue of Holocaust memory and its uses during the *Historikerstreit*, the heated debate over the role of the Holocaust in German history and society, prompted the survivor and historian Saul Friedländer (b. 1932), among others, to establish the journal *History & Memory* in 1989.

Interestingly enough, social scientific works on the Holocaust have exerted a significant influence on historians, from the Latvian American professor of psychology David Pablo Boder (1886–1961) and the political scientist Raul Hilberg (1926–2007) to Jan T. Gross, a Polish American sociologist who renewed our understanding of Nazi-occupied Poland and Polish-Jewish relations (Boder 1949; Hilberg 1961; Gross 2001, 2008). One recent example illustrates the impact of such thought-provoking work. In his 2016 book, *Ordinary Organizations: Why Normal Men Carried Out the Holocaust*, the German sociologist Stefan Kühl argued that membership in "ordinary" Nazi organizations was a significant variable for the unfolding genocide. His writing allows us to showcase three broader tendencies that this volume embraces. First, as Holocaust studies became increasingly institutionalized, social scientists—first psychologists, then sociologists and political scientists—responded to historians' frameworks, rather than reasoning outside them. For various reasons, most of these social scientific milestones received positive reviews from historians and inspired research within Holocaust studies rather than in their home disciplines. In the case of Kühl's work, fellow social scientists pointed out contextualization issues, the problematic definition of "ordinary," and the applicability of the sociologist Niklas Luhmann's system theory (Kühl 2016; Holzinger 2020). Nevertheless, Kühl's book is one of the few works in the German-speaking social sciences that have tackled Nazi Germany and the Holocaust, a state of affairs that equally applies to the West's overall social sciences (Suderland and Christ 2019; Messina 2017; Halpert 2007).

Second, and unlike Kühl, social scientists have now increasingly embraced the general shift undertaken by Holocaust historians, moving from a focus on National Socialism and perpetrators to interethnic violence and Jewish perspectives. For instance, the political scientists Jeffrey S. Kopstein and Jason Wittenberg positioned Jan T. Gross's study of the Jedwabne pogrom within a comparative landscape of communal violence during the summer of 1941. Meanwhile, in 2017 the political scientist Evgeny Finkel outlined the first typology of Jewish responses to the persecution (Kopstein and Wittenberg 2018; Finkel 2017; Soyer 2014). In that sense, the work of the political scientist Daniel Jonah Goldhagen, arguing that "ordinary" Germans acted out of widespread "eliminationist antisemitism," proved an exception to overall fruitful discussions about perpetrators (Moses 1998). Third, just as Kühl himself did, social science research has now grounded itself in regional and local archives, often using the wealth of documents scattered across Eastern Europe. In this volume, it is telling that the sociologist Rachel L. Einwohner sets out to retrieve "missing voices" instead of data points. Social science research has taken a historical turn.

By systematizing these evolutions, this book enriches Holocaust studies significantly. As a historian, I see two chief benefits of engaging with this vibrant cohort of social scientists. First, these scholars ask themselves the same methodological questions as historians, which involves reflecting on the effect of teaching and quantifying the Holocaust (Hilton and Patt 2020). Second, historians' traditional care for empiricism and opposition to "abstract theory" fails to account for chapters in this book that master national languages and integrate new and old documentation into theoretical frameworks. Take, for example, the subject of Holocaust remembrance. Establishing a detailed record of the events was necessary to confront resurgent Holocaust denial in the 1980s and 1990s. But nowadays, such denial has given way to distortions most ably analyzed by social scientists. In her chapter on actors in post-Communist Serbia, Croatia, and

Lithuania, the political scientist Jelena Subotić calls it "memory appropriation." Like the political scientists Zvi Gitelman and Volha Charnysh (respectively writing about legitimizing myths in East European states in general and Holocaust memory in Poland in particular), Subotić aptly combines historical analysis with memory studies (Dutceac Segesten and Wüstenberg 2017).

Furthermore, the dynamics of "memory appropriation"—the roots of which Subotić detects in tensions between the West, keen to "universalize" the Holocaust, and Eastern European countries, with their post-Soviet conflicts—echo scholarly debates about scales. They play out between the universal and the particular, or between sweeping macro- and granular microlevels. With the adoption of the cultural, spatial, and visual turns, it seems legitimate for social scientists to question the extent to which another fine-grained reconstruction of this SS unit or that civil administration in a Nazi-occupied territory will give rise to new insights (Stone 2012). To be sure, much factual knowledge remains to be unearthed from archives, and necessarily so. By "insights," however, I mean striking a balance between exhausting available sources and exploring the specific links between places, events, and social groups (Moses 2008). Admittedly, such connections that bring historians and social scientists closer together prove more challenging for historians of the modern era, with its sheer wealth of documents, than for, say, historians of the ancient Silk Road or medieval Europe. This initial effort to sift through and not ignore contradictory sources adds to the suspicion that many social scientists have about historians' focus on "description," which is only a preliminary step in their case studies. Reading through this collective volume, one realizes that, precisely because of this wealth of available documentation, historians need more training in quantitative and computational methods. Here, the road map outlined in *History as Social Science*, a joint venture commissioned by the National Academy of Sciences and the Social Science Research Council, remains as compelling as it did back in 1971. It noted that about three-quarters of historians claimed that at least one social science field was "particularly important" to their interest. But historians of Europe and North America were also those with the least social science training (Landes and Tilly 1971; Lemercier and Zalc 2019).

Despite all of these disciplinary differences, however, developments within the social sciences and history allow the fields to find more common ground. Most historians would contend that narration is not at odds with explanation (Maza 2017; Banner 2012; Hewitson 2014; Evans 2000). From the three core principles of political science—comparison, theory development, and generalization—historians can retain comparison (Kreuzer 2020; Slater and Ziblatt 2013). More specifically, Holocaust historians have incorporated sociological concepts, mostly derived from Bourdieu or Foucault, into their study of Nazi camps. Quantitative aspects have traditionally played an important role in studies on slave labor, German firms and insurance sectors, and postwar commissions (Hájková 2018; Browning and Hayes 2019; Grossmann, Edele, and Fitzpatrick 2017; Buggeln 2014). For their part, social scientists now understand mass violence as a political and social process. It seems to me that the underlying rational choice theory, the favorite brainchild of North American social scientists, has now somewhat lost its overall appeal. This evolution can only please historians, who have shifted focus away from bureaucratic, rational decision-making processes since the 1980s. In the same vein, a growing number of social scientists now offer a range of variables that account for the persecution of Jews in Vichy France (Balcells and Solomon 2020; Zalc 2020; Sémelin 2019; Mercklé and Zalc 2018). Perhaps the most fundamental agreement between historians and social scientists can be thematic: the Holocaust was a socially rooted genocide that evolved both transnationally and locally. Precisely because this volume starts from this point, common ground emerges, and all contributors tackle the interdependence between spatial units and observations of genocidal violence and social processes in a way more accessible to historians. As you will discover, such scholarship is diverse in its methods and multilayered in its interpretations. Below, I will offer just two perspectives that consider more systematically different scales of analysis and variations of a social, economic, and political nature across Nazi-occupied Europe.

Historians study all geographical levels of the Holocaust, but the book's focus on the micro and meso levels calls for closer attention. The contributors usefully divide the "Holocaust" into shorter episodes. Case studies range from the Warsaw and Vilna ghettos to Amsterdam, swaths of Eastern Europe, wartime France, post-Soviet nations, and Western Europe. Each chapter dwells on a specific theme—survival, church authority, gender, various forms of resistance, interethnic violence, intergenerational transmission of Holocaust memory—rather than remaining at the nation-state level (Burzlaff 2020). At the micro level, after his work on deportations to the Nazi death camps, the mathematician Lewi Stone, cooperating with the historian Stephan Lehnstaedt, uncovers a phenomenon of medical resistance in the Warsaw ghetto that remains hidden from the official Nazi record (Stone 2019; Katz 2019). Mathematical modeling allows Stone and Lehnstaedt to highlight how public health leadership and Jewish doctors and nurses helped flatten the curve of typhus in 1943, a topic that has an immediate resonance after the outbreak of the COVID-19 pandemic. On the other side of the geographical spectrum, in the first quantitative study of its kind, the political scientist Susan Welch examines gender in deportations from Western Europe. She finds that on more than 1,100 transports to Auschwitz and other camps, women were far more highly represented than men among the overall 550,000 West European Jews. The data (albeit somewhat spotty in Eastern Europe because of the death camps' presence and genocidal warfare) promises valuable additions to our understanding of the gendered plight of Jews in the Holocaust (Waxman 2017).

To be sure, there is still much to be done in these social scientific studies to achieve geographical breadth and analytical depth, which corresponds for historians to transnational history and microhistory (Zalc and Bruttmann 2017). The greatest potential for new insights may lie in comparative studies at the meso level—that is, everything between microstudies of cities, camps, and ghettos and the macro approach of Timothy D. Snyder's 2010 *Bloodlands*, understood as the area of Eastern Europe where up to fourteen million people lost their lives between 1932 and 1945. Looking back to 2010, what is surprising is not that a senior historian moved from archival work to a sweeping reinterpretation of the first half of twentieth-century Eastern Europe—a shift in scope that a historian is expected to perform in the course of an ideal career. Instead, Snyder's conceptualization of a space of genocide and mass violence and his comparative lens have stimulated the field, if only to push back on his claims (Snyder 2010).

Therefore, collaborations between historians and social scientists are particularly relevant for two issues that remain underexplored. The first deals with the social history of the Nazi occupation. For Jews, to what extent did the length and degree of one's exposure to Nazi violence shape one's choices and behaviors? For non-Jews, to what extent did it lead to their participation in or restraint from said violence? How do we systematically evaluate the persecution's intimate aspects after the summer of 1941, such as the so-called *Judenjagd* in Eastern Europe, the face-to-face stage of the extermination in rural microcosms? The role of ethnicity and the environment has also received relatively little attention (Domańska and Małczyński 2020). If one accepts "history" as the study of social change, the chapters in this volume help us envision such transformations for individuals: for example, with a life course approach or through narrative-interpretive analyses (Goldberg 2017). Other authors focus on institutions, including bishops in Vichy France, or specific themes, such as ethnic violence and political competition, in the political scientist Jeffrey S. Kopstein's chapter. This agenda-setting volume inspires much food for thought for the social history of Nazi Europe that largely remains to be written.

The second chief benefit for historians stems, I believe, from the close attention that social scientists pay to variations, paving the way for a middle ground between law-like regularities and historians' attention to specificity. It is a truism that the Holocaust unfolded very differently across various countries, regions, even cities—hence the importance of understanding both Nazi policies and social processes on the ground (Bloxham 2009). The combination of different scales of analysis not only allows for a more careful understanding of how local and communal factors played a role in the Holocaust's unfolding, but also dismisses one-size-fits-all approaches to the origins and variety of Nazi violence and—above all—the absence of neighbor-on-neighbor violence in specific communities (Bartov 2018). As these social scientists describe, a more systematic approach is all the more important since we now know how much locality and prewar experiences influenced, if not outweighed altogether, any sense of identity across Nazi Europe. For instance, more or less deeply seeded antisemitism and cultural essentialism ("the Germans," "the Poles," etc.) do not account for the stark contrasts in the persecution across the European continent. To explain such variations, scholars have begun paying attention to internal differences among social groups. In my own research on how Jews survived in and around eight cities across the Nazi empire, variations appear not only among geographical locations, but also within one city according to Jews' prewar and wartime experiences.

In this volume, two further areas welcome such a comparative approach, starting with the political behavior of prewar communities (Rozenas and Zhukov 2019). Chapters by the political scientists Benjamin Mishkin and Daniel Solomon and the sociologist Robert Braun share a focus on selective violence and processes rooted in local contexts. Take the example of those 1,253 communities affected during the 1938 pogrom in Nazi Germany known as Kristallnacht. Solomon finds that one-third (634) of all still-existing Jewish synagogues remained undamaged; these were predominantly located in places with smaller Jewish populations and areas where the German Communist Party received less support (see also Bergholz 2019). Therefore, it seems that perceptions and social categorization equally served as triggers for violence. This book thus appeals to cultural historians skeptical of political competition arguments in favor of cultural theories of difference. Combined with the theme of "borderlands," which now enjoys the full attention of Holocaust historians, these contributions have much to bring to the metaphorical table. Braun's study of the figure of a Jewish bogeyman in children's stories, whose presence clustered around border crossings in Weimar Germany, is a good example of contextualized histories of antisemitism and xenophobia that echo recent literature on Nazi rule (Gellately 2020).

Ultimately, what the historian Elissa Bemporad (2019, 7) has dubbed "communities of violence" in the context of anti-Jewish violence in the Soviet Union between 1919 and 1945 have important implications for the Holocaust more broadly—including the war's unfolding and the genocide's legacies. Another underresearched topic is how political behaviors and past persecution spill over into subjective experience. Here, this book invites historians to study various experiences of the postwar era, such as displaced persons camps, the evolution of international law, the restitution of Jewish property, and forced resettlement (Krzyzanowski 2020; Fogg 2017).

Where do we go from here? Necessarily, there will always be some amount of mutual incomprehension between historians and social scientists. In a recent book forum on Finkel's 2017 *Ordinary Jews*, and while lauding his innovative questions, reviewers continued opposing detail and contingency to broader models and typologies (Engel 2018). But despite or precisely because of the sophistication that Holocaust scholarship has reached, this field seems well suited for exploring interdisciplinary collaborations. Such possibilities go both ways. Building on historians' meticulous work over the last four decades, social scientists have shifted focus from Nazi policies to grassroots interactions, perceptions, and lived experiences, notably from the Jewish perspective. In the wake of the digital revolution, social scientists are now participating in the "allure of the archives," the emotional experience of venturing into the past's unexpected dimensions (Farge 2013; Luft 2020). In turn, this volume allows historians to reflect further on the role of big data and computing software in general, anxieties within Holocaust studies, and the tensions of this field with comparative genocide studies in particular (Moses 2016). This book suggests that crossing academic boundaries involves analytical notions of social dynamics and fluidity. Such "histories in motion" can connect historians' empirical depth with social scientists' quantitative methods (Stone 2020).

This new generation of social scientists embraces a dynamic field. Their combined efforts are only a first thrust in possible themes, and some will miss a focus on, say, the Axis states, the newly opened Vatican archives, North Africa, or Scandinavia. This book also requires that we tie the Holocaust more systematically to other genocides and that we dislodge the equation of "Western" with "universal," particularly in cases that do not fit into explanations of utopian social projects and the modern illiberal state—settler colonialism and the interplay between mass violence and genocide are just two examples where the totalitarian state paradigm still dominates (Bachman 2020). Not least for this reason, this volume makes a compelling case for pluralist endeavors. Such an intellectual journey represents a challenge in our sophisticated but fragmented subfields, a path that will prove unfamiliar at times and rocky at first. But many topics can be approached only from a decidedly interdisciplinary angle, as the cultural anthropologist Joanna Tokarska-Bakir has shown for Polish-Jewish relations (Tokarska-Bakir 2011; Engelking 2018). Therefore, we should also encourage the input of archaeologists, cultural geographers, social psychologists, art historians, scholars of religion, anthropologists, and economists as experts on materiality, space, beliefs, meanings, and behavior, as well as the relationship between ends and limited resources (Tokarska-Bakir 2019; Sturdy Colls 2015; Chare and Williams 2019).

Given the observable spike in populist and neofascist movements in the last few years, including the politicization of "genocide," combining the efforts of historians and social scientists appears an urgent task (Moses 2019). After all, history as a collective enterprise has always been shaped by practice, which includes borrowing from other fields and shifts in historians' sensibilities regarding how the past is represented. As Paul Veyne (b. 1930), a noted French historian of ancient Rome, once wrote, progress in historiography lies "in being able to ask oneself more and more questions, but not in knowing how to answer them" (Veyne 1984, 213).

REFERENCES

Abbott, Andrew. 1991."History and Sociology: The Lost Synthesis." *Social Science History* 15 (2): 201–38.

Bachman, Jeffrey. 2020. "Cases Studied in *Genocide Studies and Prevention* and *Journal of Genocide Research* and Implications for the Field of Genocide Studies." *Genocide Studies and Prevention: An International Journal* 14 (1): 2–20.

Balcells, Laia, and Daniel Solomon. 2020. "Violence, Resistance, and Rescue during the Holocaust." *Comparative Politics* 53 (1): 161–80. https://doi.org/10.5129/001041520X15863824603010.

Banner, James M., Jr. 2012. *Being a Historian: An Introduction to the Professional World of History*. Cambridge: Cambridge University Press.

Bartov, Omer. 2018. *Anatomy of a Genocide: The Life and Death of a Town Called Buczacz*. New York: Simon and Schuster.

Beachler, Donald W. 2011. *The Genocide Debate: Politicians, Academics, and Victims*. New York: Palgrave Macmillan.

Bemporad, Elissa, 2019. *Legacy of Blood: Jews, Pogroms, and Ritual Murder in the Lands of the Soviets*. Oxford: Oxford University Press.

Bergholz, Max. 2019. "To Kill or Not to Kill? The Challenge of Restraining Violence in a Balkan Community." *Comparative Studies in Society and History* 61 (4): 954–85.

Bloxham, Donald. 2009. *The Final Solution: A Genocide*. New York: Oxford University Press.

Boder, David. 1949. *I Did Not Interview the Dead*. Chicago: University of Illinois Press.

Browning, Christopher, and Peter Hayes. 2019. *German Railroads, Jewish Souls: The Reichsbahn, Bureaucracy, and the Final Solution*. New York: Berghahn Books.

Browning, Christopher, Susannah Heschel, Michael R. Marrus, and Milton Shain, eds. 2015. *Holocaust Scholarship: Personal Trajectories and Professional Interpretations*. New York: Palgrave Macmillan.

Buggeln, Marc. 2014. *Slave Labor in Nazi Concentration Camps*. Oxford: Oxford University Press.

Burzlaff, Jan. 2020. "Confronting the Communal Grave: A Reassessment of Social Relations during the Holocaust in Eastern Europe." *Historical Journal* 63 (4): 1054–77.

Carr, Edward H. 1967. *What Is History?* New York: Vintage.

Chare, Nicholas, and Dominic Williams. 2019. *The Auschwitz Sonderkommando: Testimonies, Histories, Representations*. Basingstoke, UK: Palgrave Macmillan.

Domańska, Ewa, and Jacek Małczyński, eds. 2020. "Special Issue on the Environmental History of the Holocaust." *Journal of Genocide Research* 22 (2).

Dutceac Segesten, Anamaria, and Jenny Wüstenberg. 2017. "Memory Studies: The State of an Emergent Field." *Memory Studies* 10 (4): 474–89.

Elster, Jon. 2020. *France before 1789: The Unraveling of an Absolutist Regime*. Princeton, NJ: Princeton University Press.
Engel, David. 2018. "Analyzing Jewish Behavior during the Holocaust." *Shofar: An Interdisciplinary Journal of Jewish Studies* 36 (1): 183–89.
Engelking, Barbara. 2018. "Des rêves comme source pour l'histoire de l'Holocauste?" *Vingtième siècle: Revue d'histoire* 139 (3): 94–109.
Evans, Richard J. 2000. *In Defence of History*. New York: W. W. Norton.
Farge, Arlette. 2013. *The Allure of the Archives*. New Haven, CT: Yale University Press.
Finder, Gabriel N., and Alexander V. Prusin. 2018. *Justice behind the Iron Curtain: Nazis on Trial in Communist Poland*. Toronto: Toronto University Press.
Finkel, Evgeny. 2017. *Ordinary Jews: Choice and Survival during the Holocaust*. Princeton, NJ: Princeton University Press.
Fogg, Shannon. 2017. *Stealing Home: Looting, Restitution, and Reconstructing Jewish Lives in France, 1942–1947*. Oxford: Oxford University Press.
Fulbrook, Mary. 2018. *Reckonings: Legacies of Nazi Persecution and the Quest for Justice*. Oxford: Oxford University Press.
Gellately, Robert. 2020. *Hitler's True Believers: How Ordinary People Became Nazis*. Oxford: Oxford University Press.
Goldberg, Amos. 2017. *Trauma in First Person: Diary Writing during the Holocaust*. Bloomington: Indiana University Press.
Gross, Jan T. 2001. *Neighbors: The Destruction of the Jewish Community in Jedwabne, Poland*. Princeton, NJ: Princeton University Press.
———. 2008. *Fear: Anti-Semitism in Poland after Auschwitz*. Princeton, NJ: Princeton University Press.
Grossmann, Atina, Mark Edele, and Sheila Fitzpatrick, eds. 2017. *Shelter from the Holocaust: Rethinking Jewish Survival in the Soviet Union*. Detroit: Wayne State University Press.
Hájková, Anna. 2018. "Den Holocaust queer erzählen." In *Jahrbuch Sexualitäten*, edited by Janin Afken, Jan Feddersen, Benno Gammerl, Rainer Nicolaysen, and Benedikt Wolf, 86–110. Göttingen: Wallstein.
Halpert, Burton P. 2007. "Early American Sociology and the Holocaust: The Failure of a Discipline." *Humanity & Society* 31 (1): 6–23.
Hewitson, Mark. 2014. *History and Causality*. Basingstoke, UK: Palgrave Macmillan.
Hilberg, Raul. 1961. *The Destruction of the European Jews*. New Haven, CT: Yale University Press.
Hilton, Laura J., and Avinoam Patt, eds. 2020. *Understanding and Teaching the Holocaust*. Madison: University of Wisconsin Press.
Holzinger, Markus. 2020. "Ganz seriöse Wissenschaft? Einige Bemerkungen zur Kühl-Kontroverse über die 'ganz normalen Organisationen.'" *Zeitschrift für Genozidforschung* 18 (1): 7–29.
Katz, Steven T. 2019. "Thinking about Jewish Resistance during the Holocaust." In *Holocaust Studies: Critical Reflections*, edited by Steven T. Katz, 233–66. Abingdon: Routledge.
King, Charles. 2012. "Can There Be a Political Science of the Holocaust?" *Perspectives on Politics* 10 (2): 323–41.
Kopstein, Jeffrey S., and Jason Wittenberg. 2018. *Intimate Violence: Anti-Jewish Pogroms on the Eve of the Holocaust*. Ithaca, NY: Cornell University Press.
Kreuzer, Marcus. 2020. "Varieties of Time in Comparative Historical Analysis." In *The Oxford Handbook of Time and Politics*, edited by Klaus H. Goetz, 1–28. Oxford: Oxford University Press.
Krzyzanowski, Lukasz. 2020. *Ghost Citizens: Jewish Return to a Postwar City*. Cambridge, MA: Harvard University Press.

Kühl, Stefan. 2016. *Ordinary Organizations: Why Normal Men Carried Out the Holocaust*. Hoboken, NJ: Wiley.

Landes, David S., and Charles Tilly, eds. 1971. *History as Social Science*. Englewood Cliffs, NJ: Prentice Hall.

Lemercier, Claire, and Claire Zalc. 2019. *Quantitative Methods in the Humanities: An Introduction*. Charlottesville: University of Virginia Press.

LeRoy Ladurie, Emmanuel. 1977. "Motionless History." *Social Science History* 1 (2): 115–36.

Luft, Aliza. 2020. "How Do You Repair a Broken World? Conflict(ing) Archives after the Holocaust." *Qualitative Sociology* 43 (3): 317–43.

Luhmann, Niklas. 2005. "Positives Recht und Ideologie." In *Soziologische Aufklärung*, vol. 1, *Aufsätze zur Theorie sozialer Systeme*, edited by Niklas Luhmann, 224–55. Wiesbaden: VS Verlag für Sozialwissenschaften.

Mahoney, James, and Dietrich Rueschemeyer. 2003. *Comparative Historical Analysis in the Social Sciences*. Cambridge: Cambridge University Press.

Maza, Sara. 2017. *Thinking about History*. Chicago: University of Chicago Press.

McCants, Anne E. C. 2016. "History and the Social Sciences: Past Imperfect, Future Promising." *Social Science History* 40 (4) 525–34.

Mercklé, Pierre, and Claire Zalc. 2018. "Peut-on modéliser la persécution? Apports et limites des approches quantifiées sur le terrain de la Shoah." *Annales: Histoire, sciences sociales* 73 (4): 923–57.

Messina, Adele Valeria. 2017. *American Sociology and Holocaust Studies: The Alleged Silence and the Creation of the Sociological Delay*. Boston: Academic Studies Press.

Michman, Dan. 2020. "Characteristics of Holocaust Historiography and Their Contexts since 1990: Emphases, Perceptions, Developments, Debates." In *A Companion to the Holocaust*, edited by Simone Gigliotti and Hilary Earl, 211–33. Hoboken, NJ: Wiley.

Moses, A. Dirk. 1998. "Structure and Agency in the Holocaust: Daniel J. Goldhagen and His Critics." *History and Theory* 37 (2): 194–219.

———. 2002. "Conceptual Blockages and Definitional Dilemmas in the 'Racial Century': Genocides of Indigenous Peoples and the Holocaust." *Patterns of Prejudice* 36 (4): 7–36.

———. 2008. "Toward a Theory of Critical Genocide Studies." In *Online Encyclopedia of Mass Violence*. April 18, 2008. http://bo-k2s.sciences-po.fr/mass-violence-war-massacre-resistance/en/document/toward-theory-critical-genocide-studies.

———. 2016. "Anxieties in Holocaust and Genocide Studies." In *Probing the Ethics of Holocaust Culture*, edited by Claudio Fogu, Wulf Kansteiner, and Todd Presner, 332–54. Cambridge, MA: Harvard University Press.

———. 2019. "'White Genocide' and the Ethics of Public Analysis." *Journal of Genocide Research* 21 (2): 201–13.

Rittner, Carol, and John K. Roth, eds. 2020. *Advancing Holocaust Studies*. New York: Routledge.

Rozenas, Arturas, and Yuri M. Zhukov. 2019. "Mass Repression and Political Loyalty: Evidence from Stalin's 'Terror by Hunger.'" *American Political Science Review* 113 (2): 569–83.

Sémelin, Jacques. 2019. *The Survival of the Jews in France, 1940–1944*. New York: Hurst.

Sewell, William H., Jr. 2005. *Logics of History: Social Theory and Social Transformation*. Chicago: University of Chicago Press.

Slater, Dan, and Daniel Ziblatt. 2013. "The Enduring Indispensability of the Controlled Comparison." *Comparative Political Studies* 46 (10): 1301–27.

Snyder, Timothy D. 2010. *Bloodlands: Europe between Hitler and Stalin*. New York: Basic Books.

Soyer, Michaela. 2014. "'We Knew Our Time Had Come': The Dynamics of Threat and Microsocial Ties in Three Polish Ghettos under Nazi Oppression." *Mobilization: An International Quarterly* 19 (1): 47–66.

Stone, Dan. 2012. "Introduction: The Holocaust and Historical Methodology." In *The Holocaust and Historical Methodology*, edited by Dan Stone, 1–19. New York: Berghahn Books.

———. 2020. "Structure and Fantasy: Genocide and the Homogenization of Identity." In *Logics of Genocide: The Structures of Violence and the Contemporary World*, edited by Anne O'Byrne and Martin Shuster, 246–63. London: Routledge.

Stone, Lewi. 2019. "Quantifying the Holocaust: Hyperintense Kill Rates during the Nazi Genocide." *Science Advances* 5 (1): eaau7292. https://doi.org/10.1126/sciadv.aau7292.

Sturdy Colls, Caroline. 2015. *Holocaust Archaeologies: Approaches and Future Directions*. Cham: Springer.

Suderland, Maja, and Michaela Christ. 2019. "National Socialism as a Research Topic in German-Language Sociology—Thoughts on a Hesitant Development." *Journal of Holocaust Research* 33 (3): 191–211.

Tokarska-Bakir, Joanna. 2011. "How to Exit the Conspiracy of Silence? Social Sciences Facing the Polish-Jewish Relations." *East European Politics and Societies* 25 (1): 129–52.

———. 2019. *Pogrom Cries: Essays on Polish-Jewish History, 1939–1946*. Berlin: Peter Lang.

Veyne, Paul. 1984. *Writing History: Essay on Epistemology*. Middletown, CT: Wesleyan University Press.

Walser Smith, Helmut. 2008. *The Continuities of German History: Nation, Religion, and Race across the Long Nineteenth Century*. Cambridge: Cambridge University Press, 2008.

Waxman, Zoë. 2017. *Women in the Holocaust: A Feminist History*. Oxford: Oxford University Press.

Zalc, Claire. 2020. *Denaturalized: How Thousands Lost Their Citizenship and Lives in Vichy France*. Cambridge, MA: Harvard University Press.

Zalc, Claire, and Tal Bruttmann, eds. 2017. *Microhistories of the Holocaust*. New York: Berghahn Books.

Part I
SITES OF VIOLENCE

3

POGROM VIOLENCE AND VISIBILITY DURING THE KRISTALLNACHT POGROM

Daniel Solomon

This chapter centers on an empirical puzzle: why did participants in the Kristallnacht pogrom of November 1938 refrain from damaging or destroying one-third of the active synagogues in Germany?[1] On November 9, Joseph Goebbels encouraged state officials assembled in Munich to stoke violence against Jewish communities throughout Germany, an order that gave participants little basis for restraint. Even so, the curious fact of restraint—that is, the absence of violence—during Kristallnacht is a longstanding question in the historiography of the pogrom. Steinweis (2009, 57), for example, contrasts the popular image of totalizing violence with a variable pattern of antisemitic attacks: "Viewed in its entirety, the pogrom seemed frenzied and chaotic, yet it did possess a certain unifying structure and rhythm. . . . Even as it was a nationwide event possessing certain unifying characteristics, the Kristallnacht was an aggregation of hundreds of individual, local pogroms, each of which unfolded according to a unique convergence of factors." Systematic research provides for rigorous testing of this pattern.[2]

I introduce and summarize the tentative results of a study that addresses this gap. In defining pogroms as a distinct type of informal, group-selective (Straus 2015) violence, I draw four major explanations for that violence from scholarship about riots, genocide, civil war, and other closely related forms of contention: its symbolic uses, competition, intergroup hatreds, and weak "bridging" bonds between social groups. Violence during Kristallnacht was most severe and most likely in municipalities in which the Jewish population share was largest, and pogrom organizers attacked the greatest number of synagogues where there was also a high concentration of Weimar-era electoral support for the German Communist Party. These findings offer strong support for the idea of the symbolic logic of pogrom violence, and moderate support for explanations for variation in violence that center on political competition.

This chapter proceeds in four parts. First, I briefly survey competing explanations for pogrom violence. Second, I elaborate on the design and findings of my Kristallnacht research. Third, I describe two outstanding theoretical problems in my empirical approach to the Kristallnacht case that my research illustrates but leaves unresolved: (1) the multiple interpretations of causality that underpin statistical studies of subnational variations in violence, and (2) the heterogeneity of Jewish social roles and cultural practices in Weimar- and Nazi-era Germany. These theoretical problems have specific implications for my findings about the causes of pogrom violence, but they also pertain to more general challenges surrounding the social science of the Holocaust. I conclude by discussing pathways for future research and the implications of my tentative findings for social science research about the Holocaust and the practice of preventing pogrom violence.

Explaining Pogrom Violence

The events of Kristallnacht are a case of pogrom violence, which I define as a relatively brief episode of multiple violent acts against a specific social community, by an informal group but involving some pattern of state involvement. Although historians typically associate the term "pogrom" with a bounded wave of antisemitic violence in the Eastern European Pale of Settlement during the late nineteenth and early twentieth centuries (Klier and Lambroza 1992), researchers of other, closely related episodes of collective violence also use the term to describe group-selective violence in non-European contexts and against non-Jewish communities (e.g., Lumpkins 2008; Ghassem-Fachandi 2012). Additionally, researchers use other terms to describe events that share the definitional characteristics of pogroms, such as race riots (McLaughlin 2005), ethnic riots (Horowitz 2001), and collective or communal violence (Tambiah 1997).

Pogroms involve the leadership and coordination of organizers and actions of participants against targets associated with a recognizable social group. Pogrom organizers rely on a network of violence "specialists" (Brass 1997; Lower 2011) to initiate and sustain violence. During pogrom episodes beyond the Kristallnacht case, however, variable patterns of violence are common across multiple political and social contexts. In the Indian state of Gujarat, for example, state-authorized Hindu nationalist violence (Ghassem-Fachandi 2012) against the area's Muslim population in 2002 was more severe in some towns than in others (Berenschot

2012). Similar variations in violence occurred in the starkly distinct case of Poland's eastern borderlands, where skeletal state institutions in the summer of 1941 could neither constrain nor authorize violence (Kopstein and Wittenberg 2018).

In this project, I explore four prevailing explanations in the literature on pogroms and similar forms of violence: (1) its symbolic uses, (2) intergroup hatreds, (3) competition, and (4) weak "bridging" bonds between social groups. Below, I describe the logic of each explanation and observable hypotheses that follow from each.

Symbolic Violence

Pogrom organizers use symbols to encourage action by would-be participants (Snow and Benford 1992). As in other social movements, the most obvious referential symbols are visual insignia or public rhetoric that movement organizers use to rally their members. Although theorists of symbolic action differentiate between symbolic and physical violence (e.g., Bourdieu 1991), the violence of a pogrom episode is itself a symbolic practice. Because pogroms typically occur in public, pogrom violence is a form of "violent display" (Fujii 2017) in which organizers aim to both displace and harm members of the targeted group. In this process of public violence, the pogrom episode reclaims public space for the organizers at the expense of members of the targeted community (Feldman 1991).

The symbolic logic of pogrom violence implies that violence will occur where that symbol's social meaning is most salient—that is, where the groups that pogrom organizers seek to target are most visible. These visible populations provide pogrom organizers with a compelling symbol of the social "other" that the organizers seek to displace through violence.

> *H1: Areas with a relatively large population of the targeted group will experience higher levels of group-selective violence after the onset of a pogrom.*

Political Competition

Pogroms are also forms of public contestation. Violence often follows preexisting patterns of political and social competition. In India, for example, Hindu and Muslim political parties have used collective violence to appeal to different majority and minority constituencies. The electoral incentives of competing parties shape decisions to mobilize or prevent costly violence. Wilkinson (2004) finds a greater risk of ethnic rioting where elections are more competitive, whereas pogrom organizers in Hindu or Muslim party strongholds have fewer incentives for collective violence. These competitive incentives also interact with local systems of patronage (Berenschot 2011, 2020).

The best measure of violence as a function of political threat is the combined concentration of the pogrom organizers' political opponents and the group targeted by the pogrom. If the competition hypothesis holds, pogrom organizers will use their opponents' political strength as a pretense for violence against the targeted group.

> *H2: Areas with both higher levels of electoral support for the political opponents of pogrom organizers and a relatively large population of the targeted group will experience higher levels of group-selective violence after the onset of a pogrom.*

A second strain of competition-based arguments draws on "group-threat," or "power-threat," theories of intergroup conflict (e.g., Spilerman 1971; Olzak 1992). These theories interpret violence as a product of the social anxieties of the pogrom organizers. Group-threat theories predict that violence will occur where and when pogrom organizers and participants perceive the targeted group as threatening to their social or economic status. For proponents of group-threat theories, conditions that encourage the subjective *perception* of threat—rather than the objective possibility of collective deprivation—explain the onset of violence. Kopstein and Wittenberg (2018) show that antisemitic pogroms in contested areas of Poland's eastern borderlands were most likely to break out in localities with a higher concentration of pre–World War II support for Jewish nationalist parties, whom Polish and Ukrainian nationalists saw as a threat to their own territorial claims.

Labor-market theories of group threat imply that rapid changes in migration or economic displacement also precede these perceived status threats (Tolnay and Beck 1995). In Tulsa, Oklahoma, for example, the 1921 race riots took place during a period of emergent Black economic success that left White Tulsa residents anxious about potential future unemployment and social dislocation (Ellsworth 1992). In London's Notting Hill neighborhood, race riots against Afro-Caribbean residents in 1958 occurred after local landlords evicted White tenants to make way for a growing migrant population (Pilkington 1988). As these cases demonstrate, rates of demographic change are a useful alternate measure of social competition.

> *H3: Areas with a recent increase in the relative size of the targeted population will experience higher levels of violence after the onset of a pogrom.*

Deep-Seated Hatreds

Pogroms also occur amid popular and elite animosity toward the targeted group. Although the empirical record contradicts extreme essentialist predictions of ubiquitous and ever-present violence where "hatreds" are most pronounced (Varshney 2009), more moderate arguments predict that a higher concentration of people for whom animosity toward the targeted group is a salient political preference will lead to more violence (Horowitz 1985). Violence after a pogrom's onset should occur where the ideological companions of pogrom organizers enjoy a relatively high degree of political and social support.

> H4: *Areas with higher levels of electoral support for ethnonationalist parties will experience higher levels of group-selective violence after the onset of a pogrom.*

The conflict recurrence literature also indicates that patterns of hateful violence are cyclical; places that have experienced violence in the recent past are more likely to experience a new episode of mass violence (Walter 2004; Das 1990; Ulfelder and Valentino 2008). In their study on the long-term effects of antisemitic pogroms in medieval Germany, Voigtländer and Voth (2012) show that German localities that experienced collective violence in the fourteenth century were more likely to also experience antisemitic violence during the Weimar and Nazi periods.

> H5: *Areas with higher levels of previous violence against the targeted group will experience higher levels of group-selective violence after the onset of a pogrom.*

Weak Civil Society

Although pogroms often represent a sharp departure from previous forms of abuse against the targeted group, they also emerge from preexisting associations within and between groups. Pogrom organizers rely on social networks to distribute information about violent activities and encourage participation in violence (Horowitz 2001; Scacco 2008). Varshney (2002) points to the dual role of civic associations in either encouraging or restraining Hindu-Muslim riots in India. In areas in which Hindu and Muslim groups were relatively segregated, civic associations were less able to stem the onset of ethnic violence. Communities in which these groups were more integrated, by contrast, experienced less violence because they established "peace committees" that addressed contentious social and political topics without resorting to violence. Comparative cases show that these cross-cutting peace committees are a common means of violence prevention in conflict-prone societies (Kaplan 2017; Jose and Medie 2015).

"Bridging" networks, which organize communities across various forms of social difference, inoculate societies against the outcomes that opposite "bonding" groups encourage (Chenoweth and Perkoski 2019). Bridging theories of violence prevention emphasize the causal importance of *collective* association. Where bridging organizations are dominant, local leaders may be more likely to oppose mobilization by pogrom organizers. An active member of an organization devoted to encouraging cross-cultural collaboration, for example, has social incentives to protect and advocate for members of other cultural groups that a member of a "bonding" organization devoted to the preservation of a specific cultural identity does not have.

Absent comprehensive data about organizational life itself, popular support for political pluralism is a viable proxy for organizations capable of opposing political violence. Pluralist groups should protect against the outbreak of violence; risks of violence are greater where those parties are weaker.

> H6: Areas with higher levels of electoral support for pluralist parties will experience lower levels of group-selective violence after the onset of a pogrom.

Data and Research Design: The Kristallnacht Pogrom

The pogrom was a decisive moment in the destruction and collapse of Jewish civil society and religious life in Germany. Its scope was extensive: in addition to those within the Weimar-era borders of the German Reich, pogrom violence also targeted Jewish communities in annexed areas of Austria and Czechoslovakia. Jewish communities had experienced recurrent pogroms and antisemitic protests during the Weimar and early Nazi periods, but the scale, diversity of tactics, and extent of desecration during Kristallnacht had no modern precedent (Bergmann, Hoffmann, and Smith 2002). In addition to attacking synagogues, pogrom participants targeted Jewish individuals, homes, businesses, and other ritual sites, and security forces and local law enforcement arrested and deported Jewish residents to concentration camps across Germany (Ross and Gruner 2019).

The proximate trigger for the pogrom was the assassination of a German diplomat, Ernst vom Rath, by Herschel Grynzspan, a Polish Jew, in Paris in the morning of November 7, 1938. That evening, officials distributed fabricated reports of an international Jewish conspiracy to local German press shops and, by extension, local party functionaries (Heiber 1957). The main direct participants in the attacks were a combination of Nazi security and paramilitary forces, members of the Nazi Party's Sturmabteilung paramilitary units, and party members, local youth groups, and "ordinary" German citizens who joined in the violence toward the end of November 10, the second day of nationwide violence (Siemens 2017, 195–97).

Below, I describe the variables and estimation strategy that I use to test plausible explanations for variation in violence during the pogrom.[3] I measure all variables at the municipality (*Gemeinde*) level.

Outcome Variables

SYNAGOGUE ATTACKS

To study nationwide patterns of violence during the pogrom, I use a new geocoded dataset about synagogue attacks throughout Germany on the nights of November 9 and 10, 1938. I record these data at the synagogue level. I draw the data from a memorial publication by the Beth Ashkenaz Synagogue Memorial Project, a Tel Aviv–based effort to record German Jewish communities whose members, cultural practices, and communal institutions the Nazi government destroyed from 1933 through 1945. The project's publications (Synagogue Memorial Beth Ashkenaz 2003, 2014) synthesize the findings of documentation efforts by local community groups and German historians of the Holocaust and German Jewry (Grellert 2007); the data that I use in this project draw only from its 2003 publication.

A 2003 draft of the project's synagogue memorial publication (Synagogue Memorial Beth Ashkenaz 2003) includes the cities, states, and current-to-2003 addresses of synagogues and prayer houses that served a Jewish community in Germany at some date prior to the Kristallnacht pogrom.[4] Based on this address information, I use the Google Maps (ggmap) package in the R software program to identify the spatial point (latitude and longitude) of each site. I then use a spatial "nearest neighbor" algorithm to match each synagogue to the nearest municipal centroid, or geographic center. I use this matched list to create three municipal-level measures of violence during Kristallnacht: (1) the number of synagogues attacked, (2) the percent of synagogues attacked, and (3) a binary measure of whether or not a synagogue was attacked in the municipality.

The geocoded dataset includes 2,238 synagogue observations, although only 1,890 of these sites were still active in 1938. Communities deactivated synagogues to sell the building and property, or in response to previous local episodes of antisemitic violence or accidental causes such as fire (Synagogue Memorial Beth Ashkenaz 2014). Local pogrom participants damaged or destroyed 1,253 (66 percent) of all active synagogues; in 637 (34 percent) of the synagogues, there is no evidence of attacks.[5]

Attacks on synagogues were one among several violent strategies that Kristallnacht participants employed against Germany's Jewish population (Ross and Gruner 2019). In further research about a subset of municipalities in which synagogues were attacked, I will address the determinants of attacks on private Jewish homes, public violence against Jewish individuals and businesses, and mass deportations to concentration camps in areas where participants also attacked synagogues (Solomon 2021).

Explanatory Variables

The hypotheses above correspond to six explanatory variables that may account for spatial variation in synagogue attacks. Most variables describe a political or social feature of the Weimar Republic, the regime that ruled Germany from the end of World War I in 1918 to the Nazi Party's rise to power in 1933. I infer the social characteristics and collective political preferences of German localities in 1938 from pre-1933 data about the Weimar era (Hänisch 1988).

JEWISH POPULATION SHARE IN 1933 (H1)

For the relative size of the targeted group, I use the municipal-level Jewish population share as calculated in the 1933 census.[6] In municipalities throughout Germany, Jewish population size was an aggregate indicator of other measures of visibility for which I lack systematic data, such as the scale of Jewish associations, the proliferation of sites of religious worship, and Jewish business activities (Wallach 2017).

VOTE SHARE OF THE COMMUNIST PARTY IN THE SEPTEMBER 1930 FEDERAL ELECTION (H2)

For electoral support for the political opponents of the pogrom organizers, I use the Communist Party (KPD) vote share in the September 1930 election. The KPD was the Nazi Party's diametric electoral and paramilitary opponent, both at the polls and in pitched street fights that accompanied electoral politics throughout the Weimar era (Schumann 2012). To assess political competition against perceived Jewish Communists as a potential explanation for violence during Kristallnacht, I estimate the multiplicative effect of combined electoral support for the KPD and relatively high Jewish population share on synagogue attacks.

CHANGE IN JEWISH POPULATION SHARE (H3)

For increase in the relative size of the targeted population, I subtract the Jewish population share in 1925 from the Jewish population share in 1933. A positive value of this variable indicates an increase in the Jewish population share, whereas a negative value indicates that the Jewish population declined in relative size.

VOTE SHARE OF THE ANTISEMITIC COALITION (H4)

For electoral support for ethnonationalist groups, I use the combined vote share of the two main ethnonationalist parties—the Nazis and the German National Peoples' Party (DNVP)—that contested the September 1930 election. In the late Weimar period, both the Nazi Party and the DNVP jockeyed for support among right-wing nationalist constituencies (Chanady 1967; Ziblatt 2017, 297–333). In the September 1930 election more than others, both parties embraced explicit antisemitic platforms and promoted themselves as opponents of the pluralist Weimar order.

POGROMS IN THE FOURTEENTH CENTURY AND 1920S (H5)

For past violence against the targeted group, I use historical patterns of pogrom violence against German Jews. I include variables for both medieval-era and Weimar-era episodes of antisemitic violence. These variables follow Voigtländer and Voth's (2012) finding that pogroms in response to conspiracies surrounding the spread of the fourteenth-century Black Death plague are positively associated with multiple measures of Weimar- and Nazi-era antisemitism.

VOTE SHARE OF THE SOCIAL DEMOCRATIC PARTY (H6)

For electoral support for pluralist parties, I use the Social Democratic Party (SPD) vote share during the September 1930 election. Throughout the Weimar period, the SPD adopted the combined mantles of republicanism and political pluralism. Aside from the KPD, the SPD was the only consistent public opponent of widespread antisemitic rhetoric among right-wing German parties. It also condemned prominent episodes of antisemitic violence during the Weimar era.

In the model I present here, I also include two covariates—logged population size and the predicted strength of local radio signals—that are typically associated with pogrom violence.[7] I also use *Länder* fixed effects to account for unobserved characteristics of some regions that may have influenced the intensity of violence (Pepinsky, Goodman, and Ziller 2020).

Given the competing theories that I describe above, these variables make up the most efficient explanatory model of pogrom violence. The following potential correlates of mobilization during Kristallnacht, however, also merit additional research beyond this chapter's limited scope: (1) religious affiliation (Heilbronner and Mühlberger 1997), (2) Nazi Party membership (Brustein and Falter 1995), (3) distance to regional Nazi Party headquarters that may have aided in the coordination of violence (Steinweis 2009, 54), and (4) more direct measures of bridging and bonding civil society for the subset of German municipalities for which data are available (Satyanath, Voigtländer, and Voth 2017). Additionally, aggregating synagogues by municipal borders rather than by their proximity to municipal centroids may change the results.

Results

I display the coefficients and standard errors for the models in table 1. The nonstandardized coefficients in model 1 indicate the average change in the outcome variable that results from a one-unit change in the explanatory variable. The standardized coefficients in models 2 and 3 indicate the effect of a one-standard-deviation increase in the explanatory variable on the value of the outcome variable. For ease of interpretation, I estimate each model using ordinary-least-squares (OLS) or linear regression. Following convention, my threshold for statistical significance is p = 0.05.

The regression results provide strong evidence that pogrom violence is greatest where the population targeted by the organizers is most visible.[8] The effect of the relative size of the Jewish population on the proportion, occurrence, and extent of synagogue attacks (models 1, 2, and 3, respectively) is positive and statistically significant. The substantively large effect of Jewish population share is notable. A 1 percent increase in the Jewish population share of a municipality results in a 4.52-point increase in the average proportion of attacked synagogues (model 1), while a one-standard-deviation increase in Jewish population share (approximately 3 percent) increases the likelihood of a synagogue attack (model 2) by 21.4 percent and the number of synagogues attacked (model 3) by 39.4 percent.

The results also provide some evidence that pogrom violence is associated with multiple forms of political and social competition, although the direction of those effects is ambiguous. A combined one-standard-deviation increase in Communist support and Jewish population share increases the number of synagogues attacked by 22 percent. Contrary to expectations, however, municipalities in which the Jewish population share grew from 1925 to 1933 are associated with a lower likelihood of violence and a lower number of synagogue attacks. The effects of these coefficients are all statistically significant. The interactive effect of Communist support and Jewish population share on the proportion and extent of synagogue attacks is not statistically significant. This finding suggests that power-threat theories may explain how widespread violence becomes after a pogrom begins, but not the basic fact of its onset or the severity of violent mobilization.

TABLE 3.1 Ordinary least squares estimates for variation in synagogue attacks during Kristallnacht

	PROPORTION OF SYNAGOGUES ATTACKED	LIKELIHOOD THAT SYNAGOGUES WERE ATTACKED	NUMBER OF SYNAGOGUES ATTACKED
	(1)	(2)	(3)
Jewish pop. share, 1933	4.519***	0.214***	0.394***
	(1.297)	(0.045)	(0.142)
KPD share, 1930	0.458	0.021	−0.083
	(0.283−)	(0.021)	(0.067)
Jews * KPD	−20.498*	−0.027	0.220***
	(10.619)	(0.023)	(0.071)
Jews (1933) / Jews (1925)	−1.761	−0.110***	−0.274**
	(1.179)	(0.041)	(0.127)
Antisemitic share, 1930	−0.514*	−0.069**	0.033
	(0.281)	(0.034)	(0.106)
Pogroms, 1349	0.037	0.019	−0.022
	(0.039)	(0.016)	(0.050)
Pogroms, 1920s	0.041	−0.0003	−0.058
	(0.089)	(0.014)	(0.045)
SPD share, 1930	0.016	−0.004	−0.071
	(0.133)	(0.018)	(0.055)
Pop., 1933 (log)	0.022	0.102***	0.602***
	(0.014)	(0.023)	(0.071)
Radio, 1938	−0.004	−0.041	0.288***
	(0.003)	(0.031)	(0.098)
Radios * Antisemitic share	0.011	0.042	−0.136
	(0.012)	(0.040)	(0.127)
Constant	0.673***	0.748***	0.972***
	(0.133)	(0.046)	(0.145)
Länder fixed effects	Yes	Yes	Yes
N	774	827	827
R^2	0.115	0.137	0.267

Notes: All models employ ordinary least squares regression. Coefficients for model 1 are not standardized; coefficients for models 2 and 3 are standardized. All observations are at the municipal (*Gemeinde*) level. The outcome variable in model 1 is the share of all active synagogues destroyed during Kristallnacht. The outcome variable in model 2 is a binary measure of synagogue attacks for each municipality, where 1 indicates that participants attacked synagogues in the municipality and 0 indicates that they did not. The outcome variable in model 3 reflects the count of synagogues that participants attacked during Kristallnacht. Significance thresholds: *p < .1; **p < .05; ***p < .01. Standard errors in parentheses.

Discussion

This analysis demonstrates that the symbolic theories of violence merit additional attention from scholars concerned with explaining patterns of political violence and contention. As I discuss above, however, two plausible mechanisms make a targeted group's visibility important for the strategic goals of pogrom organizers: what the group signifies to others about the dominance of pogrom organizers and their constituents, and the group's salience for pogrom organizers as an object of contention. The group's relative size is the coarse measure of their visibility that does not differentiate between these two mechanisms. Clarifying how visibility contributes to the processes of domination and mobilization during pogroms requires additional information about the interaction between the group's prominence and the political and social positions of those who organize violence against them.

Two additional shortcomings merit discussion. First, this study's emphasis on structural explanations for violence does not account for the dynamic diffusion of violence across space and time. The results of the multivariate regression analysis that I present here captures one logic of causal explanation: the characteristics of particular locations that make them more likely than others to experience violence after a pogrom's onset. These "covering laws" (Tilly 2001) of pogrom variation necessarily overlook the sequence of events and decisions that led Nazi officials and informal groups to escalate antisemitic violence on the evening of November 9, 1938. This analytic choice papers over the *process* of pogrom onset: why did Nazi officials encourage the repertoire of violent tactics that participants employed during Kristallnacht, and why against Germany's Jews rather than other groups whom they had marked as political outliers? Although the antisemitic rhetoric of the Nazi government and our collective memory of the Holocaust leave the impression that these patterns were inevitable, the multiple strategic and tactical choices that localities across Germany confronted mean that the precise conditions that motivated anti-Jewish mobilization during Kristallnacht require further explanation.

The second shortcoming emerges from the positivist underpinnings of this analysis. The task of measuring visibility presumes an observable difference between more and less visible populations that is analytically separate from the various political, social, and cultural contexts that gave that visibility meaning. As the interpretivist tradition of pogrom research demonstrates (Brass 1997; Tambiah 1997), the actions and practices of pogrom participants and targets themselves generate different meanings of threat, visibility, and other social processes that shape violence. To explain why and how pogroms occur, future research should combine the general patterns of variation on which this analysis centers with the context-specific ways that actors made sense of those patterns.

This interpretive move requires particular attention to the diversity of Jewish communal relations and cultural practices in pre-1933 Germany. Jewish communities maintained a variety of networked relationships with their neighbors in nearby population centers. For example, small Jewish communities that were unable to form a recurring *minyan*—a group of ten adults, often men, required for daily prayer services—often formed joint synagogue communities with Jews of neighboring towns. Others maintained common cemeteries and *chevrot kadisha*—Jewish burial societies—for the sake of logistical and financial efficiency (Synagogue Memorial Beth Ashkenaz 2014). What it meant to "be Jewish" also varied from town to town, depending on many factors including the extent of Jewish communal involvement in local politics, the availability of assimilationist versus orthodox religious denominations, the presence of Zionist or antinationalist political movements, and regional variations in historical access to secular or non-Jewish institutions of education and social welfare.

These are interpretive differences in the content of Jewishness in Germany, but they also have obvious implications for the credibility of the explanatory models that I present here. To illustrate: Compare the vaulted architecture of the Reform synagogue at Augsburg to its Orthodox counterpart at Halberstadt. The former cast a more impressive shadow in Augsburg's town center, but its presence and role in the city's local Jewish community was as obvious as the latter's contributions to Halberstadt's. Do these variations do any explanatory work, or is a coarser measure of visibility sufficient? Further research should examine whether and how these interpretive differences change the precision or accuracy of the explanations that I test in this chapter.

Further research should examine how the precise historical context of the Kristallnacht pogrom shapes these findings. The political context of consolidated Nazi rule may explain why the perception of "Jewish threat" is a more consistent explanation for pogrom violence in 1941 Poland and Ukraine (Kopstein and Wittenberg 2018) than in 1938 Germany. In the Kristallnacht case, formal state actors and informal paramilitary groups were central to the mobilization of violence; in the regions of Eastern Europe, whose local politics the Nazi military's anti-Soviet invasion upended, formal state institutions were all but absent. What role does the state play in pogrom mobilization across different political contexts? How does this role interact with those of the other informal groups that participate in pogroms?

Empirically, this study presents another example of the potential applications of the extensive historical record about the "array of event categories" (King 2012,

326) that make up the Holocaust. Social scientists theorizing and testing existing explanations for violence benefit from the documentary record about the events and experience of antisemitic violence in mid-twentieth-century Europe. Compiling this record has been a searching and nonlinear enterprise, involving victimized communities themselves, those who organized and participated in violence against them, justice processes that sought to rectify these atrocities, and multiple generations of researchers who have adjudicated between these often-conflicting sources. Social science research about the Holocaust requires the same caution about sources of bias and threats to causal inference in data collection and analysis that underpin the contemporary study of violence (Balcells and Solomon 2020). Using these data also poses ethical dilemmas about the political and social positions of researchers (Subotić 2020) and the care with which we interpret often-conflicting archival material about sensitive and traumatizing events (Luft 2020).

These findings also offer a way forward for resolving the tension between rationalist and culturalist explanations for violence (Brubaker and Laitin 1998) and the gathering of systematic data to assess descriptive patterns of performance and spectacle (Fujii 2009, 2017).

Finally, these tentative findings offer practical implications for groups facing risks of mass violence and those—both locally and globally—who seek to assist them. In both the global model of human rights work and more localized varieties of contention against large-scale violence, much advocacy suggests that a more visible spotlight on vulnerable groups will result in less or less severe group-selective violence (Hafner-Burton 2008). These findings imply, however, that the visibility for which these groups strive may be a double-edged sword. Future research should assess whether intervening conditions such as preexisting relations between targeted groups and the constituents of pogrom organizers may mitigate or exacerbate the risks of group-selective violence against visible groups.

REFERENCES

Adena, Maja, Ruben Enikolopov, Maria Petrova, Veronica Santarosa, and Ekaterina Zhuravskaya. 2015. "Radio and the Rise of the Nazis in Prewar Germany." *Quarterly Journal of Economics* 130 (4): 1885–1939. https://doi.org/10.1093/qje/qjv030.

Alicke, Klaus-Dieter. 2008. *Lexikon Der Jüdischen Gemeinden Im Deutschen Sprachraum Gebundenes Buch*. Gütersloh, Germany: Gütersloher Verlagshaus.

Aly, Götz, and Karl Heinz Roth. 2004. *The Nazi Census: Identification and Control in the Third Reich*. Philadelphia: Temple University Press.

Balcells, Laia, and Daniel Solomon. 2020. "Violence, Resistance, and Rescue during the Holocaust." *Comparative Politics* 53 (1): 161–80. https://doi.org/10.5129/001041 520X15863824603010.

Berenschot, Ward. 2011. "The Spatial Distribution of Riots: Patronage and the Instigation of Communal Violence in Gujarat, India." *World Development* 39 (2): 221–30.
———. 2012. *Riot Politics: Hindu-Muslim Violence and the Indian State*. New York: Columbia University Press.
———. 2020. "Patterned Pogroms: Patronage Networks as Infrastructure for Electoral Violence in India and Indonesia." *Journal of Peace Research* 57 (1): 171–84. https://doi.org/10.1177/0022343319889678.
Bergmann, Werner, Christhard Hoffmann, and Helmut W. Smith. 2002. *Exclusionary Violence: Antisemitic Riots in Modern German History*. Ann Arbor: University of Michigan Press.
Bourdieu, Pierre. 1991. *Language and Symbolic Power*. Cambridge, MA: Harvard University Press.
Brass, Paul R. 1996. *Riots and Pogroms*. New York: Springer.
———. 1997. *Theft of an Idol: Text and Context in the Representation of Collective Violence*. Princeton, NJ: Princeton University Press.
Braun, Robert. 2019. *Protectors of Pluralism: Religious Minorities and the Rescue of Jews in the Low Countries during the Holocaust*. Cambridge: Cambridge University Press.
Brubaker, Rogers, and David D. Laitin. 1998. "Ethnic and Nationalist Violence." *Annual Review of Sociology* 24 (1): 423–52. https://doi.org/10.1146/annurev.soc.24.1.423.
Brustein, William, and J. W. Falter. 1995. "Who Joined the Nazi Party? Assessing Theories of the Social Origins of Nazism." *Zeitgeschichte* 22 (3–4): 83–108.
Bulutgil, H. Zeynep. 2016. *The Roots of Ethnic Cleansing in Europe*. Cambridge: Cambridge University Press.
Chanady, Attila. 1967. "The Disintegration of the German National Peoples' Party, 1924–1930." *Journal of Modern History* 39 (1): 65–91.
Chenoweth, Erica, and Evan Perkoski. 2019. "A Source of Escalation or a Source of Restraint? An Empirical Investigation of How Civil Society Affects Mass Killings." HKS Working Paper No. RWP19-027. Social Science Research Network. September 11, 2019. https://doi.org/10.2139/ssrn.3451355.
Das, Veena. 1990. *Mirrors of Violence: Communities, Riots and Survivors in South Asia*. Oxford: Oxford University Press.
Ellsworth, Scott. 1992. *Death in a Promised Land: The Tulsa Race Riot of 1921*. Baton Rouge: LSU Press.
Feldman, Allen. 1991. *Formations of Violence: The Narrative of the Body and Political Terror in Northern Ireland*. Chicago: University of Chicago Press.
Fox, Nicole, and Hollie Nyseth Brehm. 2018. "'I Decided to Save Them': Factors That Shaped Participation in Rescue Efforts during Genocide in Rwanda." *Social Forces* 96 (4): 1625–48. https://doi.org/10.1093/sf/soy018.
Fritzsche, Peter. 2009. *Life and Death in the Third Reich*. Cambridge, MA: Harvard University Press.
Fujii, Lee Ann. 2009. *Killing Neighbors: Webs of Violence in Rwanda*. Ithaca, NY: Cornell University Press.
———. 2013. "The Puzzle of Extra-lethal Violence." *Perspectives on Politics* 11 (2): 410–26.
———. 2017. "'Talk of the Town': Explaining Pathways to Participation in Violent Display." *Journal of Peace Research* 54 (5): 661–73. https://doi.org/10.1177/0022343317714300.

Ghassem-Fachandi, Parvis. 2012. *Pogrom in Gujarat: Hindu Nationalism and Anti-Muslim Violence in India.* Princeton, NJ: Princeton University Press.

Hafner-Burton, Emilie M. 2008. "Sticks and Stones: Naming and Shaming the Human Rights Enforcement Problem." *International Organization* 62 (4): 689–716.

Hänisch, Dirk. 1989. "Inhalt und Struktur der Datenbank 'Wahl- und Sozialdaten der Kreise und Gemeinden des Deutschen Reiches von 1920 bis 1933.'" *Historical Social Research* 14 (1): 39–67. https://doi.org/10.12759/hsr.14.1989.1.39-67.

Heiber, Helmut. 1957. "Der Fall Grünspan." *Vierteljahrshefte für Zeitgeschichte* 5 (2): 134–72.

Heilbronner, Oded, and Detlef Mühlberger. 1997. "The Achilles' Heel of German Catholicism: 'Who Voted for Hitler?' Revisited." *European History Quarterly* 27 (2): 221–49. https://doi.org/10.1177/026569149702700203.

Horowitz, Donald L. 1985. *Ethnic Groups in Conflict.* Berkeley: University of California Press.

———. 2001. *The Deadly Ethnic Riot.* Berkeley: University of California Press.

Jose, Betcy, and Peace A. Medie. 2015. "Understanding Why and How Civilians Resort to Self-Protection in Armed Conflict." *International Studies Review* 17 (4): 515–35. https://doi.org/10.1111/misr.12254.

Kaplan, Oliver. 2017. *Resisting War: How Communities Protect Themselves.* Cambridge: Cambridge University Press.

King, Charles. 2012. "Can There Be a Political Science of the Holocaust?" *Perspectives on Politics* 10 (2): 323–41.

Klier, John Doyle, and Shlomo Lambroza. 1992. *Pogroms: Anti-Jewish Violence in Modern Russian History.* Cambridge: Cambridge University Press.

Kopstein, Jeffrey, and Jason Wittenberg. 2018. *Intimate Violence: Anti-Jewish Pogroms on the Eve of the Holocaust.* Ithaca, NY: Cornell University Press.

Lower, Wendy. 2011. "Pogroms, Mob Violence and Genocide in Western Ukraine, Summer 1941: Varied Histories, Explanations and Comparisons." *Journal of Genocide Research* 13 (3): 217–46. https://doi.org/10.1080/14623528.2011.606683.

Luft, Aliza. 2020. "How Do You Repair a Broken World? Conflict(ing) Archives after the Holocaust." *Qualitative Sociology* 43 (3): 317–43. https://doi.org/10.1007/s11133-020-09458-9.

Lumpkins, Charles L. 2008. *American Pogrom: The East St. Louis Race Riot and Black Politics.* Athens: Ohio University Press.

McLaughlin, Malcolm. 2005. *Power, Community, and Racial Killing in East St. Louis.* New York: Palgrave Macmillan.

Olzak, Susan. 1992. *The Dynamics of Ethnic Competition and Conflict.* Stanford, CA: Stanford University Press.

Pepinsky, Thomas B., Sara Wallace Goodman, and Conrad Ziller. 2020. "Does Proximity to Nazi Concentration Camps Make Germans Intolerant? Modeling Spatial Heterogeneity and Historical Persistence." Social Science Research Network. Last revised April 14, 2020. https://doi.org/10.2139/ssrn.3547321.

Pilkington, Edward. 1988. *Beyond the Mother Country: West Indians and the Notting Hill White Riots.* London: Tauris.

Ross, Steven J., and Wolf Gruner, eds. 2019. *New Perspectives on Kristallnacht: After 80 Years, the Nazi Pogrom in Global Comparison.* West Lafayette, IN: Purdue University Press.

Satyanath, Shanker, Nico Voigtländer, and Hans-Joachim Voth. 2017. "Bowling for Fascism: Social Capital and the Rise of the Nazi Party." *Journal of Political Economy* 125 (2): 478–526. https://doi.org/10.1086/690949.

Scacco, Alexandra. 2008. "Who Riots? Explaining Individual Participation in Ethnic Violence." September 2008. https://citeseerx.ist.psu.edu/viewdoc/download?doi=10.1.1.615.3726&rep=rep1&type=pdf.

Schumann, Dirk. 2012. *Political Violence in the Weimar Republic, 1918–1933: Fight for the Streets and Fear of Civil War*. New York: Berghahn Books.

Siemens, Daniel. 2017. *Stormtroopers: A New History of Hitler's Brownshirts*. New Haven, CT: Yale University Press.

Snow, David A., and Robert D. Benford. 1992. "Master Frames and Cycles of Protest." In *Frontiers in Social Movement Theory*, edited by Aldon D. Morris and Carol McClurg Mueller, XXX–YYY. New Haven, CT: Yale University Press.

Solomon, Daniel. 2021. "The Logic of Pogrom Violence: Evidence from Kristallnacht." OSF. Last updated September 5, 2021. https://osf.io/d2s5k/.

Spilerman, Seymour. 1971. "The Causes of Racial Disturbances: Tests of an Explanation." *American Sociological Review* 36 (3): 427–42. https://doi.org/10.2307/2093083.

Steinweis, Alan E. 2009. *Kristallnacht 1938*. Cambridge, MA: Harvard University Press.

Straus, Scott. 2007. "What Is the Relationship between Hate Radio and Violence? Rethinking Rwanda's 'Radio Machete.'" *Politics & Society* 35 (4): 609–37. https://doi.org/10.1177/0032329207308181.

———. 2015. *Making and Unmaking Nations: War, Leadership, and Genocide in Modern Africa*. Ithaca, NY: Cornell University Press.

Subotić, Jelena. 2020. "Ethics of Archival Research on Political Violence." *Journal of Peace Research* 58 (3): 342–54. https://doi.org/10.1177/0022343319898735.

Synagogue Memorial Beth Ashkenaz. 2003. *List of Germany's Synagogues of the 20th Century*. Jerusalem: Synagogue Memorial Beth Ashkenaz.

———. 2014. *Pogrom Night 1938—a Memorial to the Destroyed Synagogues of Germany*. Jerusalem: Synagogue Memorial Beth Ashkenaz.

Tambiah, Stanley J. 1997. *Leveling Crowds: Ethnonationalist Conflicts and Collective Violence in South Asia*. Berkeley: University of California Press.

Tilly, Charles. 2001. "Mechanisms in Political Processes." *Annual Review of Political Science* 4 (1): 21–41. https://doi.org/10.1146/annurev.polisci.4.1.21.

Tolnay, Stewart Emory, and E. M. Beck. 1995. *A Festival of Violence: An Analysis of Southern Lynchings, 1882–1930*. Urbana: University of Illinois Press.

Ulfelder, Jay, and Benjamin Valentino. 2008. "Assessing Risks of State-Sponsored Mass Killing." Social Science Research Network. November 7, 2010. https://papers.ssrn.com/abstract=1703426.

Varshney, Ashutosh. 2002. *Ethnic Conflict and Civic Life: Hindus and Muslims in India*. New Haven, CT: Yale University Press.

———. 2009. "Ethnicity and Ethnic Conflict." In *The Oxford Handbook of Comparative Politics*, edited by Carles Boix and Susan C. Stokes, 274–94. https://doi.org/10.1093/oxfordhb/9780199566020.003.0012.

Voigtländer, Nico, and Hans-Joachim Voth. 2012. "Persecution Perpetuated: The Medieval Origins of Anti-Semitic Violence in Nazi Germany." *Quarterly Journal of Economics* 127 (3): 1339–92. https://doi.org/10.1093/qje/qjs019.

Wallach, Kerry. 2017. *Passing Illusions: Jewish Visibility in Weimar Germany*. Ann Arbor: University of Michigan Press.

Walter, Barbara F. 2004. "Does Conflict Beget Conflict? Explaining Recurring Civil War." *Journal of Peace Research* 41 (3): 371–88. https://doi.org/10.1177/0022343304043775.

Welch, David. 2008. *The Third Reich: Politics and Propaganda*. New York: Routledge.

Wilkinson, Steven I. 2004. *Votes and Violence: Electoral Competition and Ethnic Riots in India*. Cambridge: Cambridge University Press.

Yanagizawa-Drott, David. 2014. "Propaganda and Conflict: Evidence from the Rwandan Genocide." *Quarterly Journal of Economics* 129 (4): 1947–94.

Ziblatt, Daniel. 2017. *Conservative Parties and the Birth of Democracy*. Cambridge: Cambridge University Press.

4

HISTORICAL LEGACIES AND JEWISH SURVIVAL STRATEGIES DURING THE HOLOCAUST

Eugene Finkel

One of the most understudied aspects of the Holocaust is the individual and community-level response to persecution. The early stereotype of victims "going like lambs to the slaughter" is not just morally problematic; it is also empirically wrong. Jewish responses to the Holocaust varied on both individual and communal levels. In recent decades, scholars of political violence have extensively analyzed the microlevel dynamics of civil wars, riots, uprisings, and mass killings (e.g., Kalyvas 2006; Varshney 2002; Weinstein 2007; Wood 2003). This analysis, however, mostly focuses on the behavior of perpetrators of violence and almost completely overlooks the strategies adopted by the victims. The analytical literature on the Holocaust and genocides more broadly is also mostly concerned with the conduct and motivation of the perpetrators (Browning 1993; Goldhagen 1996; Straus 2006). At the same time, the many excellent community histories and biographies produced by historians (e.g., Engelking and Leociak 2009; Epstein 2008; Kobrin 2010; Peled 1993) do not, and indeed cannot, make any general claim about Jewish behavior beyond the locality or the person they analyze.

Why should social science scholars and Holocaust researchers care about the variation in Jewish behavior, the survival strategies adopted by the victims, and the choices they made? The reasons are both analytical and normative. Focusing on this level of analysis cannot explain why the Holocaust happened (Finkel and Straus 2012), but it will immensely enrich our understanding of *how* it happened and what its outcomes were. Genocide is a dynamic and relational process, and its trajectories and outcomes cannot be fully understood by concentrating solely on perpetrators.

From the moral perspective, analyzing the victims restores their voice and agency. Even if the choices they made were largely choiceless and death was the most likely outcome regardless of the behavior they adopted, choices they were nonetheless, and scholars ought to try to understand and analyze them, not just describe them.

In this contribution and elsewhere (Finkel 2015, 2017), I ask what explains the different patterns of behavior adopted by civilians targeted by mass violence. To answer this question, I analyze Jewish behavior during the Holocaust at the individual and community levels. More specifically, I do so by comparing the large, important, yet understudied Jewish communities of Minsk, Kraków, and Białystok. My research is based on both rich archival material and five hundred survivors' testimonies from the video archives of the Fortunoff collection, the US Holocaust Memorial Museum, Yad Vashem, the USC Shoah Foundation, and others.

These case studies were chosen because of their similarities in a number of important features. The three cities are comparable in the size of their prewar Jewish communities and their percentages of Jews. During the Nazi occupation, they had ghettos enclosed by a physical barrier and were located in the "zone of extermination" (Fein 1979, 26)—no Jews were supposed to be spared in each locale. They were also important Nazi administrative and government centers. Yet despite these similarities, in Białystok almost no one escaped the ghetto, whereas in Minsk thousands fled. The Jewish underground attacked Germans outside the ghetto in Kraków but staged a rebellion within the ghetto walls in Białystok. In Minsk the internal organization of the ghetto was chaotic and its leadership corrupt, while the Białystok ghetto was known for its order and efficiency.

The Strategies

What did the Jews do under Nazi rule and which strategies could they adopt in the hope of surviving the Holocaust? I build on the previous attempts to categorize Jewish behavior (Bauer 1989; Hilberg 2003) as well as broader typologies of human actions in other contexts (e.g., Hirschman 1970) and propose the following list of strategies that the Jews could and did engage in during the Holocaust: (1) cooperation and collaboration, (2) coping, (3) evasion, and (4) resistance.

Cooperation and *collaboration* mean working with the enemy by either participating in or facilitating the persecution. The key distinction between cooperation and collaboration is the intended goal of the actions taken. Those who merely cooperated with the Nazis desired to preserve the community and its members; those who collaborated knowingly acted to the detriment of the community's or individual Jews' survival. *Coping* means confronting the danger and trying to survive while staying put, without leaving one's community or country, engaging in cooperation or collaboration with the perpetrators, or resisting them. *Evasion* is an attempt to escape persecution by fleeing: leaving the community, emigrating, or assuming a false identity. Finally, *resistance* is involvement in organized activity that is aimed at physically or materially harming the perpetrators.

The typology is meant to serve an analytical, not moral, purpose. No matter how one evaluates collaboration with the Nazis from a normative standpoint, it is still crucial to understand that people who engaged in this strategy did so for a reason, and it is incumbent on social scientists to understand those reasons and motivations.

The Argument

I argue that the explanation for these differences across cities depended less on what the Nazis did and more on legacies of pre–World War II regimes under which the Jews lived. The three cities had an overlapping but also divergent experience of being governed by the main states and regimes that existed in Eastern Europe prior to the Holocaust. Minsk was part of the Russian Empire, replaced by the USSR; Kraków was governed by the Austro-Hungarian Empire and then by Poland; Białystok experienced the Romanov, Polish, and Soviet rules.

More specifically, it was the impact of several state policies that had the most bearing on which survival strategies the Jews chose. The first policy was education, especially primary and secondary education policies and whether Jewish children were schooled in ethnically mixed or ethnically segregated schools. Where the state promoted or even required ethnically mixed educational institutions, Jews spoke the majority's language, were familiar with the local culture, and could pass as non-Jews. They also had friends, teachers, even school janitors from the other ethnic group, whom they could approach and ask for help in their time of need. The second policy was the state's encouragement of the Jews' economic activities outside the Jewish community. Where that happened, Jews had non-Jewish friends, coworkers, or clients to whom they could turn for help. The third policy was the state's attitude toward the Jews' political activism and whether ethnic Jewish parties were allowed or discouraged. Having ethnically mixed political parties created a pool of people more willing to help the Jews they knew from political work. It also created a pool of local-level elites or political activists who saw Jews as their base and often helped their constituencies at great personal risk.

On the other hand, ethnically based political competition, as Kopstein and Wittenberg (2018) demonstrate, led to hostile relations. Finally, the viability of Jewish resistance was determined by the patterns of pre–World War II state repression. At the individual level, I argue that people with pre-Holocaust political experience were overrepresented among the Jewish Councils (Judenrat) and the Jewish resistance groups.

The Austro-Hungarian Empire and the USSR promoted the integration of Jews—not because they, especially the USSR, were liberal or pro-Jewish, but what mattered was the result, not the intention. The Russian Empire and the interwar Polish state did nothing to promote such integration. The outcome was that policies that were enacted even before Hitler was born influenced how Jews behaved under the Nazi occupation. Kraków experienced the Austro-Hungarian Empire's ethnic integration policies in the late nineteenth and early twentieth centuries. The twenty years of the interwar Polish state control slowed down but did not reverse these processes. In Minsk, twenty years of the Soviets' quite brutal social engineering completely erased the two centuries of Tsarist anti-Jewish policies. Many Kraków Jews spoke perfect Polish and had ethnically mixed social networks. Minsk Jews were even more integrated into the Soviet society than the Kraków Jews were into the Polish. But the flip side of integration was that the organized Jewish community was nonexistent in Minsk and weak in Kraków. Białystok, on the other hand, was first part of the Russian Empire and then part of interwar Poland—neither of which promoted the integration of Jews into non-Jewish societies. There, the Jews generally did not speak Polish and their relations with non-Jews were extremely hostile, but the Jewish community was cohesive and well organized. Thus, it was not any one particular regime or time period that could explain the adoption of survival strategies within and across communities, but the overlapping, combined effects of the different polities that governed what Snyder (2010) powerfully labels "Bloodlands."

In the following sections, I demonstrate how pre–World War II regimes and the educational, economic, and repression policies these regimes adopted shaped Jewish behavior in each of the three communities.

Cases in Brief

Minsk

Germany invaded the USSR on June 22, 1941. Initially most people believed the Soviet propaganda assurances that the enemy would be swiftly defeated and knew little about the real situation on the front lines. Following the German air raid on June 24, many realized the danger and tried to escape. Most refugees were stopped by quickly advancing German units and sent back. The city itself was occupied on June 28. On July 19, German authorities ordered the establishment of a ghetto and began requiring Jews to wear a round yellow patch. Leaving the ghetto without permission or being outside the ghetto without wearing the patch was punishable by death. Housing was scarce and hunger was prevalent in the crowded ghetto (Epstein 2008, 87–88).

The first large-scale massacre (*Aktion* in German parlance) took place on November 7, 1941. It was followed by mass killings on November 20, 1941, March 2, 1942, and July 28–31, 1942, and throughout August 1943. In each massacre, thousands were shot and gassed. By October 1, 1943, there were only two thousand Jews left in the ghetto. On October 20–21, 1943, the ghetto was liquidated, and its last inhabitants killed or deported.

Kraków

Germany invaded Poland on September 1, 1939. On September 6, German troops entered Kraków. The persecution of Jews began almost immediately. Starting December 1, 1939, Jews were required to wear a Star of David. In April 1940, the Germans ordered the expulsion of the Kraków Jews; only about ten thousand were to remain in the city. Yet the order was never fully implemented. Many more than the envisaged ten thousand remained, most of those expelled simply moved to the outskirts of Kraków, and numerous Jews managed to eventually return to the city.

On March 3, 1941, the German authorities announced the establishment of a ghetto that was enclosed by a wooden fence and a brick wall. Even though the ghetto was crowded and food was scarce, Kraków Jews enjoyed relative safety until June 1942 when the first mass deportation to the Belzec death camp took place. A week later, a new deportation was conducted. The next Aktion took place on October 28, 1942. The ghetto then was divided into two sections: Ghetto A for those who were able to work, and Ghetto B for all others. The final liquidation of the ghetto began on March 13, 1943. The able-bodied from Ghetto A were marched to the Płaszów labor camp. The remaining Jews were either murdered on the spot or transported to Auschwitz.

Białystok

Germany occupied Białystok for the first time on September 15, 1939. Because Białystok was located in the territory destined to join the USSR as part of the Molotov-Ribbentrop Pact, on September 22, 1939, the Germans withdrew and the Red Army entered the city. German troops returned on June 26, 1941, and immediately started persecuting Jews. Around eight hundred were herded into the Great Synagogue and burned there. On July 3 and 12, mass shootings took place. After that, mass killings stopped for twenty months.

On July 26, 1941, the creation of the ghetto was announced. The ghetto was surrounded by a high fence topped with barbed wire. Life in the ghetto was harsh but, until February 1943, relatively safe. The first major deportation to the death camps started on February 5, 1943, and lasted for the whole week. In July 1943 the Germans decided to liquidate the ghetto. On August 16 the Białystok ghetto inhabitants were ordered to assemble at the deportation point. The underground rebelled, but the rebellion was put down by the German troops. Most Białystok Jews were deported to death camps; those chosen for work were sent to labor camps.

Cooperation and Collaboration

In the Minsk ghetto, the main collaboration and cooperation bodies were the Jewish Council (Judenrat) and the Order Service (Ordnungsdienst), generally known as the Jewish Police. In addition, there was the Special Operations Unit, which worked closely with the Nazi security services. The Germans also had a network of paid Jewish informers in the ghetto. The establishment of the Judenrat was one of the first German actions after occupying the city. The first Jewish Council head, Il'ia Mushkin, was chosen simply because he happened to be the only person who spoke at least some German among a group of Jews randomly seized on the street.

In this, the appointment of the Judenrat chair made Minsk different from ghettos established in Poland, where prewar communal and political leaders were appointed or volunteered to take the position. Yet because of Soviet policies that gradually disbanded all Jewish communal bodies, and because ethnically Jewish Communists were the first to be killed by the Nazis, German authorities had to improvise. Mushkin was widely regarded as a decent and honest person committed to helping the ghetto population. He was arrested in February 1942, tortured, and killed. Mushkin was followed by Moshe Yoffe, a German-speaking refugee from Poland. In a desperate and suicidal move, Yoffe warned the ghetto population about the July 1942 Aktion and was immediately killed.

After Yoffe's death, the Judenrat ceased to function, and the Jewish police became the most powerful Jewish institution in the ghetto. Most ghetto survivors considered the Jewish police and its Special Operations Unit to be traitors and willing Nazi agents. The Minsk ghetto Jewish police were dominated by Jewish refugees from Poland. Here again the legacies of the Soviet prewar policies help explain this reality. Soviet Jews who experienced firsthand Stalin's Great Terror knew that taking the lead, as the Soviet saying went, was dangerous, and therefore they did not seek to stick out. Polish Jews, on the other hand, had no problem being first movers and, against the background of their small numbers in the ghetto, were substantially overrepresented among collaborators. More crucially, this behavior was believed to increase one's survival chances, even at the expense of others. Service in the police, and collaboration more generally, provided refugees—people who were cut off from their kinship and social support networks—with sources of income and influence.

As in Minsk, in the Kraków ghetto the main cooperation and collaboration bodies were the Jewish Council, later replaced by the Jewish Commissariat, and the Jewish police. German security services also created a network of paid Jewish informers in the city. Initially the Judenrat was headed by Dr. Mark Bieberstein, an educator, and his deputy, Wilhelm Goldblat. Bieberstein's tenure as the Judenrat chair was short. He was replaced by Artur Rosenzweig, a lawyer and the former secretary of the Kraków city bar association. During the Aktion of June 1942, Rosenzweig refused to provide the Germans with the demanded deportees, and paid for this act of insubordination with his life. When Rosenzweig was killed, the Jewish Council was dissolved and replaced by the Commissariat, headed by Dawid Gutter.

The real power, however, rested with the Jewish police. Initially it consisted of forty servicemen, the vast majority of whom were unpaid volunteers who lived off the business opportunities (mainly bribes and smuggling) made possible by their status and connections. The Kraków ghetto police became notorious under the leadership of Symche Spira. Spira started his career in the ghetto as a low-level clerk in the Judenrat, and when the Jewish police force was organized, applied to be transferred to the force. He was immediately liked by the German supervisors for his ruthlessness, obedience, and willingness to carry out any order, and he was quickly promoted. The Jewish police were widely despised by their fellow ghetto inmates. Some survivors even claimed that they were worse than the Germans (Edward S. 1991; Meringer-Moskowicz 1996).

Why did these Kraków Jews collaborate with Germans? Not one of them did so for ideological reasons. Rather, their key motivation was the belief that collaboration increased their chances of survival (Chwalba 2011, 353; Pankiewicz 1987, 67). Service in the Jewish police also provided its members with numerous enrichment opportunities that could be easily translated into benefits such as better food and clothing and the ability to buy fake documents and to pay for shelter outside the ghetto, thus presumably making it more likely that they would survive. The expectation that collaboration would lead to survival proved to be futile, but Jews who chose this behavior had no way of knowing that at the time.

Like the other two ghettos, Białystok also had a Jewish Council and a Jewish police force. In addition, it also had a number of private collaborators who were the German security services' informers. The Białystok ghetto Jewish Council was a stronger and more capable institution than its Minsk and Kraków counterparts. For more than two years, the council worked tirelessly and quite efficiently to shield, and if possible save, what was left of Białystok's Jewish community.

The Białystok ghetto Jewish Council was established by the Nazis in late June 1941, immediately after the German occupation of the city. German authorities summoned the city's chief rabbi, Gedaliah Rosenmann, and appointed him the Judenrat chair. The selection of Rosenmann is not surprising, given Białystok's political situation prior to the German takeover. As Jewish communal institutions had been dismantled by the Soviets who ruled the city in 1939–41, the rabbi was the most visible remaining Jewish public figure in the city.

Rosenmann, in turn, appointed Ephraim Barasz, the former general manager of the Białystok pre–World War II Jewish Community Council, to be his deputy and the acting chair of the Judenrat. After Barasz's appointment, Rosenmann, the de jure Judenrat chair, assumed a largely ceremonial role. Almost all other Judenrat members were also public figures in the city's Jewish community (Blumental 1962, chap. 1; Shilhav 1961, 10–45).

Throughout the existence of the Białystok ghetto, Barasz was its undisputed leader. As with many other Judenrat chairs, Barasz's key goal was securing the survival of his ghetto, and he had a clear vision of how to achieve that. His was a two-pronged strategy of cooperating with the local German authorities and making the ghetto so indispensable to the German war effort that its liquidation would become unthinkable. Having graduated from a German university, Barasz knew how to approach the local German authorities. Some officials, who were known in the ghetto as "good Germans," helped Barasz out of human decency, personal sympathy, or patriotic feelings, because they recognized the importance of ghetto workshops and factories to the German war effort. Others were bribed.

The strategy *almost* worked. Barasz was able to keep his ghetto intact when most other ghettos were liquidated. While Barasz believed that cooperation with the Germans meant the best chance to save the ghetto as a whole, he was also certain that such behavior would lead to his own death. He had no doubt that the Germans were going to lose the war, and he told his secretary that he expected to be executed when the Soviets returned (Levkowitcz 1980, 7). To save the community, he was willing to sacrifice his life. The ghetto also had Jewish police. In many ghettos, including Kraków and eventually Minsk, the police were de facto independent from, and often more powerful than, the Judenrat. But in Białystok, which had a strong and competent Judenrat, the Jewish police were firmly subordinate to the Judenrat. During the February 1943 Aktion, the behavior of the

Jewish police members was by and large irreproachable. During the deportation, the Jewish police refrained from taking part in rounding up fellow Jews, leaving the dirty work to the Germans, and they are largely remembered by the survivors as decent people.

Resistance

Cooperation with and resistance to the Nazis are located on opposite ends of the behavioral spectrum. Yet the two strategies share substantial similarities. First, both behaviors were shaped by the pre–World War II policies of the regimes under which the Jews lived. Second, similarly to Judenrat leaders, resisters were drawn primarily from the ranks of politically active yet substantially younger Jews.

The Minsk ghetto was a resistance hub. Almost immediately after the city was occupied by the Nazis, numerous small and uncoordinated underground initiatives emerged. They were directed mainly by idealistic and naive Communist Party youth branch members and low-level Communist cadres. These people, however, had no real understanding of how to operate and survive in the underground, and most either ceased their activities or were caught and executed by the Nazis.

Some older Communist cadres also contemplated resistance. But as disciplined party members who had lived through the horrors of Stalin's Great Terror, they simply could not bring themselves to create any organizational structure without an explicit order from above. The attitude of Communist refugees from Poland—people who were repressed in their homeland and had worked for many years in the underground—was different. Less accustomed to rigid Soviet discipline, they were willing to act unsupervised by party higher-ups. Moreover, they had the skills to operate and survive in the underground.

Among the Polish-Jewish Communists was Hersh Smolar, a high-ranking activist with decades of underground work under his belt. In the ghetto, Smolar encountered other Communist cadres, whom he knew and trusted. Eventually an underground organization was formed under Smolar's leadership. Virtually all of the leadership and prominent members of the resistance were activists from the Communist Party and its youth branch (Epstein 2008, 110–47; Smolar 1989, 25).

The Polish-Jewish Communists' previous underground experience was crucial for the organization's survival. The internal security rules instituted by Smolar allowed the Jewish underground to survive despite the Germans' repeated efforts to crush it. After Soviet partisan units had been organized around Minsk, the underground started smuggling members into the forests. The resistance continued to operate in the city until the majority of its cadres relocated to the forests and continued fighting from there.

The Minsk ghetto underground, while ostensibly Communist and focused mainly on helping the Soviet Union win the war, did invest efforts in saving Jews qua Jews, especially after it became clear that the ghetto's days were numbered. The main expression of this attempt to save as many Jewish lives as possible was the creation of the Jewish partisan detachments that, unlike the non-Jewish units, had both military and civilian components. The most important of these detachments was "Unit 106," commanded by Shalom Zorin, who escaped the Minsk ghetto to the forest in late 1941. The unit consisted of a large family camp where Jewish children, women, and men who were unfit for combat—mostly Minsk ghetto escapees—were placed, as well as a fighting squad that protected the family camp and engaged in other missions.

In Kraków, Jewish organized resistance emerged only in 1942, after almost three years of Nazi rule. Eventually, two Jewish resistance organizations emerged—the predominantly Communist Iskra ("Spark" in Polish) and the Fighting Organization of the Jewish Halutz Youth (Organizacja Bojowa Żydowskiej Młodzieży Chalucowej), more widely known as the Hehalutz Halochem ("Fighting Pioneer" in Hebrew).[1] The emergence and conduct of both groups can be directly traced to their leaders' pre–World War II political activism and exposure to state repression. Iskra was founded by Heszek Bauminger. When World War II broke out, Bauminger joined the Polish army, became a POW, and eventually made his way to Soviet-occupied eastern Poland, where he became a devoted Communist. When Germany invaded the USSR, Bauminger joined the Red Army. In the fall of 1941, he once again became a POW in eastern Ukraine. He escaped the POW camp and managed to return to Kraków, where he started a resistance group.

In addition to Bauminger, another figure playing a key role in Iskra's activities was Gola Mire, an experienced Communist activist whom Bauminger met in eastern Poland, where she had escaped from the Nazis. When Mire also made it back to Kraków, she renewed her contacts with Bauminger and quickly became one of Iskra's leading figures (Peled 1993, chap. 3).

Iskra was as a small but well-organized group engaged in anti-German sabotage and nightly stealth assaults on off-duty servicemen. Under Mire's influence, Iskra also merged with the armed wing of the Communist Polish Workers' Party, the Gwardia Ludowa, becoming its Jewish (and arguably its most active) unit in the city. Yet Iskra's small manpower was simply insufficient to conduct anything more ambitious than small-scale sabotage, so Mire decided to join forces with the Zionist underground organization, the Hehalutz Halochem (HH).

The HH originated from Akiba, the largest of the youth Zionist movements in Kraków. During the early stages of the Nazi rule the top priority for the movement was not resistance but educational activities. The movement also received permission to operate an agricultural farm in Kopaliny, where many activists eventually moved. The farm existed until fall 1942. As the news about mass killings and deportations of entire communities started to reach the farm, the Akiba leaders realized that the threat had become both lethal and immediate (Maher 2010), and the decision to launch an armed underground was finally reached (Davidson Draenger 1996, 37–38).

In the fall of 1942, the farm was liquidated and its residents returned to the ghetto. Initially the HH included only Akiba members, but later other Zionist youth movements joined as well. According to the preserved roster of the organization, out of ninety-seven members, only six did not belong to a Zionist youth movement (Peled 1993, app. 10).

Because the Zionists were not subject to state repression in prewar Poland, HH members had no idea whatsoever about the basics of underground work. The group leadership recognized this weakness but had neither the time nor the resources to come up with a solution. Mire, whom some of the HH leaders knew as an accomplished underground activist, was able to convince the two Jewish undergrounds to join forces and conduct a major anti-German operation, which later became known as the Cyganeria bombing. On the evening of December 22, 1942,[2] the fighters of the HH and Iskra, disguised as Poles, bombed the Cyganeria coffee house, packed with German servicemen, killing a number of them and wounding many more. Unfortunately for the Jewish underground, the HH was betrayed from inside when Germans recruited some of its members as agents, and most fighters were swiftly arrested.

In Białystok several Jewish resistance groups emerged as well, but because of different pre-Holocaust conditions, the trajectory of resistance in the city differed from that of both Kraków and Minsk. Shortly after the German occupation of Białystok, a joint Polish-Jewish Communist underground was established. Its key goal was to assist the Soviet Union in its struggle against the Nazis. It is not surprising that the Communists were the first movers in the resistance. All the other movements and organizations had been disbanded and decapitated by the Soviets during the two years of their rule in 1939–41. Furthermore, because the Communist Party was subject to state repression in interwar Poland and its members already possessed the resister's toolkit, the Białystok Communists were in a good position to launch the resistance immediately after German occupation.

The Zionist organizations, unlike the Communists, were largely inactive during this early period. To a large extent this was an outcome of the Soviet repression of non-Communist groups, which left the Zionists disorganized and leaderless because many prominent Zionists escaped the city or were exiled. One such leader was Chajka Grosman, who moved to Vilnius, where numerous Zionist youth movements' activists gathered during the Soviet occupation period. The German occupation of Vilnius and the mass shootings that followed convinced many young Zionists that the Jewish people were facing a coordinated extermination policy rather than localized atrocities, and therefore organized resistance was required. It was decided that Grosman should return to her hometown to organize resistance among the Zionist youth.

Following Grosman's return, a Zionist underground also started to coalesce in the city under her leadership and that of Mordechai Tenenbaum, another Zionist leader who arrived in Białystok from Warsaw. In Minsk, the underground consisted almost exclusively of Communists and saw its goal as aiding the USSR in its struggle against Germany. Open rebellion inside the ghetto to protect Jewish honor and signal to the world that the Jews were fighting back *as Jews* was not even seriously considered. In Kraków, the Zionist HH wanted to fight inside the ghetto to defend the Jews' honor and dignity but was convinced by the more skilled Iskra to conduct an operation that promoted the goals of the Communists and was presented as a Polish, rather than a Jewish, action. In Białystok the situation was different. There, the Zionists not only outnumbered the Communists in the underground but also possessed considerable skills, because the Soviet authorities had forced Zionist movements to operate clandestinely when eastern Poland was a part of the USSR in 1939–41. The Communists and the Zionists joined forces, and on August 16, 1943, during the ghetto's final liquidation, the Jews fought back, as Jews, inside the ghetto.

Coping vs. Evasion

The analysis of collaboration and resistance clearly demonstrates the impact of pre–World War II repression policies adopted by different regimes. But these were the strategies adopted by the most visible number of Jews, who were numerically small. The majority of Jews targeted by the Nazis' extermination policies chose between coping with the emerging situation inside the ghetto and trying to escape. To understand the choice between evasion and coping, we ought to look at prewar policies that promoted or discouraged the integration of Jews into the broader society.

Throughout most of the ghettos' existence, coping was arguably the most prudent behavior. As the mass murder progressed, however, there was a growing understanding among the Jews that simply trying to survive inside the ghetto was unlikely to ensure survival. Collaboration was morally questionable, while engaging in organized armed resistance required a certain set of skills and qualities that most Jews simply did not possess. Evasion was the main behavioral alternative to coping. Yet the majority of Jews chose to stay put. Why was this the case?

Successful coping across the three ghettos consisted of a combination of three things: finding employment, securing access to food, and preparing a hideout. In all three domains, people who were less integrated into the non-Jewish societies and had mainly intraethnic, predominantly Jewish social milieus and networks usually fared better. Furthermore, psychologically, less assimilated Jews found life inside the ghetto easier than their more assimilated coethnics.

In Minsk, the twenty years of Soviet rule completely remade the tsarist-era social networks. As Minsk Jews became more integrated into the non-Jewish society, their social networks evolved. Communal institutions, support bodies, and even the very sense of common identity also disappeared among many. As a result, coping in the Minsk ghetto was more individual- than community-based. It was chaotic and it was desperate. There was no guiding force or body to organize the community and to ensure mutual help. Acquaintances and friends outside the ghetto could offer little help, simply because leaving the ghetto was a high-risk action punishable by death. The older generation attempted to revive the city's pre-Soviet robust Jewish community, with its intraethnic solidarity and support networks (Bemporad 2013, 85), but this was a lost battle. The changes that the Minsk Jewish community had undergone were too far-reaching to reverse in such a short period.

The situation in Kraków was similar to that in Minsk. Interwar Poland did not encourage the integration of Jews into the broader society, but the polity that preceded it, the Austro-Hungarian Empire, did. Under the Habsburg rule, many Kraków Jews received their education in ethnically mixed schools, adopted Polish and German as their first languages, and participated in ethnically mixed business enterprises. The policies adopted by the Polish state in the interwar period slowed down but ultimately did not reverse this process of integration (though not assimilation) of Kraków Jews into the broader society. As a result, in the Kraków ghetto, coping was atomized and centered on the individual and the family, though to a lesser degree than in Minsk because communal institutions, weak as they were, still existed in the city. And the more integrated into the non-Jewish society a person was, the more challenging was his or her coping inside the ghetto.

In Białystok, the situation was different. Neither the imperial Russian nor the interwar Polish government promoted the integration of Jews into the broader society, which allowed strong Jewish communal institutions and identities to persist until the beginning of World War II. As a result, the Białystok Jewish community was robust, cohesive, and endowed with exceptionally strong local identity (Kobrin 2010), institutions, leadership, and support networks. In the Białystok ghetto, no one died of starvation, while numerous cases of hunger were reported in Minsk. The health situation in the ghetto was also tolerable, and the most vulnerable, such as orphans and the elderly, were efficiently cared for by the community.

Had the Germans decided to leave the Białystok ghetto intact, coping would have clearly been a winning strategy. But when the decision was made in Berlin to liquidate the ghetto, Jewish Białystok was doomed. For the weaker, more heterogeneous and divided Jewish communities of Minsk and Kraków, coping, especially at the communal level, was a challenging endeavor. Yet when overall survival—rather than successful coping inside the ghetto as long as the Nazis allowed it to exist—is considered, this was not necessarily a bad thing. For the mirror image of coping was evasion, and people who had a hard time coping in the ghetto because they had more Slavic than Jewish ties and friendships were more successful in looking for shelter and salvation outside it. When the coping strategy collapsed in one ghetto after another, the very factors that had made coping so tough made evasion easier.

We will never know how many Jews chose evasion: hiding outside the ghetto walls, escaping, or assuming a false identity. What is clear, however, is that there were vast differences between the ghettos in that respect. Possibly as many as ten thousand Jews successfully escaped from the Minsk ghetto. A smaller, though still substantial, number of Jews did so in Kraków. And almost no one chose this strategy in Białystok.

Historians agree that it was hard, but not impossible, to escape the ghettos. Thousands did so on a daily basis to trade and smuggle food. The main danger was not the act of escape itself but surviving outside the ghetto, on the so-called Aryan side. Scholars also agree that all of the racial pseudoscience notwithstanding, in Eastern Europe Germans could not tell Jews from non-Jews. Thus, the key was to be able to pass as a non-Jew culturally, behaviorally, and linguistically, so as not to be identified and betrayed by hostile members of the Slavic population (Paulsson 2002). In other words, survival outside the ghetto was a function of human and social, rather than physical, geography.

These abilities, in turn, were shaped by the pre-Holocaust regimes under which each of the three cities existed. Pre–World War II state policies determined the degree of Jews' integration into the broader society and the interethnic relations in each community. When governments allowed and promoted ethnically mixed schools, neighborhoods, workplaces, and parties, the result was a higher integration of Jews into the society. This integration inevitably led to constant, even if not always very close, contacts between Jews and non-Jews and created interethnic social networks that could later be mobilized for successful evasion.

Granovetter (1973, 1363–69) demonstrates that "weak ties," such as in the workplace or via business and school contacts, provide people with invaluable opportunities for various benefits and reduce "interracial distance." The more interethnic weak ties one had, the higher one's likelihood of choosing evasion.

In Minsk, the twenty years of Soviet rule endowed numerous Jews with the tools needed for successful evasion. Jews were increasingly educated in ethnically mixed schools and thus spoke local languages fluently and without an accent. Religion was actively suppressed, and as a result many Jewish males were not circumcised, thus removing the telltale sign of their origin. Furthermore, unlike in more traditional societies such as Poland, younger people were not even expected to know Christian prayers and traditions; just speaking the language and playing the part was often enough. And even more importantly, ethnically mixed schools, clubs, and workplaces substantially increased the number of people whom escaping Jews could approach for help. Not everyone did, and many Jews were betrayed, but survival on the Aryan side was virtually impossible without a network of helpers.

Evasion in Kraków was more limited than in Minsk but still followed a similar pattern. Most Jews in the city spoke Polish, and the Habsburg policies of ethnic integration led to ethnically mixed social networks and workplaces, though to a lesser degree than in the USSR. Yet even Jews who spoke flawless Polish were usually ignorant about the most basic features of Christian faith, which were crucial for passing as Poles. The Jews' more limited number of friends and acquaintances on the Aryan side, and their unfamiliarity with the most foundational religious components of Catholic Polish identity, bedeviled successful evasion. Even despite these hurdles, however, hundreds if not thousands chose to escape the ghetto and try to survive outside it.

In Białystok only a handful did. Before World War II, Białystok was a polarized and segregated city with hostile interethnic relations. Most Jewish children had virtually no non-Jewish acquaintances, let alone friends. Unlike the Austro-Hungarian monarchy in Kraków, the Russian Empire did not promote ethnically integrated schools in Białystok, and the differences between the cities persisted throughout the interwar period when both were a part of the Polish state. Few Jews in the city, mainly those from middle- and upper-class families, were fluent in Polish. Even the Jews who spoke Polish well had few, if any, non-Jewish contacts, because they usually went to schools where the language of instruction was Polish but all students were Jewish. Mixed neighborhoods did exist in the city but were rare.

The segregation between the Jewish and Polish communities in Białystok proved to be detrimental to the survival chances of many Jews. Those who did manage to escape the ghetto were mostly Jewish refugees from other parts of Poland who moved to Białystok after 1939. Unlike local Jews, many of these people spoke Polish and could pass as non-Jews. Even after the ghetto was liquidated, there were Jews who considered it too risky, indeed unthinkable, to move to the Aryan side. They hid in bunkers and cellars for months with almost no food or water, simply because going to the Aryan side was perceived as suicidal. And because of the city's lack of any meaningful integration of Jews into the broader community, it really was.

Modern social science can contribute to the better understanding of the Holocaust in several ways. First, social scientists' focus on variation in outcomes can lead to new and previously unexplored crucial questions, such as the one I have addressed in this chapter. Second, the social sciences are well equipped to not only describe but also classify different types of behavior, thus leading to the typology of survival strategies I have suggested. Third, the comparative method, a staple of social science research but also one relatively rarely used by historians, can uncover new factors that influenced how the Holocaust evolved on the ground and what its outcomes were. Finally, the focus on political and social factors helps scholars better understand the Holocaust for what it really was—an act of large-scale *political* violence, driven and shaped by politics.

REFERENCES

Bauer, Yehuda. 1989. *Jewish Reactions to the Holocaust*. Tel Aviv: MOD Books.
Bemporad, Elissa. 2013. *Becoming Soviet Jews: The Bolshevik Experiment in Minsk*. Bloomington: Indiana University Press.
Blumental, Nachman. 1962. *Darko Shel Yudenrat: Teudot Migeto Bialistok*. Jerusalem: Yad Vashem.
Browning, Christopher. 1993. *Ordinary Men: Reserve Police Battalion 101 and the Final Solution in Poland*. New York: Harper Perennial.
Chwalba, Andrzej. 2011. "The Ethnic Panorama of Nazi-Occupied Krakow." *Polin: Studies in Polish Jewry* 23:349–56.
Davidson Draenger, Gusta. 1996. *Justyna's Narrative*. Amherst: University of Massachusetts Press.
Edward S. 1991. "Edward S. Holocaust Testimony." Fortunoff Archive, New Haven, CT.
Engelking, Barbara, and Jacek Leociak. 2009. *The Warsaw Ghetto: A Guide to the Perished City*. New Haven, CT: Yale University Press.
Epstein, Barbara. 2008. *The Minsk Ghetto, 1941–1943: Jewish Resistance and Soviet Internationalism*. Berkeley: University of California Press.
Fein, Helen. 1979. *Accounting for Genocide: National Responses and Jewish Victimization during the Holocaust*. New York: Free Press.
Finkel, Evgeny. 2015. "The Phoenix Effect of State Repression: Jewish Resistance during the Holocaust." *American Political Science Review* 109 (2): 339–53.
———. 2017. *Ordinary Jews: Choice and Survival during the Holocaust*. Princeton, NJ: Princeton University Press.
Finkel, Evgeny, and Scott Straus. 2012. "Macro, Meso, and Micro Research on Genocide: Gains, Shortcomings, and Future Areas of Inquiry." *Genocide Studies and Prevention* 7 (1): 56–67.

Goldhagen, Daniel Jonah. 1996. *Hitler's Willing Executioners: Ordinary Germans and the Holocaust*. New York: Knopf.
Granovetter, Mark. 1973. "The Strength of Weak Ties." *American Journal of Sociology* 78 (6): 1360–80.
Hilberg, Raul. 2003. *The Destruction of the European Jews*. 3rd ed. New Haven, CT: Yale University Press.
Hirschman, Albert. 1970. *Exit, Voice, and Loyalty*. Cambridge, MA: Harvard University Press.
Kalyvas, Stathis. 2006. *The Logic of Violence in Civil War*. New York: Cambridge University Press.
Kobrin, Rebecca. 2010. *Jewish Bialystok and Its Diaspora*. Bloomington: Indiana University Press.
Kopstein, Jeffrey S., and Jason Wittenberg. 2018. *Intimate Violence: Anti-Jewish Pogroms on the Eve of the Holocaust*. Ithaca, NY: Cornell University Press.
Levkowitcz, Hadasah. 1980. "Interview with Hadasah Levkowitcz." Oral History Division Archive, Jerusalem.
Maher, Thomas. 2010. "Threat, Resistance, and Collective Action." *American Sociological Review* 75 (2): 252–72.
Meringer-Moskowicz, Nachum. 1996. "Nachum Meringer-Moskowicz Testimony." Oral History Division Archive, Jerusalem.
Pankiewicz, Tadeusz. 1987. *The Cracow Ghetto Pharmacy*. New York: Holocaust Library.
Paulsson, Gunnar. 2002. *Secret City: The Hidden Jews of Warsaw, 1940–1945*. London: Yale University Press.
Peled, Yael. 1993. *Krakov HaYehudit, 1939–1943*. Tel Aviv: Beit Lohamei Hagetaot.
Shilhav, Yaakov Moshe. 1961. "Haminhal Hayehudi Haatsmi (Hayudenrat) Begeto Biyalistok." MA thesis, Hebrew University of Jerusalem.
Smolar, Hersh. 1989. *The Minsk Ghetto: Soviet-Jewish Partisans against the Nazis*. New York: Holocaust Library.
Snyder, Timothy. 2010. *Bloodlands: Europe between Hitler and Stalin*. New York: Basic Books.
Straus, Scott. 2006. *The Order of Genocide: Race, Power, and War in Rwanda*. Ithaca, NY: Cornell University Press.
Varshney, Ashutosh. 2002. *Ethnic Conflict and Civic Life: Hindus and Muslims in India*. New Haven, CT: Yale University Press.
Weinstein, Jeremy. 2007. *Inside Rebellion: The Politics of Insurgent Violence*. New York: Cambridge University Press.
Wood, Elisabeth. 2003. *Insurgent Collective Action and Civil War in El Salvador*. New York: Cambridge University Press.

5

A COMMON HISTORY OF VIOLENCE?

The Pogroms of Summer 1941 in Comparative Perspective

Jeffrey S. Kopstein

In the weeks following the German attack on the Soviet Union in summer 1941, local inhabitants in hundreds of cities and villages attacked their Jewish neighbors and fellow citizens. They beat them, tormented them, raped them, stole their possessions, and frequently murdered them in the most brutal manner. This intercommunal violence occurred in a brief spurt but stretched over a very broad territory of tremendous ethnic and religious diversity.

These kinds of atrocities did not happen everywhere. In a study of the eastern borderlands of occupied Poland undertaken with Jason Wittenberg, I found that less than 10 percent of the communities where Jews lived—that is, where such events could have taken place—actually experienced neighbor-on-neighbor pogroms in the summer of 1941 (Kopstein and Wittenberg 2018). Yet such proportions merely make the question motivating historical inquiry all the more puzzling. Why there and not elsewhere? Why some cities and towns and not others? In a region running from the Baltic to the Black Sea, the pogroms unleashed by the German invasion lasted approximately one month. By the beginning of August 1941, the ghettoization of the Jews in the borderlands had begun, and by September the organized extermination of the Jews by the Germans was well underway.

A few examples from across the region illustrate the class of events in question. In the Lithuanian city of Kovno (Kaunas) on June 25, 1941, a German army photographer witnessed a pogrom in which a Lithuanian man beat to death forty-five to fifty people with a crowbar, one by one, over the course of around forty-five minutes. Onlookers, women and children included, clapped. When he finished, they sang along as he played the national anthem on an accordion (Klee, Dressen, and Riess 1988, 31). This was one act in a much larger pogrom.

On July 7, some two hundred kilometers to the south, the Polish residents of Radziłów, in the Białystok region, drove the town's Jews into a barn and burned them alive (Dmitrów, Machcewicz, and Szarota 2004, 216). Identical incidents occurred nearby in Wąsosz two days before and in Jedwabne three days after, when Jews were forced by local Poles to march through the city streets before being murdered en masse while peasants from surrounding villages brought carts, expecting to loot Jewish property (Gross 2001, 90–110).

Moving southward to what had been interwar Romania, on June 28 in Iași a multiday pogrom began with widespread local participation, killing hundreds and injuring thousands (Zwieback 2003). In the Bukovinian town of Sadagura (Sadgora), a pogrom on July 6 led by a local schoolmaster resulted in the murder of more than one hundred Jews. He and his band of peasants raped, beat, and looted the property of the Jews of three small towns before killing nearly all of them in a forest. According to Radu (2000, 98), "One witness testified that a baby's sobs could be heard coming from the mass grave for quite some time."

In Western Ukraine as well, local Ukrainians engaged in anti-Jewish violence. Some of these pogroms, above all the complex and brutal events in L'viv on June 30 and July 1, 1941, have attracted scholarly attention (Himka 2011); others are known but have received far less scrutiny. In the Volhynian town of Tuczyn, a Jewish eyewitness reported that "the local Ukrainians made a pogrom against the Jews of the townlet. . . .. Wielding iron bars, axes and other instruments, they beat up Jews, looted and rioted. The toll was 70 killed and a large number of wounded including women and children" (Spector 1990, 64, 66). Two days before the Tuczyn pogrom, on July 4, in the Eastern Galician town of Bolekhiv, after the Soviets had evacuated but before the Germans had arrived, local Ukrainians killed some of the town's Jewish residents, indiscriminately shooting them and dumping their bodies in the local river (Mendelsohn 2006, 78). In Nezvys'ko, a village near the Romanian border, peasants under the leadership of a Ukrainian priest and a local doctor "took the Jews from the neighboring villages . . . and together with Jews from Niezwiska itself, a few hundred people, locked them in the basement of a school and adjacent buildings and during the night they drowned them, throwing them from the ferry into the water. Father Golduniak took active part in this, chasing the Jews with a stick onto the ferry. Around 200 people lost their lives" (AŻIH 301–1434).[1]

Three factors figure prominently in the scholarship on the pogroms of 1941 in Western Ukraine: (1) the role of the Germans, especially the Einsatzgruppen; (2) the impact of twenty-one months of brutal Soviet rule, especially the massacres of People's Commissariat for Internal Affairs (NKVD) prisoners preceding the Soviet departure; and (3) the role of local nationalists in organizing and/or carrying out the pogroms. In what follows, after defining and identifying what happened, I then assess the role of the Germans, the Soviets, and the Organization of Ukrainian Nationalists. Although all three of these factors carry some causal weight, none of them—either together or separately—are completely satisfactory. Gaining a deeper understanding of the pogroms requires moving beyond the international and national level into a deeper engagement with local political and communal factors. As shown in Kopstein and Wittenberg's (2018) study, what appears to best account for the communal-level geographic distribution of pogroms is a variant of the classic power-threat hypothesis first put forward to account for race relations in the United States (Blalock 1967): where political polarization was high, where the Jewish community was large, and where Jews pressed for national equality in the decades before 1941 (as expressed in the vote for Jewish nationalist parties), locals used the opportunity provided by the chaos of the first weeks of the German occupation to rid themselves of their political rivals, and the likelihood of a pogrom rose steeply.

But is this account portable? Does it help us to explain anti-Jewish pogroms in other times and places? The vast majority of "exclusionary violence" in Jewish history took place under nondemocratic conditions, and therefore one could argue that mass politics constitute a scope condition for the theory. Does the power-threat thesis give us purchase on earlier anti-Jewish violence? What follows is an exercise in comparative history cast through the lens of social science. I first sift through various possible causes of the pogroms of 1941 in order to settle on what seems to be the most powerful account, one that stresses underlying political conflicts between ethnic majorities and Jewish minorities, conflicts that preceded the violence itself, sometimes by decades. Second, having established the logic of the power-threat hypothesis, I then compare the pogroms of summer 1941 to two other instances of localized anti-Jewish violence from history—one in Alexandria 38 CE and the second in Valencia in 1391—in order to explore whether the facilitating conditions for pogroms found on the eve of the Holocaust reflect common patterns. As we shall see, in these cases, too, the question of political "ownership" played a crucial and underappreciated role in the onset of pogroms, suggesting that anti-Jewish violence is less about hatred or cultural difference than about political conflict.

The Pogroms of 1941 in Western Ukraine
The Germans

Pogroms in the sense of locally based anti-Jewish violence involving nonstate actors had occurred before in much of Eastern Europe. There is a common explanatory tension in the historiography on pogroms of earlier eras (1880–1920), revolving around the question, who is pulling the strings? To what extent was anti-Jewish violence in cities, towns, and villages driven by external stimuli from outside the communities versus antagonisms within them? (Klier and Lambroza 1992).

The question of external versus internal stimuli in 1941 leads us directly to the role of the invading Germans. The general presence of German army units, police battalions, and mobile killing units in the region is indisputable. What remains hotly contested is the exact nature of their involvement. Did the Germans inspire, organize, or compel locals to carry out these pogroms? The Nazi leadership had clearly decided that Jews in territories captured during this phase of the war would be treated ruthlessly.

The documentary record nevertheless makes clear that at this stage of the war, the Germans preferred others to do their dirty work for them and were keenly interested in using locals for "self-cleansing" of "Communists and Jews." The Germans, for their part, were keen to film and photograph the massacres as proof that the locals shared their hatred of the Jews. Internal German communications make explicit reference to "pogroms." On June 29, SS-Gruppenführer Reinhard Heydrich sent off a telegram to the heads of the Einsatzgruppen reminding them of what had already been discussed in person: "Nothing is to be put in the way of the self-cleansing actions of anti-communist and anti-Jewish circles in the newly occupied areas. On the contrary, without trace they are to be unleashed and, when necessary, to be intensified and steered onto the right path." (quoted in Musiał 2004, 336).

Even with these orders in hand, the evidence is clear that the Germans frequently failed to set off pogroms and expressed frustration where they could not (Ainsztein 1974, 251). A further piece of information casts doubt on the notion that this was purely a German affair: in many localities, pogroms occurred in the chaos before the Germans arrived, after they had left, or with very little German help (Golczewski 2008, 91).

The similarities of pogrom rituals across cities and towns may suggest a German script, but the Germans did not force anyone to follow this script. Above all, the presence or absence of the Germans does not help us distinguish between pogrom and nonpogrom locations within Western Ukraine. The German invasion and general presence appears to have been a facilitating condition, but it was neither a sufficient nor, in many cases, even a necessary one.

The Soviet Occupation

The pogroms took place within a restricted time frame: June and July 1941. They also occurred within a specific geographic space—the borderlands—in territories occupied by the Soviets from 1939 to 1941. No significant pogrom activity occurred east of these lands, in the pre-1939 Soviet Union itself (Dumitru and Johnson 2011).

What about Soviet rule made the newly acquired territories so susceptible to pogrom violence? For many, Soviet rule had become one long ordeal of degradation and humiliation. It marked the end of national independence for Poland and ultimately thwarted the national aspirations of patriotic Ukrainians. Soviet authorities expropriated property and arrested, imprisoned, and deported local elites of all ethnic groups, and showed a callous disregard for local languages and religious traditions.

Much ink has been spilled on the welcome given to Soviet soldiers as they entered communities in Western Ukraine. Although generalization is hazardous, most scholars agree that the Soviets were met by the Jews with relief, by Ukrainians with a measure of hope (for genuine autonomy and ethnic advantage), and by Poles with a good deal of fear (as the conquered *Staatsnation*). Of course, not all Jews, Ukrainians, and Poles fit these categories, but they are probably appropriate characterizations of the "median" reaction. A minority of Jews and Ukrainians (and a smaller number of Poles) greeted the Soviets enthusiastically (Bauer 2007).

Were Jews distributional beneficiaries of Soviet rule? Some were, but the vast majority were not. What is clear is that the big initial losers of the occupation were ethnic Poles, who immediately lost "ownership" of the state. They were replaced by local Ukrainians and Jews, as well as officials arriving from the East. Polish schools became Ukrainian.

Nationalization of Polish and Jewish businesses quickly followed, artisans were compelled to join cooperatives, and virtually the entire spectrum of political parties (Polish, Ukrainian, and Jewish) and civic organizations disappeared overnight. Religious institutions faced new and draconian kinds of restrictions. In his account of Brzezany, Shimon Redlich (2002, 85) reports that "various kinds of restrictions and harassment now affected local churches and synagogues. Of all the synagogues only two, the Large Synagogue and Rabbi Yidel's synagogue, continued to function under the Soviets. The others became residential quarters for Jewish refugees. The main entrances to Polish churches and to the Ukrainian church in the center of Brzezany were closed. People had to enter through the back doors. Services were severely limited and electricity was cut off to some churches during midnight Christmas prayers." Many Ukrainians initially looked on the new order as a chance for genuine autonomy, but most were quickly disabused of this by the reality of Soviet rule. The new rulers quickly removed cherished national symbols, replaced Ukrainian narratives with "internationalist" ones, and doled out police and other bureaucratic functions along political rather than ethnic lines.

How did Soviet rule affect interethnic relations? Before turning to this question, it is important to be realistic about the communities before the arrival of the Soviets. The 1930s saw a significant deterioration in relations between Poles, Ukrainians, and Jews in Volhynia and Eastern Galicia. The period between the collapse of Poland in September 1939 and the establishment of Soviet rule in Western Ukraine entailed a measure of violence between Poles and Ukrainians and by Ukrainians against Jews (Redlich 2002, 86; Bauer 2009, 33). In towns temporarily occupied by German soldiers in the first half of September, Germans themselves carried out selective persecutions. Although some Jews did flee to the German part of Poland after the arrival of the Soviets, a far larger number poured eastward over the new Soviet frontier in search of physical security, swelling the Jewish population in many towns in what had now become Western Ukraine.

On ethnic relations under the Soviets, Henryk Szyper's unpublished memoir captures some of the highlights from a Jewish standpoint (AŻIH 301–4654). Reporting from L'viv, Szyper writes that the economy deteriorated immediately, well below the level of what the Soviets called "fascist" pre-1939 Poland: "The inept Soviet propaganda did not help. It did not explain the need for sacrifice; instead it continued to refer to 'landlord's Poland' and contrast it with the paradise of the USSR." In fact, with the signing of the German-Soviet Nonaggression Pact in August 1939, negative stories about Germany stopped appearing in the Soviet press. Szyper notes that "all Ukrainian and Polish grievances against the Bolsheviks found their expression in antipathy toward the Jews, who were seen as accomplices. After all, Jews were 'close' and the Bolsheviks 'far away.' It was easier to express anger against the former for the sins of the latter."

Szyper also directly addresses the question, "How indeed did the Jews behave under Soviet rule and did they deserve the blame?" After acknowledging the abuses of local Communists who were "comprised of minorities" (by which he means Ukrainians and Jews), he pointedly remarks, "But whenever the Soviets repressed the population they repressed the Jews just as much. So, in 1940 many prominent Jewish merchants and landlords, as well as industrialists, were deported east to the provinces. Among officers and their families, Jews were not spared." According to Snyder (2010, 140), of the 21,892 Polish officers killed during 1940, "some eight percent of the victims were Jews, corresponding to the proportion of Jews in eastern Poland."

Still, for Szyper and many others like him, an unquestionable achievement of Soviet rule was, as Szyper put it, "factual emancipation and equalization of political citizenship." It was this simultaneous experience of terror and emancipation that Ukrainians and especially Poles did not always share with their Jewish fellow citizens. Jews and Ukrainians were now allowed to apply for and hold offices and positions that had been previously barred to them. In fact, most accounts indicate that after Jews had been favored in some administrative posts initially, by mid-1940 most had been replaced by Ukrainians. To take but one example, of the 476 members of the L'viv city soviet in December 1940, 252 were Ukrainians, 121 Poles, 76 Jews, and 27 members of other nationalities (Yones 2004, 48). Scholars have replicated these findings for other bureaucracies and political institutions in Western Ukraine.

What mattered, however, was not reality but perception. As Christoph Mick (2010, 458–77) notes in his study of L'viv, Jewish behavior under the Soviets was largely seen through the lens of older prejudices and stereotypes, and any evidence contradicting these older views was largely ignored. "Privileging of Jews is an exaggeration if one looks at this objectively," Szyper writes before he turns to the heart of the matter: "Many idiocies were uttered, however, by narrow minded morons whom you will find in any population, Jewish too. For instance, a director of a store would now say to a Pole who may have voiced a complaint, 'There is no more free Poland, your time is over. It is our time.' I heard the same shouted by a woman to a city plumber who was carrying out repairs. Such idiots were numerous." Even with this serious "self-criticism," in the end, according to Szyper, "the average person, a Pole or Ukrainian, could not forgive the Jews their equality. This had to be avenged."

Soviet repression affected all three ethnic groups, although at different times and with different intensities. Of the 66,563 individuals arrested in Western Ukraine between September 1939 and May 1941, 22,045 were Poles, 23,210 were Ukrainians, and 13,164 were Jews. In two nights alone, April 12 and 13, 1940, approximately 8,000 Poles from L'viv were deported to the interior of the Soviet Union, and on the next night, April 14, Jewish politicians and Zionist leaders were arrested and sent eastward (Mick 2007, 250). And perhaps most critically, of the 20,094 prisoners in custody in Western Ukraine on June 10, 1941 (the majority Ukrainian but a number of them Poles and Jews), approximately 4,500 were deported to the East, 7,000 suspected petty or serious criminals remained in prisons temporarily, and more than 8,700 in the hands of the NKVD were murdered just before the Germans arrived (Hryciuk 2007, 183).

In many testimonies, the discovery of corpses by arriving German military units is linked to the violence that followed. In L'viv, Germans and local Ukrainians forced Jews to dig up corpses from mass graves and retrieve them from jails before they incited a pogrom against the Jewish population of the city. Pogroms unfolded in a similar fashion in Sambir, Stryj, Boryslav, Zolochiv, and other towns in Eastern Galicia.

Did the prison massacres cause the pogroms? The NKVD massacres, where they occurred, probably made the pogroms bloodier than they otherwise might have been. But the location of NKVD prisons and pogrom locations do not map neatly onto each other. The number of pogrom locations (126), moreover, far exceeds the number of NKVD massacres. These murders were therefore a sufficient but not a necessary condition for pogrom violence. There is no evidence that Soviet rule was any worse in villages and towns where pogroms occurred than in those where they did not. In small towns and villages especially, Jews were taken by complete surprise by the pogroms and drew no connection to Soviet rule. Some even wrote to German military authorities in search of relief (Pohl 1996, 65).

Ukrainians (as opposed to Jews) who collaborated with Soviet authorities were largely spared the retribution of their fellow Ukrainians. According to one eyewitness, in July 1941 soldiers returning to Bolekhiv wearing Soviet uniforms, for example, were killed only if they were Jews (Mendelsohn 2006, 195). And in L'viv, Szyper notes, "somewhat tacitly all Ukrainians agreed to peace. Nobody was attacked for participating in the Soviet administration." In short, the evidence indicates that the pogroms were less the product of anti-Soviet than anti-Jewish sentiments. This observation raises the question of nationalism and antisemitism.

Nationalism, Antisemitism, and the Role of the OUN

Nationalist networks figure prominently in both eyewitness and scholarly accounts of the pogroms of summer 1941 (Struve 2015). There is no doubt that these networks were deeply rooted in Eastern Galicia. During the interwar period, the major cities were hotbeds of nationalist politics—Polish, Jewish, and Ukrainian. In L'viv, approximately 84 percent of Poles cast their votes for the anti-Ukrainian and antisemitic Endejca in 1922. For Stanislaviv and Ternopil, the proportions were 75 and 70 percent, respectively. The vast majority of Jews (nearly 80 percent) voted for the Galician Zionists, and the Ukrainian population, already mobilized into nationalist politics, boycotted the election altogether in these same cities, in protest against Polish rule. Relations were mostly cordial but never easy between Ukrainians and Jews in interwar Poland; Jewish parties, especially the Eastern Galician Zionists, attempted (not always successfully) to preserve their neutrality in the dispute between Poles and Ukrainians (Honigsman 2001, 87–100).

Ukrainian political parties—dominated by the moderate Ukrainian National Democratic Organization (UNDO)—ultimately entered Polish politics, but they enjoyed little success in reversing discriminatory Polish linguistic, economic, educational, and religious policy. Violence constituted the main nonparliamentary alternative. The Ukrainian Military Organization, under the leadership of Ievhen Konovalets, had tried during the 1920s to dislodge the Poles from Eastern Galicia, but its campaign of burning Polish estates, destroying buildings, sabotaging railroads and telegraph lines, and even political assassination ultimately failed. In 1929, again under Konovalets's leadership, the Organization of Ukrainian Nationalists (OUN) was founded in Vienna, with underground cells in Poland and abroad. During the 1930s, the Polish government responded with a series of "pacification campaigns," which entailed mass arrests, the closing or banning of Ukrainian cultural institutions, and the imprisonment of the OUN's leading cadres. The OUN fiercely resisted any attempts to compromise; it intimidated UNDO moderates with threats and violence. At the same time, the OUN carried out attacks against Jews, Jewish shops, and Jewish religious institutions, attacks that increased in number in the late 1930s (Bruder 2007, 101, 104).

Geopolitics created a community of interest between German revisionists and Ukrainian nationalists of all stripes (Golczewski 2010). Ideology, however, cemented relations between the OUN and the Nazis. From the outset, the OUN was anti-Communist, antisemitic, anti-Polish, and deeply influenced by European fascism (Bruder 2007; Carynnyk 2011). Scholars continue to debate whether the OUN is rightly categorized as a fascist or integral nationalist organization. OUN politicians frequently deviated from German positions in the 1930s; some were ardent antisemites, but others viewed Jewish questions as a distraction. In April 1941, the OUN declared the Jews to be "the most secure support of the ruling Moscow regime and the avant-garde of Moscow imperialism" but explicitly abjured pogrom violence against Jews. By June, however, the German line had changed, and so had the OUN's. The prospect of statehood was too tempting and it therefore willingly followed the Germans into their ideology of mass extermination.

What occurred next seems clear enough. German intelligence in the run-up to Operation Barbarossa instructed the OUN to organize local militias throughout Ukraine. These militias, where successfully created (primarily in Western Ukraine), were instrumental in carrying out the pogroms (Pohl 2007, 309–10). Immediately after the German invasion and until the end of July 1941, OUN leaflets called for the elimination of the Jews, the Soviets, and other enemies (Bruder 2007, 125). Pohl (1996, 49) refers to an OUN-B meeting in L'viv on July 19, 1941, where Stepan Levanskyi, the propaganda chief of the OUN-B, said, "Concerning the Jews, all methods should be accepted that lead to their extermination." Iaroslav Stets'ko, who had proclaimed Ukrainian statehood in the name of the OUN-B and thereafter was arrested by the Germans, declared in custody his "support for the destruction of the Jews and the expedience of bringing German methods of exterminating Jewry to Ukraine" (Berkhoff and Carynnyk 1999, 171).

The evidence of OUN and OUN-organized militia participation in these pogroms is also compelling. Jewish survivor testimony frequently refers to Ukrainian nationalists and militia officials, wearing blue and yellow armbands, being among those assisting the Germans, or committing atrocities without any German prompting or even presence. In his testimony about the L'viv program, Janisław Korczynsky recalled, "On the second day after the Germans came in, I saw a group of Ukrainians with yellow and blue armbands, and they were taking a group of Jewish men and women, around 70 people, to the prison by Zmarstynowskiej Street" (AŻIH 301–1809). Other accounts, such as Richard Ryndner's (also from L'viv), Erna Klinger's from Boryslav, Swerwyn Dobroszklanaka's from Rivne, Dr. Grossbard's from Kulykiv, and Szaje Feder's from Kolomyia, name the "Ukrainian militia" (AŻIH 301–18, 310–1091, 301–1222, 301–1398) as the main perpetrators of the pogroms in early July. OUN advance groups had organized these militias.

The case against the OUN seems solid. On July 1, 1941, as the OUN-B's Iaroslav Stets'ko proclaimed the new national Ukrainian state in L'viv, several hundred meters away, Jewish men, women, and children were being murdered by elements of the Ukrainian militia in what had been NKVD prisons. And yet, any account of the pogroms in Western Ukraine as primarily OUN operations misses something important. The OUN at this point in time undoubtedly wanted to kill Jews, if only to demonstrate its unity with German plans, and it sought to induce Ukrainians to take part. As an organization, however, it was spread thinly throughout a large region (Grelka 2005, 270). Just as the Einsatzgruppen were incapable of killing the East European Jews on their own, quickly and efficiently, so too was the OUN outmatched by the scale of the task it confronted. Some local inhabitants may have joined the OUN-led local administrations out of conviction after a few representatives arrived on the scene. Like Henryk Szyper's friends in L'viv, however, some Ukrainians wore the yellow and blue armbands, as Szyper notes, after having "only days before having praised the Soviet fatherland."

Damning as the case against the OUN may be, excessive focus on its role risks overlooking an essential feature of these pogroms: their mass character and the participation of broad segments of the Ukrainian public. Many accounts speak of popular participation and looting both by neighbors and by Ukrainian peasants from surrounding villages. German and Jewish accounts indicate just how chaotic these events were; they encompassed many more perpetrators, bystanders, and rescuers (and sometimes people who switched roles amid the violence) than could possibly have been members or even long-term sympathizers of the OUN. Crediting OUN-centric accounts, while understandable from the standpoint of internal Ukrainian or diaspora politics, risks blaming a few leaders or activists for what transpired and thereby letting off the hook entire communities who, in a minority of locations in Western Ukraine, either stood by without lifting a finger or actively participated in violence against their fellow citizens. They also fail to highlight the majority of Ukrainian communities that refused to heed the sirens of extremist nationalism, communities where pogroms did not occur.

Nationalism and antisemitism certainly played an important role in June and July 1941, but just how important the presence of nationalist networks was in determining where pogroms did and did not occur remains an open question. With OUN activists spread out over hundreds of towns and villages with orders to incite pogroms, in the end they managed to do so in less than 10 percent of Western Ukrainian localities.

Pogroms as Political Violence: A Return to the Local

Antisemitism on its own cannot account for why pogroms occurred in some communities but not in others. There is no evidence that antisemitism was more deeply embedded in cities or towns that experienced pogroms in summer 1941. There is also no evidence that the OUN was more present on the ground or more ensconced in these communities. As for the Germans, the Einsatzgruppen were everywhere but thinly spread; the horrors of Soviet rule appear to have been no worse where pogroms broke out than where they did not. The Germans may have wished to use the NKVD massacres to incite Ukrainians to violence against Jews, but the evidence shows that they did not need to do this, as pogroms broke out in many towns where no massacres occurred.

What are we to make of these pogroms? Are they even part of the Holocaust? The temptation to include them within the Holocaust, or to see them as a "prelude" to it, is driven largely by our knowledge of the horrors that would come next. But such knowledge was unavailable to victims, perpetrators, and bystanders at the time. Nobody knew in the summer of 1941 that there would be a Holocaust. Most of the violence during the pogroms (with few exceptions) did not indicate genocidal intent. The Germans had not yet decided on whether or how all Jews would be killed (this would occur only at the Wannsee Conference in January 1942). Even the term "pogrom" itself, widely used in contemporaneous accounts to describe the violence in June and July 1941, suggests a pre-Holocaust script or conceptual vocabulary for understanding what happened even after the Holocaust had occurred.

What, then, was the meaning of the pogroms of summer 1941? Why engage in these exercises in public humiliation and brutality? Let us return to the simple statement made at the outset of this chapter: pogroms occurred in less than

10 percent of the localities in Western Ukraine where Jews resided. In other places, pogroms either were stopped, in many cases by local Ukrainian heroes, or never got off the ground in the first place. What distinguished these two very different kinds of localities?

The differences antedated the Soviet and Nazi horrors. One important difference was political affiliation. Pogrom locations tended to have large Jewish populations who were proportionately far more mobilized into Zionist politics in the 1920s and 1930s than communities where pogroms did not occur. At this stage in its development, Zionism, rather than a clear call for emigration to a state that did not yet exist, was a new kind of assertive Jewish politics that demanded, above all, ethnic equality and national rights for the Jews as Jews. It signaled a clear unwillingness to integrate into either the Polish or Ukrainian national-building projects as they were defined at the time. Where pogroms occurred, Jews and Ukrainians lived in different political universes well before the Soviets arrived. These communities lacked the bare minimum of intercommunal solidarity that could have prevented violence once those advocating it took control.

For ordinary Ukrainians in specific kinds of local contexts, the pogroms constituted an initial opportunity to put the Jews as political competitors back in their place (hence the rituals of public humiliation) and, above all, to achieve national dominance at the local level once and for all. OUN leaders wanted to be rid of the Jews because they viewed them as hostile to the Ukrainian national project, as born foes to the "rebirth" of the nation (Carynnyk 2011) and natural opponents of an "independent Ukraine." It stands to reason that they were much more likely to find willing local partners where Jews had already committed to their own competing nation-building project. Non-Jewish civilian populations in certain kinds of communities could have seen the lawless atmosphere as an ideal and perhaps unique opportunity to rid themselves of political competitors in anticipation of a future autonomous national life. This was certainly the message the Germans and their Ukrainian counterparts in the OUN wanted to convey as they tried to incite local populations to attack their Jewish neighbors.

In their accounts of the pogroms of 1941, historians have focused on hatred, revenge, avarice, and simple human depravity. Crucial as these motives were, they are more constants than variables. That is, one can find antisemitism, a desire to avenge the crimes of the Soviet occupation, greed for "Jewish wealth," and base criminality in virtually every town where Jews and non-Jews lived side by side, including places that never experienced a pogrom. What social science brings to the discussion is an appreciation of the context in which these motives—which run the entire range of human subjectivity—could or could not be acted on.

CHAPTER 5

Alexandria 38 CE

As a student of politics, I have drawn our attention to the political backstory of each town as a facilitating or impeding condition. But can this focus help us understand pogroms in other times and places? One may question whether it is proper to use the term "pogrom" to talk about the anti-Jewish riots that broke out in Alexandria in 38 CE under the rule of Governor Flaccus while Gaius (also known as Caligula) sat in Rome. But the term has been used by specialists at least since the 1930s to characterize the riots, and the latest edition of the only firsthand account of the events, the Greco-Jewish philosopher Philo's *In Flaccum*, carries the subtitle "The First Pogrom" (Van der Horst 2003).

The context for the pogrom is clear enough. With the weakening of Alexandrian governor Flaccus after Gaius's ascent to power, the local Greek elite used the visit of the new Judean tetrarch Agrippa, himself a Jew on his way to Judea, to press for Flaccus's permission to use force against the Jewish population in ousting it from neighborhoods where Jews had not traditionally resided. The pogrom lasted several days and entailed beatings, murder, and other ritualized humiliations such as desecrating Jewish places of worship, forcing the city's Jewish women to eat pork, and public punishment by scourging (a form of torture normally reserved for "aliens").

Philo himself does not offer a theory for why the pogrom occurred. But scholars have identified the main reasons. Three groups lived in the city: Greeks, Jews, and Egyptian peasants. Although only the Greeks possessed full rights of citizenship, the Jews had certain communal privileges and rights as well, including the right to free worship: they prayed for, but not to, the emperor. They nonetheless had to pay the head tax, like the Egyptian peasantry. Greeks and Egyptians had long resented the Jews for having sided with the conquering Romans and for the Jews' continued attempts to upgrade their citizenship status, both communally and as individuals. Potential Jewish citizenship is what really drove the intercommunal conflict in Alexandria (Tcherikover 1959, 312–13).

What about antipathy toward the Jews? Multiple sources of anti-Jewish prejudices in the Hellenistic world have been documented: distrust of the Jews' all-powerful yet invisible god, coupled with their refusal to worship the emperor or his likeness; their refusal to dine with others, which sparked charges of misanthropy; the practice of circumcision; and their supposed clannishness (Schäfer 1997; Gruen 2002). But these same scholars are quick to tell us that these prejudices on their own could not have caused the pogrom because they had long been around, and such outbreaks of intercommunal violence were exceedingly rare. In short, the violence seems to have been much more situational, instrumental, and political than cultural, religious, or inherent. When the opportunity presented itself with the weakening of public authority, Alexandria's Greeks and Egyptians were less interested in wiping out the Jews than in asserting their own preeminence by putting the Jews back in their place (quite literally, since one of the main results of the violence was residential resegregation). The onset of Roman rule sparked a competition over communal ownership and citizenship, and this competition, rather than cultural difference or antisemitism, drove the conflict. The conflict, in short, was about politics.

Several pieces of evidence support this assertion. First, the immediate trigger for the pogrom was the Jewish king Agrippa's visit. His stopover on his way to Judea occasioned public expressions of pride among the city's Jews, who still had more than a touch of residual patriotism for their homeland. Alexandria's Greeks organized a parody of this visit in theatrical fashion with a local fool, Carrabas, dressed up as Agrippa just before the onset of anti-Jewish violence. Second, Philo's account references the local Greek interest in restricting Jewish citizenship and "ownership." Greek "nationalist" organizations had long been present and active in stoking resentment against the city's Jews, but the governor's weakened position and the mobilization around Agrippa's visit provided the opportunity for organization (Bergmann and Hoffmann 1987). Third, in a letter addressed to both the Greek and Jewish communities written in 41 CE, Claudius, Gaius's successor, first admonishes the Alexandrians "to behave gently and kindly toward the Jews." He then advises the Jews "not to aim at more than they have previously had . . . and not to intrude themselves into the games presided over by the gymnasiarchoi and the kosmetai, since they enjoy what is their own, and in a city *which is not their own* they possess all good things" (quoted in Schäfer 1997, 187; italics added). This letter, one of the only documents directly dealing with the Alexandrian disturbances apart from Philo's account, strongly indicates that the essence of the conflict, as well as of the pogrom itself, was about "ownership" of the local polity (Barclay 1996, 58) and concern with demographic balance (Gruen 2002, 81). Thus, even in this ancient polity where intercommunal relations were not subject to democratic electoral competition, the case anticipates the core of the "ethnic political threat" hypothesis that informs so much of the literature on racial violence in the United States and ethnic violence in other contexts (Blalock 1967).

The violence in Alexandria, while carnivalesque and escaping the control of those instigating it, was less irrational than instrumental. Of course, hatred of Jews mattered and could be a phenomenon only because their distinctive customs, practices, and ties to fellow Jews outside Alexandria marked them as a group apart. Perhaps anti-Judaism constitutes a necessary condition for the pogrom, but the crowd moved from hatred to violence for political reasons (Bergmann and Hoffmann 1987).

Valencia 1391

The context for Valencia's anti-Jewish riot of 1391—also referred to as a "pogrom" in the secondary literature—would seem to be a straightforward, if more extreme, version of the Christian antisemitic mob exacting revenge for the passion of Christ that Jewish communities had periodically confronted for centuries (MacKay 1972). But both the timing and the scale of the violence set this pogrom apart. For one thing, it occurred not during holy week but in the summer, indicating causes separate from or beyond run-of-the-mill Christian anti-Judaism. Even more telling are the differences in scale. The riot amounted to an ethnic cleansing, as after 1391 hardly any Jews remained in Valencia. The pogrom itself occasioned a forced mass conversion of Jews to Christianity, creating a huge class of conversos, which ultimately led to the momentous expulsions of 1492.

The violence began in Seville in June 1391 and spread throughout Castile and the Crown of Aragon, reaching Valencia on July 6. The script remained similar in most cases (Wolff 1971). Youths milled about outside the Jewish ghettos calling for the Jews to convert or die. From there it escalated when the ghettos themselves were infiltrated. In Valencia, attackers used drainpipes and openings in walls to enter the Jewish quarter, raping, looting, and killing its inhabitants once inside. Three hundred Jews died and the remaining ones mostly converted to Christianity (Baer 1966, 100). The story, upon first reading, seems to be one of Christianity confronting Jews and violating its own prohibition against forced conversion.

Does it make sense to characterize what occurred in Valencia (and in many other locations in Iberia in the summer of 1391) as motivated by anything other than dislike or hatred of Jews? Modern historians, as it turns out, do not primarily tell a religious or cultural story about 1391; instead they relate it in much more political terms. The particulars and the language may have been Christian, but the main factors involved the social and political role of the Jews within Spain's late Middle Ages. As Mark Meyerson, David Nirenberg, and others have noted, the Jews were considered the king's "treasure," his patrimony, existing outside the law regulating the relationship between kings and people (Nirenberg 2014, 75). The Jews performed "work" for the king, in Nirenberg's terms, not only as a source of taxation and service, but also in defining the king as being outside the law. Their position as the king's patrimony induced opponents of royal absolutism to define the Crown, and to characterize royal overreach, as Judaizing and such kings as Judaizers. Precisely because Jews represented royal power at its most absolute, they could be used to represent that power and even exercise it.

Temporal royal power itself could be defined in these terms, a reality that left Jews in a precarious position should the actual power of the king ever be brought into question, or if the position of the Crown were weakened—as happened in 1391 in Seville, first with the death of Juan I of Castile, leaving a minor as heir. Sensing royal weakness, both bourgeois and noble enemies throughout both Castile and the Crown of Aragon sought to redefine the relationship between kings and people through an attack on the Jews. The Jews, in other words, were caught up in a constitutional battle.

Throughout the thirteenth and fourteenth centuries, Christians questioned Jewish "power" as the king's servants in society and in the economy. Churches never ceased calling for conversion. But popular distaste and religious anti-Jewish instigation remain a constant rather than a variable and therefore cannot account for why the violence moved from ritualized and sporadic to widespread and devastating in the summer of 1391. This required royal sovereignty and the Jews' position within it being brought into question. Where sovereign authority remained resolute, such as in Morvedre, Jews could be and were protected in 1391 (Meyerson 2004, 210–71). These pogroms were less about Christianity than about royal absolutism and resistance to its assertion.

Although the case of 1391 does not easily fit the more "political," as opposed to cultural or religious, model of pogrom violence that I am proposing here, we can easily redirect our attention to the competing sovereign claims of would-be absolutist kings versus people, and the Jews' position within this relationship as a strategic partner or enemy. Putting the matter this way does not eliminate Christian antisemitism as a factor in the anti-Jewish pogroms of 1391—as Meyerson (2004, 279) notes, such a move would be "folly"—but it does place it in its proper perspective as a language, a vocabulary for understanding Jews' place within a situation of dangerous dual sovereignty, rather than the master account of anti-Jewish violence in the Middle Ages.

Comparing the Holocaust with other events remains a morally and analytically fraught undertaking. Analysis leading to the claim that "this, or something like this, has happened before" can all too easily become an exercise in Holocaust trivialization or obfuscation. Jelena Subotić's (2019) depiction of post-Communist governments' repeated attempts to peddle the theory of a "double genocide," in which the atrocities of the Soviet era and the Nazi-led Holocaust become moral equivalents, underscores the problem of inappropriate analogy.

If we refuse to compare, however, historical research on the Holocaust may never be incorporated into the mainstream of political science. Historical analogies constitute the core of so much theoretically driven empirical work across the social sciences. The risk of abjuring analogy completely is that the Holocaust becomes an increasingly distant (and decreasingly relevant) moral compass or an indescribable event of antiquarian interest, a regulative warning rather than the object of serious social scientific research.

Even once we have decided that comparison is appropriate, that still leaves open the question of what exactly we are comparing. Beyond the question of morality, the enormity of the Holocaust has hindered its integration into the mainstream of political violence research. It unfolded over several years across multiple countries in Europe and beyond. As Holocaust research has progressed, the event has become larger and more complicated and thus in principle even less amenable to being incorporated into social science. The analytical problems may be no less intractable than the moral ones.

One way forward has been suggested by Charles King: breaking down the Holocaust into multiple, discrete episodes. "Rather than being one big thing," King (2012, 326) observes, "the Holocaust might now be described as an array of event categories." Once we consider the matter this way, the Holocaust ceases to be only "one case" but turns into multiple events that, taken together, we see as one. Each of its parts may be compared with analogous events in other times and places. The purpose of such a comparison is not only to use the Holocaust as a source of data for empirical generalization, but also to point to the limits of analogy, the specificities of the Holocaust, and scope conditions for generalizable theory. This chapter, then, has been one such exploratory exercise, a comparison of the neighbor-on-neighbor violence of 1941 to the exclusionary anti-Jewish violence of earlier eras. The purpose of the comparison is not primarily to say "this happened before," but rather to point to commonalities in background conditions associated with pogroms.

The "politics" of Alexandria 38 CE or Valencia 1391 are not identical with the politics leading up to 1941, where the ownership of the state depended on mobilizing ethnic groups into electoral politics. The age of mass democracy, of parties competing for power in relatively free and fair elections, translated ethnic and religious demography into political power far more directly and efficiently than politics in the premodern world. But the existence of parties and free elections, the above analysis indicates, does not in itself constitute a confining scope condition for a political theory of pogroms. Even in Alexandria 38 CE and Valencia 1391—that is, even in eras far before the advent of mass democracy—competing ethnic and religious communities keenly experienced the politics of political ownership. Under conditions of perceived threat to their political dominance, non-Jews could lash out with restorative or transformational violence. These considerations suggest that the pogroms of 1941 shared as many features with the "traditional" anti-Jewish violence that preceded them as they did with the genocidal violence that followed.

REFERENCES

Ainsztein, Reuben. 1974. *Jewish Resistance in Nazi-Occupied Eastern Europe with a Historical Survey of the Jew as a Fighter and Soldier in the Diaspora*. New York: Barnes and Noble.
Baer, Yitzhak. 1966. *A History of the Jews in Christian Spain*. Vol. 2. Philadelphia: Jewish Publication Society.
Barclay, John M. G. 1996. *The Jews in the Mediterranean Diaspora*. Berkeley: University of California Press.
Barkan, Elazar, Elizabeth A. Cole, and Kai Struve, eds. *Shared History—Divided Memory: Jews and Others in Soviet-Occupied Poland, 1939–1941*. Leipzig: Leipziger Universitätsverlag.
Bauer, Yehuda. 2007. "Sarny and Rokitno in the Holocaust: A Case Study of Two Townships in Wolyn (Volhynia)." In *The Shtetl: New Evaluations*, edited by Steven T. Katz, 253–88. New York: New York University Press.
———. 2009. *The Death of the Shtetl*. New Haven, CT: Yale University Press.
Berg, Nicolas. 2015. *The Holocaust and the West German Historians: Historical Interpretation and Autobiographical Memory*. Translated and edited by Joel Golb. Madison: University of Wisconsin Press.
Bergmann, Werner, and Christhard Hoffmann. 1987. "Kalkül oder Massenwahn: Eine soziologische Interpretation der antijüdischen Unruhen in Alexandria 38 n. Chr." In *Antisemitismus und Jüdische Geschichte: Studien zu Ehren von Herbert A. Strauss*, edited by Rainer Erb and Michael Schmidt, 15–46. Berlin: Wissenschaftlicher Autorenverlag.
Berkhoff, Karel C., and Marco Carynnyk. 1999. "The Organization of Ukrainian Nationalists and Its Attitudes towards Germans and Jews: Iaroslav Stets'ko's 1941 Zettiepys." *Harvard Ukrainian Studies* 23 (3–4): 149–82.
Blalock, Hubert M. 1967. *Toward a Theory of Minority-Group Relations*. New York: John Wiley.
Bruder, Franziska. 2007. *"Den ukrainischen Staat erkämpfen oder sterben!" Die Organization Ukrainischer Nationalisten (OUN) 1928–1948*. Berlin: Metropol Verlag.
Carynnyk, Marco. 2007. "The Palace on the Ikva: Dubne, September 18th, 1939 and June 24th, 1941," in Barkan, Cole, and Struve, *Shared History—Divided Memory*, 263–301.
———. 2011. "Foes of Our Rebirth: Ukrainian Nationalist Discussions about Jews, 1929–1947." *Nationalities Papers* 39 (3): 315–52.
Dmitrów, Edmund, Paweł Machcewicz, and Tomasz Szarota. 2004. *Die Beginn der Vernichtung: Zum Mord an den Juden in Jedwabne und Umgebung im Sommer 1941*. Osnabrück: Fibre Verlag.
Dumitru, Diana, and Carter Johnson. 2011. "Constructing Interethnic Conflict and Cooperation: Why Some People Harmed Jews and Others Helped Them during the Holocaust in Romania." *World Politics* 63 (1): 1–42.
Friedman, Philip. 1980. *Roads to Extinction: Essays on the Holocaust*. New York: Jewish Publication Society of America.
Golczewski, Frank. 2008. "Shades of Grey: Reflections on Jewish-Ukrainian and German-Ukrainian Relations in Galicia." In *The Shoah in Ukraine: History, Testimony, and Memorialization*, edited by Ray Brandon and Wendy Lower, 114–55. Bloomington: Indiana University Press.
———. 2010. *Deutsche und Ukrainer 1914–1939*. Paderborn: Ferdinand Schöningh.

Gordon, Peter E. 2020. "Why Historical Analogy Matters." *New York Review of Books*, January 7, 2020. https://www.nybooks.com/daily/2020/01/07/why-historical-analogy-matters/.

Grelka, Frank. 2005. *Die ukrainische Nationalbewegung unter Deutscher Besatzungsherrschaft 1918 und 1941–1942*. Wiesbaden: Harrassowitz Verlag.

Gross, Jan T. 2001. *Neighbors: The Destruction of the Jewish Community in Jedwabne, Poland*. Princeton, NJ: Princeton University Press.

Gruen, Erich S. 2002. *Diaspora: Jews amidst Greeks and Romans*. Cambridge, MA: Harvard University Press.

Himka, John-Paul. 2011. "The Lviv Pogrom of 1941: The Germans, Ukrainian Nationalists, and the Carnival Crowd." *Canadian Slavonic Papers* 53 (2–3–4): 209–43.

Honigsman, Jakob. 2001. *Juden in der Westukraine*. Konstanz: Hartung-Gorre.

Hryciuk, Grzegorz. 2007. "Victims, 1939–1941: The Soviet Repressions in Eastern Poland." In Barkan, Cole, and Struve, *Shared History—Divided Memory*, 173–200.

King, Charles. 2012. "Can There Be a Political Science of the Holocaust?" *Perspectives on Politics* 10 (2): 323–41.

Klee, Ernst, Willi Dressen, and Volker Riess, eds. 1988. *"The Good Old Days": The Holocaust as Seen by Its Perpetrators and Bystanders*. Old Saybrook, CT: Konecky and Konecky.

Klier, John D., and Shlomo Lambroza, eds. 1992. *Pogroms: Anti-Jewish Violence in Modern Russian History*. Cambridge: Cambridge University Press.

Kopstein, Jeffrey S., and Jason Wittenberg. 2018. *Intimate Violence: Anti-Jewish Pogroms on the Eve of the Holocaust*. Ithaca, NY: Cornell University Press.

MacKay, Angus. 1972. "Popular Movements and Pogroms in Fifteenth-Century Castile." *Past and Present*, no. 55, 33–67.

Meyerson, Mark D. 2004. *Jews in an Iberian Frontier Kingdom: Society, Economy, and Politics in Morvedre, 1248–1391*. Leiden: Brill

Mendelsohn, Daniel. 2006. *The Lost: A Search for Six of Six Million*. New York: HarperCollins.

Mick, Christoph. 2007. "Only the Jews Do Not Waver." In Barkan, Cole, and Struve, *Shared History—Divided Memory*, 245–62.

———. 2010. *Kriegserfahrungen in einer multiethnischen Stadt: Lemberg 1914–1947*. Wiesbaden: Harrassowitz Verlag.

Musiał, Bogdan. 2004. "The Pogrom in Jedwabne: Critical Remarks about Jan T. Gross's *Neighbors*." In *The Neighbors Respond: The Controversy over the Jedwabne Massacre in Poland*, edited by Antony Polonsky and Joanna B. Michlic, 304–43. Princeton, NJ: Princeton University Press.

Nirenberg, David. 2014. *Neighboring Faiths: Christianity, Islam, and Judaism in the Middle Ages and Today*. Chicago: University of Chicago Press.

Pohl, Dieter. 1996. *Nationalsozialistische Judenverfolgung in Ostgalizien 1941–1944*. Munich: Oldenbourg.

———. 2007. "Anti-Jewish Pogroms in Western Ukraine—a Research Agenda." In Barkan, Cole, and Struve, *Shared History—Divided Memory*, 305–13.

Radu, Ioanid. 2000. *The Holocaust in Romania: The Destruction of Jews and Gypsies under the Antonescu Regime, 1940–1944*. Chicago: Ivan R. Dee.

Redlich, Shimon. 2002. *Together and Apart in Brzezany*. Bloomington: Indiana University Press.

Schäfer, Peter. 1997. *Judeophobia: Attitudes toward the Jews in the Ancient World*. Cambridge, MA: Harvard University Press.

Snyder, Timothy. 2010. *Bloodlands: Europe between Hitler and Stalin*. New York: Basic Books.
Solonari, Vladimir. 2010. *Purifying the Nation: Population Exchange and Ethnic Cleansing in Nazi-Allied Romania*. Baltimore: Johns Hopkins University Press.
Spector, Shmuel. 1990. *The Holocaust of the Volhynian Jews, 1941–1944*. Jerusalem: Yad Vashem.
Struve, Kai. 2015. *Deutsche Herrshaft, ukrainischer Nationalismus, antijüdische Gewalt: Die Sommer 1941 in Wesukraine*. Oldenbourg: De Gruyter.
Subotić, Jelena. 2019. *Yellow Star, Red Star: Holocaust Remembrance after Communism*. Ithaca, NY: Cornell University Press.
Tcherikover, Victor. 1959. *Hellenistic Civilization and the Jews*. New York: Atheneum.
Van der Horst, Pieter W. 2003. *Philo's Flaccus: The First Pogrom; Introduction, Translation, and Commentary*. Leiden: Brill.
Wolff, Philippe. 1971. "The 1391 Pogrom in Spain: Social Crisis or Not?" *Past and Present* 50 (1): 4–18.
Yones, Eliyahu. 2004. *Smoke in the Sand: The Jews of Lvov in the War Years*. Jerusalem: Geffen.
Zwieback, Jacques. 2003. *Der Todeszug von Iași*. Konstanz: Hartung-Gorre Verlag.

6

MASS VIOLENCE WITHOUT MASS POLITICS

Political Culture and the Holocaust in Lithuania

Benjamin Mishkin

When the German Army invaded the eastern borderlands of Poland in the summer of 1941, no fewer than 219 pogroms broke out (Kopstein and Wittenberg 2018). Polish civilians and police, unaffiliated with any formal state apparatus, killed their Jewish neighbors by the thousands. In many cases they did this without much instigating by German soldiers. Victims, perpetrators, and bystanders all interpreted this violence through the prism of "pogroms" of earlier eras. Once the initial wave of pogroms died down, it would take the Germans the next four years of ghettoizing, shooting, transporting, and gassing to eliminate almost 90 percent of the 3.3 million Polish Jews (Yad Vashem n.d.).

By contrast, when, in the summer of 1941, German soldiers also invaded Lithuania, Lithuanian participation in the initial massacres was overwhelmingly dominated by subaltern paramilitaries—variously labeled Lithuanian Activists' Front (LAF) members, white armbanders, partisans, or later on as members of local police forces—as instigators and as the *genocidaires* themselves. These paramilitaries were present for the overwhelming majority of significant massacres formally documented. Even many anecdotal accounts of small-scale killings make note of the presence of organized paramilitary units in the towns. Lithuanians not mobilized into some sort of proto-state-sanctioned organization, however loosely, do not appear to have been the first movers in the genocide. The fact that would-be murderers felt the need to identify with these militias suggests something unusual in the sociopolitical dynamics of the Holocaust in Lithuania. As the killing went on, the Lithuanian paramilitaries took on more responsibility for the genocide under the direction of the Germans, and spontaneous participation by ordinary Lithuanians became less and less central. The annihilation of Lithuania's Jews became a distinctly bureaucratic affair, drained of almost all mass political participation.

This chapter seeks to understand why the killing by Jewish citizens' fellow countrymen took such a unique form in Lithuania as compared with Poland, given that the two countries were otherwise similar in so many ways. Both emerged as independent nation-states in the wake of the First World War and the collapse of the Russian, German, and Austro-Hungarian Empires. Both had experimented with liberal parliamentarianism in the years after independence, only to fall back into right-wing authoritarianism within a decade. Both were predominantly Catholic. Both had substantial Jewish populations. In both countries, Jews were disproportionately represented in cities and in commerce. The Soviet Union occupied both or part of both countries for a time before the Nazis launched Operation Barbarossa in June 1941.

The key difference, I maintain, was the variation in prewar political culture in the two countries. Whereas both countries eventually became right-wing dictatorships of varying degrees of enlightenment, in Poland, some form of party politics, however circumscribed, continued. This continuity in party politics facilitated ethnic-based mobilization against Jews that would later contribute to the outbreak of pogroms (Kopstein and Wittenberg 2018). By contrast, politics in Lithuania, after initial parliamentary enthusiasm in the years immediately following independence in 1918, settled into a distinctly authoritarian elite-centered political pattern. By December 1926, a right-wing military putsch had installed the Lithuanian nationalist Antanas Smetona as president after a left-wing coalition won a parliamentary majority in July of that year. Multiparty democracy came to an end and parliamentary elections were suspended until 1935, when the ruling party, the Lithuanian Nationalists Union, and its youth wing, Young Lithuania, were the only parties allowed to operate and run in the "election." By this point, what contentious politics in Lithuania meant was a series of attempted military putsches. In 1939, the Security Department wrote a report for Smetona in which it counted seventeen such attempts. The department also summed up Lithuanian political culture, or lack thereof: "Our political action lacks political culture" (Balkelis 2018, 161).

Lithuanian politics was an elite affair led by a semi-enlightened despot whose main challenge came from his militarized, increasingly fascist Right. When it came time to carry out a genocide, the demobilized population provided meager raw material for mobilization; instead a large number of aggrieved and armed right-wing paramilitarists were ready to collaborate with a would-be foreign sponsor.[1] Anti-Jewish violence would be explicitly centered on these right-wing paramilitary organizations.

I begin this chapter by explaining how the Lithuanian part of the genocide took place, initially perpetrated largely by far-right paramilitarists and then, in the later weeks and months, by the Lithuanian police in conjunction with the Germans. I then elaborate the argument about the role of contrasting political cultures in Poland and Lithuania in the interwar period and show how these differences mirror differences in how the killing was carried out by the respective subaltern collaborators.[2] I conclude by highlighting areas for further research and discuss how the argument demonstrates the usefulness for Holocaust research of small-N cross-case comparisons familiar to social scientists.

How Did the Non-Jewish Lithuanians Kill Their Jewish Neighbors?

Existing accounts of the Holocaust in Lithuania suggest that the summer of 1941 was characterized by an outbreak of civilian pogroms similar to other instances in history, and to the one that was occurring in Poland during the same time period (Kopstein and Wittenberg 2018, 116; Arad 1976, 239). But these Lithuanian pogroms should be understood as distinct in form from those in Poland carried out by Poles, such as the massacre in Jedwabne. The key difference was the overwhelming role of organized Lithuanian far-right militias, which had roots in Lithuania's interwar political culture. In 1941 these militias worked in alliance with the Nazis. It was these organized paramilitary militias that constituted the driving force of Lithuanian collaboration. Without them, Lithuanian collaboration would likely have taken on a much different nature. These groups not only instigated civilian participation in killings but, more importantly, largely carried out the killings themselves under varying degrees of German supervision. Lithuanian citizens unattached to some form of partisan group, by contrast, do not seem to have been the first movers in killing their neighbors, as they appear to have been in many cases in Poland and in Ukrainian Galicia.

Several pieces of evidence testify to the central role of the paramilitaries in the Lithuanian collaboration and to the relatively low ratio of spontaneous civilian-led pogroms. First, this is how direct participants and witnesses characterized the events. SS commander Franz Walter Stahlecker wrote a report to his superior, Heinrich Himmler, in which he explained the central and effectively necessary role of both the Germans and the Lithuanian partisans in the killings:

> In Lithuania this was achieved for the first time by *partisan activists* in Kauen [Kovno]. To our surprise it was *not* easy at first to set in motion an extensive pogrom against Jews. Klimaitis, the leader of the *partisan*

> *unit* mentioned above, who was designated for this purpose primarily, succeeded in launching pogroms on the basis of advice given to him by a *small* advanced detachment operating in Kauen. In the first pogrom during the night of June 25 to 26, *the Lithuanian partisans* did away with more than 1,500 Jews, set fire to several synagogues or destroyed them by other means, and burned down a Jewish residential quarter consisting of about 60 houses. . ... After the disarmament of the partisans the self-cleansing actions ceased necessarily. (Arad 1976, 239; "Trial" 1947, 122; italics added)

This may have been a commander trying to take more credit than he deserved, but it would seem odd to tell Heinrich Himmler that there were people who did not hate Jews enough to murder them. That the killings were in fact carried out by partisans suggests that first the partisans and then their allies carried out the pogroms, and this order matters a great deal for how we understand their outbreak.

Contemporary Jewish and non-Jewish Lithuanian eyewitnesses also make frequent mention of the role of partisan groups in the killings, even if they also highlight the role of apolitical opportunists. Helena Buivodaite Kutorgiene, a Lithuanian doctor and diarist, wrote at the time, "All this nationalism is sickening.... [T]o the ranks of the 'Activists' or those so called 'Partisans,' joined—along with foolish youth who were captivated by the slogan 'Free Lithuania'—also the dregs of society whose sole desire was robbery and killing" (quoted in Cohen 1999, 31). One victim, Khone Boyarski, a Jewish Lithuanian living in the village of Butrimonys in the Alytus district in southern Lithuania, wrote an account of what transpired in the period after the German invasion. He gave the letter to a non-Jewish Lithuanian woman, who preserved it and passed it on to a Jewish survivor after the war. In the letter, Boyarski makes mention of the partisans immediately after first describing the arrival of the Germans: "Early in the morning, on Tuesday the 24th of June [It must have been the 23rd] we went out into the street and saw that the town was already full of German soldiers. Already there were 'Partisans'— Lithuanian bandits wearing **WHITE ARMBANDS WITH SWASTIKAS** and without a moment's delay they began to rob and beat Jews. They could already do anything they wanted to a Jew" (quoted in Cohen 1989, 365; emphasis and brackets in the original). Boyarski makes numerous additional references to the partisans as the main perpetrators of the killings he heard about. While he frequently refers to them as "bandits," his descriptions imply an unmistakable degree of centralization and organization in these groups. He notes how the leader of one group had assumed the title of commander of the local police station (Cohen 1989, 366). Even when he refers to this group as **"THIEVES AND**

HOOLIGANS" (emphasis in the original), he also explains that they were led by a commander who had been a Lithuanian captain and, crucially, that they identified themselves as "partisans" (Cohen 1989, 365). These comments underscore the relatively high degree of formal organization by these genocidaires, at least when compared to Polish pogromists. Most importantly, Boyarski's descriptions place responsibility for the violence almost exclusively on these partisan units, as opposed to describing them as (seemingly) uncoordinated civilian riots.

The Holocaust Atlas of Lithuania (n.d.) provides a second source of evidence of the central role that formalized Lithuanian units played in the genocide, as opposed to its comprising spontaneous civilian pogroms. The researchers have collected an impressive amount of detail on 230 instances of mass killings of Jews in Lithuania between 1941 and 1944, identifying the perpetrators of 199 of these killings. Of those 199, just 2 list Lithuanian "civilians" as perpetrators. One of these cases is the June 7, 1941, Lietukis Garage massacre, in which Lithuanian white armbanders and civilians tortured and murdered an estimated sixty Jews using iron bars, wooden sticks, and water hoses; the Atlas lists Germans as being present at the massacre. The second is the mass murder of the 192 Jewish men of Kudirkos Naumiestis in southwestern Lithuania. For the remaining 197 events, the perpetrators were some combination of white-armband groups, partisans, Lithuanian police, and, of course, Germans. This holds true regardless of how many Jews were killed in each episode, and from the beginning of the genocide in June 1941 to the end in 1944.

This documentation may be unable to account for the more subtle ways in which civilians may have contributed to the genocide—for instance, by identifying neighbors to partisan murderers or by joining the white armbands directly at the last minute. But even with such civilian participation, it is noteworthy that there was still a need for the white armbands in order for the murders to occur. Perhaps even more important, civilians did not appear to feel authorized or encouraged to kill without membership in the white armbands. Given the atmosphere of violence, if Lithuanians had wanted to engage in spontaneous pogroms without participation in organized partisan groups, little would have prevented them from doing so. Yet they refrained from initiating pogroms of the sort documented in Poland during the same weeks.[3]

Data from the "Holocaust by Bullets" memorial project also highlights the central role of the Lithuanian paramilitaries. Of the fifty-two killings in Lithuania publicly documented so far, mention of involvement by white-armband partisan paramilitarists is made in eighteen cases (Yahad—in Unum n.d.). In the remaining thirty-four cases, no publicly available information about the precise perpetrators exists beyond references to Germans. By contrast, the only mention of civilians *qua* civilians highlights their role as assistants in digging ditches or collecting looted goods of the victims after their deaths. Eyewitnesses, of course, have reason to downplay the participation of their neighbors, but the degree to which the paramilitarists, even of Lithuanian origin, figure in the accounts of the genocide is nevertheless striking.

Over the course of 1941, Lithuanian participation in the genocide became more associated with national-level organized paramilitary and police politics. Immediately following the invasion, former officers identified with the Smetona regime took the lead in organizing Lithuanian military units for service with the Germans. Among these were the newly formed provisional government's minister for internal affairs, Colonel Jonas Šlepetys, and the commandant of Kaunas, Kazys Bobelis. Within a month of the invasion, however, a clique of officers associated with the Iron Wolf, a group that had been associated with the radical anti-Bolshevist and antisemitic Augustinas Voldemaras and his failed coup in 1934, staged something of a putsch within the Lithuanian security forces. On the night of July 23–24, members of the Iron Wolf ousted Šlepetys and Bobelis and other officers associated with the Smetona regime. While the Smetona officials had cooperated fully with the genocide until that point, the members of the Iron Wolf were even more aligned with German eliminationist intentions (MacQueen 1998, 38). They now set the tone.

The precise procedures of the killing after the initial paroxysm of violence also highlight the degree to which the genocide was a distinctly "state-centric" phenomenon divorced from the need for mass civilian mobilization. The procedure was for Lithuanian local police to gather together the Jews of a given town and then notify the head of the uniformed Lithuanian police, Vladas Reivytis, who would then contact the Germans. Reivytis had to issue so many identical commands to his local police that he had the instructions printed on mimeographed forms, with blank spaces for the relevant locality (MacQueen 1997, 100). Once informed, the Germans dispatched a squadron of eight to ten SS men to lead units of no more than two hundred Lithuanians—the Germans prohibited larger units to forestall the impression of an independent Lithuanian army (MacQueen 1998, 37)—to the town to murder the Jews. Local police would often assist with the killing (MacQueen 1998, 40). This pattern repeated itself until there were no more Jews left to kill.

In sum, then, the evidence is strong that, in the summer of 1941, Lithuanians killed Jews, hundreds of thousands of Jews, on their own, without Germans putting a gun to their heads to do so. But the violence did not resemble the pogroms occurring at about the same time in Poland or Ukraine. Rather, the Lithuanian portion of the genocide was an organized paramilitary affair with roots in a militarized prewar Lithuanian elite and exile politics. In the overwhelming number of documented cases, popular participation in the genocide was channeled into some sort of paramilitary or police formation, even early on. Outside of these formations, there does not seem to have been an exceptionally large degree of popular participation in the actual acts of killing.

Lithuanian vs. Polish Interwar Political Culture

These contrasting "styles" of the subaltern genocides in Lithuania and Poland—Nazi-aligned far-right partisans methodically killing Jews, as opposed to unaffiliated civilian-led outbreaks of violence along premobilized ethnic lines—is a reflection of the relatively demobilized state of politics in the second half of the Lithuanian interwar period as compared with Poland. By the end of the period, it was apparent even to Lithuanians themselves that they lacked a culture of popular participation in (non)democratic politics. No genuine elections occurred after 1926, and popular contentious politics remained sporadic and ineffective, the result no doubt of authoritarian repression. For instance, after a peasant rebellion in Suvalkija in 1935 following a collapse in agricultural product prices, the regime simply deployed the army and police to repress the unrest. Even more extreme, the state simply banned political parties other than the state-led Lithuanian Nationalists Union (LNU), explicitly blocking democratic participation. When the state held the first parliamentary election in ten years in 1936, apart from the LNU and its youth wing, Young Lithuania, no other parties were permitted to register or compete. In effect, the elite had constructed a one-party state. Reflecting either the weakness of civil society or the success of the regime's repression, or both (or gaps in the archives), historians have failed to find any sign of sustained mass demonstrations opposing the institution of what in effect was a demobilized one-party state.

By contrast, Józef Piłsudski's Poland resisted the imposition of a state party. Piłsudski himself participated in a free and fair election in 1928 after taking power in a coup (in which his own party failed to capture a parliamentary majority), something that Smetona never considered. Even with increasing authoritarianism, especially after Piłsudski's death in 1935, Polish interwar politics appear to have maintained a sense of popular participation. The elections that occurred after 1928, even if in some sense "managed," avoided dwindling into purely one-party farces. Some space remained for alternative parties to mobilize, even when it became increasingly risky to do so.

While a full discussion of the origins of Smetona's and Piłsudski's different approaches to mass democracy is beyond the scope of this chapter, at least one plausible hypothesis is their different personas and places in their respective publics' imaginations. It seems reasonable to assume that Piłsudski maintained significant mass popularity due to his status as a Polish military hero from World War I, and thus stood to benefit from appealing to a mass audience, even if the expression of mass preferences was limited by an authoritarian state. In contrast with Piłsudski's martial charisma, Smetona cut a decidedly less rousing figure. An intellectual, he made his name in Lithuanian independence at least in part through publishing a book on Lithuanian grammar. He would later serve as a professor of art theory and history and philosophy at the University of Lithuania. That such a man adopted a strategy of limiting popular mobilization is perhaps not surprising.

But what Lithuania lacked in popular participation in the latter two-thirds of the interwar period it made up for in palace intrigue. Smetona himself came to power through a coup in 1926, which overthrew the recently elected leftist coalition government (Balkelis 2018, 159). Smetona was lucky, however; he avoided the same fate he imposed on his predecessor. Between late 1918 and early 1939, the Security Department documented seventeen attempted putsches and coups. Two took place in the contested (with Germany) territory of Klaipeda (Memelland), but the other plots were hatched within Lithuania proper. Smetona's suppression of mass politics did not cause the epidemic of putsch attempts, but those attempts did increase significantly in number after he took power: four had occurred before his takeover, while thirteen took place afterward (Balkelis 2018, 161). In virtually all of them, the main player was the right-wing military, which Smetona relied on to repress such mass politics as the peasants' rebellion in 1935. That Smetona never adjusted his selectorate toward one based more in the mass public suggests additional grounds to believe that his leadership style was based as much on personal preferences as on rational calculation.

Smetona never extricated himself from the intrigues of praetorian politics, and this fact proved crucial in the organization and nature of the Holocaust in Lithuania. The Jewish question itself also played out on this stage. Antisemitic, protofascist politics also became a game of palace intrigue. Far-right groups, rather than organizing as political parties in search of votes even within sham elections, confined themselves to paramilitary-type organizations and worked within national institutions such as the military.[4]

The fate of one of the main groups, the Secret Union of Officers (SUO), demonstrates both the praetorian style of Lithuanian politics and these elite leaders' central role in the genocide to come. The SUO consisted of First World War veterans who generally pushed a strong Lithuanian nationalist line. The SUO had been the central actor in Smetona's rise to power, which came on the heels of the previous, newly installed left-wing government's firing of two hundred conservative-oriented army officers. By the late 1920s, however, the SUO split between those leaning toward more explicit Italian-style fascism, calling themselves the "Iron

Wolf," and those who supported Smetona's more moderate course, which included, for instance, support for Jewish educational and religious autonomy and contributions to rabbinical salaries (Balkelis 2018, 161). Founded in 1927, the Iron Wolf was ostensibly a youth sports organization but was actually a vehicle for protofascism. Emblematic of the cramped, elite-driven politics of the period, the fight over the group was a fight for the loyalty of military officers rather than the public. While Smetona maintained the loyalty of the senior officers, his own prime minister, the charismatic Augustinas Voldemaras, was a central figure within the Iron Wolf, and was becoming increasingly popular among the more junior ranks (Vaičikonis 1984).

Voldemoras's relationship with Smetona soured after an attempt on the former's life in May 1929, after which he drew closer to the Iron Wolf. Smetona removed him as prime minister that September and placed him under police surveillance. In the meantime, the Iron Wolf went underground but did not leave the Lithuanian political scene for very long. In 1934, the group launched a coup against Smetona and sought to install Voldemaras as his successor. The coup failed and Voldemaras was imprisoned for four years. The Iron Wolf leadership decamped to Berlin, by now under Nazi control, and became a central node in the exile community. The Soviet takeover in 1940 created a second wave of nationalist exiles, who came to be known, in Berlin and at home in Lithuania, as the Lithuanian Activists' Front (LAF). These new refugees linked up with the Iron Wolf. The two groups were hungry for power, and the relations between them would prove fractious after the Nazi invasion and both groups' return to Lithuania. For the time being, however, they continued to court Nazi sponsorship (Kwiet 1998, 14).

After the invasion, the Iron Wolf, the LAF, and other associated right-wing groups such as the Riflemen's Union formed the backbone of Lithuanian collaboration in the genocide, under the umbrellas of white armbanders, partisans, and later police forces. Mobilization into the genocidal ranks built on these existing sociopolitical structures rather than mass organizations. The groups, however, did succeed in channeling popular energies and desires for anti-Jewish violence into them, and this accounts for the relative absence of civilian-led pogroms. In testimony to Soviet investigators after the war, Adolfas Galdikauskas explained the nature of his recruitment into the genocide, in a statement worth quoting at length:

> Three or four days after the Nazis entered Rietavas, Jonas Abukevicius, a high school teacher and lieutenant of the Lithuanian army, together with Leonas Kontvainis, a doctor, gathered all the former members of the Riflemen's Union on the premises of the school and told us that we had to form a detachment to fight Soviet activists, Jews and red partisans.

> After a couple of days I and other former riflemen came to the security police, where we met Abukevicius, Kontvainis and a few unfamiliar Germans. Detailed questionnaires were filled out for us at the Gestapo and we signed that we were willing to join the Lithuanian Activists' Front organization, in other words, a detachment of white partizans [sic] to fight the Bolsheviks. There and then we received sleevebands with the letters "LAF."
>
> Two days after, we were armed at the police station.... ("Testimonies of Murderers" 1999, 65)

Galdikauskas's statement highlights the role of interwar junior officers (Abukevicius), interwar right-wing-affiliated quasi-paramilitary groups (the Riflemen's Union) as a focus of recruitment, and the fluid boundaries between different Lithuanian security formations (police, partisans, white armbanders, the LAF). In doing so, it draws attention to the degree to which recruitment depended on formal institutions forged in the interwar period. This was a far cry from the unaffiliated Polish murderers of, for example, Jedwabne. In Poland, where the target of interwar political mobilization was civilians, it was civilians who formed the backbone of subaltern violence. In Lithuania, by contrast, these same energies were channeled through paramilitaries with roots in the interwar praetorian political culture.

We cannot know whether Lithuanian civilians, in the absence of already radicalized and mobilized indigenous paramilitaries, would have taken up arms against their neighbors in the manner that occurred in Poland. Perhaps the reason there appears to be no Lithuanian Jedwabne unassociated with a partisan force is that these partisans did it before civilians had a chance and before the Germans stepped in. What we can say is that the style of collaboration in Lithuania coincided with the most lethal genocide of any European country. Less than 5 percent of Lithuanian Jews survived (Hollander 2006, 38).

Lithuania stands out in the Holocaust in Eastern Europe not just in that it was an especially eager would-be client state but because it had the sociopolitical structures that enabled particularly seamless collaboration and catastrophically efficient genocide. These structures—namely, a complex of right-wing paramilitaries led by leaders near the apex of the Smetona-era political structure—dated to the interwar period's depopularization and demobilization of national politics under Antanas Smetona. Ironically, this lack of an organized civilian mass politics in the interwar period gave way to an especially lethal form of mass violence.

This argument about the patterns of violence that come in the wake of authoritarian regimes is relevant both to scholars of the Holocaust and to other social scientists. For Holocaust scholars, substantively, this research is part of a broader effort to link up prewar conditions with wartime outcomes, in particular in relatively overlooked areas such as the Baltics. The mass killings are another example of King's point (in chapter 1 of this volume) that mass murders have local and social roots and are based in state politics that evolve over time. For social scientists more generally, the findings suggest the possibility of the importance of authoritarian legacies for crucial outcomes of interest in other places and at other times.

Even so, there are limitations to my argument about the different patterns in the Holocaust between Lithuania and Poland and the role of varying prewar cultures of popular mobilization and elite politics. First, it could be argued that my definition of "pogrom" is too narrow. These were, after all, chaotic events, even if led by paramilitaries. Second, perhaps the distinction between paramilitary mass shootings and nonparamilitary anti-Jewish riots is a distinction without a difference. I argue, however, that it deforms the definition of "pogrom" to combine into one category killings carried out by organized, nearly professionalized subaltern killing squads explicitly allied with the invading power and killings carried out by untrained civilians relatively unaffiliated with any formal organizational structure. That one coincided with the most efficient subcase of genocide in the Holocaust would also seem an additional reason to treat the two phenomena somewhat separately. It goes without saying that these differences were likely irrelevant to the victim. This seems to be a conceptual and perhaps moral question that empirical research can only be auxiliary to in answering.

This chapter also has been able to only scratch the surface of some already existing sources that may shed more light on the nature of the killings, especially in the countryside, such as the Koniuchowsky Papers (Valone 2014). Knowing with greater certainty that the reports of partisan involvement in killings, as suggested by the eyewitness testimonies cited above, apply to the countryside writ large would lend the argument greater weight.[5] In particular, further research could shed light on the phenomenon, noted in many reports, of civilians slipping on white armbands before joining paramilitary violence. I maintain that even if this phenomenon were quite widespread, it would still speak to the role that prewar structures played in how non-Jewish Lithuanians killed their Jewish neighbors. Why put on a white armband at all? Did this higher degree of even symbolic organization help account for Lithuania's extreme lethality? If not, why not? By contrast, if further research could demonstrate significant variation in the degree to which civilians joined in paramilitary violence that could be predicted by local prewar political currents, this would call into question my emphasis on a culture of demobilization and the role of national-level variables.

In addition, as with all cultural explanations, the argument risks assuming a coherence behind the culture of Lithuanian paramilitary politics that may be better categorized as the outcome of strategic interactions over material or power-political resources at the individual level. I recognize this limitation but do not think a cultural argument precludes a more precise specification of the nature of the strategic interactions that gave it its seeming stability. Perhaps game-theoretic explanations seem appropriate for understanding the choices the Lithuanian regime made to maintain power through popular demobilization given an apparent set of alternatives just over the border in Poland. The ample literature on external threat, ethnicity, and coup-proofing (e.g., McMahon and Slantchev 2015) seems as good a place as any to begin to look for more specific answers to the dynamics of interwar Lithuanian politics.

Finally, methodologically, this chapter demonstrates the usefulness of a small-N cross-case comparative approach to Holocaust studies, which others have already used in their research (Hollander 2006), and the limitations of a dogmatic quantitative microlevel approach, popular in recent research in political violence (Balcells and Stanton 2021). Viewing the Holocaust as a series of events (as illustrated in the introduction to this volume) demands both small- and large-scale comparisons and the methods to make them. Thankfully, small-N comparative approaches—defined as research that compares a small number of cases to draw causal inferences, as opposed to "large-N" research, which typically compares across a sufficient number of cases to enable statistical analysis—have a rich history in social science (Brady and Collier 2010). Keeping this methodological approach in mind can only help scholars make the most of social science to better understand the Holocaust.

REFERENCES

Arad, Yitzhak. 1976. *The "Final Solution" in Lithuania in the Light of German Documentation.* Jerusalem: Yad Vashem.

Balcells, Laia, and Jessica A. Stanton. 2021. "Violence against Civilians during Armed Conflict: Moving beyond the Macro- and Micro-Level Divide." *Annual Review of Political Science* 24 (1): 45–69. https://doi.org/10.1146/annurev-polisci-041719-102229.

Balkelis, Tomas. 2018. *War, Revolution, and Nation-Making in Lithuania, 1914–1923.* The Greater War. Oxford: Oxford University Press.

Brady, Henry, and David Collier. 2010. *Rethinking Social Inquiry: Diverse Tools, Shared Standards.* Edited by Henry E. Brady. 2nd ed. Rowman and Littlefield.

Cohen, Nathan. 1989. "The Destruction of the Jews of Butrimonys as Described in a Farewell Letter from a Local Jew." *Holocaust and Genocide Studies* 4 (3): 357–75. https://doi.org/10.1093/hgs/4.3.357.

———. 1999. "The Attitude of Lithuanians towards Jews during the Holocaust as Reflected in Diaries." *Lithuania: Crime and Punishment*, January 1999.

Hollander, Ethan J. 2006. "Swords or Shields? Implementing and Subverting the Final Solution in Nazi-Occupied Europe." PhD diss., University of California, San Diego.

"Holocaust Atlas of Lithuania." Accessed May 6, 2022. http://www.holocaustatlas.lt/EN/.

Kopstein, Jeffrey S., and Jason Wittenberg. 2018. *Intimate Violence: Anti-Jewish Pogroms on the Eve of the Holocaust*. Ithaca, NY: Cornell University Press.

Kwiet, Konrad. 1998. "Rehearsing for Murder: The Beginning of the Final Solution in Lithuania in June 1941." *Holocaust and Genocide Studies* 12 (1): 3–26. https://doi.org/10.1093/hgs/12.1.3.

Levinson, Joseph, ed. 2006. *The Shoah (Holocaust) in Lithuania*. Vilnius: Vilna Gaon Jewish State Museum.

MacQueen, Michael. 1997. "Nazi Policy toward the Jews in the *Reichskommissariat Ostland*, June–December 1941: From White Terror to Holocaust in Lithuania." In *Bitter Legacy: Confronting the Holocaust in the USSR*, edited by Zvi Gitelman, 91–103. Bloomington: Indiana University Press.

———. 1998. "The Context of Mass Destruction: Agents and Prerequisites of the Holocaust in Lithuania." *Holocaust and Genocide Studies* 12 (1): 27–48.

McMahon, R. Blake, and Branislav L. Slantchev. 2015. "The Guardianship Dilemma: Regime Security through and from the Armed Forces." *American Political Science Review* 109 (2): 297–313. https://doi.org/10.1017/S0003055415000131.

"Testimonies of Murderers." 1999. *Lithuania: Crime and Punishment*, January 1999.

"Trial of the Major War Criminals before the International Military Tribunal ("Blue Series"): Volume 2." 1947. Library of Congress. https://www.loc.gov/rr/frd/Military_Law/pdf/NT_Vol-II.pdf.

Truska, Liudas. 2004. "The Crisis of Lithuanian and Jewish Relations (June 1940–June 1941)." In *The Preconditions for the Holocaust: Anti-Semitism in Lithuania (Second Half of the 19th Century—June 1941)*, edited by Liudas Truska and Vygantas Vareikis, XXX–YYY. Vilnius: Margi Raštai.

Vaičikonis, Kristina. 1984. "Augustinas Voldemaras." *Litanus: Lithuanian Quarterly Journal of Arts and Science* 30 (3). http://www.lituanus.org/1984_3/84_3_06.htm.

Valone, T. Fielder. 2014. "Rescued from Oblivion: The Leyb Koniuchowsky Papers and the Holocaust in Provincial Lithuania." *Holocaust and Genocide Studies* 28 (1): 85–108. https://doi.org/10.1093/hgs/dcu019.

Yad Vashem. n.d. "Murder of the Jews of Poland." Accessed January 18, 2020. https://www.yadvashem.org/holocaust/about/fate-of-jews/poland.html.

Yahad—in Unum. n.d. "in Evidence: The Map of Holocaust by Bullets." Accessed September 16, 2020. https://yahadmap.org/en/#map/.

Part II

NEW USES FOR OLD DATA ON ANTISEMITISM AND THE HOLOCAUST

7

TERRITORIAL LOSS AND XENOPHOBIA IN THE WEIMAR REPUBLIC

Evidence from Jewish Bogeymen in Children's Stories

Robert Braun

A rapidly expanding body of work—ranging from studies of anti-immigrant attitudes in the contemporary world (Koopmans and Olzak 2004) to subnational analysis of antisemitism going back as far as the early fifteenth century (Becker and Pascali 2019; Charnysh and Finkel 2017)—tries to explain why xenophobia varies across space. This research frequently focuses on how political (Blalock 1982; King and Brustein 2006; Kopstein and Wittenberg 2018) and economic threats (Olzak 1994; Brustein 2003) posed by outsiders translate into xenophobia among insiders. The popularity of both threat approaches notwithstanding, evidence in support of either is rather mixed (Bélanger and Pinard 1991; Williams 1994).

Following macrolevel theories on the formation of exclusive nationalism (Mann 2005; Midlarsky 2005; Brubaker 1996; Hiers, Soehl, and Wimmer 2017), I will move beyond economic and political threat models and highlight the role of geopolitical fears. In particular, I will argue that spatial variation in xenophobia is in part driven by territorial loss due to military defeat. Two reinforcing mechanisms link loss of territory to hostility toward outsiders. First, territorial loss hardens ethnic fault lines, unleashing aggressive and exclusive forms of nationalism (Mann 2005; Brubaker 1996). Second, geopolitical decline activates collective feelings of loss that generate extreme responses (Midlarsky 2005). Taken together, these feelings and fault lines produce spatial landscapes in which those inside the state but outside the ethnic community are attractive scapegoats for broader social problems facing the nation (Hiers, Soehl, and Wimmer 2017).

I develop this argument through a study of antisemitism in Weimar Germany. Out of dissatisfaction with existing measures of antisemitism that often incorrectly assume that the presence of Jews is required for anti-Jewish sentiments to emerge (Charnysh 2015), I have developed a new dataset that captures over-time and geographical variation in antisemitic attitudes utilizing research conducted by folklorists. It traces antisemitism in 19,828 localities by looking at the prevalence of Jewish bogeymen in *Kinderschreck* (children's fright), an oral tradition that deploys fear to induce obedience in children. The data show that regions surrounding lost territories in Weimar Germany formed hotbeds of antisemitism. This finding has important implications for the study of xenophobia, in its suggestion that geopolitical threats work together with economic and political fears in producing hostility toward outsiders.

The remainder of this chapter is structured as follows. In the next section, I will give an overview of how territorial loss played out in Weimar Germany and theorize how these developments can be linked to xenophobia. The third section introduces the folklore data and statistical methods deployed to study this relationship. Following that, I deploy spatial econometrics and a difference-in-differences design to show that resentment toward Jews indeed clustered near lost territories. The conclusion discusses the generalizability of this study as well as its implications for the study of German history, antisemitism, and ethnic relationships more broadly.

Territorial Loss and Xenophobia

The Treaty of Versailles that ended World War I seriously challenged Germany's sovereignty, as it forced the country to cede control of Eupen-Malmedy, Alsace-Lorraine, a portion of Schleswig-Holstein, parts of Upper Silesia, Danzig, the Polish Corridor, and all recent military gains, either directly or, in the case of East Prussia and Schleswig-Holstein, after popular plebiscites. In addition, Germany had to demilitarize the Rhineland and pay the Allied powers reparations to compensate for losses caused by the war. When the Germans defaulted on their payments, Belgium and France occupied the Rhineland in response (Mommsen 1998).

Macroscholarship on nationalism suggests that this geographical contraction probably left an important imprint on German regions in at least two ways. First, lost territories shape their surroundings by acting as focal points for aggressive nationalist mobilization. As lost territories symbolize international rivalry and cross-border influence, nationalist entrepreneurs see them as places where territory can be won or lost for the nation in the future. Subsequently, lost territories activate mobilization by radical nationalist groups that aim to defend the nation-state against outsiders or people who defy national categories (Mann 2005). This hardening of national fault lines is further reinforced by the nearby presence and repatriation of coethnics who live in lost territories but resent their new and ethnically different rulers (Brubaker 1996).

Second, geographic contraction increases the salience of national decline, producing shared feelings of loss. In times of crisis, lost territories amplify the perception of international threat and lost national status. As loss generates extreme responses, locals will become more likely to attribute their increased perceived social problems to forces located outside the nation, making them more susceptible to xenophobic scapegoating (Midlarsky 2005).

In addition, the convergence of loss and hardened ethnic fault lines will have important consequences for how people conceive the relationship between state and nation (Wimmer 2002). The modern state is supposed to protect and serve the nation. Lost territory, however, draws attention to the fact that the state is not able to uphold this promise, loosening the connection between shared ethnicity and shared citizenship (Hiers, Soehl, and Wimmer 2017). This process of detachment, in turn, makes hostility toward those inside the state but outside the nation more attractive and feasible.

Was there a spatial relationship between the rise of antisemitism and lost territory, as the above theories seem to imply? To investigate this proposition, we need refined data on both local antisemitism and geographic contraction.

Data and Methods

Existing subnational analyses of antisemitism in Europe before the Holocaust often rely on pogrom data (Kopstein and Wittenberg 2011; Voigtländer and Voth 2012) or votes for parties that embraced antisemitic rhetoric (Heilbronner 1990). Pogrom data suffers from three shortcomings. First, pogroms are an extreme form of antisemitism. Yet anti-Jewish sentiments are likely to exist even in the absence of pogroms. Second, pogroms cannot take place in the absence of Jewish targets. Deploying pogroms as a proxy therefore assumes a local Jewish presence as a precondition for the emergence of antisemitism, something that remains an open empirical question (Charnysh 2015). Third, pogroms are not a pure measure of local sentiments toward Jews, as they also tap the capacity to mobilize and in some cases the presence of instigation by movement entrepreneurs.[1] Consequently, pogroms tell us about organized forms of antisemitic violence but do not fully capture latent and nonviolent sentiments.

Whereas data on pogroms are too narrow, electoral data are overly broad. Openly antisemitic parties often had more comprehensive policy platforms that were anchored in economic and cultural issues unrelated to Jews or Judaism. As a consequence, it is not clear whether a vote for a party that openly embraces antisemitism does indeed capture xenophobic sentiments of the voter or not. This is further complicated by the fact that one and the same political party would often vary the extent to which it played up its antisemitism at a local level. Catholics, conservatives (Kauders 1996), nationalists (Heilbronner 1990), and even liberal campaigns (Kurlander 2002) would espouse antisemitism in one place but not another. Assuming that votes for one party mean the same everywhere therefore seems unwarranted.

Given these shortcomings, I will exploit fine-grained data on antisemitic themes in children's stories collected by folklorists to investigate the territorial decline thesis. This source taps both latent and less extreme forms of antisemitism and does not require the presence of Jews for antisemitism to appear. Moreover, the data have an over-time dimension that enables us to explore antisemitism through time and space. Below, I will describe the folklorist data in more detail before discussing the measurement of lost territories.

Main Variables

The collapse of the German empire, hatred toward the Versailles Treaty, destabilizing economic transformations, and social unrest shattered German trust in modern progress, producing an "explosive spiritual vacuum" (Kurlander 2017, 63). In part, this void was filled by a renaissance in occult beliefs, folklore, and mythology as folk tales centered on national myths, stereotypes, and symbols allowed Germans to deal with the burdens of postwar life by providing a lens through which to perceive daily struggles (Mosse 1987). These stories, filled with supernatural and natural monsters such as cannibals, witches, vampires, magicians, and demons, instilled a romantic sense of German identity while at the same time constructing a range of imagined enemies that threatened national values (Leschnitzer 1956; Grober-Glück 1974).

This chapter zeros in on the genre of folk tales known as *Kinderschreck* (children's fright) to capture local variation in popular antisemitism. Kinderschreck was an oral tradition of storytelling widespread in Central Europe during the nineteenth and twentieth centuries. It was deployed by parents to discipline children through the inducement of fear. The setup of Kinderschreck stories was both brief and basic, involving only two components: a spatial location and a bogeyman. Parents would tell their children to stay away from a certain place (a water line, cornfields, etc.) because otherwise a bogeyman would come and get them. Kinderschreck tales frequently featured rather innocent depictions of fantasy figures or animals that acted as bogeymen. In some villages, however, the bogeymen was the "Forest Jew," "Blood Jew," or "Wandering Jew" (Beitl 1933; Mannhardt 1884).

I build on data collection efforts by folklorists to map where and when Jewish bogeymen started appearing in German history. Folklore studies was established as a professional discipline by the Grimm brothers, who, in addition to collecting and publishing children's stories, had a deep interest in documenting different oral and material traditions that existed in German lands. Over time, the collection of materials became more and more professional (Peßler 1932). The work of the Grimm student Wilhelm Mannhardt is particularly noteworthy, as he was probably the first to start collecting folklore through systematic expert surveys in a large number of European villages (Mannhardt 1884). Mannhardt's approach inspired many and culminated in the *Atlas Der Deutschen Volkskunde* (ADV) (Schmoll 2009).

This research project, funded by Deutsche Forschungsgemeinschaft (the German equivalent of the National Science Foundation), was grandiose for its time. The study was based on expert surveys in almost twenty thousand German localities between 1930 and 1935. For each of these localities, the ADV sent questionnaires to prescreened and preselected local experts who were able to write independently and had lived in the surveyed community for a prolonged period of time. The 1930, 1931, and 1932 surveys included questions on Kinderschreck stories in the region and explicitly asked about the bogeyman featuring in these tales (Zender 1958).[2] The Nazi takeover and World War II abruptly ended the analysis of the questionnaires from the early 1930s.[3]

But the original surveys survived the war and are currently located in the basement of the Abteilung Kulturantropologie of the Rheinische Friedrich-Wilhelms University in Bonn, Germany. During the summer of 2017 and 2018, I received permission to access the survey material, which had not been touched for over twenty years. During this period, I hand-coded the answers to the Kinderschreck questions. The resulting dataset included information on bogeymen reported by 50,356 experts living all over Germany. This database was transformed into a locality-level dataset with 19,828 observations. For 5.620 percent of these localities, at least one expert reported the presence of a Jewish bogeyman.

As individual judgment is prone to systematic biases, reliability is a major concern when using expert-based measures (Maestas 2016). In order to assess the reliability of the ADV experts, I exploit the fact that we have multiple reports from different experts living in the same locality. This allows us to determine how frequently different experts report the same bogeymen. If experts are likely to report the same bogeymen for the same locality, we can be more certain that measurement is reliable. Table 7.1 reports the reliability scores for localities with two or more expert surveys. These scores vary from 0 to 1, with 1 denoting a large similarity between reports. Regardless of what reliability measure we use, the variance between experts is extremely low, providing us with more confidence in the reliability of their reports.

TABLE 7.1 Reliability of reports on Jewish bogeymen

RELIABILITY MEASURE	3 RESPONDENTS	2 RESPONDENTS
Percent agreement	.9935	.9937
	(.001)	(.001)
Brennan and Prediger	.9869	.9873
	(.001)	(.001)
Cohen/Conger's Kappa	.9269	.9301
	(.006)	(.006)
Scott/Fleiss's Kappa	.9263	0.9301
	(.006)	(.006)
Gwet's AC	.9928	.993
	(.001)	(.001)
Krippendorff's Alpha	.9275	.9301
	(.006)	(.006)
Villages	14,176	16,350

Note: Standard errors in parentheses

To further assure that individual difference between experts is not driving our results, I compared a random sample of experts who reported the presence of Jewish bogeymen with a random sample of experts who did not. For each of these samples, I have coded individual characteristics such as age, profession, religion, birthplace, and the number of years the respondent was living in the relevant locality. Figure 7.1 displays a simple difference in means tests for almost one thousand respondents. As we can see, in terms of age, regional expertise, or professional background, experts who reported the presence of Jewish bogeymen are not significantly different from those who did not.

The geocoded Kinderschreck data is paired with data on lost territories by calculating the logged distance from each town to the nearest lost territory. Locations of the latter are obtained by intersecting German shapefiles from right before World War I and 1921, the year in which the East Prussian and Schleswig plebiscites were finalized. The lost territories are depicted in figure 7.2 below.

Empirical Strategy

Border regions have distinct histories and experience unique demographic, political, economic, and military dynamics that can be plausibly linked to antisemitism (Dower et al. 2018). To investigate the independent influence of the attraction and perception mechanisms on the clustering of antisemitism, we therefore need to consider a wide range of confounders. Let's go back in time and start with the long-term legacies that borderlands carry.

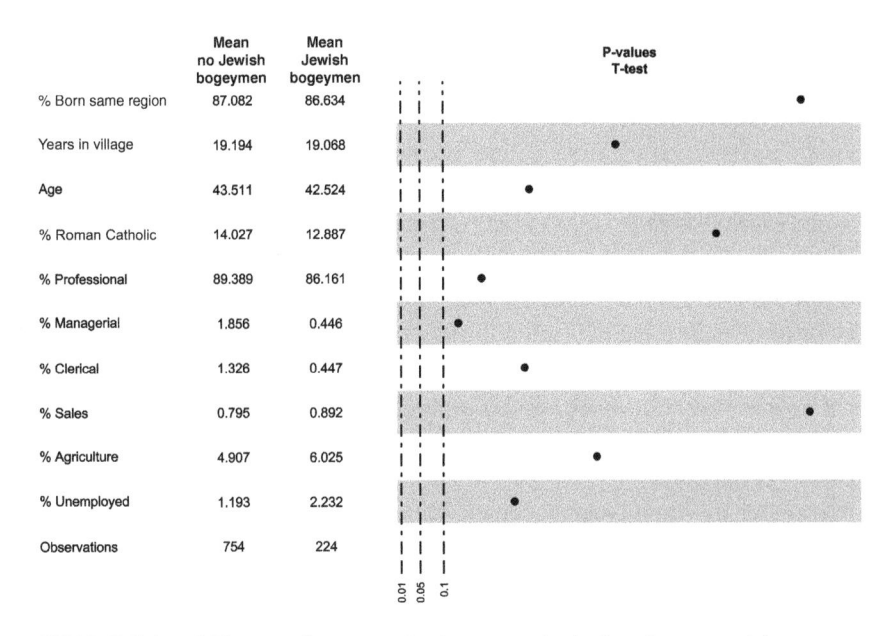

	Mean no Jewish bogeymen	Mean Jewish bogeymen
% Born same region	87.082	86.634
Years in village	19.194	19.068
Age	43.511	42.524
% Roman Catholic	14.027	12.887
% Professional	89.389	86.161
% Managerial	1.856	0.446
% Clerical	1.326	0.447
% Sales	0.795	0.892
% Agriculture	4.907	6.025
% Unemployed	1.193	2.232
Observations	754	224

FIGURE 7.1. Difference in means tests respondents (random sample)

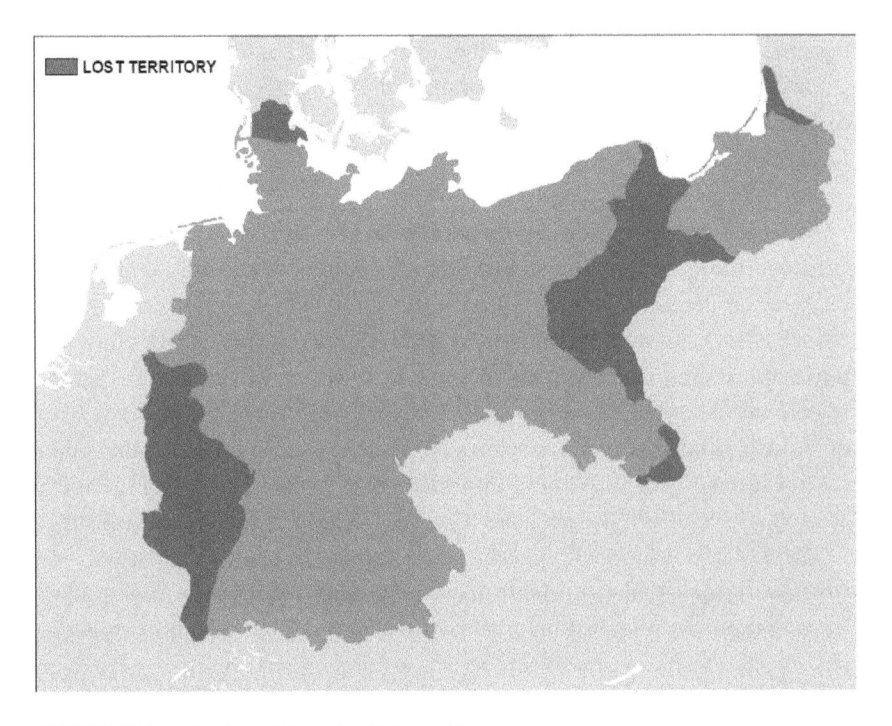

FIGURE 7.2. Territorial loss in Weimar Germany

The history of the Jews is closely intertwined with that of border regions. Because of comparative advantage in moneylending and trade, Jews have historically played an important role in forging connections between different localities, transcending dividing lines between empires, principalities, and later nations. Throughout history, Gentile responses to Jews in border regions have varied widely. Starting at least as early as the fourteenth century, Jews were seen as alien agents who undermined local economies by exploiting local entrepreneurs, activating waves of violence targeting Jews in times of economic disruptions (Johnson and Koyama 2017). On the other hand, some regions celebrated the complementary role Jews played in strengthening the local economy, producing a more tolerant climate (Becker and Pascali 2019). There is an abundance of evidence suggesting that (in)tolerance toward outsiders produced by early economic relationships can persist in border regions for centuries. Particularly relevant for this study, Voigtländer and Voth (2012) have demonstrated that cities that experienced pogroms in 1349 were more antisemitic during the Weimar Republic. Follow-up research, however, has revealed that persistence of antisemitic attitudes was much weaker in Catholic parts of Germany (Becker and Pascali 2019). In these regions, Jewish complementarity in forging trade relationships was deemed more important, since religious prescriptions prevented Gentiles from engaging in moneylending themselves. I construct two measures to tap legacies of (in)tolerance. First, based on data collected by Voigtländer and Voth, I mark each locality within a 31.06-mile radius of a pogrom in 1349. Second, to capture the divergence between Catholic and Protestant regions, I also mark localities within 31.06 miles of major Catholic trade hubs.[4] Data are obtained from Becker and Pascali (2019).

Moving from ancient legacies to more temporally proximate causes, researchers across the globe have shown that ethnic animosity follows out of immediate political competition (Biggs and Dhattiwala 2012; Wilkinson 2004). An important branch of this approach focuses on the dynamic relationship between increased power threats and intergroup conflict (Olzak 1994). These theories predict that resentment is more likely when outsiders start to threaten the political status of insiders (Kopstein and Wittenberg 2018). Empirical support for this political threat model has been found in a wide range of cases, including twentieth-century antisemitism (Brustein and King 2004; Kopstein and Wittenberg 2011).

Across Central Europe in general and Weimar Germany in particular, Jews were associated with the leadership of left-wing parties (Brustein and King 2004). Initially these parties relied on cross-national networks to mobilize, producing new socialist and Communist hotbeds near the border (Applegate 1990; Lapp 1997). To make sure that this clustering is not driving the relationship between border regions and antisemitism, I control for *the rise* in the percentage of votes for the Communist and socialist parties between 1924 and 1928, a time period in which right-wing politicians explicitly linked major left-wing gains in electoral strength to Judaism (King and Brustein 2006). Work on ethnic violence suggests that narrow win margins between parties can also activate elite instigation of ethnic resentment (Biggs and Dhattiwala 2012; Wilkinson 2004). In additional models, I added controls for vote margins between right- and left-wing parties and votes for far-right parties. This did not alter the main results and led to a poorer model fit.

It is important to note that left-wing mobilization can also have a mitigating effect on xenophobia. Left-wing movements in Weimar strongly supported pluralism and were embedded in collective associations that brought together Jews and Gentiles. Civic networks that bridge ethnic divides can stem the emergence of intergroup hostility (Scacco and Warren 2018). In line with this, Solomon (2019) shows that Kristallnacht attacks were less prevalent in localities with strong left-wing movements. I therefore control for the percentage of votes that Communists and socialists received in the year 1928. Data for both political proxies are obtained from the massive data collection project supervised by Falter and Hänisch (1990).

Instead of focusing on political threats, the scapegoating approach theorizes a relationship between xenophobia and economic challenges. This classic theory suggests that xenophobia rises because outsiders are blamed for the economic problems facing local communities (Scheepers, Gijsberts, and Coenders 2002; Olzak 1994). This approach dovetails well with historical scholarship on economic antisemitism in interwar Germany that links antisemitism to economic modernization and crisis. The rise of capitalism, industry, and liberalism emancipated the Jews economically, politically, and socially. While Jewish social mobility elicited fear among Gentiles, their prominent position in trade and finance produced resentment (Niewyk 2018).

Because of market volatility and the presence of international competition nearby, some of Weimar's border regions experienced heightened economic instability (Schnabel 1982; Applegate 1990; Lapp 1997). To assure that these distinct economic problems are not confounding the relationship between lost territory and antisemitism, I condition on the unemployment rate in 1932, logged GDP in the same year, and decline in GDP between 1928 and 1932. While the first two measures are culled from the 1936 census, the third measure is constructed by Spenkuch and Tillman (2018) to capture the consequences of the global financial crises.

The end of World War I was perhaps the biggest source of local instability in border regions, as it destroyed parts of social life, temporarily uprooted economic relationships, and seriously damaged national pride. The Far Right directly framed Jews as playing a role in these processes. The infamous stab-in-the-back myth took this to its extreme and claimed that Jews and Jews alone were responsible for German defeat (Vascik and Sadler 2016). It therefore seems plausible that exposure violence during World War I may have been driving the clustering of antisemitism near border regions.[5]

To deal with this issue, I construct three measures to capture exposure to warfare. First, I coded localities that were within a 31.06-mile radius of a World War I battle, according to Clodfelter (2002).[6] Second, I condition on the percentage of the population receiving veterans' benefits in 1929, as digitized by Adena et al. (2015). Third, I utilize population data compiled by Falter and Hänisch (1990) to measure the decline in population during the five years immediately following the end of the war.

Last but not least, to make sure I am not comparing localities that are completely different in terms of ethnic, religious, and economic composition, I control for logged population size as well as the percentage of (1) Jews, (2) Catholics, (3) seculars, (4) the population employed in trade, (5) the population employed in industry, (6) the population employed in agriculture, and (7) votes for parties that represent the interests of ethnic minorities in the baseline model.[7] The first seven measures, all based on the 1925 census, are culled from data collected by Falter and Hänisch (1990). The latter measure is taken from the 1887 Reichstag election, the last year for which votes for minority parties have been recorded.[8]

Conventional statistical analysis assumes independence of observations. The bogeymen data deployed in this chapter are likely to violate this assumption, as oral traditions tend to diffuse through space (Grober-Glück 1974). Spatial dependence creates autocorrelation and typically introduces bias in standard errors and coefficients. To account for spatial autocorrelation, I deploy spatial filtering (Murakami and Griffith 2019). This approach absorbs autocorrelation in the residuals through the inclusion of Moran's eigenvectors as synthetic controls on the right-hand side of the statistical model. In addition, I allow the standard errors to be correlated within counties by using clustered standard errors. Since the presence of bogeymen is a binary outcome, I deploy a logistic link function.

Analysis

Main Results

The thesis developed in this chapter would lead us to expect that antisemitic bogeymen cluster near lost territories. As a first cut at the data, I mapped all the localities in the dataset and marked those with Jewish bogeymen. Figure 7.3

TABLE 7.2 Summary statistics for analysis of bogeymen

VARIABLE	OBS	MEAN	STD. DEV.	MIN	MAX
Main variables					
Jewish bogeymen	19,829	.056	.230	.000	1.000
Proximity to lost territory (logged)	19,831	3.056	1.797	.000	7.023
Demographic controls					
Population, 1925 (logged)	19,829	10.851	.567	7.363	13.892
% Jews, 1925	19,829	.355	.448	.000	10.471
% Ethnic minority votes, 1887	19,829	.398	4.422	.000	99.600
% Catholics, 1925	19,829	33.346	37.633	.304	99.759
% Nonreligious, 1925	19,829	1.636	1.740	.000	17.290
% Trade, 1925	19,829	10.778	5.318	.000	43.832
% Industry, 1925	19,829	31.131	15.359	.000	79.567
% Agrarian, 1925	19,829	39.184	18.642	.000	83.649
Legacies					
Pogrom, 1349 (50 km radius)	19,829	.415	.369	.000	1.000
Tolerant trade city, 16th century	19,829	.288	.453	.000	1.000
Political controls					
% Left Wing Votes, 1928	19,829	23.902	12.035	1.887	60.874
Δ % Left-wing votes, 1924–28	19,829	2.929	3.688	-21.825	28.447
Economic controls					
% Unemployment, 1932	19,829	11.874	6.147	1.734	40.524
Income (logged), 1932	19,829	7.85	.173	7.251	9.519
Δ Income 1928–32 (logged)	19,829	.070	.224	-.804	2.449
War controls					
WWI battle (50 km radius)	19,829	.093	.290	.000	1.000
% War veterans' pensions, 1929	19,829	.470	1.67	.000	28.778
Δ Population, 1919–25 (logged)	19,829	1.901	1.133	-3.985	5.714

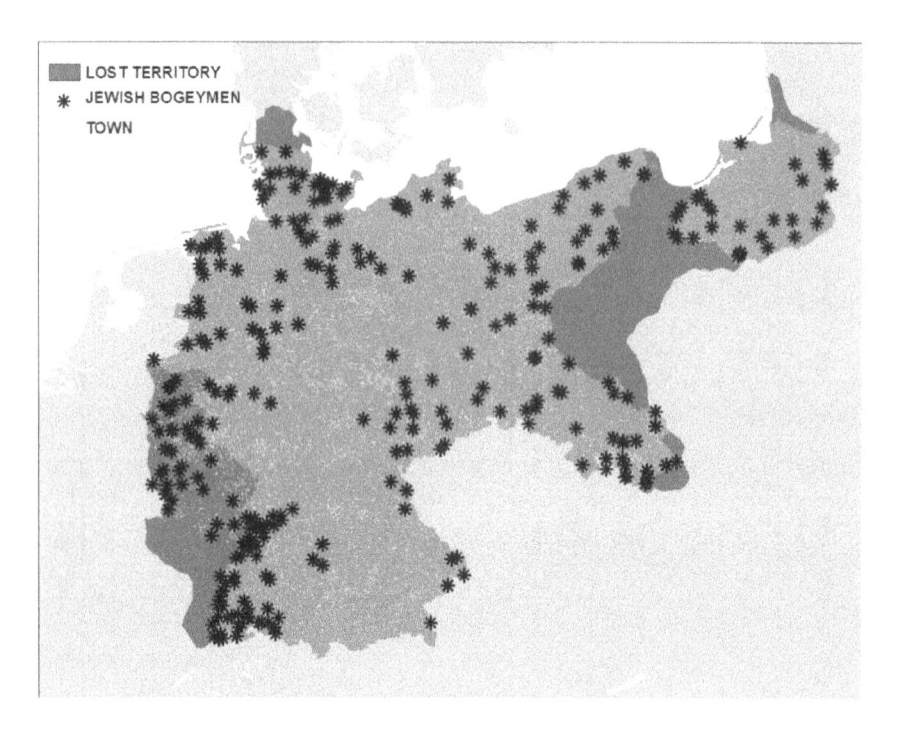

FIGURES 7.3 AND 7.4. Jews, Jewish bogeymen, and lost territory in Weimar Germany

reveals that Jewish bogeymen tend to be more prevalent near territories lost to France, Poland, and Denmark than in the center of the country. Figure 7.4, in turn, displays the geographical distribution of Jewish citizens living in Weimar Germany in 1925. There does not seem to be a particularly strong overlap between the presence of antisemitic themes in children's stories and Jews, suggesting that antisemitism without Jews was quite prominent (Charnysh 2015).

A more systematic investigation of the relationship between lost territory and ethnic fear requires the evaluation of a counterfactual claim: would the presence of Jewish bogeymen be lower if no lost territory were nearby? In observational settings, these types of claims are hard to assess because regions are likely to vary along multiple other dimensions related to both xenophobia and geopolitical dynamics. Border regions often have distinct histories of tolerance as well as conflict and undergo distinct demographic economic, political, and military transformations that can be plausibly linked to the outbreak of antisemitism (Dower et al. 2018). I statistically analyze the relationship between bogeymen and proximity to lost territory while keeping constant (1) demographic composition,

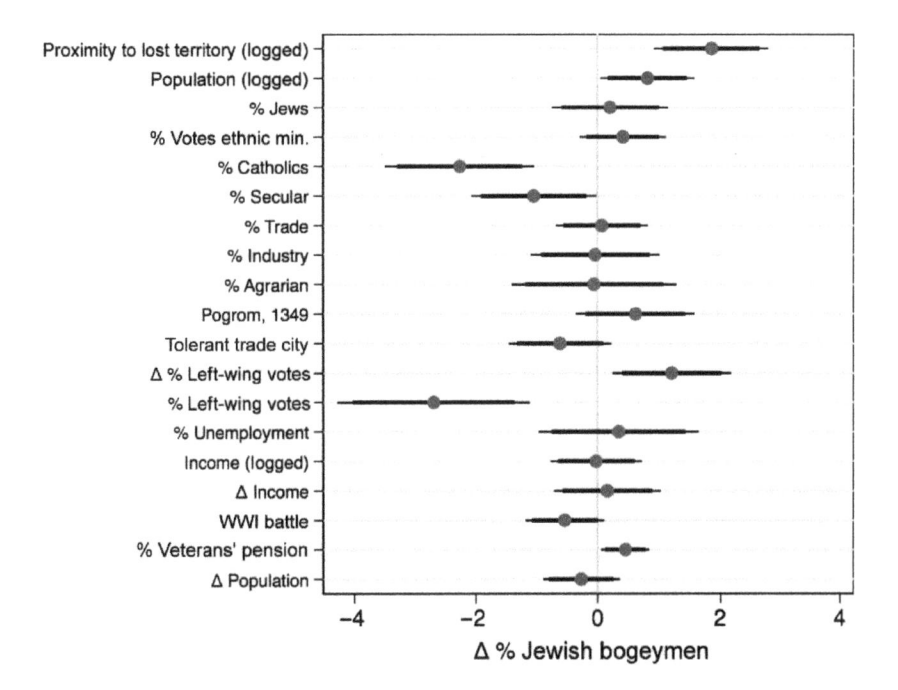

FIGURE 7.5. The effect of increasing variables one SD on the % of local communities with Jewish bogeymen, with 90 and 95 percent confidence intervals

(2) legacies of hate and tolerance, (3) economic problems, (4) political threats, and (5) exposure to World War I.

We can find the results of this analysis in figure 7.5, which reveals that Jewish bogeymen appeared most frequently in populous, Protestant, right-leaning towns that had recently experienced an upsurge in left-wing voting and had a relatively high proportion of veterans' pensions. Somewhat surprisingly, historical legacies and economic conditions appear to be unrelated to antisemitism. Importantly, and in line with the geopolitical thesis put forward in this chapter, increasing proximity to lost territory with one standard deviation increases the prevalence of Jewish bogeymen by 2 percent, a considerable effect given that, on average, only 5 percent of all localities experienced this form of xenophobia. The strength of the effect is roughly comparable with that of religion and the rise of the political Left, factors that are often assumed to be the key drivers of anti-Jewish attitudes (King and Brustein 2006; Becker and Pascali 2019). As we saw in figure 7.4 above, there does not appear to be a relationship between Jewish presence and antisemitism, driving home the point that existing studies that rely on pogrom data often overestimate this relationship.

Difference-in-Differences

It is plausible that border regions located between countries were already more antisemitic before the outbreak of World War I. To make sure that prewar differences in antisemitism are not driving my results, I deploy a basic difference-in-differences framework, using the abovementioned 1865 expert survey conducted by Wilhelm Mannhardt (1884), which provides information on Kinderschreck for 1,608 localities. The original survey was digitized based on source material held by the Staatsbibliothek Berlin Preussischer Kulturbesitz.[9]

Pairing the Weimar data from the ADV with Mannhardt's 1865 survey allows us to explore the clustering of Jewish bogeymen before and after territorial loss. Figure 7.6 shows the percentages of localities with Jewish bogeymen in 1865 and 1930–32 by region, using a 6.21 buffer to mark regions that are close to lost territories. Two things immediately stand out. First, one can note the overall increase in Jewish bogeymen between 1865 and 1930–32. This pattern can be plausibly linked to two factors: the overall increase in antisemitism mentioned above and an uptick in nationalist mythmaking. Second, the upward trend in antisemitism is much stronger in localities near lost territories. Jewish bogeymen are 6 percent more likely to be found in border regions. Taken together, these observations support the idea that proximity to lost territory had an independent and positive influence on the production of antisemitism.

We can evaluate this relationship more systematically with a basic difference-in-differences setup, where we model the interactions of time and explanatory

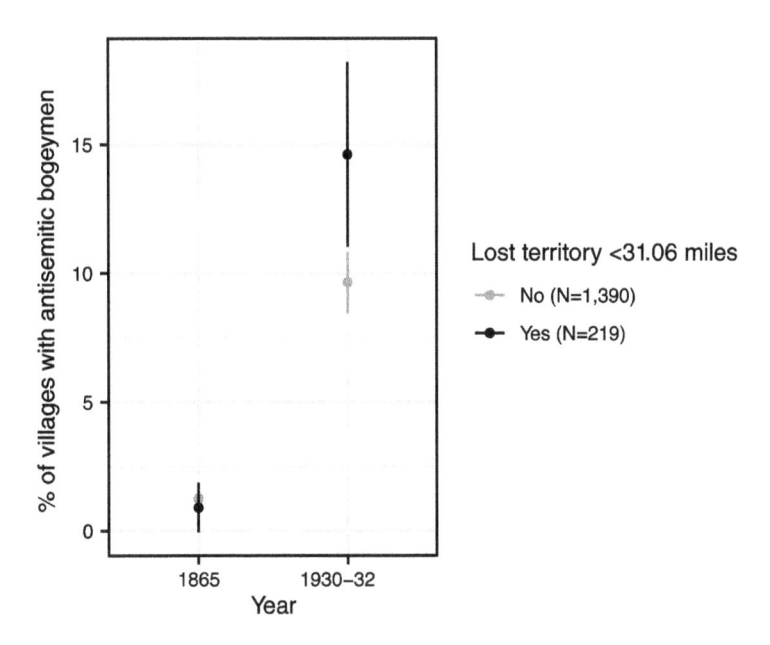

FIGURE 7.6. Percentage of villages with Jewish bogeymen by region, before and after World War I, with 95 percent confidence intervals

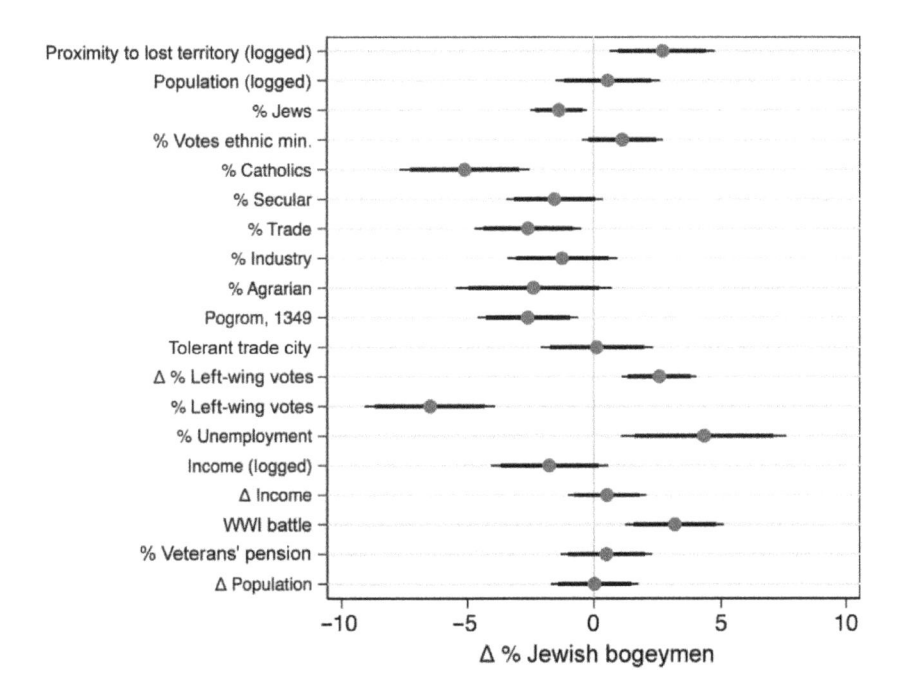

FIGURE 7.7. Difference-in-differences: The effect of increasing variables one SD on the percentage of local communities with Jewish bogeymen, with 90 and 95 percent confidence intervals

variables while including time and locality fixed effects as well as standard errors clustered at the locality level. Figure 7.7 below displays the effect of lost territory for the difference-in-differences setup. Increasing proximity to lost territories with one standard deviation leads to a 3 percent higher probability of Jewish bogeymen. All in all, the results for all other covariates are in line with those of the spatial statistical analysis presented earlier. Again, there is some evidence that political threats activate xenophobia, while economic factors are less important. One noticeable difference, however, is that the presence of Jews now even has a negative effect on the presence of Jewish bogeymen. This suggests that Jewish presence may have had an effect on prewar antisemitism but was less important after territorial loss emerged.

A considerable body of work on xenophobia has identified political and economic sources of resentment. The findings in this chapter provide clear support for the former threat theory but not the latter. More importantly, the main analysis reveals the importance of geopolitical threats in general and territorial loss in particular in shaping xenophobic dynamics.

This finding allows us to move beyond the existing threat literature in two distinct and important ways. First, this chapter joins a growing body of work that situates intergroup dynamics in the context of broader cleavage structures (Braun 2019) through the demonstration that conflict between nations activates borders within nations. While existing research, in part driven by methodological choices, often looks at how relationships between insiders and outsiders influence mutual resentment, this chapter suggests that intersections within one insider group (i.e., borders between Gentiles) alone can activate hatred toward a third group (i.e., the Jews) by shaping emotions and hardening ethnic fault lines. Second, instead of zeroing in on domestic sources of threat, a geopolitical framework draws attention to the fact that international relations between countries shape the formation of domestic xenophobia, forging connections between macro- and microlevel sources of ethnic conflicts within and between nations (Hiers, Soehl, and Wimmer 2017).

The findings also provide the microfoundations for macrosociological theories on the rise of nationalism and ethnic conflict. The shift from empire to nation-state has produced intensified political exclusion along ethnic lines (Wimmer 2002). This chapter suggests that this shift was particularly strong in areas near lost territories and identifies important mechanisms that specify how this shift materialized at a local level. It identifies how the rise of emotions and fault lines at the margins of the state are important in shaping the forms that ethnic exclusion in the political center might take.

The exclusion of Jews is a case in point. While most historians and some social scientists have always recognized the early roots of antisemitic thought (Niewyk 2018; Voigtländer and Voth 2012), a majority of social scientists argue that the importance of deep-seated hatreds is perhaps overstated (Kopstein and Wittenberg 2018). The over-time analysis of Jewish bogeymen reveals that although the antisemitic theme of the Jew as a border-transcending actor is ancient, its influence varies through time and space. Fear of Jews as measured in children's stories became stronger after the establishment of the nation and mainly concentrated in contested regions. The geopolitical threat framework put forward in this chapter therefore shows how ancient xenophobic themes about border transcendence and disloyalty interact with contemporary spatial configurations to produce hatred toward outsiders near places that symbolize decline and loss.

Finally, this chapter also breathes new life into the now-debunked geographical interpretation of German history. This controversial approach claims that Germany's precarious geographical location in Central Europe played an important role in the emergence of the Third Reich and the Holocaust. Bordering enemies on all sides, Germany could not afford democracy and was forced to embrace radical nationalist authoritarianism (Evans 2006). The findings in this chapter should not revitalize this somewhat teleological geographic thesis, but they do shed light on how pressure at Germany's distinct borders produced a xenophobic climate that could be exploited by radical movements at a local level.

This brings us to the generalizability of the lost territory thesis. Although further research is required, there is suggestive evidence that the mechanisms outlined in this chapter may travel well beyond the confines of the unique German case and operate in other instances during which the nation-state was under pressure. When we travel to Eastern Europe, we find that the rise of aggressive antisemitism was closely aligned with distinct patterns of territorial exchanges that took place in the border regions of Hungary, Czechoslovakia, Ukraine, and Bulgaria (Segal 2016). Outside the realm of antisemitism, research on the Armenian genocide indicates that conflict between nationalist Turks and the Armenians was most salient along borderlines because of fear of international influences and territorial decline (Bloxham 2005).

Let us conclude with an important suggestion for further research. A close inspection of the spread of Jewish bogeymen in figure 7.3 reveals that antisemitism also clustered alongside less contentious borders in the Northwest and South of the country. This seems to suggest that border regions more broadly, and not only those adjacent to lost territory, provide a fertile breeding ground for xenophobia. Further research is required to explore this dynamic (Braun 2020).

REFERENCES

Adena, Maja, Ruben Enikolopov, Maria Petrova, Veronica Santarosa, and Ekaterina Zhuravskaya. 2015. "Radio and the Rise of the Nazis in Prewar Germany." *Quarterly Journal of Economics* 130 (4): 1885–939.

Applegate, Celia. 1990. *A Nation of Provincials: The German Idea of Heimat.* Berkeley: University of California Press.
Becker, Sascha, and Luigi Pascali. 2019. "Religion, Division of Labor, and Conflict: Anti-Semitism in Germany over 600 Years." *American Economic Review* 109 (5): 1764–804.
Beitl, Richard. 1933. *Untersuchungen zur Mythologie des Kindes.* Münster: Waxmann Verlag.
Bélanger, Sarah, and Maurice Pinard. 1991. "Ethnic Movements and the Competition Model: Some Missing Links." *American Sociological Review* 56 (4): 446–57.
Biggs, Michael, and Raheel Dhattiwala. 2012. "The Political Logic of Ethnic Violence: The Anti-Muslim Pogrom in Gujarat, 2002." *Politics & Society* 40 (4): 483–516.
Blalock, Hubert. 1982. *Race and Ethnic Relations.* Hoboken, NJ: Prentice Hall.
Bloxham, Donald. 2005. *The Great Game of Genocide: Imperialism, Nationalism, and the Destruction of the Ottoman Armenians.* Oxford: Oxford University Press.
Braun, Robert. 2019. *Protectors of Pluralism: Religious Minorities and the Rescue of Jews in the Low Countries during the Holocaust.* Cambridge: Cambridge University Press.
———. 2020. "Bloodlines: National Border Crossings and Antisemitism in Weimar Germany." *American Sociological Review* 56 (4): 446–57.
Brubaker, Rogers. 1996. *Nationalism Reframed: Nationhood and the National Question in the New Europe.* Cambridge: Cambridge University Press.
Brustein, William. 2003. *Roots of Hate: Anti-Semitism in Europe before the Holocaust.* Cambridge: Cambridge University Press.
Brustein, William, and Ryan King. 2004. "Anti-Semitism as a Response to Perceived Jewish Power: The Cases of Bulgaria and Romania before the Holocaust." *Social Forces* 83 (2): 691–708.
Charnysh, Volha. 2015. "Historical Legacies of Interethnic Competition: Anti-Semitism and the EU Referendum in Poland." *Comparative Political Studies* 48 (13): 1711–45.
Charnysh, Volha, and Evgeny Finkel. 2017. "The Death Camp Eldorado: Political and Economic Effects of Mass Violence." *American Political Science Review* 111 (4): 801–18.
Clodfelter, Micheal. 2002. *Warfare and Armed Conflicts: A Statistical Reference to Casualty and Other Figures.* Jefferson, NC: McFarland.
Dower, Paul Castañeda, Evgeny Finkel, Scott Gehlbach, Dmitrii Kofanov, and Steven Nafziger. 2018. "Religious Polarization and Conflict: Evidence from Imperial Russia." Working paper, University of Wisconsin, Madison.
Evans, Richard. 2006. *The Third Reich in Power.* New York: Penguin.
Falter, Jürgen, and Dirk Hänisch. 1990. "Election and Social Data of the Districts and Municipalities of the German Empire from 1920 to 1933." GESIS Data Archive, Cologne. ZA8013 data file.
Grober-Glück, Gerda. 1974. *Motive und Motivationen in Redensarten und Meinungen: Textband.* Marburg: Elwert.
Heilbronner, Oded. 1990. "The Role of Nazi Antisemitism in the Nazi Party's Activity and Propaganda: A Regional Historiographical Study." *Leo Baeck Institute Year Book* 35 (1): 397–439.
Hiers, Wesley, Thomas Soehl, and Andreas Wimmer. 2017. "National Trauma and the Fear of Foreigners: How Past Geopolitical Threat Heightens Anti-immigration Sentiment Today." *Social Forces* 96 (1): 361–88.
Johnson, Noel, and Mark Koyama. 2017. "Jewish Communities and City Growth in Preindustrial Europe." *Journal of Development Economics* 127:339–54.

Kauders, Anthony. 1996. *German Politics and the Jews: Düsseldorf and Nuremberg, 1910–1933*. Oxford: Oxford University Press.
King, Ryan, and William Brustein. 2006. "A Political Threat Model of Intergroup Violence: Jews in Pre–World War II Germany." *Criminology* 44 (4): 867–91.
Koopmans, Ruud, and Susan Olzak. 2004. "Discursive Opportunities and the Evolution of Right-Wing Violence in Germany." *American Journal of Sociology* 110 (1): 198–30.
Kopstein, Jeffrey S., and Jason Wittenberg. 2011. "Deadly Communities: Local Political Milieus and the Persecution of Jews in Occupied Poland." *Comparative Political Studies* 44 (3): 259–83.
———. 2018. *Intimate Violence: Anti-Jewish Pogroms on the Eve of the Holocaust*. Ithaca, NY: Cornell University Press.
Kurlander, Eric. 2002. "The Rise of Völkisch-Nationalism and the Decline of German Liberalism: A Comparison of Liberal Political Cultures in Schleswig-Holstein and Silesia 1912–1924." *European Review of History: Revue européenne d'histoire* 9 (1): 23–36.
———. 2017. *Hitler's Monsters: A Supernatural History of the Third Reich*. New Haven, CT: Yale University Press.
Lapp, Benjamin. 1997. *Revolution from the Right: Politics, Class, and the Rise of Nazism in Saxony, 1919–1933*. Leiden: Brill.
Leschnitzer, Adolf. 1956. *The Magic Background of Modern Anti-Semitism: An Analysis of the German-Jewish Relationship*. New York: International Universities Press.
Lixfeld, Hannjost. 1994. *Folklore and Fascism: The Reich Institute for German Volkskunde*. Bloomington: Indiana University Press.
Maestas, Cherie. 2016. "Expert Surveys as a Measurement Tool: Challenges and New Frontiers." In *The Oxford Handbook of Polling and Survey Methods*, edited by Lonna Atkeson and Michael Alvarez, http://www.oxfordhandbooks.com/view/10.1093/oxfordhb/9780190213299.001.0001/oxfordhb-9780190213299-e-13. Oxford: Oxford University Press.
Mann, Michael. 2005. *The Dark Side of Democracy: Explaining Ethnic Cleansing*. Cambridge: Cambridge University Press.
Mannhardt, Wilhelm. 1884. *Mythologische Forschungen aus dem Nachlasse, von Wilhelm Mannhardt*. Strasbourg: KJ Trübner.
Midlarsky, Manus. 2005. *The Killing Trap: Genocide in the Twentieth Century*. Cambridge: Cambridge University Press.
Mommsen, Hans. 1998. *The Rise and Fall of Weimar Democracy*. Chapel Hill: University of North Carolina Press.
Mosse, George. 1987. *Masses and Man: Nationalist and Fascist Perceptions of Reality*. Detroit, MI: Wayne State University Press.
Murakami, Daisuke, and Daniel Griffith. 2019. "Eigenvector Spatial Filtering for Large Data Sets: Fixed and Random Effects Approaches." *Geographical Analysis* 51 (1): 23–49.
Niewyk, Donald. 2018. *Jews in Weimar Germany*. Abingdon: Routledge.
Olzak, Susan. 1994. *The Dynamics of Ethnic Competition and Conflict*. Palo Alto, CA: Stanford University Press.
Peßler, Wilhelm. 1932. "Die geographische Methode in der Volkskunde." *Anthropos* 5:707–42.
Scacco, Alexandra, and Shana Warren. 2018. "Can Social Contact Reduce Prejudice and Discrimination? Evidence from a Field Experiment in Nigeria." *American Political Science Review* 112 (3): 654–77.

Scheepers, Peer, Mérove Gijsberts, and Marcel Coenders. 2002. "Ethnic Exclusionism in European Countries: Public Opposition to Civil Rights for Legal Migrants as a Response to Perceived Ethnic Threat." *European Sociological Review* 18 (1): 17–34.
Schmoll, Friedemann. 2009. *Die Vermessung der Kultur: Der "Atlas der deutschen Volkskunde" und die Deutsche Forschungsgemeinschaft, 1928–1980*. Wiesbaden: Franz Steiner Verlag.
Schnabel, Thomas. 1982. *Die Machtergreifung in Südwestdeutschland: Das Ende der Weimarer Republik in Baden und Württemberg 1928–1933*. Stuttgart: Kohlhammer.
Segal, Raz. 2016. *Genocide in the Carpathians: War, Social Breakdown, and Mass Violence, 1914–1945*. Palo Alto, CA: Stanford University Press.
Solomon, Daniel. 2019. "The Symbolic Logic of Pogrom Violence: Evidence from Kristallnacht." Working paper, Georgetown University.
Spenkuch, Jörg, and Philipp Tillmann. 2018. "Elite Influence? Religion and the Electoral Success of the Nazis." *American Journal of Political Science* 62 (1): 19–36.
Vascik, George, and Mark Sadler. 2016. *The Stab-in-the-Back Myth and the Fall of the Weimar Republic: A History in Documents and Visual Sources*. London: Bloomsbury.
Voigtländer, Nico, and Hans-Joachim Voth. 2012. "Persecution Perpetuated: The Medieval Origins of Anti-Semitic Violence in Nazi Germany." *Quarterly Journal of Economics* 127 (3): 1339–92.
Wilkinson, Steven L. 2004. *Votes and Violence: Electoral Competition and Ethnic Riots in India*. Cambridge: Cambridge University Press.
Williams, Robin. 1994. "The Sociology of Ethnic Conflicts: Comparative International Perspectives." *Annual Review of Sociology* 20 (1): 49–79.
Wimmer, Andreas. 2002. *Nationalist Exclusion and Ethnic Conflict: Shadows of Modernity*. Cambridge: Cambridge University Press.
Zender, Matthias. 1958. *Atlas der deutschen Volkskunde: Neue Folge*. Marburg: Elwert.

8

DEFEATING TYPHUS IN THE WARSAW GHETTO

A Scientific Look at Historical Sources

Lewi Stone and Stephan Lehnstaedt

The genocide of European Jews in World War II was carried out not only directly by bullets and in extermination camps, but also indirectly by the conditions that the Germans imposed on the Jews: the combination of starvation, disease, and work to total exhaustion proved fatal for hundreds of thousands. This was true in almost all camps and ghettos, the size of which also determined the death rates.

In Warsaw, the site of the largest ghetto in German-occupied Eastern Europe, with at times almost 450,000 people, approximately 100,000 died before deportations to the gas chambers at the Treblinka extermination camp began in July 1942 (Berestein and Rutkowski 1958). A major typhus epidemic that broke out in 1941 proved to be catastrophic. Our chapter examines the causes of its occurrence, its course, and its end. This is of particular relevance given the COVID-19 pandemic that began in 2020, since the lethality and contagiousness of typhus also gave it pandemic status in Europe at the time. Yet very few studies have set out to document, in a quantitative manner, the course of the typhus epidemic in the Warsaw ghetto.

Based on the historical sources, we first try to reassess the number of individuals who were infected over the course of the typhus epidemic and the number of those who died. We do this by making use of a detailed study of the often-contradictory literature, combined with mathematical principles commonly used in epidemiological modeling. Subsequently, we search for explanations for the end of the epidemic at the beginning of winter 1941–42, an occurrence considered completely surprising and inexplicable at the time. Our findings assess the commitment and actions of the Judenrat and the devotion and success of the ghetto's professional medical practitioners.

Typhus and the Germans before the Holocaust

Wars and epidemics have a centuries-old common history. Wandering armies, the many dead, the lack of hygiene and crowded living conditions, and, last but not least, the hunger and starvation, all offered ideal conditions for the spread of dangerous contagious diseases. Typhus (not to be confused with typhoid fever) is one of the most notorious. Although believed to be present already in ancient times, it was first described as an independent disease with tens of thousands of dead during Napoleon's invasion of Russia in the nineteenth century (Vasold 2004).

From the biological viewpoint, typhus is a bacterium (*Rickettsia prowazekii*) spread by its vector, the human body louse (*Pediculus humanus humanus*), which transmits the disease to its human host. The lice multiply prolifically under conditions of poor hygiene, filth, overcrowding, and cold weather. They have a twelve-day life cycle and embed themselves in the clothes of the human host, their victim. They bite the host four to six times a day to consume blood and lay eggs. The thousands of lice biting at the same time can cause major irritation and itching, especially since the bites can cause an allergic and inflammatory reaction. The itching encourages the human host to scratch, which in turn can lead to breaks in the skin. The typhus bacterium is then passed via the infected feces of the lice, as it enters the host's body through the scratches. When the host dies, the lice search for a new host, thereby spreading the disease.

Lice are incapable of jumping, flying, or rapid movements, so while the host is alive they spread largely through human contact. This helps explain why typhus outbreaks most commonly occur in situations where large groups of people live in unsanitary conditions, such as in periods of war, famine, or natural disasters. Confined areas such as prisons, refugee centers, and slums are particularly notorious for typhus epidemics.

After the host is infected, symptoms usually appear in twelve to fourteen days, the typical incubation period. Often a high fever develops with headache, muscle pains, and/or nausea. On many occasions, and in the Warsaw ghetto, abdominal pains were mistaken for appendicitis and sufferers had their appendices needlessly removed. Another common symptom is the purple rash that appears extensively on the body of the host. As the disease progresses, the victim becomes weak and sometimes delirious, and this may lead to unconsciousness or a coma. Death can result, sometimes even within a few days for the worst cases, with death rates of 20–40 percent being the norm. Death rates may be higher in poor, undernourished populations. Suicides are not unheard of, with reports of sufferers jumping through windows in agony.

Little was known scientifically about typhus until 1903. At that time, the French scientist Dr. Charles Nicolle became director of the Pasteur Institute in Tunis and devoted his research to understanding the transmission of typhus. As part of his daily routine, it was not uncommon for Nicolle to step over dead bodies of typhus-infected patients that lay at the entrance of his medical clinic. From witnessing how bathing and a change of clothes appeared to stop diseased patients from infecting others, in 1915, through scientific tests, Nicolle finally reached the conclusion that lice spread the disease (Schultz and Morens 2009). This was an important breakthrough because typhus spread through most of Europe especially in the cold winters, killing millions of people and crossing national and continental boundaries. Nicolle was awarded the Nobel Prize in 1928 for his work.

The First World War brought a new, catastrophic outbreak of the disease. In Serbia and among the Austro-Hungarian troops and their prisoners, approximately 150,000 fell ill with the disease, and about 30,000 of them died in the first few months of 1915 (Soubbotitch 1918, 33). Typhus did not remain isolated in prisoner-of-war camps. In 1918–22, an epidemic in revolutionary Russia claimed an estimated two and a half million lives (Mühlens 1923, 21). In the eyes of racists, these occurrences provided further proof that Eastern Europeans were teeming with vermin and constituted a dangerous risk.

Moreover, antisemites considered Jews to be the main disease vectors. Jews were commonly portrayed with lice hidden in their caftans and beards in the most demonizing way. Religious male Jews frequently considered their beards an important part of their religious identity. The occupying Germans quickly seized on this and forced many to shave as a form of entertainment, while justifying it on "scientific" grounds. Typhus provided the opportunity to breathe new life into classical antisemitic prejudices. The Germans had, in fact, already initiated hygiene programs for Jews in the occupied East during World War I, in essence declaring Judaism to be unhygienic (Weindling 2000, 97–104).

Revisionist Germans attributed Germany's defeat in World War I to a "stab in the back" from those who opposed the war and, for nationalist devotees of a vision of national purity, to hygiene. In the democratic Weimar Republic, such patterns of interpretation had little practical relevance, but they were eagerly taken up and developed further by all opponents of the "system," not least by Adolf Hitler and his National Socialists. His antisemitism combined a pseudoscientific racial doctrine with ideas of hygiene, in which the Jews were no longer regarded as mere carriers of disease, but became the disease itself. As early as

1925 in *Mein Kampf*, Hitler had called the Jews "parasites" and written, "One has ruthlessly to use all military means to annihilate this pestilence" (Hitler 2016, 473; Weindling 1989, 489–92).

After 1933, this prejudice became a government program and Jew hatred became official politics, without, of course, limiting itself to its medical manifestation. To cleanse the *Volkskörper* (people's body), the National Socialists initially enforced the emigration of Jews. At the same time, they prepared for war to revise the borders of 1918 and secure "living space" in the East. There they would encounter millions of Slavs and Jews, and for each a corresponding population policy had to be developed. Scientists like Peter-Heinz Seraphim (1938) wrote the basic doctrine on this matter. In his study titled *Jewry in Eastern European Space*, he elaborated the notion of an eternal struggle between Jews and Christians over the rule of cities and, more generally, the world. He argued that Jews had settled in core areas of towns—in ghettos—and then spread slowly but steadily, subjugating other urban inhabitants. In his eyes, ghettos constituted out-of-control incubators of a Jewish "disease," overflowing with crime and epidemics. Leading SS officials thoroughly absorbed Seraphim's work; his interpretation provided the grounds for Reinhard Heydrich's initial refusal of Hermann Göring's proposal to erect new ghettos (Michman 2011, 45–60).

Notwithstanding his reservations, on September 21, 1939, Heydrich, as head of the SS Reichssicherheitshauptamt (Reich Security Main Office), wrote in his infamous "Schnellbrief" about "concentrating" the Jews of occupied Poland (Friedrich 2011, 88–93). He did not call these residential patterns "ghettos" but "concentration cities," where Jews from the surrounding area were to be gathered in order to deport them from the Polish western territories further to the east. This temporary approach differed from Göring's 1938 idea, as Heydrich already envisaged deportations and thus avoided establishing ghettos in each place Jews resided. Ghettos were to be for larger towns, while rural Jewish communities were to be dissolved entirely (Lehnstaedt 2016).

It remains an unresolvable paradox that even for the National Socialists, ghettos were on the one hand a cause of disease, but on the other hand a "necessary" measure to prevent its spread. The actual ghettoization therefore depended very much on the regional occupying authorities. In Warsaw in particular, the fear of typhus can be identified as the central motivation, as the overcrowded and poor parts of the city center mainly inhabited by Jews were seen as a potential source of epidemics. In November 1939, this paranoia about disease motivated the establishment of a *Seuchensperrgebiet* (epidemic exclusion zone), which German soldiers were prohibited from entering. The *Warschauer Zeitung* wrote of "parasites" and "hygienically unsound subjects, whose faces reflect inferiority."[1] And so the residential segregation of Jews was understood as a service to the Gentile community, defending them from disease and dirt. These were powerful stereotypes and German doctors therefore urged the formation of ghettos (Walbaum 1942). Protecting the health of Jews was not a consideration, which explains why better nutrition or housing conditions were rarely proposed (Browning 1988, 21–23). In fact, German plans called for extracting as much food as possible from occupied Poland. Jews, therefore, would be left to starve.

The arguments reinforced themselves, for example when the head of the health administration in the *Generalgouvernement*, Jost Walbaum, noted in May 1940 the eradication of typhus in annexed western Poland because the Jews there had been deported to the East—where the disease now posed a greater threat. In Warsaw, when previous measures failed to offer significant protection, the health administration pressed for the erection of an "epidemic wall" (Weindling 2000, 274). In November 1940 this became a reality. Warsaw's Jews were now crammed into an area of initially about 307 hectares (3.07 square kilometers) designated as a ghetto. Poles living there were expelled (Sakowska 1999, 37, 55–57). The resulting prohibition of contact between the Jewish and Polish populations placed a heavy economic burden on the ghetto, already an object of German plunder: the means to obtain sufficient food, hygiene products, and medicines all but disappeared.

Of course, doctors were not alone in pushing for the ghettoization of the Jews—but in the case of Warsaw they were the driving force. They lobbied incessantly for separation and repeatedly combined medical arguments with economic and racial antisemitism (Browning 1988, 23). At the same time, they promoted typhus research in Warsaw's State Hygiene Institute, where Robert Kudicke had replaced Ludwik Hirszfeld, the eminent Polish-Jewish bacteriologist and Nobel Prize nominee, who moved to the ghetto with other colleagues. The Kudicke-led institute, however, never achieved any major research successes (Werther 2004, 58–60).

Typhus in the Warsaw Ghetto

Under the disastrous conditions created by the Germans, typhus appeared and began to develop into an epidemic. Concern grew when some 70,000 Jews from the surrounding towns were forced into the ghetto in winter 1940–41, increasing the already existing problems of overpopulation and lack of supplies. By May 1941, the ghetto's population swelled to some 440,000. Hirszfeld had no doubts about what lay ahead. In an ironic counterpoise to the German view, he noted that during World War II, typhus was created by the Germans, precipitated by lack of food, soap, and water: "You could say that typhus is a German disease, because in our country, it was remarkably correlated with German occupation. When one concentrates 400,000 wretches in one district, takes everything away from them, and gives them nothing, then one creates typhus. In this war, typhus is the doing of the Germans" (Hirszfeld 2010, 211).

Table 8.1 shows the official registered dataset specifying monthly cases of typhus in the Warsaw ghetto. The dataset indicates a total of 20,370 typhus cases between the ghetto's opening in 1939 and the deportations to Treblinka in July 1942. This constituted less than 5 percent of the ghetto's population and consisted of 1,842 cases that occurred in the minor epidemic of 1940, and 18,528 cases for the larger second epidemic, mostly in 1941. The latter outbreak erupted almost immediately after the ghetto was sealed in November 1940. Chaim Kaplan, in his diary of the Warsaw ghetto, noted, "Typhus is destroying us and them. When two friends meet and one tells the other of the illness of a third, he never identifies the disease, for that is understood anyway; it must be the sickness that is now prevalent. The same applies when anyone dies; the cause must be typhus. The number of fatalities is enormous. Some families have lost half their number. Everyone knows someone who has succumbed to this horrible disease and there is no end to the toll it is taking" (Katsh 1999, 269). Many similar descriptions strongly indicate that the total number infected was far greater than 5 percent of the population, as reported in the Judenrat statistics.

In fact, the official dataset of the numbers infected conflicts with reports from all of the best epidemiologists and medical professionals in the ghetto, who suggest that there were far more. Here we can provide definitive and unequivocal evidence for the true typhus case numbers. Professor Jakub Penson, head of the typhus ward at the ghetto's main hospital on Czyste Street, wrote in his war crimes testimony that "another epidemic broke out in June 1941 and continued until June 1942. It spread not only in 'transit camps' [for] homeless people, like the first epidemic had done, but it swept all over the Ghetto, infecting about 100,000 people. This epidemic was a lot more acute than the first one, with a

TABLE 8.1 Registered official reported monthly cases of typhus compiled by the Judenrat

REPORTED	JAN	FEB	MARCH	APRIL	MAY	JUNE	JULY	AUG	SEPT	OCT	NOV	DEC
1939												88
1940	191	214	3398	407	335	123	68	18	0	0	0	0
1941	57	129	201	241	367	841	1,742	1,805	2,492	3,438	2,156	1,980
1942	1,220	787	478	319	208	67						

Note: The true number of cases was four to five times larger, according to medical reports (see text).

Sources: Reports for the Germans by the Warsaw Judenrat. Jan Grabowski, ed., *Ludność żydowska w Warszawie w latach 1939–1943: Życie—walka—zagłada* (Warsaw: DiG, 2012); statistics for 1941 alone on p. 859.

death rate of 20 per cent (in the first one it was 10 per cent); during that time, about 20,000 people died of typhus" (Penson 1946).

Dr. Mordechai Lenski, who was on location in the ghetto hospitals, wrote that "according to my estimate, the number of [typhus] patients should be set at about 100,000." He added, "From September 1939 to September 1942, 80,000 persons died of disease, and of these, 18,000 died of starvation" (Lenski 1975, 288). Dr. Henryk Fenigstein, another physician from the Warsaw ghetto and its hospital, suggested that by November 1941, some 15 percent of ghetto inmates had typhus—or roughly 70,000 people (Roland 1992, 137).

With so many dying and ill, it is no wonder that the huge outbreak of the typhus epidemic was also noted by some who were not medical experts. The ghetto chronicler Emmanuel Ringelblum wrote on August 26, 1941, "Now, the middle of August, there are some six or seven thousand patients in [private] apartments, and about nine hundred in hospitals" (Sloan 1958, 155). This was repeated by the economist Jerzy Winkler, from the Judenrat's Statistical Division, who wrote that "to understand the numbers and the intensity of typhus, doctors say that the actual number of typhus patients treated secretly at home was 7 times higher" (Winkler 1942, 15). Note that according to the official numbers in table 8.1, there were 1,805 typhus cases in August 1941, which is 25 percent of the more accurate estimate of cases mentioned by Ringelblum (7,000–8,000 cases). This again provides support for estimating a reporting rate in the vicinity of 25 percent.

Of course, the German occupiers repeatedly commented on health conditions in the ghetto. But only a few of them, like Wilhelm Hagen, the chief medical officer in Warsaw and a trained epidemiologist who specialized in typhus and tuberculosis, really understood what was going on. Hagen estimated that 20–25 percent of typhus cases were reported (Hagen 1978, 179–81).

It seems very reasonable to accept an estimate of approximately 25 percent for the reporting rate: since some 18,530 cases were reported for the major epidemic, this implies a true typhus case count of 74,000 to 93,000 for the larger of the two epidemics. These numbers were further confirmed by historians after the war. Thus in 1971, the medical historian Dr. Ryszard Zabłotniak (1971, 4), when reviewing the professional epidemiological literature, suggested that "over 100,000 persons suffered from this disease. In all likelihood about 25,000 Jews died of typhus." Professor Yisrael Gutman, a historian of the ghetto who reviewed many accounts and further material, wrote that "in the course of that year [1941] 14,661 [typhus] cases were reported, but for all practical purposes even this official figure is far from exact, and it is assumed to have represented only 25 to 30 percent of the actual number of cases (some estimates go as high as over 100,000 cases)" (Gutman 1989, 106).

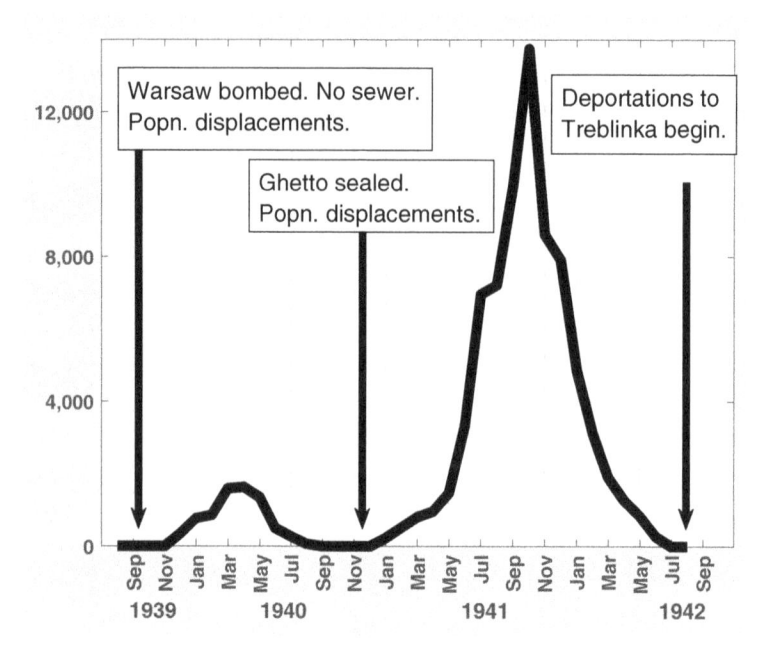

FIGURE 8.1. Typhus epidemics in the Warsaw ghetto: the number of new monthly "reconstructed" typhus cases

We have plotted the Judenrat data from table 8.1 after assuming this 25 percent reporting rate. (That is, the registered data in table 8.1 are multiplied by a factor of four.) The resulting graph in figure 8.1 thus gives an indication of the population dynamics of the typhus epidemic as it evolved over time. The underlying assumption here is that at least the trend in the official registered case numbers is a reasonable proxy (up to a scale factor) for the true numbers.

Fighting Typhus

With the German authorities most interested in the disease not spreading beyond the ghetto, the job of quelling the epidemic fell to the Judenrat. But this presented a dilemma. German responses to an outbreak could be draconian. The head of the ghetto, Adam Czerniaków, sought to avoid providing the Germans with a pretext for taking matters into their own hands. When they did, a single individual coming down with typhus would sometimes lead to quarantines for entire buildings containing hundreds of residents, lasting two or three weeks. During quarantine, food supplies were cut off for "infected" buildings. Most, if not all, Jewish medical doctors opposed the Nazis' brutal tactics in quarantining, bathing, and disinfecting, which in practice served only to humiliate the Jewish residents rather than to improve the situation.[2] As Hirszfeld (2010, 195) wrote, "Did not sealing houses for three weeks mean death by starvation for most people? And the disinfection was carried out in such a way that it destroyed everything. Did that not mean complete ruin?" He argued that the Nazi approach was intended "only to cover up a new barbaric act"—namely, ghettoization itself.

The fear of German "countermeasures" to the epidemic—which in the view of the Germans merely proved that all Jews were notorious spreaders of disease—also severely suppressed the numbers of officially reported cases of typhus (see table 8.1). It was more prudent for the Judenrat to "fudge" the numbers in this way. After all, when typhus cases appeared in August 1941 in the Kovno ghetto, the Nazis burned to the ground the entire ghetto hospital together with its living doctors, nurses, and patients (Baumslag 2005, 107). Warsaw's Jewish leaders clearly understood that the presence of typhus was not something to advertise.

In the Warsaw ghetto, doctors and nurses tended to the sick to the point of complete physical and mental exhaustion. All official measures required permission from the Germans, who had placed the ghetto under the authority of the Warsaw district authorities. Warsaw's German *Stadthauptmann* [city major] was subordinate to the Health Department. That department included a municipal medical officer—from February 1941 to February 1943 the aforementioned Wilhelm Hagen, who formally supervised the ghetto's health care system but without actually being privy to all of the details (Engelking and Leociak 2009, 234).

Hagen's approach later in 1941 became quite pragmatic. He frequently accepted suggestions from the medical authorities of the ghetto, such as Hirszfeld's plea to care for typhus patients at home if at all possible, so that a further spread in the completely overburdened hospitals would be prevented; the quarantine then only affected individual apartments. Hagen also permitted the extensive lectures that Hirszfeld held twice per week for several hundred doctors and numerous nurses, ostensibly exclusively for the prevention of epidemics, but actually regarding treatment as well.

These lectures indicate the presence of an unofficial health care system that paralleled the official one. The latter emanated from the Health Department of the Jewish Council (Department XV), under Dr. Izrael Milejkowski, and included not only the hospital on Czyste Street and the Bersohn and Bauman Children's Hospital, but also several smaller health centers. It was financed by an extra tax levied by the Judenrat on the ghetto, a tax that was also used to finance a smaller laboratory to conduct research especially on epidemics and malnutrition.

A Health Council was initially an advisory group, but its members later worked as managers. The council was later headed by Hirszfeld—whose appointment was met with enthusiasm by the doctors who had previously been involved there (Engelking and Leociak 2009, 234).

An estimated 46,500 people worked in the ghetto's health sector in the summer of 1942, including some 800 doctors of various specialties, most of whom received private patients to supplement their income. In addition, there were more than a dozen pharmacies, all under the control of the Judenrat. The pharmacies were charged with rationing the drug supply, but the Germans allowed only a fraction of what was needed to enter the ghetto. An experimental vaccination was also sporadically available to some in the ghetto, but this was expensive, difficult to obtain, and often ineffective (Allen 2014).

Little else remained to fight typhus but draconian hygiene measures enforced by the house committees and resulting in constant inspections by Judenrat employees: they inspected for dirty kitchens and toilets, bed sheets, and dishes, and emphasized proper food storage. Homes were fumigated, but these measures were unpopular and, in the eyes of epidemiologists like Hirszfeld, not very useful. Inspections and fumigation may have worked with minor local outbreaks but were ineffective in ghetto conditions (Engelking and Leociak 2009, 237–39, 283).

Theories for Explaining the Epidemic's Unexpected Collapse in Late October 1941

The curtailing of the epidemic at the end of October 1941, as seen in figure 8.1, remains an enigma, puzzling both ghetto doctors and chroniclers. In a previous article (Stone et al. 2020), we used state-of-the-art epidemiological modeling to try to understand this decline at the beginning of winter, exactly when typhus should have accelerated. We found it impossible to fit the dataset in figure 8.1 using realistic epidemiological parameters. A good fit could be achieved only if we assumed that more than three hundred thousand ghetto residents were infected with typhus over the period of the epidemic. But as we know from the above, such a count would be three times larger than the actual number of infected residents. Further modeling led to the conclusion that there must have been an epidemiological or behavioral intervention that led to the epidemic's demise in the months before November 1941. In fact, our modeling revealed that in the absence of this intervention, the typhus epidemic would have been far larger—possibly three times larger—and would have continued on through winter, peaking in January.

The decline is not due to some irregularity or inaccuracy in data collection (see table 8.1). Regarding the unusual curtailment of the epidemic, Ludwik Hirszfeld (2010, 216) writes that "by a peculiar coincidence the epidemic began to decline when the new Health Council was organized. We tried to ensure that outbreaks centered in specific buildings and apartments ebbed spontaneously [rather like contact tracing and isolation]. We didn't spread the epidemic by taking totally inappropriate measures. I don't think however that this was the only reason for the decline. But public opinion ascribed the improvement to the new leadership and the new spirit in the Health Council."

Confirming again the unusual curtailment, Emmanuel Ringelblum stated clearly in his November 1941 note, "The typhus epidemic has diminished somewhat—just in the winter, when it generally gets worse. The epidemic rate has fallen some 40 percent. I heard this from the apothecaries, and the same thing from the doctors and the hospitals. This is really an irrational phenomenon; there's no explaining it rationally. The only possible explanation is that most of the people in the refugee centers, which are the chief centers of the epidemic, have already had the disease. Another explanation is that poor people wear heavy clothing in the winter, so the lice can't get at them easily. At any rate the epidemic has lessened" (Sloan 1958, 229).

Including Hirszfeld's response above, there are several alternative arguments mentioned by Ringelblum and others as to why the epidemic diminished:

1. The simplest and most common hypothesis advanced is that the course of the epidemic fits the characteristic pattern of all epidemics and died out naturally. For example, Lenski writes that "the fall of the epidemic on its own, without improvement in the sanitary conditions, surprised the medical doctors. It seems that in terms of the epidemiological dynamics there is a limit to an epidemic even when it occurs in the worst sanitary conditions" (Silberklang 2009, 127).

In our study (Stone et al. 2020), we examined this hypothesis carefully using classical epidemic modeling principles. As mentioned, the only way it is possible for the data of the major outbreak in 1941 to follow a standard epidemic curve is if more than three hundred thousand residents of the ghetto were infected in total. But such a possibility would contradict the opinion of all of the key epidemiologists in the ghetto: that roughly one hundred thousand people were infected. Furthermore, Lenski's explanation would imply that the epidemic died out naturally due to a lack of susceptibles remaining in the population that would be required to keep it going. But the modeling does not support this—it shows a plentiful supply of susceptibles at the end of the epidemic. Moreover, the 1941 outbreak was followed by another, third epidemic of typhus in late 1942. Given this occurrence, it is hard to accept that the 1941 outbreak depleted most of the susceptible population.

2. A second hypothesis, which Offer (2015, 347) attributes to Hirszfeld, is that in October 1941, "strangely the epidemic ... retracted spontaneously after around a third to half [of the] 450,000 residents became infected from the disease." We have been unable to locate this passage in Hirszfeld's writings. From our perspective, it appears to be erroneous, as it would imply that 150,000–220,000 residents were infected by October 1941 when the epidemic turned around and was then only 60 percent complete. It would also imply that typhus infected a total number between 250,000 and 366,000 residents. As we have shown, the total number never reached anything near this level by October 1941, and in reality was likely closer to a third of this number. We therefore reject this hypothesis.

3. A third hypothesis, somewhat related, is that, according to Offer (2015, 347), in Hirszfeld's "opinion, the reason for the latter [hypothesis 2] is that most of the workers and residents of refugee houses were infected (up to 100%), such that all of that specific population, which were the primary source of typhus, had already been infected, and the epidemic had retracted from there." This last possibility is interesting, but from the reading of diaries and statistics in the six regions of the ghetto, lice infestation was widespread and typhus was rampant everywhere, among rich and poor. The "first sparks of disease," noted Bernard Goldstein (1949, 73), "spread like a forest fire throughout the entire ghetto."

In fact it has often been pointed out that typhus affected the rich populations more than the poor (Trunk 1989, 18). Even if the refugee houses had all been infected, it is hard to accept that the epidemic would suddenly collapse overnight. In the period from January to October 1941, not more than 60,000–70,000 residents were infected. A disease like typhus would require at least 50 percent (~225,000) of the residents to become infected before the epidemic reaches its height and turns around from population herd immunity. It is hard to believe the refugee houses could have this impact when there were so many remaining susceptibles (~390,000) in the population and such poor conditions elsewhere in the ghetto.

Moreover, Hirszfeld (2010, 229) notes that in August 1941, "when I arrived in the district, there were still twelve thousand deportees alive, living in deportee houses," while official Judenrat statistics speak of 10,421 living in TOZ homes (Towarzystwo Ochrony Zdrowia Ludności Żydowskiej, or the Society for

Safeguarding the Health of the Jewish Population) in May 1941.[3] This is 3 percent or less of the full population of 450,000, and it is very unlikely that this 3 percent could be responsible for the crash in the epidemic.

But even if it were, one might ask why these 3 percent lost their infective ability by October or November 1941. It is understood that the living quarters of these "deathpoints," just like the poorest parts of the ghetto on Krochmalna Street, were being specifically targeted for cleanliness during the intense period of the epidemic (Roland 1992, 138).

Defeating Typhus in the Warsaw Ghetto: Some Explanations

There is no single explanation for the end of the epidemic in the Warsaw ghetto. Obviously the Germans deserve no credit. Instead it was the combination of several factors, each presenting challenges in measuring its relative effectiveness but each of which deserves mention.

Education

From May 1941, the Jewish Health Department and Health Council initiated a large number of sanitary courses for house wardens, covering a range of topics from human anatomy and public hygiene to infectious diseases. In July, courses in sanitary training started. Between February and August 1941 there were 264 talks on the fight against epidemics, with up to five hundred people attending each. There also were nineteen courses of sanitary training, in which more than nine hundred people participated (Engelking and Leociak 2009, 248–55).

Improved Food Rations

Initially the German ghetto administration was led by "attritionists" with the goal of liquidating the ghetto population through starvation. This changed in May 1941, when the new "productionist" ghetto commissioner, Heinz Auerswald, was appointed with the intention of building a self-sufficient and self-sustaining ghetto economy. The productionists believed that sources of labor should not be wasted and that therefore some component of the ghetto residents should be given minimal food and nutrition so they could work. Thus in mid-1941, the ghetto conditions improved with some increases in food aid. In addition, for a short period, Auerswald turned a blind eye to food smugglers (Browning 1988, 26).

This improved nutrition helped boost the resistance of the population to the disease, by strengthening the immune system of better-fed residents.

The community soup kitchens established by the Jewish self-help organizations were an important part of this story. According to Trunk's (1989, 12) account, "In April 1940 an average of 59,314 plates of soup were distributed daily; in July 1941 the number was 117,500. By the end of September the number came to nearly 130,000 plates of soup daily. Later the number declined.... In January 1942, the number was still 80,000 daily." As the historian Gutman (1989, 106) noted, "It would not be an exaggeration to state that in Jewish Warsaw, where almost one hundred thousand victims succumbed to death, mostly from starvation and disease, from the beginning of the war until July 1942, a similar or perhaps even greater number prevailed until that fatal date, owing largely or decisively to the dedicated aid of the corps of relief workers" and self-help relief agencies operating.

Disposal of Waste and General Hygiene

The Germans initially prohibited the disposal of rubbish and household waste. Thus as Stanisław Adler (1946) writes,

> The epidemic intensified not only because people were herded in from different places, or because of the cramped living conditions or extreme starvation resulting from the impossibility of regular provision of food, but also because, despite continual requests submitted by the *Judenrat* the Germans did not permit the disposal of rubbish and household waste. Month by month, in each courtyard, more and more piles of decomposing waste grew. The burning of rubbish or its transport into burnt-out buildings was a palliative which did not solve the problem at all. This situation did not change until the middle of 1941, when the Nazis eventually permitted waste disposal from the quarter.

Other examples of typhus epidemics have shown that, indeed, improved hygiene practices can curb an epidemic. For example, in the town of Shargorod in German-occupied Transnistria, which suffered a typhus epidemic in the ghetto in early 1942, once "a cleaning service and a workshop for the manufacture of soap had been established in the ghetto, as well as public lavatories and baths, the number of typhus victims dropped and the epidemic was curbed" (Arad 2009, 273).

An Awareness of Social Distancing

This last point is the most difficult to assess, though many prominent historians and diarists of the Warsaw ghetto comment on the awareness of social distancing.

Chaim Kaplan, for instance, wrote in October 1941, "Last year permission was granted to open the schools but this was never put into effect. The reason given then was the typhus epidemic which was still raging through the ghetto. A large concentration of children in one place would be likely to spread the disease. On the face of it, this seemed a justifiable argument. But it was ... [more the Nazis'] desire to deprive Jewish children of an education" (Katsh 1999, 273). The public schools reopened in October 1941. The Judenrat, Kaplan recorded, "expected a large enrolment but they were disappointed. The poor cannot afford the fees, and the well-to-do are afraid to expose their children to the children of the poor, who might be carriers of disease" (273). And in another passage: "There is a great confusion of pedestrians, street vendors, overloaded porters, carriages and delivery carts, beggars and all sorts of creatures whose proximity you cannot bear for fear of lice. The fear of lice obsesses all of us, for the tiny creatures are the carriers of typhus" (128).

Stanisław Adler pointed out that

> the extent of the traffic and masses of people who used this artery cannot be described and these crowded conditions contributed greatly to the spread of the typhus epidemic which decimated the Quarter.... Lice infestation was everywhere. Merely walking a hundred meters along the street exposed one to great danger. One had only to brush against a person infested with lice to discover these dangerous vermin in the evening while examining each piece of clothing; ... The children of the streets contributed most to the spread of the epidemic. They were everywhere, running at dizzying speed through the crowds, rubbing against every pedestrian. (Adler 1982, 33–35)

"From time to time," he also wrote, "somebody passing by brushes against me. I am horrified because so many people are infected with lice.... The danger of that infection [typhus] terrifies me" (Adler 1982, 304).

This fear and need to distance was well observed by others too. Bernard Goldstein (1949, 80) recalled, "The street was packed with people: death, death, and more death; yet there was no end to the overcrowding. People elbowed their way through the noisy throngs, fearing to touch each other, for they might be touching typhus." And even younger ghetto inhabitants like Mary Berg (2007, 66) commented on social distancing: "The chief carrier of this terrible disease [typhus] is the clothes louse, and it is hard to avoid encountering this repulsive insect. It is enough to walk in the street and rub against someone in the crowd to become infested."

During the COVID-19 pandemic, we have come to understand the vast destructive powers of contagious diseases and their ability to inflict massive damage on human populations—huge death tolls, the tearing apart of societies, the resulting chaos on the scale of nations, and the disruption of global order. We pay more attention to the role of public health and the science of epidemiology. In this chapter, we have tried to demonstrate how epidemics and pandemics had similar impacts during World War II and in the Holocaust in particular. This phenomenon is poorly understood and rarely discussed in the literature.

The schematic in figure 8.1 encapsulates some of the key points we have made. The figure and the timeline visually illustrate the unusual way in which history and disease intersected in the Warsaw ghetto period (1940–42).

In a cruel but perhaps predictable irony, many of the Germans' harshest measures regarding the ghetto and the epidemic coincided with the most sacred Jewish holidays. The bombing of Warsaw, particularly the Jewish areas, in September 1939 was especially strong on Rosh Hashanah and Yom Kippur, and this was followed by a minor typhus outbreak as the sewer system was destroyed. The synagogues were closed in January 1940 to prevent the spreading of epidemics. On Yom Kippur, October 12, 1940, the establishment and opening of the ghetto were officially announced. When the ghetto was sealed in November 1940, it was a matter of two months before the first typhus cases arrived with the large numbers of refugees forcibly resettled into the ghetto. The sealing of ghettos severed all economic ties with the outside world. Additionally, food was cut off, and death by starvation ensued so that by March 1941, many thousands were dying per month. When combined with overcrowding and lack of basic sanitation resources, this set off a massive typhus outbreak—the very epidemic the Germans feared yet created by their own actions.

The outbreak peaked in November 1941 and was curtailed presumably due to the anti-epidemic efforts of the Jewish Health Council, the ghetto's doctors and health workers, and the efforts of the voluntary aid organizations. While difficult to prove definitively, examining the epidemic dynamics "under the microscope" makes it seem unlikely that the epidemic ebbed by chance or because it naturally "burned out." In the absence of anti-epidemic efforts, the epidemic would have been three times as large and would have peaked only in January 1942.

Returning to figure 8.1, we see that the very last embers of the epidemic still burned in June 1942. It was at this point, on July 22, after about 100,000 ghetto Jews had died from disease and starvation, that the Nazis initiated their new and efficient "fast-track" method to exterminate the Warsaw ghetto population. On Tisha B'Av (July 22), the day marking the calamity of the destruction of the First and Second Temples in Jerusalem (traditionally considered the saddest day of the Jewish calendar), deportations to the gas chambers of Treblinka began. Within less than two months, more than 260,000 Jews from the Warsaw ghetto had been taken by train to Treblinka and exterminated in this mass-killing center.

As Ryszard Zabłotniak (1971, 10) emphasized, the enormous efforts made in the health sphere during the fateful years of 1941 and 1942 in the Warsaw ghetto were at the insistence of the Jewish Health Council, "so that future generations could not say we stood by and did nothing."

REFERENCES

Adler, Stanisław. 1946. "Testimony for the Warsaw District Commission for the Investigation of German Crimes." Chronicles of Terror. https://zapisyterroru.pl/dlibra/results?q=adler&action=SimpleSearchAction&mdirids=&type=-6&startstr=_all&p=0.

———. 1982. *In the Warsaw Ghetto, 1940–1943: An Account of a Witness; The Memoirs of Stanislaw Adler*. Jerusalem: Yad Vashem.

Allen, Arthur. 2014. *The Fantastic Laboratory of Dr. Weigl: How Two Brave Scientists Battled Typhus and Sabotaged the Nazis*. New York: W. W. Norton.

Arad, Yitzhak. 2009. *The Holocaust in the Soviet Union*. Lincoln: University of Nebraska Press.

Baumslag, Naomi. 2005. *Murderous Medicine: Nazi Doctors, Human Experimentation, and Typhus*. Westport, CT: Praeger.

Berestein, Tatjana, and Adam Rutkowski. 1958. "Liczba ludności żydowskiej i obszar przez nią zamieszkiwany w Warszawie w latach okupacji hitlerowskiej." *Biuletyn Żydowskiego Instytutu Historycznego* 26:73–114.

Berg, Mary. 2007. *The Diary of Mary Berg: Growing Up in the Warsaw Ghetto*. Oxford: Oneworld.

Browning, Christopher. 1988. "Genocide and Public Health: German Doctors and Polish Jews, 1939–41." *Holocaust and Genocide Studies* 3 (1): 21–36.

Engelking, Barbara, and Jacek Leociak. 2009. *The Warsaw Ghetto: A Guide to the Perished City*. New Haven, CT: Yale University Press.

Friedrich, Klaus-Peter, ed. 2011. *Die Verfolgung und Ermordung der europäischen Juden durch das nationalsozialistische Deutschland*. Vol. 4, *Polen, September 1939–Juli 1941*. Munich: Oldenbourg.

Goldstein, Bernard. 1949. *The Stars Bear Witness*. New York: Viking.

Gutman, Yisrael. 1989. *The Jews of Warsaw, 1939–1943: Ghetto, Underground, Revolt*. Bloomington: Indiana University Press.

Hagen, Wilhelm. 1978. *Auftrag und Wirklichkeit: Sozialarzt im 20. Jahrhundert*. Munich: Banaschewski.

Hirszfeld, Ludwik. 2010. *The Story of One Life*. Translated and edited by Marta A. Balińska and William H. Schneider. Rochester, NY: University of Rochester Press.

Hitler, Adolf. *Mein Kampf*. 2016. Edited by Christian Hartmann, Thomas Vordermayer, Othmar Plöckinger, and Roman Töppel. Munich-Berlin: Institut für Zeitgeschichte.

Katsh, Abraham, ed. 1999. *Scroll of Agony: The Warsaw Diary of Chaim A. Kaplan*. Bloomington: Indiana University Press.

Lehnstaedt, Stephan. 2016. "Jewish Spaces? Defining Nazi Ghettos Then and Now." *Polish Review* 61 (4): 41–56.

Lenski, Moredecai. 1975. "Problems of Disease in the Warsaw Ghetto." *Yad Vashem Studies* 3:283–93.

Michman, Dan. 2011. *The Emergence of Jewish Ghettos during the Holocaust*. Cambridge: Cambridge University Press.

Mühlens, Peter. 1923. "Die russische Hunger- und Seuchenkatastrophe in den Jahren 1921–22." *Zeitschrift für Hygiene und Infektionskrankheiten* 99:1–45.
Offer, Miriam. 2015. *White Coats inside the Ghetto: Jewish Medicine in Poland during the Holocaust*. [In Hebrew.] Jerusalem: Yad Vashem.
Penson, Jakub. 1946. "Testimony for the Łódź District Commission for the Investigation of German Crimes." Chronicles of Terror. https://www.chroniclesofterror.pl/dlibra/results?q=penson&action=SimpleSearchAction&mdirids=&type=-6&startstr=_all&p=0.
Roland, Charles G. 1992. *Courage under Siege: Starvation, Disease and Death in the Warsaw Ghetto*. Oxford: Oxford University Press.
Sakowska, Ruta. 1999. *Menschen im Ghetto: Die jüdische Bevölkerung im besetzten Warschau 1939–1943*. Osnabrück: Fibre.
Schultz, Myron G., and David M. Morens. 2009. "Charles-Jules-Henri Nicolle." *Emerging Infectious Diseases* 15 (9): 1519–22.
Seraphim, Peter-Heinz. 1938. *Das Judentum im osteuropäischen Raum*. Essen: Essener Verlagsanstalt.
Silberklang, David, ed. 2009. *Mordechai Lenski: A Physician inside the Warsaw Ghetto*. Jerusalem: Yad Vashem.
Sloan, Jacob, ed. 1958. *Notes from the Warsaw Ghetto: From the Journal of Emmanuel Ringelblum*. New York: McGraw-Hill.
Soubbotitch, Voyislav. 1918. "A Pandemic of Typhus in Serbia in 1914 and 1915." *Proceedings of the Royal Society of Medicine* 11:31–39.
Stone, Lewi, Daihai He, Stephan Lehnstaedt, and Yael Artzy-Randrup. 2020. "Extraordinary Curtailment of Massive Typhus Epidemic in the Warsaw Ghetto." *Science Advances* 6 (30): eabc0927.
Trunk, Isaiah. 1989. *Epidemics and Mortality in the Warsaw Ghetto, 1939–1942*. Berlin: De Gruyter Saur.
Vasold, Manfred. 2004. "Die Fleckfieberepidemie von 1813/14 im mainfränkischen Raum." *Würzburger medizinhistorische Mitteilungen* 23:217–32.
Walbaum, Jost. 1942. "Gesundheitswesen." In *Das Generalgouvernement*, edited by Max du Prel, 190–94. Würzburg: Triltsch.
Weindling, Paul. 1989. *Health, Race and German Politics between National Unification and Nazism, 1870–1945*. Cambridge: Cambridge University Press.
———. 2000. *Epidemics and Genocide in Eastern Europe: 1890–1945*. Oxford: Oxford University Press.
Werther, Thomas. 2004. "Fleckfieberforschung im Deutschen Reich 1914–1945: Untersuchungen zur Beziehung zwischen Wissenschaft, Industrie und Politik unter besonderer Berücksichtigung der IG Farben." PhD diss., Marburg University.
Winkler, Jerzy. 1945. "Gehenna Żydów Polskich pod okupacją hitlerowską." Żydowski Instytut Historyczny Warsaw, ARing I/45.
Zabłotniak, Ryszard. 1971. "Epidemia duru plamistego wśród ludności Żydowskiej w Warszawie w latach II wojny światowej." *Biuletyn Żydowskiego Instytutu Historycznego* 80:3–22.

9

HOLOCAUST SURVIVAL AMONG IMMIGRANT JEWS IN THE NETHERLANDS

A Life Course Approach

Peter Tammes and Andrew J. Simpkin

In many academic studies on the Holocaust, the focus has been on the initiators and perpetrators (namely, the Nazis and their collaborators), the circumstances under which Jews were persecuted involving bystanders and locality-level characteristics, or resistance and rescuers. This has resulted in detailed descriptive studies on the Nazi occupation, the actors involved, and the destruction process of Jews, and, less commonly, in comparative studies associating national or local factors with survival rates. A relatively recent development in Holocaust research is the emphasis on microhistory to be able to study Jewish agency or Jewish responses to the Nazi persecution (e.g., Finkel 2017; Stone 2017; Zalc and Bruttmann 2016).

Despite the Nazis' ideology and their "machinery" to identify, isolate, deport, and kill Jews (Hilberg 1985, 54), many Jews living in Nazi-occupied territory survived. It seems therefore appropriate to study differences in survival from the perspective of the victims, the individual Jews, and to follow their (re)actions in response to life-threatening events and situations they faced during the Nazi regime. Within social history, the social sciences, demography, and epidemiology, the life course approach is often used to study the impact of a change in position, role, or status on a certain outcome. This chapter's aim is to improve our understanding of differences in Jewish survival chances by applying a life course approach.

Our objective is to examine whether immigrant Jews in the Netherlands had different experiences related to isolation, deportation, and victimization than Dutch-born Jews. Examining differences in these experiences could reveal underlying mechanisms for Jewish immigrants' better survival chances, as shown in previous studies (e.g., Tammes 2007). Using immigrants' motives, opportunities, and restrictions in the life course approach, we formulated hypotheses on Jewish immigrants' experiences during the Nazi persecution. To test these hypotheses, we used data from administrative sources to construct life histories for about 1,300 Jews, including both survivors and victims, living in eight Dutch municipalities before the beginning of systematic or regular deportations to concentration and destruction Nazi camps abroad in July 1942. Logistic regression and survival analyses were used to analyze these data.

A Life Course Approach to the Study of Holocaust Survival

A life course approach explores the continuity and change of human lives in relation to personal connections, social structure, and historical forces (Elder, Johnson, and Crosnoe 2003). The life courses of humans are life trajectories, and these are made up of transitions (Elder, Johnson, and Crosnoe 2003). A transition often involves changes in position, role, or status—for example, leaving the parental home, becoming a parent, or retiring (Elder, Johnson, and Crosnoe 2003). Turning points involve a substantial change in the direction of one's life—for example, returning to school during midlife.

This chapter's focus is on the life trajectories of Jews under the Nazi regime. These trajectories were embedded in the context of intensifying stages in the Nazi persecution of Jews, such as political-legal discrimination, the appropriation of Jewish assets, the isolation of Jews, and destruction as the final stage (Hilberg 1985, 54). Others, such as Fein (1979, 62, 266), refined these stages, stating that discrimination was possible only after the identification and registration of Jews, and isolation only after the segregation of Jews. Despite the Nazi ideology, the "destruction process," and the "machinery of destruction" (Hilberg 1985, 53–57), numerous Jews living in Nazi-occupied territory survived. Although the Netherlands showed the highest Holocaust victimization rate among the Nazi-occupied countries in Western Europe—about 73 percent of the Jewish population were killed (Hirschfeld 1991, 165)—still about thirty-eight thousand Jews survived, while thousands of victims had tried to escape through hiding, fleeing, or otherwise. Focusing on the life trajectories of Jews in the Netherlands during the occupation years, five general principles of the life course approach (Elder, Johnson, and Crosnoe 2003, 10–14) provided us direction in identifying differences in these trajectories that may be related to higher survival chances among immigrants.

The first principle, lifespan development, is aimed at taking a long-term perspective (Elder, Johnson, and Crosnoe 2003, 11). Choices and behavior can be better understood by considering experiences in earlier stages of life (Kok 2007, 205). For research into the Holocaust, one can think of prewar decisions on marriage partners (that is, marrying a non-Jew) and religious affiliation (conversion to Christianity). These decisions earlier in the lifespan may have influenced transitions in positions and status during the Nazi occupation.

The second principle, agency, emphasizes that individuals construct their own life course through the choices and actions they take within the opportunities and constraints of history and social circumstances (Elder, Johnson, and Crosnoe 2003, 11–12). The Nazi persecution of Jews in the Netherlands is portrayed as "cat and mouse play" (Presser 1965, 1:56, 211–12, 459, 2:110) and the Jews as "outlaws in a cage" (Herzberg 1985, 108) under the Nazi regime. Nonetheless, Jews had choices regarding survival strategy, such as cooperation, compliance, coping, evasion, and/or resistance (Finkel 2017), shaping their trajectories under Nazi rule.

The third principle, time and place, states that the life course of individuals is embedded in and shaped by the historical times and places they experience over their lifetime (Elder, Johnson, and Crosnoe 2003, 12). Migrants living in the occupied Netherlands are a special case, as many had fled Nazi German territory in the 1930s. Migrants' experiences of antisemitism and the life-threatening situations in the country they had fled in the 1930s or even earlier may have shaped their decisions and actions and hence their trajectories when deportations of Jews from the Netherlands began.

The fourth principle, timing, suggests that the consequences of certain transitions or events vary according to their timing in a person's life (Elder, Johnson, and Crosnoe 2003, 12–13). The systematic deportation starting in July 1942 can be seen as the main event triggering decisions and actions that strongly influenced transitions in positions and status. The impact of this event on deciding survival strategy may have depended, for example, on someone's marital status or age.

The fifth principle, linked lives, stresses that human lives are lived interdependently and that transitions in one person's life often entail transitions in other people's lives as well (Elder, Johnson, and Crosnoe 2003, 13–14). Significant others in this study were family members. During the Nazi occupation, some Jews were granted a temporary exemption from internment and deportation. Often this implied that other members of the family were then also exempted; therefore, such an exemption could impact more life trajectories under the Nazi regime.

Within life course epidemiology, transitions or exposures are events influencing morbidity or mortality risk, and difference in exposures may account for inequalities in health and mortality (Kuh et al. 2003). Different "chains of risk" or causal models are distinguished to determine the impact of exposures on health outcomes. The life course causal model most suitable for this study on Holocaust survival seems to be the accumulation model. Within this model, an adverse experience or exposure in each of the stages in the chain increases the risk of being killed in a cumulative or additive fashion. The "trigger effect" in our model is the start of the systematic deportation to concentration and killing camps abroad in July 1942. If Jews were not (temporarily) exempted from deportation, went into hiding, or escaped to safer countries, the risk of being interned in transit camp Westerbork or concentration camp Vught increased. Being in these camps increased the risk of being deported to a Nazi camp abroad, while arrival in such a camp increased the risk of becoming a Holocaust victim (see figure 9.1).

Based on the accumulation model and the five general principles of the life course approach, we formulated five hypotheses for differences between immigrant and Dutch-born Jews in the risk of experiencing an adverse event for each of the stages in the chain to becoming a Holocaust victim. Antisemitic legislation from 1933 onward, culminating in Kristallnacht (or the Night of Broken Glass) on November 9–10, 1938, was a watershed for Jews living in Nazi German territory (Moore 1986, 18). Many Jews who had fled to the Netherlands may have had stronger motives to escape and had been hiding or fleeing more often than Dutch-born Jews when systematic deportation started in July 1942 (Hypothesis 1). An argument against this hypothesis is that many Jewish immigrants had lived only for a few years in the Netherlands before the Nazi occupation and were not integrated enough into Dutch society to find ways to hide or flee (Blom 1989, 146). Many Jewish immigrants were integrated into the network of the Dutch Committee for Jewish Refugees. During the Nazi occupation, this committee became part of the Jewish Council, which was assigned the responsibility for all Jews in the Netherlands. On behalf of the occupier, this council was in the position to exempt thousands of Jews temporarily from internment and deportation,

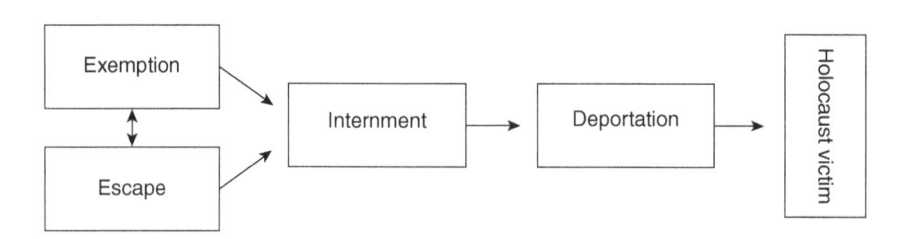

FIGURE 9.1. Life course causal model for becoming a Holocaust victim

or to grant a so-called *Sperre*, a temporary exemption from deportation (Presser 1965, 1:287–97).

The overrepresentation of immigrants in the Jewish Council may have resulted in immigrants being (temporarily) exempted from deportation relatively more often than Dutch-born Jews (Hypothesis 2). A temporary exemption may have given Jews more time to find a hiding place or an escape route to safer countries. As a result, immigrants may have been less likely to be interned than Dutch-born Jews (Hypothesis 3). It has been said that within the transit camp Westerbork, German Jews occupied better positions while they did their best to save German inmates from being deported (Moore 1997, 261–63; Mechanicus 1989, 28). This situation may have resulted in immigrants being less at risk of being deported to Nazi camps abroad than Dutch-born Jews (Hypothesis 4). Impression-based evidence suggests further that Dutch Jews suffered more in Nazi camps than Jews of another nationality (Presser 1965, 2:429). This may have resulted in more immigrants than Dutch-born Jews surviving deportation to Nazi camps abroad (Hypothesis 5).

Berger (1995, 2010) applied a narrative approach in a life course study using information from in-depth interviews with two family members who survived the Holocaust: his father and his uncle. One of them survived several Nazi camps, while the other survived through reclassification of his Jewish status and by hiding. Based on the information from the interviews, Berger constructed for both relatives sequences of positions, roles, or statuses. Despite the many life stories such as postwar memories, (reworked) real-time diaries or letters, and the many postwar interviews, Berger's narrative life course approach has not been applied much. Our study followed up on Berger's application of the life course approach to Holocaust survival, though it used data from administrative sources, allowing us to include both survivors and victims while applying statistical methods for data analyses to test the five formulated hypotheses. In a pilot study on about four hundred adult Amsterdam-born Jews, using data from administrative sources such as the Jewish Council index cards, Tammes (2012) explored the systematic collection and coding of data from these cards into a database and showed the validity of these data for quantitative research. Thereafter, Keesing, Tammes, and Simpkin (2019) used these cards, among other sources in their study on the Holocaust survival of about nine hundred *Kindertransport* children in the Netherlands.

Sources and Data

We have built upon Tammes's immigrant database, including detailed information on migrant and Dutch-born Jews in seven Dutch municipalities (Tammes 2007). For this study, we excluded one of the seven municipalities and included

Jews from two other municipalities, Culemborg and Nijmegen, increasing the number of Jews to 1,318 living in eight municipalities.[1] These eight municipalities are more or less spread across the southern and middle parts of the Netherlands: Culemborg, Wisch, and Nijmegen are located in the province of Gelderland; Heerlen is in the province of Limburg; Leidschendam, Voorburg, and Woerden are located in the province of South Holland; and Zeist is in the province of Utrecht.

Predictors: Immigrant Status and Date of Immigration

Using the municipality registration lists of Jewish inhabitants in 1941 provided us with information on place of birth. This allowed us to determine who was an immigrant. For the original six municipalities in the database, information on the date of immigration and country of origin for immigrants was added by using data retrieved from the local population registries or mentioned in local studies. Culemborg and Nijmegen were added to this database, as their registration lists of Jewish inhabitants included place of birth as well as information on date of arrival and previous living place. Migration information on a registration list of Jewish inhabitants is rare but helpful, as this information is nowadays difficult to retrieve from local population registries due to stricter privacy regulations. But some Jewish immigrants living in Culemborg or Nijmegen arrived first in another Dutch municipality before they moved to one of these places. For these Jews, we used online data from several local population registries if accessible, and the online source "Namenlijst Nijmegen 1939–1944" to determine their date of immigration to the Netherlands.[2]

Outcome 1: Hiding and Fleeing

In the course of 1941 and 1942 many anti-Jewish regulations were introduced to limit travel and movement, employment, and meeting non-Jews. Particularly after systematic deportations started in mid-July 1942, many Jews tried to escape internment and deportation through hiding or fleeing to safer countries such as Switzerland.[3] Around the same time, the Jewish Council created individual index cards to record some personal and other information, such as arrival in Westerbork and deportation to Nazi camps abroad (Schütz 2019).[4] When Jews arrived in Westerbork, their barrack number was recorded on these cards; Jews who were caught in hiding or while fleeing were often put in barrack 67, providing us an indication of their attempted escapes. Furthermore, notes on these cards related to postwar tracing activities, such as an *o* in the left upper corner, indicated that someone had been hiding, providing us another indication of who had tried to escape. If a card contained neither these indications (barrack 67 or *o*) nor information on internment and deportation, and these Jews were not mixed-married or converted to Christianity, then such an "empty" card could indicate that a particular Jew had escaped Nazi persecution.[5] To confirm this, we used information from four detailed local studies, providing us with names of those who made either a failed or a successful escape. Two local studies used as a source the *Algemeen politieblad* (General police journal). If homes of Jews were deserted when they were arrested or when Jews did not turn up for transportation to Westerbork or Vught, local burgomasters, such as the burgomaster in Woerden (Ultee 1999, 30–31), published notifications of a "missing person" in this journal (Presser 1965, 2:261). For Nijmegen, the commissar for the province of Gelderland had published these notifications, and these are included in the earlier-mentioned source "Namenlijst Nijmegen 1939–1944." Detailed local studies on Jews in Wisch (Kooger 2001) and in Heerlen (Van Rooij-Trienekens 1998) mentioned who had been hiding or fleeing, mainly based on stories from local eyewitnesses or persons who had been involved. To test our hypothesis on hiding and fleeing, we focused on Jewish inhabitants in these four municipalities, using the information both in the local studies and on the index cards.

Outcome 2: Exemption from Deportation

The Nazi occupiers in the Netherlands initially exempted all Jews married to a non-Jew, or so-called mixed-married Jews, from deportation. These Jews, though, were still at risk if they did not comply with the many anti-Jewish regulations introduced during the German Nazi occupation, while their exemption status was continuously discussed (Stuldreher 2007, 223–42, 277–344). Likewise, Jews who had converted to Christianity before Nazi Germany invaded the Netherlands were initially exempted from deportation.[6] But after church protests against the deportation of Jews at the end of July 1942, the Nazi occupiers rounded up a few hundred Jews who were converted to Catholicism (Presser 1965, 1:260–61). Some municipal registration lists recorded who was mixed-married or had converted to Christianity. To determine who was mixed-married or converted in the other municipalities, we used, respectively, the lists of mixed-married Jews made up in September and November 1942, and the list of Jews who had converted to Christianity made up in September 1942.[7] We noticed during our research that for several mixed-married or converted Jews, the Jewish Council had not created an index card; this may indicate that they were never targeted by the Nazis.

From the summer of 1942 onward, the Jewish Council granted some Jews (temporary) exemption from deportation. About 17,500 Jews were granted a Sperre as they or a nuclear family member held a position in the (local) Jewish

Council. Furthermore, about 6,700 Jews were granted a Sperre as they or a nuclear family member had a certain job, such as a diamond or metal worker. In addition, a few other smaller groups of Jews were also granted a Sperre, such as Jews from Nazi-allied countries. All of these exemptions, however, appeared to be temporary, and all eventually became invalid during 1943 (Presser 1965, 1:287–97). To determine who in our datafile was granted a Sperre, we used the index cards (Schütz 2019).

Information in some local studies suggests that a few Jews were temporarily exempted because they or a family member was ill and therefore *Transportunfähig* (not able to be moved on medical grounds) (Boot 1967, 141; Van Rooij-Trienekens 1998, 48, 58, 60).[8] We did not find such exemptions in the administrative sources we used, and have not included this information from local studies in our research to avoid measurement bias.

Outcomes 3 to 5: Date of Internment, Deportation, and Death

For the arrival date in internment camps—for instance, transit camp Westerbork, concentration camp Vught, or prison camps such as Amersfoort or Scheveningen—we used the information on the index cards. These same cards also provided us information on the date of deportation. A few Jews were caught in Belgium or France when they tried to flee to Switzerland or Spain and were deported from Mechelen transit camp or Drancy internment camp. This information was recorded after the war on the index cards, and further information was gathered from other sources such as the Memoriaal van de Deportatie der Joden uit Belgie (Memorial of the Deportations of Jews from Belgium) (Klarsfeld and Steinberg 1982). To determine the date of death, all Jews in our datafile were compared to postwar death lists such as *In Memoriam-Lezecher* (SDU 1995) and the Digital Jewish Monument to determine who had not survived the Nazi occupation and was killed by the Nazis and who had died from natural causes.[9] For a few Jews, however, we could not find dates of internment, deportation, or death. Besides this, some Jews either were killed in Mauthausen due to an earlier roundup in the autumn of 1941 in the eastern part of the Netherlands, had died of natural causes, or had moved before the systematic deportation began in July 1942. These Jews were excluded from the analyses, as our focus is on events from July 1942 onward.

The overall deportation and death percentages in this study are about 61 percent and 59 percent, respectively. This is lower than the national overall percentages of about 76 percent and 73 percent, respectively. Deportation and death rates among Dutch municipalities vary hugely but were generally higher in the biggest cities (Tammes 2019, web appendix). Local percentages of Holocaust victims in this study ranged from 35 percent for Woerden and Zeist to 75 percent for Nijmegen. Likewise, differences in Holocaust victimization among immigrant and Dutch-born Jews could vary between municipalities. The local study on Heerlen, for example, shows that relatively more immigrant than Dutch-born Jews were killed (Van Rooij-Trienekens 1998, 65). In this study, however, we analyzed all Jewish inhabitants living in the eight municipalities together.

Study Design and Method of Analysis

Our data were based on sociodemographic information on Jewish inhabitants registered in 1941. Since these local registrations took place before the systematic deportations to Nazi camps abroad began, we did not know from these registrations who was killed or had survived the Nazi occupation, and hence our study did not suffer from selection bias. An important source was the individual Jewish Council index cards on which information was continually recorded, such as being granted a Sperre and dates of internment and deportation. Using postwar death lists, we were able to determine who had not survived the Holocaust and when and where these victims were killed. Most of the collected and linked data for this study can be considered as prospective data, which is well suited to a longitudinal study.

To test Hypothesis 1, we have an outcome of having tried to escape Nazi persecution through hiding or fleeing. Since, for many Jews, we did not have a clear date when they tried to escape, this was a binary outcome and was therefore modeled using logistic regression. To test Hypothesis 2, we have an outcome of being exempted from deportation because of (1) being mixed-married or converted, or (2) having been granted a Sperre. These were binary outcomes and were again modeled using logistic regression. We reported odds ratios (ORs) from these models, where a ratio of 1 means no effect of the tested variable (i.e., immigrant), above 1 implies that migrants were more likely to have tried to escape or to have been exempted from deportation, and less than 1 corresponds to migrants being less likely to have tried to escape or to have been exempted from deportation.

To test Hypotheses 3 through 5, we treated internment, deportation, and victimization as a time-to-event variable—namely, that we have both an event (for example, interned/not interned) and a time of internment (month and year). Those Jews not interned are said to be censored at the end of the time of study. Internment, deportation, and victimization were all modeled using a Cox proportional hazards model (Cox 1972), which is the most commonly used approach for time-to-event variables. For each variable under examination, we estimated a hazard ratio (HR). A hazard ratio of 1 represents no effect of the variable being tested on the outcome (i.e., immigrant), below 1 means a protective effect, and above 1 means a harmful effect.

We used 95 percent confidence intervals (95% CI) to provide evidence as to whether our sample results are likely to infer population effects for all Jews represented by this sample. Where a 95 percent confidence interval is fully above or below 1, this suggests evidence for an association between the variable of interest and the outcome. We also reported p-values but did not use a stringent cutoff of 0.05 to determine a population effect. We used a strength of evidence approach (Sterne and Davey Smith 2001), whereby smaller p-values suggest stronger evidence for a population effect.

Differences in local survival rates are associated with some locality-level characteristics, such as degree of collaboration among policemen in the local police force, local religious composition, and date of local transport of Jews to transit camp Westerbork (Tammes 2019; see also Braun 2019). For example, Tauber (2004, 7–28) described in his postwar memoirs how he, together with many other Jews in Nijmegen, had to leave their homes for Westerbork in mid-November 1942, while Silber (1997, 60–61) described in his war diary that his family received a call-up at the end of August 1942 to leave for Westerbork the next day. Therefore, we take clustering at the municipality level into account in our analyses when testing Hypotheses 1 to 3.

Furthermore, we adjusted all of our analyses for confounding factors such as age, gender, and marital status; this information was recorded or derived from information on the local registration lists. In addition, in the analysis on hiding and fleeing, we included whether someone was exempted from deportation because of being mixed-married or converted or being granted a Sperre. In the analysis on internment, we again included whether someone was exempted from deportation; after testing the proportional hazard assumption of the Cox model, we included the Sperre as a time-varying covariate. In the analysis on deportation, we included the period of internment (i.e., between July and December 1942, between January and August 1943, or after August 1943), as the number of trains leaving transit camp Westerbork varied over time. In the analysis on date of death, we included the year of deportation, as later deportation may have increased survival.

Of the 1,318 Jews in our datafile, we excluded thirty Jews from our analyses because they had moved or had died before the start of systematic deportation in July 1942, and another five for whom key data were missing, such as date of immigration. For another fourteen Jews, we knew they had been interned, but we did not know their date of internment; they were excluded from the analyses testing Hypothesis 3. For another sixteen Jews, we knew they had been interned and deported, but we did not know their deportation date; they were excluded from

TABLE 9.1 Descriptive statistics: The number and percentage of Jews experiencing each of the outcomes relating to our five hypotheses

	HYPOTHESIS 1: ESCAPING			HYPOTHESIS 2: TEMPORARY EXEMPTION			HYPOTHESIS 2: EXEMPTION			HYPOTHESIS 3: INTERNMENT			HYPOTHESIS 4: DEPORTATION			HYPOTHESIS 5: VICTIMIZATION		
	Total in analysis	Attempted escape		Total in analysis	Sperre		Total in analysis	Mixed married / converted		Total in analysis	Interned		Total in analysis	Deported		Total in analysis	Killed	
	N	n	Pct.	N	n	Pct.	N	n	Pct.	N	n	Pct.	N	n	Pct.	N	n	Pct.
Nonmigrants	473	151	32%	870	121	14%	870	67	8%	864	593	69%	588	549	93%	560	541	97%
Immigrants	259	108	42%	413	23	6%	413	50	12%	405	218	54%	221	210	95%	214	199	93%
Total	732	259	35%	1,283	144	11%	1,283	117	9%	1,269	811	64%	809	759	94%	774	740	96%
Nonmigrants	473	151	32%	870	121	14%	870	67	8%	864	593	69%	588	549	93%	560	541	97%
Migrated before 1933	87	30	34%	113	8	7%	113	11	10%	111	67	60%	67	64	96%	66	60	91%
Migrated between 1933 and Oct. 1938	96	50	52%	169	8	5%	169	25	15%	167	79	47%	80	76	95%	77	73	95%
Migrated after Oct. 1938	76	28	37%	131	7	5%	131	14	11%	127	72	57%	74	70	95%	71	66	93%
Total	732	259	35%	1,283	144	11%	1,283	117	9%	1,269	811	64%	809	795	94%	774	740	96%

the analyses testing Hypothesis 4. For another Jew who was deported and killed, we did not know the date of death; this person was excluded from the analyses testing Hypothesis 5. Table 9.1 presents some descriptive statistics for each outcome, as well as the number of Jews included in the analyses, as this varied, since, for example, not all interned Jews were deported, while the analysis concerning escaping Nazi persecution was based only on Jews in four municipalities.

Results

The results testing Hypothesis 1, on escaping Nazi persecution, are shown in table 9.2; these results were controlled for age, gender, marital status, and having ever been exempted from deportation. There was no strong evidence to support the hypothesis that, in general, immigrant Jews were more likely to have (successfully or unsuccessfully) tried to escape Nazi persecution through hiding or fleeing. When considering periods of arrival, however, Jews arriving in the Netherlands between 1933 and October 1938 were 82 percent more likely to have tried to escape than Dutch-born Jews (OR 1.82, 95% CI 1.08 to 3.08). This result supports our hypothesis.

TABLE 9.2 Estimates of odds ratios (OR) for the association between immigrant status and the likelihood of trying to escape Nazi persecution through hiding or fleeing

	MODEL 1		MODEL 2	
	OR (95% CI)	p-value	OR (95% CI)	p-value
Constant	0.70 (0.24, 2.05)	0.517		
Migrant (ref. Dutch-born)	1.15 (0.79, 1.69)	0.463		
Constant			0.70 (0.26, 2.07)	0.522
Immigration (ref. not migrated)				
Born abroad, migrated before 1933			0.62 (0.34, 1.14)	0.126
Born abroad, migrated 1933–Oct. 1938			1.82 (1.08, 3.08)	0.025
Born abroad, migrated after Oct. 1938			1.19 (0.66, 2.13)	0.568

Note: The analyses also included age, gender, marital status, and ever having been temporarily exempted from internment and deportation due to (1) a Sperre, or (2) mixed marriage or conversion to Christianity.

The results testing Hypothesis 2, on receiving (temporary) exemption from deportation, are presented in table 9.3; these results were controlled for age, gender, and marital status. Compared to Dutch-born Jews, migrant Jews were 64 percent less likely to have been granted a Sperre (OR 0.36, 95% CI 0.22 to 0.58), rejecting our hypothesis. When investigating different periods of arrival, it appears that the association was strongest in those Jews arriving in the Netherlands after 1933. There was only weak evidence for an association when comparing Dutch-born Jews to migrant Jews arriving before 1933 (OR 0.52, 95% CI 0.24 to 1.11). Compared to Dutch-born Jews, however, those Jews arriving between 1933 and October 1938 were 72 percent less likely (OR 0.28, 95% CI 0.13 to 0.60), and those arriving after October 1938 were 66 percent less likely (OR 0.34, 95% CI 0.15 to 0.76), to have been granted a Sperre. There was no strong evidence that immigrants were more likely to be exempted on grounds of mixed marriage or conversion to Christianity than Dutch-born Jews. This result does not support our hypothesis.

The results testing Hypothesis 3, on internment, are presented in table 9.4; these results are controlled for age, gender, marital status, and having ever been exempted from deportation. There was some weak evidence for a decreased risk of internment among migrant Jews compared to Dutch-born Jews, indicating some support for our hypothesis. Based on the available data, Jews who migrated to the Netherlands had a 29 percent reduced risk of being interned. But when using these data to make claims about all such Jews in the Netherlands, we consider the 95 percent confidence interval to give a range of plausible values. Our model suggests anywhere from a 51 percent decreased risk of internment to a 2 percent *increased* risk of internment (HR 0.71, 95% CI 0.49 to 1.02). There was no strong evidence for an association between migrant status and risk of internment when considering the period of arrival of migrant Jews into the Netherlands.

The results testing Hypothesis 4, on deportation, are presented in table 9.5; these results were controlled for age, gender, marital status, and period of internment. There was no strong evidence for a difference in risk of deportation between immigrant and Dutch-born Jews, even when considering the period of migration. These results do not support our hypothesis.

The results testing Hypothesis 5, on being killed in Nazi camps abroad, are presented in table 9.6; these results were controlled for age, gender, marital status, and year of deportation. Compared to Dutch-born Jews, migrant Jews had an 18 percent reduced risk of being killed in these camps (HR 0.82, 95% CI 0.69 to 0.96), supporting our hypothesis. When investigating different periods of arrival, there was some weak evidence for a reduced risk for migrants arriving in the Netherlands before 1933 (HR 0.76, 95% CI 0.58 to 1.00) and for Jews arriving

TABLE 9.3 Estimates of odds ratios (ORs) for the association between immigrant status and the likelihood of being temporarily exempted from internment and deportation

	TEMPORARY EXEMPTION: SPERRE				EXEMPTION: MIXED MARRIAGE OR CONVERSION TO CHRISTIANITY			
	Model 1		Model 2		Model 1		Model 2	
	OR (95% CI)	p-value	OR (95% CI)	p-value	OR (95% CI)	p-value	OR (95% CI)	p-value
Constant	0.08 (0.04, 0.15)	<0.001			0.02 (0.01, 0.05)	<0.001		
Migrant (ref. Dutch-born)	0.36 (0.22, 0.58)	<0.001			1.12 (0.72, 1.73)	0.615		
Constant			0.08 (0.04, 0.15)	<0.001			0.02 (0.01, 0.05)	<0.001
Immigration (ref. not migrated)								
Born abroad, migrated before 1933			0.52 (0.24, 1.11)	0.090			1.25 (0.61, 2.56)	0.548
Born abroad, migrated 1933–Oct. 1938			0.28 (0.13, 0.60)	0.001			1.20 (0.69, 2.09)	0.526
Born abroad, migrated after Oct. 1938			0.34 (0.15, 0.76)	0.009			0.92 (0.47, 1.78)	0.808

Note: The analyses also included age, gender, and marital status.

TABLE 9.4 Estimates of hazard ratios (HRs) for the association between immigrant status and the risk of being interned

	MODEL 1		MODEL 2	
	HR (95% CI)	p-value	HR (95% CI)	p-value
Migrant (ref. Dutch-born)	0.71 (0.49, 1.01)	0.056		
Immigration (ref. not migrated)				
Born abroad, migrated before 1933			0.88 (0.73, 1.06)	0.169
Born abroad, migrated 1933–Oct. 1938			0.58 (0.31, 1.10)	0.098
Born abroad, migrated after Oct. 1938			0.74 (0.52, 1.07)	0.111

Note: The analyses also included age, gender, marital status, and ever having been temporarily exempted from internment and deportation due to (1) a Sperre, or (2) mixed marriage or conversion to Christianity.

TABLE 9.5 Estimates of hazard ratios (HRs) for the association between immigrant status and the risk of being deported to Nazi camps abroad

	MODEL 1		MODEL 2	
	HR (95% CI)	p-value	HR (95% CI)	p-value
Migrant (ref. Dutch-born)	1.00 (0.85, 1.18)	0.983		
Immigration (ref. not migrated)				
Born abroad, migrated before 1933			1.23 (0.94, 1.60)	0.133
Born abroad, migrated 1933–Oct. 1938			0.99 (0.78, 1.27)	0.952
Born abroad, migrated after Oct. 1938			0.88 (0.68, 1.13)	0.311

Note: The analyses also included age, gender, marital status, and period of internment.

after October 1938 (HR 0.79, 95% CI 0.61 to 1.03). There was no strong evidence for a reduced risk for Jews arriving between 1933 and October 1938.

By reading war diaries, postwar memoirs, and biographies, we can learn about escaping Nazi persecution, coping with life in camps such as Westerbork and Vught, and sometimes the horror of deportation and life in Nazi concentration

TABLE 9.6 Estimates of hazard ratios (HRs) for the association between immigrant status and the risk of being killed in Nazi camps abroad

	MODEL 1		MODEL 2	
	HR (95% CI)	p-value	HR (95% CI)	p-value
Migrant (ref. Dutch-born)	0.82 (0.69, 0.96)	0.017		
Immigration (ref. not migrated)				
Born abroad, migrated before 1933			0.76 (0.58, 1.00)	0.056
Born abroad, migrated 1933– Oct. 1938			0.89 (0.69, 1.14)	0.359
Born abroad, migrated after Oct. 1938			0.79 (0.61, 1.03)	0.080

Note: The analyses also included age, gender, marital status, and year of deportation.

camps. But we can get a better understanding about Holocaust survival or victimization and differences in Jewish survival chances when combining and comparing individual life histories. In this study, we applied a life course approach that shaped the hypotheses to be tested, directed the collection and gathering of information from administrative sources, and framed the study design and the statistical analyses.

The analysis of the life histories of about 1,300 Jews living in eight Dutch municipalities has revealed possible explanations for immigrants' better survival chances. Immigrants, particularly those arriving in the Netherlands between 1933 and October 1938, were more likely to go into hiding or to find escape routes to safer countries. Despite immigrant Jews in this study being less likely to be granted a Sperre, there was some evidence that they had a reduced risk of being interned in transit, concentration, or prison camps in the Netherlands; this may be due to their higher likelihood of trying to escape Nazi persecution through hiding or fleeing. Although there was no significant difference between interned immigrants and Dutch-born Jews in being deported to concentration and killing camps abroad, immigrants had a reduced risk of being killed in these camps. These results suggest that immigrants had different survival strategies than Dutch-born Jews, cumulating in an overall better survival chance for immigrants.

Although the eight municipalities in this study were spread across the southern and middle parts of the Netherlands, generalizability of the study's findings may be limited, since they involved less than 1 percent of the Jewish population and did not include Jews from Amsterdam, the Hague, or Rotterdam. Nonetheless, these findings show that the application of a life course approach using data from historical sources in statistical analyses can contribute to our understanding of Holocaust survival. The application of a life course approach can be expanded by including Jews from other places or Jews working in the same branch (Skorczewski and Siertsema 2020), and by including other events and experiences before the summer of 1942, such as moving between places, reclassification of Jewish status, emigration attempts, being sent to work camps, or experiencing early local roundups. Information on these events and experiences can be found in national, regional, and local archives, since the Nazi occupiers left a paper trail of correspondence with Dutch officials and others alongside administrative data on the persecution of Jews. Scholars using this information together with information from individual sources, such as diaries and postwar interviews, in studies applying a life course approach—whether qualitative, quantitative, or mixed-method research—can improve our knowledge of the Holocaust and Jewish survival strategies.

REFERENCES

Berger, Ronald. 1995. "Agency, Structure, and Jewish Survival of the Holocaust: A Life History Study." *Sociological Quarterly* 36 (1): 15–36.

———. 2010. *Surviving the Holocaust: A Life Course Perspective*. New York: Routledge.

Bijsterveld, Arnoud-Jan. 2016. *House of Memories: Uncovering the Past of a Dutch Jewish Family*. Hilversum: Uitgeverij Verloren.

Blom, Johannes C. H. 1989. "The Persecution of Jews in the Netherlands: A Comparative Western European Perspective." *European History Quarterly* 19:333–51.

Boot, Joost, J. G. 1967. *Burgemeester in bezettingstijd*. Apeldoorn, Netherlands: Semper Agendo.

Braun, Robert. 2019. *Protectors of Pluralism: Religious Minorities and the Rescue of Jews in the Low Countries during the Holocaust*. Cambridge: Cambridge University Press.

Cox, David R. 1972. "Regression Models and Life Tables." *Journal of the Royal Statistical Society*, series B (Methodological), 34:187–20.

Elder, Glen H., Monica K. Johnson, and Robert Crosnoe. 2003. "The Emergence and Development of Life Course Theory." In *Handbook of the Life Course*, edited by Jeylan T. Mortimer and Michael J Shanahan, 3–19. Boston: Springer.

Fein, Helen. 1979. *Accounting for Genocide: National Responses and Jewish Victimization during the Holocaust*. New York: Free Press.

Finkel, Evgeny. 2017. *Ordinary Jews: Choice and Survival during the Holocaust*. Princeton, NJ: Princeton University Press.

Hilberg, Raul. 1985. *The Destruction of the European Jews*. New York: Holmes and Meier.

Hirschfeld, Gerhard. 1991. "Niederlande." In *Dimension des Völkermords: Die Zahl der jüdischen Opfer des Nationalsozialismus*, edited by Wolfgang Benz, 52–72. Munich: Munchen Verlag.

Keesing, Miriam, Peter Tammes, and Andrew J. Simpkin. 2019. "Jewish Refugee Children in the Netherlands during World War II: Migration, Settlement, and Survival." *Social Science History* 43 (4): 785–811.

Klarsfeld, Serge, and Maxime Steinberg. 1982. *Memoriaal van de deportatie der joden uit België*. Brussels: Vereniging der Joodse Weggevoerden in België.

Kok, Jan. 2007. "Principles and Prospects of the Life Course Paradigm." *Annales de démographie historique*, no. 1, 203–30.

Kooger, Hans. 2001. *Het oude volk: Kroniek van joods leven in de Achterhoek, Liemers en het grensgebied*. Doetinchem: Staring Instituut/Mr. H. J. Steenbergenstichting.

Kuh, Diana, Yoav Ben-Shlomo, J. Lynch, John Hallqvist, and Chris Power. 2003. "Life Course Epidemiology." *Journal of Epidemiology and Community Health* 57 (10): 778–83.

Mechanicus, Philip. 1989. *In Dépôt: Dagboek uit Westerbork*. Amsterdam: Van Gennep.

Moore, Bob. 1986. *Refugees from Nazi Germany in the Netherlands, 1933–1940*. Dordrecht: Martinus Nijhoff.

———. 1997. *Victims and Survivors: The Nazi Persecution of the Jews in the Netherlands 1940–1945*. London: Arnold.

Presser, Jacques. 1965. *Ondergang: De vervolging en Verdelging van het Nederlandse Jodendom, 1940–1945*. 2 vols. The Hague: Staatsuitgeverij.

Schütz, Raymund. 2019. "Syllabus Workshop Joodse Raadcartotheek." Version 3. https://www.academia.edu/42656283/Joodse_Raad_Cartotheek_en_Arolsen_Archives_03_V.

SDU. 1995. *In Memoriam-Lezecher*. The Hague: Sdu Uitgeverij.

Silber, Salomon. 1997. *Een joods gezin in onderduik. Dagboek*. Kampen: Uitgeverij Kok.

Skorczewski, Dawn, and Bettine Siertsema. 2020. "'The Kind of Spirit that People Still Kept': VHA Testimonies of Amsterdam's Diamond Jews." *Holocaust Studies* 26 (1): 62–84.

Sterne, Jonathan A. C., and George Davey Smith. 2001. "Sifting the Evidence—What's Wrong with Significance Tests?" *BMJ* 322:226–31.

Stone, Dan. 2017. "A Victim-Centred Historiography of the Holocaust?" *Patterns of Prejudice* 51 (2): 176–88.

Stuldreher, Coen. 2007. *De legale rest: Gemengd gehuwde Joden onder de Duitse bezetting*. Amsterdam: Boom.

Tammes, Peter. 2005. *"U draagt geen ster": De vervolging van joodse inwoners in Bergen (NH) tijdens de Tweede Wereldoorlog*. Bergen: Uitgeverij Bonneville.

———. 2007. "Jewish Immigrants in the Netherlands during the Nazi Occupation." *Journal of Interdisciplinary History* 37 (4): 543–62.

———. 2012. "De levensloopbenadering in Holocaustonderzoek: Verschillen in overlevingsduur onder Amsterdamse joden tijdens de Duitse bezetting." In *Leren van historische levenslopen*, edited by Koen Matthijs, Jan Kok, and Hilde Bras, 119–44. Leuven: Acco Uitgeverij.

———. 2019. "Associating Locality-Level Characteristics with Surviving the Holocaust: A Multilevel Approach to the Odds of Being Deported and to Risk of Death among Jews Living in Dutch Municipalities." *American Journal of Epidemiology* 188 (5): 896–906.

Tauber, Fritz. 2004. *Rondom Westerbork*. Westerbork: Herinneringskamp Westerbork.

Ultee, Wout C. 1999. *We mogen nergens heen, we moeten naar Vught: De Joodse inwoners van Woerden, 1930–1947*. Heemtijdinghen: Orgaan van de Stichts-Hollandse Historische Vereniging.

Van den Ende, Hannah. 2015. *"Vergeet niet dat je arts bent": Joodse artsen in Nederland 1940–1945*. Amsterdam: Uitgeverij Boom.
Van Rooij-Trienekens, Fiet. 1998. *Joden in Heerlen in de Tweede Wereldoorlog*. Beek-Ubbergen: De Rozet.
Zalc, Claire., and Tal Bruttmann, eds. 2016. *Microhistories of the Holocaust*. Oxford: Berghahn Books.

10

NORMALIZING VIOLENCE

How Catholic Bishops Facilitated Vichy's Violence against Jews

Aliza Luft

On July 10, 1940, the French Third Republic was dissolved and a new authoritarian government came to power. Led by Prime Minister Phillipe Pétain, the Vichy regime tried to reorganize French social life by eliminating the French Republic's civic virtues of liberty, equality, and fraternity and replacing them with a new conception of the nation, also known as the National Revolution. Characterized by the principles of work, family, and fatherland, Vichy privileged ancestry, tradition, and religion as if biologically transmitted.[1] As a result, its first targets were those considered external to the national, and supposedly *natural*, community: foreigners and Jews.

Among the Vichy regime's first decrees was the Statut des Juifs, a legislative measure intended to exclude Jews from public life in France and limit their influence. Between October 1940 and November 1941, eleven more measures restricting Jews' rights would come to be passed. By 1945, according to Adler (2001, 1067), "some four hundred laws, decrees, and police measures" targeting Jews were introduced. These exclusionary laws facilitated the incarceration, forced deportation, and eventual mass murder of approximately eighty thousand Jews from France. How did the Vichy regime obtain acquiescence from the non-Jewish French population to these violent laws?

At the heart of the Occupation and Vichy's collaboration with Nazi Germany is the question of legitimation. Marshal Pétain came to power under vexed circumstances: a vote on July 10, 1940, two weeks after France surrendered to Germany, whereby the French Third Republic collectively abdicated its democratic rights.[2] Thus, to promote his political agenda, the Vichy regime needed to accumulate legitimacy. As a result, its ability to do so—to secure, more or less, adherence from a wide swath of a population in disarray to a new national ideology that involved restrictions against fellow citizens and recently arrived foreigners who had enjoyed more lenient policies a few years prior—requires explanation. This chapter explains how the Vichy regime was able to change French politics and society so that actions and ideologies once thought beyond the pale became ho-hum parts of everyday life. Specifically, it analyzes how Vichy recruited leaders in the French episcopate as a strategy to facilitate the accumulation of legitimacy, and how French bishops responded. It also analyzes how this shift in the relationship between the government and the episcopate impacted the relationship between the episcopate's leadership and the rabbinate in France.[3]

As many historians have noted, the French Catholic Church during World War II was a "a key agent and go-between in the process of legitimation" for the Vichy government (Peschanski 2004, 409). In 1940, approximately 88 percent of France was Catholic (Bédarida 1998, 7), and politicians and civilians alike flocked to the church following the chaos of France's defeat (Drapac 1998, 142). The church became a "central player in the drama of public life" (Nord 2003, 11), while Catholicism itself became "the single most cohesive force in French society after Germany defeated France" (Drapac 1998, 28). The Catholic Church powerfully influenced how French civilians interpreted the rapidly shifting state of affairs before them, and, as a result, bishops had significant power to influence public opinion on Vichy and its collaboration with Nazis. Furthermore, as religious and moral leaders, bishops' perspectives on Jews were especially important. Many times before the start of the war, bishops protested on Jews' behalf and made prominent declarations against Hitler (Luft 2016, chap. 1). With the defeat and division of France and the occupation of half the country by Nazis, laity turned to their clergy in search of guidance. French bishops encouraged obedience to the Vichy regime and remained publicly silent until 1942 on all matters concerning Jews.

Subsequently, although this chapter focuses on the first half of World War II and the Holocaust in France, a holistic examination of the French Catholic Church during this time period demonstrates its influence on public opinion throughout the course of the war. When French bishops endorsed Vichy, they legitimized state violence by officially supporting its antisemitic policies. Later, their deviation from this stance and their protest in August 1942 of the French state's persecution of Jews delegitimized the Vichy regime and mobilized Catholics on behalf of European Jewry. Although I do not discuss it here (this protest, and its antecedents and consequences, is the subject of a book manuscript I have in preparation), French bishops' first two years of support for Vichy and their silence concerning Jews can be theorized as a "critical antecedent" (Slater and

Simmons 2010, 889) to the rupture caused by their eventual protest. Following the bishops' defections to support Jews, monthly deportation rates of Jews from France collapsed and never reached the high level of forty thousand Jews deported in 1942. It is impossible to understand this shift in the trajectory of the Holocaust in France without first understanding how bishops contributed to the legitimation of Vichy's violence against Jews in its first two years of rule.

Accordingly, I draw on primary sources collected from French diocesan and national archives, as well as French Jewish community archives, to explain how transformations in the relationship between the government and the episcopate contributed to the legitimation of the authoritarian and antisemitic Vichy regime. Drawing on Bourdieusian theories of legitimacy and political and symbolic capital, I identify four mechanisms: public endorsements, cooperation, the expression of shared values, and the use of common rhetoric. These mechanisms led to a "synchronization" of religious and political fields in France and a concomitant decline in the Catholic leadership's alignment with the rabbinate, particularly when compared with the support the former provided to the latter from 1933 to 1940 (Luft 2016, chap. 1; Gorski and Türkmen-Dervişoğlu 2013, 204). In the concluding section, I argue that French Catholic bishops' alliance with Pétain and the Vichy government played a central role in the government's attempts to legitimize its National Revolution philosophy. This included an effort to redefine who belonged to the nation and who did not, targeting, first and foremost, Jews.

Finally, and although numerous historical works have been written about this time period in France (e.g., Bernay 2012; Marrus and Paxton [1981] 1995), the social science approach pursued here allows for the development of a broader argument of how state violence becomes legitimized in formerly democratic regimes. I extend existing sociological theory with evidence from archival sources to develop a relational analysis of how meso-level actors influence authoritarian legitimation. As a result, this chapter goes beyond the specifics of the case analyzed here to consider its lessons for social scientific research on state violence. It also considers what lessons can be gleaned from this case for the present. There are numerous parallels between Vichy France and our current political moment, and I conclude this chapter with broader social scientific and contemporary arguments.

Legitimizing Violence

By mid-fall 1940, the issue of the Statut des Juifs had already been settled: the church had decided to endorse it in August, and the law was published as official state policy on October 18.[4] From early October, when the first Statut des Juifs was promulgated, to May 14, 1941, when the first roundups of Jews by French police occurred, Vichy passed twenty-six more laws and twenty-four decrees concerning Jews (Jackson 2003, 356). Of course, it can be argued that none of these laws, including that which permitted prefects to intern foreign Jews at their own discretion and that which eliminated the Crémieux Decree and stripped Jews from Algeria of their citizenship, constituted state violence compared to the extreme brutality of what was yet to come.[5]

Yet it is my contention that there is nothing "small" and certainly nothing meaningless about the "drip, drip, drip" of these decrees (Rosbottom 2014, 244). Indeed, Jews were subject to slow but steady suppression, and were forced to register themselves and their property in a mandatory census in September 1940 (occupied France) and June 1941 (unoccupied France), which would soon lead to the loss of citizenship, employment, possessions, and more—altogether, extremely violent while laying the groundwork for worse to come.[6] How did this new order of affairs emerge from the crisis of summer 1940? The construction of the idea that there was a "Jewish Problem" in France that needed to be solved, as well as the implementation of strategies to "solve" this problem, was an *accomplishment*.

This chapter, seeking to explain that accomplishment, makes two theoretical moves. First, it extends the definition of state violence to include symbolic violence. The approach is explicitly Bourdieusian: one of the most distinguishing aspects of Bourdieu's theory is his definition of the state as an institution that "successfully claims the monopoly of the legitimate use of physical *and symbolic* violence over a definite territory and over the totality of the corresponding population" (1994, 3; emphasis added). Bourdieu's attention to symbolic violence separates his view from Weber's (1978, 54) oft-cited definition, which references only physical violence. This matters, because especially during the years from 1940 to 1942, the Vichy National Revolution was an attempt at cultural (or, in Bourdieusian terms, symbolic) revolution, not least in whom it classified as rightful citizens and beneficiaries of government protection.[7] When applied to the case at hand, the classification of Jews as not belonging to the French nation, and the concomitant effort by the Vichy government to naturalize Jews as "others" deserving of special treatment, was a form of symbolic violence that paved the way for the physical violence to come.

Second, there is another aspect of Bourdieu's definition (and here, he replicates Weber), and that is its focus on *legitimacy*. According to Weber (1978, 215), three kinds of political authority legitimate domination: charismatic, traditional, and rational. Bourdieu, on the other hand, argues that legitimate political domination depends on political capital accumulation and symbolic capital accumulation (Swartz 2013, 106–11). The state is the end result of struggles in the political field to obtain positions of authority, and of struggles *by* those authorities to impose and naturalize their visions of the world as legitimate (Bourdieu 2000, 63–64). As a result, for Bourdieu, political power becomes legitimate (and political domination is obtained) when states (or state authorities) are able to impose symbolic divisions that represent social divisions. This can take two different forms: "On the objective level, one may take action in the form of acts of representation, individual or collective, meant to show up and to show off, certain realities . . . . On the subjective level, one may act by trying to change the categories of perception and evaluation of the social world, the cognitive and evaluative structures" (Bourdieu 1991, 124; see also Bourdieu 1989, 20). In this sense, the struggle for political domination entails *both* objective political power and symbolic power that legitimates domination through misrecognition. In turn, to obtain legitimate political domination, political capital and symbolic capital are required.

That legitimate political authority depends on successful accumulation of political and symbolic capital leads to the question of how it is that political authorities accumulate political and symbolic capital in the first place—how do they "[incarnate themselves] in objectivity, in the form of specific organizational structures and mechanisms, and in subjectivity in the form of mental structures and categories of perception of thought" (Bourdieu 1994, 3–4)? Building on these two theoretical moves, and with evidence collected from French national, Catholic diocesan, and Jewish community archives in France, I argue as follows: the religious nationalism of the Vichy regime was produced through four processes of alignment between the religious and political fields, made possible by the actions of religious and political elite. In turn, these alignments facilitated the accumulation of political and symbolic capital required to legitimize the "new" French state, its efforts at symbolic violence against Jews included.

The following section briefly identifies two political and two symbolic mechanisms to analyze processes of political and religious field alignment in France from 1940 to 1942 and then complements this identification of mechanisms with evidence from this time period.

Political Capital and Mechanisms

Whereas social capital is the ability to mobilize support through acquaintances and networks, political capital hinges on the objectification of this support in the form of institutionalized positions and alliances (Bourdieu 1991, 196–97; 2000, 64, 65; Bourdieu and Wacquant 1992, 119). Hence, political capital accumulation can be observed by *evaluating whether there has been an increase in public endorsements for the government and its representatives among actors who did not speak out on its behalf with similar frequency prior to the time period of interest*. This is a proxy for support through acquaintances and networks. Second, political capital accumulation can be observed by *evaluating whether acquaintances and networks have become embedded in formal state structures*. This is a proxy for support for institutionalized positions and alliances. Each of these measures is an indicator of changing relational dynamics that can be used to observe political capital accumulation. The focus is on changing objective relations that indicate political support, measured by public endorsements and institutionalized arrangements.

Symbolic Capital and Mechanisms

To legitimize authoritarianism as a form of political rule, a government must also successfully combine its political capital with symbolic capital. Unique in its emphasis on misrecognition, symbolic capital naturalizes political capital by deflecting attention away from its power dynamics (Bourdieu 1989, 23; Loveman 2005, 1655).

According to Bourdieu (1991), religion is an especially good "resource" for states and state authorities interested in accumulating symbolic capital in an effort to legitimately impose symbolic meanings and classifications. This is because religion *qua* religion is a system of symbolic meaning that "dupes people" into believing that their positions in society—and others' positions too—are "somehow natural or, worse still, divinely sanctioned" (Rey 2007, 6). In this way, religion is a form of misrecognition *par excellence*. Religion is a symbolic system that helps "create, legitimate, and reproduce unjust social orders" (7). In turn, the church, as the social institution responsible for "producing" religion, and bishops, as "specialists" of the (Catholic) religious field, play a role in consecrating the social order as legitimate.

Subsequently, symbolic capital accumulation can be observed by *evaluating whether there has been an increase in expressions of common religious and political worldviews compared with before the time period of interest*. It can also be observed by *evaluating whether there has been a conflation of religious and political symbols*. Together, both practices serve to legitimize and naturalize political systems and agendas through misrecognition, enabling the accumulation of symbolic capital in the political sphere. Each can therefore be examined to observe symbolic capital accumulation.

Data and Methods

The documents analyzed in this chapter comprise a variety of sources on the French Catholic episcopate and the Vichy government as well as the rabbinate and letters from important Jewish community leaders in France. These include private diaries, notes, and personal correspondence between bishops, with the papal nuncio Valerio Valeri, and with numerous representatives of the Vichy government. I also examine sermons, mass announcements, and publications in the *Semaine religieuse* newsletter of each diocese, as well as local publications that gave voice to the French Catholic Church, however muffled due to censorship. Finally, I consider primary documents from chief rabbis in the French rabbinate and other important Jewish community leaders, such as Jacques Helbronner, president of the Israelite Central Consistory of France from 1940 until 1943, when he was deported to Auschwitz and murdered. The data were collected from the diocesan archives in Lyon, Cambrai, and Paris, the National Center for the Church Archives of France, the archives of the Alliance Israélite Universelle, and the French National Archives. All translations are mine unless otherwise noted. Secondary sources are specified in parentheses.

Importantly, when analyzing these documents, I primarily focus on processes that indicate changing patterns of relations among the Catholic hierarchy with Vichy government authorities and the Jewish rabbinate. This requires a relational approach. Instead of examining individuals or groups as entities—for instance, "the church," "the state," or "the Jews"—I focus on the relationships between them. This approach to historical analysis allows me to identify the consequences of changing interaction patterns for Jews' experiences during the Holocaust.

Analysis: How Catholic Bishops Contributed to Vichy's Violence against Jews

Public Endorsements

Beginning in fall 1940, the church openly rallied to the regime and encouraged the laity to follow in its stead. Best known among these statements of support is Cardinal Gerlier's famous declaration, on November 19, 1940, that "Pétain is France, and France today is Pétain."[8] This statement, though not unanimously supported by all bishops, was indicative of the episcopate's formal public stance, which would be expressed time and again during this time period.[9]

For example, on January 15, 1941, the Association of Cardinals and Archbishops (ACA) met and proclaimed "total loyalty to the state and the government in France."[10] This position was endorsed by the ACA in unoccupied France two weeks later.[11] On May 4, 1941, Bishop Piguet of Clermont-Ferrand declared, "[Pétain] alleviates our misery and seeks to eradicate, through . . . himself and his glory of yesteryear, the costs of our misery."[12] Yet simultaneously, misery after misery was being heaped on Jews. Already on July 22, 1940, the Vichy government had constructed a Commission for the Revision of Naturalizations to review all grants of French citizenship since 1927. Jews were disproportionately denaturalized and deported under this policy (Zalc 2016).

Likewise, the first major roundup of Jews in Paris occurred on May 14, 1941, two months before another ACA meeting where Cardinal Gerlier called for "a sincere and complete loyalty to the established power."[13] Public endorsements for the state from the church were even evident as late as September 1, 1941, less than two weeks after 4,232 Jews were arrested in Paris by French police collaborating with German *Feldgendarmes*. These Jews were first taken to the Drancy concentration camp in northeast Paris, then deported to Auschwitz, where they were murdered. On the same day, Monsignor Jean Chollet called on the faithful to follow the marshal's plan for France: "We have no right to criticize the leader himself or his orders. The subordinate obeys without question or inquiry. . . . [I]n the name of our own religious conscience we will be the most united and the most disciplined of citizens."[14]

Several weeks later, following the Jewish High Holy Day of Yom Kippur, thirteen synagogues in Paris, Marseille, and Vichy were bombed and destroyed. In response, the Council of the Association of French Rabbis drafted a declaration for Chief Rabbi Isaïe Schwartz to submit to Cardinal Gerlier.[15] Begging for a statement of support on Jews' behalf, the rabbis wrote, "How comforting for us and for our anguished brothers would it be if we were to hear our sentiments echoed . . . invoked in the synagogues, the churches, the mosques, and if the faithful of other religions and their spiritual leaders showed their reprobation of these ungodly crimes?"[16] Gerlier replied by promising to share the letter with bishops in the free zone during the ACA's next meeting.[17] He was beginning to feel anxious about mounting violence against Jews and their institutions but ultimately declined to speak out.[18] This was a radical contrast with autumn 1933, when Jewish buildings were first ransacked and numerous bishops protested on Jews' behalf. Less than a decade prior, the grand rabbi, Israël Levi, invited all Christians to form a "front of defense for the bible" whereby Jews and Catholics would ally against Nazism, and bishops from some of France's biggest cities, including Cardinal Gerlier, responded affirmatively.

Cooperation

The relationship between church and state also changed through the inclusion of religious authorities and notable Catholics in political institutions and affairs and vice versa. The Vatican appointed Archbishop Valerio Valeri to serve as papal nuncio to Vichy, and Vichy nominated its own ambassador, Léon Bérard, as its representative to the Holy See. This confirmation of positions validated the regime, along with the incorporation of over two hundred clerics into communal and departmental leadership positions throughout France (Jackson 2003, 268; Cointet 1998, 140). For the first time since 1879, countless Catholics held positions in the government (Fouilloux 1997, 194–96). Meanwhile, Jews were purged from the state council following the first Statut des Juifs (Poznanski 2001, 43).[19]

Moreover, and in a revealing exchange of letters between Cardinal Gerlier and Archbishop Valeri in February 1941, the former debated whether to accept an offer from Vichy minister of justice Joseph Bathélemy to serve on the council of ministers as an adviser.[20] Gerlier declined but not without first offering the archbishop of Cambrai and secretary of the ACA, Émile-Maurice Guerry, to serve in his stead.[21] In Paris, Cardinal Emmanuel Suhard declined a nomination to serve on the national council in March 1941 but also sent someone in his place: his chief aide, Monsignor Roger Beaussart.[22] Several months later, Beaussart was present at the formal welcoming reception for Hermann Göring, and in a private telegram to German ambassador Otto Abetz, Suhard assured him that the clergy was "fully disposed to make its influence felt in favor of collaboration."[23] And so they did, by joining the administrative structures of the state and also by frequently participating in official political events and occasions.

Meanwhile, French rabbinical authorities struggled to affirm their prewar relationships with Catholic authorities but could not. In October 1940, Chief Rabbi Julien Weill went to Cardinal Suhard with the goal of joining both of their religious communities together in solidarity—much like before the German invasion, and against what Weill characterized as Nazi ideology that could harm them both.[24] Yet Suhard had overcome what he had earlier described in his diary as apprehension about collaboration and was confident already by mid-September that aligning with German authorities would benefit the church. In his diary, Suhard wrote, "The occupying power proves correct, and even very correct, with me. What will it be tomorrow? I think the Catholic Church can emerge from this ordeal magnified and glorified by the position she held during this ordeal."[25] As a result, when Rabbi Weill met with Suhard in Paris two weeks later and requested that the two continue in their fight against Nazism, Suhard was uninterested.

Likewise, in December 1941, Jacques Helbronner wrote a letter to Pétain, which he also delivered to Cardinal Gerlier, deploring the horrible conditions of Jews in occupied France.[26] Helbronner begged the marshal to "stop this campaign of hate" that was depriving Jews "of their rights as citizens."[27] "These persecutions," he asked, "will they ever end?"[28] In his note to Pétain, Helbronner was obsequious: "You are, with his eminence Cardinal Gerlier . . . the only comfort, the only support that I can find."[29] He implored, "Can we receive from you a word of hope?"[30] Helbronner would write twenty-six more times to Pétain in 1941, often noting his ties to Cardinal Gerlier in an effort to demonstrate his social capital, but Gerlier maintained his silence, refusing to ally with him or with Jews during this time period. Pétain only minimally replied to Helbronner on occasion, and only with curt and formal letters, never addressing the issue of Jews' suffering that Helbronner raised time and time again.

Shared Values

Once the Vichy regime's political orientation became clear, French bishops perceived that its values mirrored their own and regularly expressed this to the laity. For example, on November 19, 1940, Cardinal Gerlier proclaimed in his famous speech, "work, family, fatherland—these words are ours."[31] In December, he wrote in the *Journal des débats*, "The Marshal said one day: 'our fatherland must recover the beauty of its roots.' What is then the most beautiful of all the roots if not Christianity, which gave it birth?"[32] Gerlier echoed Pétain's speeches in these statements and declarations and, in so doing, contributed to the legitimation of a worldview that described Jews as external to the natural French community.

Significantly, the Vichy government frequently courted the episcopate in its efforts to legitimize itself to the French population, and often imitated religious discourse in its own proclamations by calling for a return to religious values. For example, Pierre Sauret, director of cults and associations at the Ministry of the Interior, authored a lengthy memo on church-state relations where he argued that it was crucial for the state to work hand in hand with the episcopate because an abandonment of religion contributed to France's defeat.[33] Pétain himself was not religious, but he, too, "was happy to embrace the Church as a bastion of social order whose objectives dovetailed with the national revolution" (Jackson 2003, 268). This extended to dismissing *laïcité*, the republic's institutionalized secularism of state education, which was the most important concern among Catholic bishops and which the new regime made an early priority by rescinding, on September 3, 1940, the 1901 Law on Associations that had banned religious orders from teaching.[34] In October, the *écoles normales* (publicly funded teacher-training schools believed to be bastions of secularism) were abolished. Suhard during this same month remarked in his diary how pleased he was about the changing laws on education.[35] In December, a law was passed that instructed "duties toward God" to be taught in public schools.[36] From its very beginnings, Vichy was prepared to work with the church, motivated by common values and beliefs about how best to reconstruct the nation.

This "harmonization" of the episcopate's and the state's worldviews is striking when considering how, numerous times, Jewish leaders sought to establish an alliance with the church by calling attention to *their* presumed-to-be-common values. For example, after the first Statut des Juifs was passed, on October 22,

Rabbi Schwartz denounced the new laws in both occupied and unoccupied France in a letter to Pétain, fervently writing that they were a form of "racial legislation, [with] principles born outside our borders, repudiated by Judaism, denied by consciousness and sentenced *ex cathedra* by the head of the Catholic Church and other Christian churches."[37] Rabbi Weill followed suit one day later.[38] These letters demonstrate how little the rabbis knew about the church's "new" worldview. Rabbis Schwartz and Weill tried to appeal to Catholic values as a form of symbolic capital that could sway the marshal's stance. Sadly, their letters instead revealed a widening divide between the episcopate and the rabbinate: the rabbis did not know that the statute had been passed with the bishops' consent.

Common Rhetoric

Finally, the change in relations between religious and political authorities in France during this time period can be seen in the shared symbolism expressed by both, including in the use of religious metaphors and prayers. Best known among these is how Pétain identified himself with Christ's sacrifice and framed his role as that of a redeemer, saving France from her sinful past and leading her into a glorious future. Three days after signing the armistice, Pétain proclaimed on the radio that he was prepared to give France "the gift of my person." When Pétain first visited Lyon, Gerlier, welcoming him, exclaimed, "France needed a chief who would lead her to her eternal destiny. God has allowed for you to be here."[39] One year later, Suhard wrote to Pétain of his "profound conviction, that God in your person, will always protect France and renew her."[40] Shortly after, at Christmas Mass in Notre Dame, he described the population's suffering under the weight of occupation as a time of "salvation," brought to France by a "unique savior." Suhard then turned to extend his Christmas greetings—in front of a crowd of hundreds—to Pétain.[41]

In addition to the symbolism of Pétain as savior, the Vichy regime also adapted religious emblems to encourage the public to support its political agenda. The contortion of Joan of Arc's image in service of the regime was especially common, such as when a propaganda poster depicted Pétain in Joan of Arc's likeness and fighting a "crusade" against "the bolshevik peril" (Pinto 2012, 18). A stained-glass window in Orléans displayed Joan of Arc alongside an image of "Orléans aux Juifs," where the latter depicted Jews dominating French civil society and destroying it. The Joan of Arc window, in contrast, proclaimed that the "figure that would embody France would be the one who would rid the country of foreigners such as the English and, especially, the Jews" (Pinto 2012, 16–17). The manipulation of Joan of Arc in the service of religious and national symbolism was yet another way in which the state co-opted religious emblems to legitimize its goals and make them appear as natural features of the French landscape.

Moreover, the church helped constitute the Vichy regime as the natural French authority through its many prayers for Pétain, as well as through its inclusion of political authorities in practices once reserved for religious officials only, and vice versa. In Le Puy, for example, the prayer read,

> Glorious leader of our country,
> Father great of heart, we love you,
> Your children's soul has been shattered,
> Yet only command, and we will follow you. (Quoted in Halls 1995, 169)

The national "prayer to *Le Maréchal*" that the government exhorted the public to proclaim likewise characterized Pétain as a Christlike figure. Modeled after the Catholic "Our Father," it ended with the injunction, "and deliver us from evil, Oh, Marshal!"

Finally, religious ceremonies, much like the Christmas Mass at Notre Dame described above, also regularly included an homage to Pétain, sometimes even in person, such as when he stopped at the Cathedral of Notre-Dame-de-l'Assomption in Clermont-Ferrand on his tour of the South in November 1940. The service included a ceremony where he walked "like a youth" up the steps of the stage, decorated with a military medal, alongside the bishop, Monsignor Piguet, who also wore a military medal and the Croix de Guerre (Le Moigne 2005, 96). Members of the hierarchy were also regularly present at the inauguration of German institutes and the funerals of known collaborationists (Burrin 1996, 220), while they simultaneously avoided ceremonies for members of the resistance. Jewish authorities were forbidden from participating in joint political and religious ceremonies. There was no common rhetoric between them; Jews were excluded entirely.

In the summer and fall of 1940, the Vichy government came to power in France through the problematic circumstances of "collective abdication" (Ermakoff 2008). Immediately, this new government endeavored to reconstruct the nation through a philosophy it called the National Revolution. But due to the vexed conditions under which it was instituted, the Vichy government required legitimacy to promote its political agenda. As a result, it appealed to the episcopate to naturalize its rule, and in so doing, it reversed decades in which the government in France strengthened itself by breaking its ties with the church. Subsequently, and as the French historian Denis Peschanski (2004, 409) explains, "the history of

France's defeat, occupation, and subsequent liberation may be read and written as a constant struggle for legitimacy ... [and] one of the main actors and arbiters of this struggle was the Catholic Church." This chapter has analyzed precisely *how* Catholic religious authorities in France facilitated the legitimation of the Vichy regime and, in simultaneously remaining publicly silent concerning violence against Jews, helped to legitimize the idea that there was a "Jewish Problem" in France.

Specifically, I begin by extending Bourdieu's idea that legitimate political domination depends on political and symbolic capital accumulation to generate a theory of how meso-level leaders contribute to the legitimation of violence. This theory asserts that, through public endorsements and cooperation, both proxies for political capital accumulation, and through the expression of shared values and common rhetoric, both proxies for symbolic capital accumulation, meso-level actors help incarnate authoritarian leaders and their violent dictates in both objective and subjective ways. This theory can—and, indeed, ought to be—tested and refined with future work on similar cases of violence. Though the details of the French case are unique, the contours are not.

In particular, with authoritarianism on the rise in once-democratic societies, with political authorities bent on reclassifying citizens as *not truly* nationals, and with the vicious targeting of immigrants and refugees, the public stances of religious and other meso-level actors can profoundly shape how civilians interpret these events and actions. Likewise, it can shape the opportunities that civilians perceive for resistance. Though this chapter does not discuss it, when French bishops defected from their support for Vichy and protested on Jews' behalf, they bolstered existing resistance movements and helped trigger a sea change in public opinion vis-à-vis the regime's legitimacy. Not only did the bishops' protest lead to a collapse in deportation rates of Jews, but it also prompted hundreds of priests, monks, and nuns to prepare false documents for Jews in hiding and to offer religious institutions as a haven for Jews in need. Catholic citizens, as well, mobilized on Jews' behalf by hiding them in religious boarding schools with their families. Hence, while French bishops' actions were shaped by their time and place, their lessons have important relevance far beyond the confines of this one case.

REFERENCES

Adler, Jacques. 2001. "The Jews and Vichy: Reflections on French Historiography." *Historical Journal* 44 (4): 1065–82.

Bédarida, Renée. 1998. *Les Catholiques dans la guerre, 1939–1945: Entre Vichy et la Résistance*. Paris: Seuil.

Bernay, Sylvie. 2012. *L'Église de France face à la persécution des juifs 1940 1944*. Paris: CNRS.

Bourdieu, Pierre. 1989. "Social Space and Symbolic Power." *Sociological Theory* 7 (1): 14–25.
——. 1991. *Language and Symbolic Power.* Cambridge, MA: Harvard University Press.
——. 1994. "Rethinking the State: Genesis and Structure of the Bureaucratic Field." Translated by Loïc J. Wacquant and Samar Farage. *Sociological Theory* 12 (1): 1–18.
——. 2000. *Pascalian Meditations.* Redwood City, CA: Stanford University Press.
Bourdieu, Pierre, and Loïc J. D. Wacquant. 1992. *An Invitation to Reflexive Sociology.* Chicago: University of Chicago Press.
Brubaker, Rogers. 1992. *Citizenship and Nationhood in France and Germany.* Cambridge, MA: Harvard University Press.
Burrin, Phillipe. 1996. *Vichy France under the Germans: Collaboration and Compromise.* New York: New Press.
Cointet, Michèle. 1998. *L'Eglise sous Vichy, 1940–1945: La repentance en question.* Paris: Perrin.
de Pury, Roland. 1978. "Les églises et les Chrétiens à l'automne 1944." *Revue du nord* 60 (238) ["Églises et Chrétiens pendant la Seconde Guerre Mondiale: Les colloques de Lyon et de Varsovie"]: 729–33.
Drapac, Vesna. 1998. *War and Religion: Catholics in the Churches of Occupied Paris.* Washington, DC: Catholic University of America Press.
Ermakoff, Ivan. 2008. *Ruling Oneself Out: A Theory of Collective Abdications.* Durham, NC: Duke University Press.
Fouilloux, Etienne. 1997. *Les Chrétiens français entre crise et libération: 1937–1947.* Paris: Seuil.
Georges, Olivier. 2003. "Un discours controversé: La réception du Maréchal Pétain à Lyon par le Cardinal Pierre-Marie Gerlier, le 20 novembre 1940." *Chrétiens et Sociétés XVIe–XXIe siècles* 10:133–49.
Goldberg, Chad A. 2007. *Citizens and Paupers: Relief, Rights, and Race, from the Freedmen's Bureau to Workfare.* Chicago: University of Chicago Press.
Gorski, Philip S., and Gulay Türkmen-Dervişoğlu. 2013. "Religion, Nationalism, and Violence: An Integrated Approach." *Annual Review of Sociology* 39 (1): 193–210.
Halls, W. D. 1995. *Politics, Society, and Christianity in Vichy France.* Providence, RI: Berg.
Jackson, Julian. 2003. *France: The Dark Years, 1940–1944.* Oxford: Oxford University Press.
Joly, Laurent. 2013. "The Genesis of Vichy's Jewish Statute of October 1940." *Holocaust and Genocide Studies* 27 (2): 276–98.
Le Moigne, Frédéric. 2005. *Les évêques français de Verdun à Vatican II: Une génération en mal d'héroïsme.* Rennes: Presses Universitaires de Rennes.
Loveman, Mara. 2005. "The Modern State and the Primitive Accumulation of Symbolic Power." *American Journal of Sociology* 110 (6): 1651–83.
Luft, Aliza. 2016. "Shifting Stances: How French Bishops Defected from Support for the Anti-Semitic Vichy Regime to Save Jews during the Holocaust." PhD diss., University of Wisconsin–Madison.
——. 2020. "Religion in Vichy France: How Meso-Level Actors Contribute to Authoritarian Legitimation." *European Journal of Sociology* 61 (1): 67–101.
Marrus, Michael, and Robert Paxton. (1981) 1995. *Vichy France and the Jews.* Stanford, CA: Stanford University Press.
Nord, Philip. 2003. "Catholic Culture in Interwar France." *French Politics, Culture, and Society* 21:1–20.

Peschanski, Denis. 2004. "Legitimacy/Legitimation/Delegitimation: France in the Dark Years, a Textbook Case." *Contemporary European History* 13 (4): 409–23.

Pinto, Minerva. 2012. "Nationalist Symbol of a Nation Divided: The Paradox of France's Joan of Arc, 1940–1944." BA thesis, Haverford College.

Poznanski, Renée. 2001. *Jews in France during World War II*. Waltham, MA: Brandeis University Press, in association with the United States Holocaust Memorial Museum.

Rey, Terry. 2007. *Bourdieu on Religion: Imposing Faith and Legitimacy*. London: Equinox.

Rosbottom, Ronald C. 2014. *When Paris Went Dark: The City of Light under German Occupation, 1940–1944*. New York: Little, Brown.

Slater, Dan, and Erica Simmons. 2010. "Informative Regress: Critical Antecedents in Comparative Politics." *Comparative Political Studies* 43 (7): 886–917.

Swartz, David. 2013. *Symbolic Power, Politics, and Intellectuals: The Political Sociology of Pierre Bourdieu*. Chicago: University of Chicago Press.

Tallett, Frank, and Nicholas Atkin, eds. 1991. *Religion, Society and Politics in France since 1789*. London: Hambledon.

Weber, Max. 1978. *Economy and Society: An Outline of Interpretive Sociology*. Translated by Guenther Roth. Edited by Claus Wittich. Berkeley: University of California Press.

Zalc, Claire. 2016. *Dénaturalisés: Les retraits de nationalité sous Vichy*. L'Univers historique. Paris: Éditions du Seuil.

11

USING THE YAD VASHEM TRANSPORT DATABASE TO EXAMINE GENDER AND SELECTION DURING THE HOLOCAUST

Susan Welch

Transporting Jews to the East, where they would be murdered en masse out of the sight of westerners, was a key part of the Holocaust.[1] In his seminal early work on the Holocaust, Raul Hilberg (1961) devoted nearly three hundred pages to the topic of planning, organizing, and carrying out deportations. Transports were not only an effective way to move people to the camps and killing sites, where they would be murdered immediately or through the brutality of the camp conditions, but an efficient way to continue the process of dehumanization and destruction that began with public policies to strip Jews of their livelihood and freedoms (Gigliotti 2010) and ended in their deaths.

This chapter uses a unique data source to help us understand the role of gender in these transports and the survival of the men and women on them. After briefly describing the role of transports in the Holocaust, I describe the Yad Vashem database, where, for the first time, information is being assembled on all known transports. Using this database, I will then compare findings on the gender composition of transports and the survival rates of those transported with the individual-level survival rates of Italian Jews who were deported.

Transports and the Holocaust

German policy on how and where Jews were to be murdered varied throughout the war, and this, of course, affected transport origins, timing, and destinations

(Cesarani 2016, 451–581). Early in the war, the relatively few transports went to eastern ghettos and some labor camps. After the invasion of the Soviet Union and Soviet-occupied Poland in June 1941, the Germans developed a plan to kill all Jews in the *Generalgouvernement* (the central part of Poland not incorporated directly into the Reich in the West nor occupied by the Soviet Union in the East). Called Operation Reinhard, the plan included building three killing camps—Belzec, Sobibor, and Treblinka—which were opened during 1942.[2] Starting in February 1942, the Nazis also began to use Auschwitz as a killing and slave labor camp for Jews (Browning 2004, 307; Cesarani 2016, 454–56). An essential part of their horrific plan was to transport hundreds of thousands of Jews to these killing sites.

Most of those transported came from the large Jewish populations in Poland and other areas of Eastern Europe. But more than 550,000 Western and Central European Jews were also transported to these killing sites and to Eastern European ghettos and labor camps. The transports came from cities and towns and from several transit camps in Western Europe.

Almost all Western European Jews who were murdered in the Holocaust were killed after being deported from their communities to eastern locations. This is in contrast with the Jews of Eastern Europe. Hundreds of thousands of *Ostjuden* were deported to and murdered in killing camps and Auschwitz, but hundreds of thousands of others were killed by bullets in their own towns and villages or nearby (Desbois 2009).[3]

Table 11.1 indicates the destinations, where known, of all the transports from Western Europe by year. The number of transports peaked in 1942, and so did the number of transports to Auschwitz, the killing camps, the ghettos, and Terezin. After 1942, ghettos were being liquidated and transports there ceased.[4] By the end of 1943, the Nazis had closed and destroyed the killing centers.

TABLE 11.1 Destination of Western European transports by year

	AUSCHWITZ	GHETTO	TEREZIN	KILLING	CONCENTRATION	TOTAL
1939–40	0	4	0	0	0	4
1941	0	46	9	0	1	56
1942	110	50	274	35	0	469
1943	92	0	149	23	2	266
1944	87	0	136	0	32	255
1945	0	0	43	0	2	45
Total	289	101	611	58	36	1,095

Note: The destination of fifteen transports remains unknown.

Gender and the Transports

Little has been written about gender and transports (but see Cole 2016; Welch 2020a, 2020b). In fact, for many years, gender was not addressed at all. In the first decades after the war, German attempts to kill all Jews made discussions of gender differences "irrelevant and even irreverent," as one writer remarked (Ringelheim 1998, 323).[5] But as more survivors came forward to tell their stories and as women's history became more mainstream, the discussion of the experiences of women in the ghettos, in camps, and in hiding became more frequent (Bos 2003; Goldenberg and Shapiro 2013; Hilberg 1992, 17, 34); Ofer and Weitzman 1999; Rittner and Roth 1998). We have discovered, as Nechama Tec (2003, 12) has written, "Even though the Germans were committed to sending all Jews to their deaths, for a variety of reasons women and men traveled toward that destination on distinct roads."

Although social scientists made seminal contributions to understanding the Holocaust in the first wave of research after the war (as luminous examples, see Adorno et al. 1950; Hilberg 1961; Kogan 1950), their interest in the Holocaust diminished after the first postwar years, and did not revive until rather recently (King 2012; and see King, chap. 1 in this volume). It is not surprising, then, that most research on gender and the Holocaust has been qualitative, based on personal testimonies through interviews, diaries, and autobiographies, ghetto histories, and other textual records. Even this work has paid little attention to the transports.

There has been sporadic documentation about the gender distributions of those on the transports. For example, diarists in the Warsaw ghetto reported that trainloads of Jews from Central and Eastern Europe pouring in were mostly women, and those on the trains to Treblinka were also mostly women (Ringelheim 1993, 338). After these massive deportations to Treblinka, those left behind were about 56 percent male, most of working age (Cesarani 2016, 526). Ringelheim (1998, 347) also reports that the transports from the Łódź ghetto were also mostly women. But the gender distribution of prisoners on transports to eastern camps and ghettos from other cities are mostly unremarked on (Trunk and Gutman 2008).

We know that gender differences in treatment persisted after individuals reached their transport destinations, though that, too, has been rarely explored. The most widely known example is the first selection at Auschwitz, where women with small children were usually sent immediately to be gassed; comparably healthy young men were usually not.[6] For most destinations, however, we do not know and may never know what happened to individuals. What became of the thousands of Berliners and Viennese dropped in the Łódź ghetto in late 1941, for example (Adelson 1991)? We know a few survived the war, but we do not know who and how many died in Łódź, nor do we know all of those who were deported to Chełmno or other camps and died there.[7] We also lack information about most of those taken directly to concentration camps. People were killed through work, starvation, random brutality, and disease, or by being sent on to other camps, not by an immediate decision on arrival.

With gender as a focus, this chapter will help fill in those gaps. We will look specifically at the gender compositions of transports sent from eight Western European nations, how those compositions varied during the war and from different origins, and, to the extent we know, the immediate and longer-term fate of Western European Jews sent to Auschwitz.

The Yad Vashem Database

The primary data for our analysis are drawn from the information contained in "Transports to Extinction: Holocaust (Shoah) Deportation Database." Established online, beginning in 2012, by Yad Vashem's International Institute for Holocaust Research, the database contains detailed information about each transport: the dates it departed and arrived, its origin and destination, the number of people on it, the route it took, and the number of survivors.[8] A narrative describes the background for each transit, with, for example, information on the state of the war, the immediate strategy for deportations in the area or country, the preparations that the prisoners were allowed or forced to make beforehand, the assembling places and conditions there, Nazi and local officials who were overseeing the transport, if known, and the place of the transport in a series from that locale, if relevant. The primary purpose of these Yad Vashem data is to record the fate of as many individual Holocaust victims as possible for the benefit of their families, communities, and posterity. But the data are immensely useful for social scientists as well.

In compiling these data, historians at Yad Vashem rely on extensive archives of official documents and survivors' testimonies in addition to published work on each specific transport, including survivors' reports, reports on national railways, the transports from that location (for example, Westerbork or Berlin), and national histories.[9] Vast amounts of information, including survivor testimony, is available for many transits; for others, almost nothing is known. For most transits, the database also includes information on how many were immediately murdered on arrival at their destination—for example, sent to the gas chambers at Auschwitz or killing sites near some ghettos—and how many prisoners are known to have survived the war. Because Yad Vashem's compilation of the data was based on extant transport, survivor, and country sources, I made only occasional use of these other sources.[10]

Information on most of the transports, though not all, includes the gender breakdown of the passengers. Sometimes there is information on the age of the prisoners, the number who survived the war, and the gender of the survivors. In many cases, complete or partial rosters of prisoners on the transports are included.

The transports in this dataset encompass all of those transported from Western Europe for whom there is information as of early 2020. The researchers at Yad Vashem continue to augment and amend the data as new information comes to light.[11]

Those who have tried to accurately measure the numbers and characteristics of individuals on transports know the near impossibility of this task. The size and composition of transports changed during the time between the initial summons and the final boarding. Often last-minute additions and deletions to the initial passenger lists were made. Some of those assigned to a transport committed suicide or died from illness between the time they were notified and when the transport left.[12] Others were able to argue their way off the transport and still others were forced onto it. After final boarding, numbers would continue to change, with deaths and escapes during the journey and occasionally stoppages at work sites to unload fit men, whose exact numbers were usually not precisely recorded.[13] Sometimes deaths en route are noted, but other times not, as when the bodies of the dead were simply taken off the train upon arrival at the destination and disposed of in the same way as others. Escapees also are not always recorded. Danuta Czech's (1997) Auschwitz compilation, for example, relied on the initial roster of the transport in recording the transport size and did not take into account changes thereafter.

Because the data are based on transports, not individuals, I cannot track all individuals, a limitation in trying to determine who survived and who were redeported from their original destinations. The Yad Vashem researchers are making great progress in providing lists of victims, but the number of people listed on many transports is larger than the number who were on the transports, and on others there is no roster at all. The rosters for the transports were amended many times, and a final reckoning may not be possible.

Those still alive are usually not included on the transport roster, presumably for privacy reasons. Despite these various limitations, this is the most complete set of information on transports during the Holocaust and, in my view, well worth exploring despite its defects.

Data and Methods

Data for this chapter are derived primarily from 1,110 transports to the East from eight nations of Western and Central Europe (Austria, Belgium, Czechoslovakia, France, Germany, Italy, Luxembourg, and the Netherlands) containing roughly 567,000 people, almost all of them Jews.[14] Of these transports, 15 were excluded from most analyses because the destination was unknown, leaving 1,095. Another 31 that carried Jews to major internal transit centers such as Drancy and Westerbork were also excluded.[15] A majority of the 1,110 transports went to Terezin in Czechoslovakia, most of the rest departed for Poland, and some carried Jews to the Baltics.[16] The unit of analysis for these data is the transport.

A more complete understanding of individual and collective fates will come when we have information about each individual on each transport. There, too, progress has been made. Serge Klarsfeld (1983) has made it part of his life's work to compile lists of every prisoner on every transport from France and from Belgium. The digital "Joods Monument" (n.d.) documents the life of every Jew living in the Netherlands who died in the Holocaust. The site is not yet easily searchable to connect people with transports, however. Perhaps the most complete compilation of individual data is that of Liliana Picciotto (2017), who, with the support of the Ricerca della Fondazione Centro di Documentazione Ebraica Contemporanea, has published a list of each Jew who lived in Italy and was deported. Each biographical entry includes information on birthplace and date and place of death, along with information about where the individual was arrested, held, transported to, and died.

It is the latter source we will use to compare some of the key findings for the Italian transports. These include information on nearly 8,600 Jews living in Italy from September 1943 to March 1945 during the German occupation.

Size, Origin, and Destination of Transports from Western Europe

Though most images of transports and survivor testimonies focus on transports of hundreds of prisoners, 36 percent of these transports from Western Europe included fifty prisoners or fewer. Many included only a handful of prisoners, and 8 percent just one. Small transports sometimes involved high-ranking members of the Jewish community or, toward the end of the war, half Jews and Jews married to Christians who had earlier been protected from deportation. Table 11.2 illustrates the distribution of transport sizes. Clusters occur around 1, 50, 100, and 1,000.

TABLE 11.2 Average number of prisoners per transport

TRANSPORT SIZES	PROPORTION OF TRANSPORTS (%)
1	8
50 or less	36
51–500	18
501–990	14
990–1,010	18
1,010 or more	14

TABLE 11.3 Number of transports from Western Europe by year

YEAR	MEAN NUMBER OF PRISONERS
1939–1940	755
1941	945
1942	617
1943	495
1944	262
1945	126

The transports from Western Europe went to thirty different destinations. More than half went to Terezin (612) and a quarter (289) to Auschwitz. Lublin (30), Sobibor (29), and Riga (24) were the next most frequent destinations.

As table 11.3 shows, the mean number of prisoners on each transport decreased significantly after 1942 as the number of Jews "available" for transport decreased. So while nearly 1,000 Jews were transported on each train in 1942, by 1945 the number was 126.[17]

Findings

For 77 percent (N = 872) of the transports, we were able to find a gender breakdown of the prisoners in the Yad Vashem database or other sources.[18] Availability of gender data differs greatly among the eight countries. In Italy and Belgium, we can identify the gender composition on all transports, while in Holland we can identify it on only 53 percent. Details from many of the transports from Westerbork are missing. Gender composition data in the other countries range between 74 percent (Czechoslovakia) and 89 percent (Luxembourg).

The 236 cases with missing gender data are disproportionately from the first three years of the war (48 percent missing) compared to the middle (22 percent), and the last two years (14 percent). Thus there is more missing gender data for transports to ghettos (54 percent) than any of the other destinations, because ghetto transports occurred only in the early years of the war.[19] The Italian data contain gender data on all but one individual.

Gender Compositions of Transports

As we anticipated, women were a majority of those transported. On the average transport, 56 percent of the prisoners were women, and women constituted a majority on 72 percent of the transports (Welch 2020b, 468). But the proportions varied greatly from country to country, ranging from 41 percent in France to 62 percent in Germany.

Country-to-country differences, especially the high proportion of women on German transports, are consistent with the fact that the prewar Nazi regime in Germany had substantially reduced the Jewish male population available for transport primarily by stimulating emigration. The low proportion of men on the French transports is likely linked to the large Jewish immigrant population of that country, which made up around 40 percent of its Jewish population (Semelin 2019, 10, 86).[20] Prewar immigrants were most likely to be men. Almost two-thirds of Jews deported from France were nonnatives (Semelin 2019, 86).[21]

Italy's convoy prisoners were almost equally divided between men and women. Women were 49 percent of the prisoners, significantly less than the overall European average. The mean proportion of women, calculated by averaging proportions of women on each transport, is almost identical to the proportion of women overall.

Obviously, the calculation of the proportion of women on each transport would not be identical to that calculated from individual data if gender distributions differed widely on transports of different sizes. For example, the average transport from Czechoslovakia held 55 percent women prisoners, but calculated on the basis of individuals on those transports, the average was closer to 57.

TABLE 11.4 Estimating the proportion of women on Italian transports

	ON EACH TRANSPORT	OVERALL (CALCULATED FROM TRANSPORT DATA)	OVERALL (CALCULATED FROM INDIVIDUAL DATA)
Mean percent of women	.492	.492	.491
N	43	7,919	7,911

Women also constituted a greater proportion of prisoners transported in 1942 and 1943, after Nazi policy turned from transporting Jews to ghettos and concentration and labor camps to sending them to killing camps and Auschwitz. Transports to those killing locations began in 1942, and during the second half of that year, transports to both the Reinhard camps and Auschwitz resulted in the greatest period of mass murder in history (Stone 2019).[22] The proportion of women on transports peaked in the second half of 1942 at 61 percent (Welch 2020b, 465). By the time the Italian deportations began, the Germans had destroyed all traces of the Reinhard camps (Arad 2018, 211–28).[23]

Gender Differences in Initial Selections

Gender differences in treatment persisted after individuals reached their transport destinations. We know most about selection at Auschwitz (Dwork and Pelt 2002; Rees 2017). On the arrival of most transports, an SS officer determined who would be immediately murdered and who would be used as slave laborers. Around 43 percent of the prisoners in an average Western European transport escaped immediate death by being selected for slave labor (Welch 2020b, 472), a higher proportion than that found in Hungarian transports, where only 25 percent survived the first selection (Gerlach and Aly 2004, 134).[24] The Yad Vashem data allow us to examine the gender distribution of that selection for the first time on a scale beyond one departure place or country.[25]

We expected a higher proportion of women than men to be executed immediately, because of the policy of sending mothers with children to be gassed, without a similar policy for men. Additionally, in many cases women were overrepresented among the aged, another group that was sent immediately to be murdered (Kaplan 1999; Ringelheim 1993; Welch 2020a). An earlier analysis of

TABLE 11.5 Number of women executed on arrival at Auschwitz, compared to men

COUNTRY TRANSPORTED FROM	% WOMEN EXECUTED ON ARRIVAL, MINUS % MEN EXECUTED
Belgium	17
Czechoslovakia	5
France	10
Germany	31
Italy	9
Netherlands	18

Note: N = 194 (transports to Auschwitz where gender composition of the transport and initial gender selection data are known). A positive number equals more women murdered on arrival. I have data on only one transport each from Austria and Luxembourg, so they are omitted.

the data for eight nations indicated that transports for all countries had a higher murder rate for women than men in that first selection (see table 11.5). Overall, only 38 percent of the women were chosen for labor, compared to 51 percent of the men.[26] The differences among countries are large, with 31 percent more German women than men being sent to the gas chamber, compared with a 5 percent difference among those from Czechoslovakia.

Because these data are based on transports, not individual characteristics, they do not allow us to test our expectation that gender differences in immediate death at Auschwitz are due to the practice of murdering women with children on arrival and to the disproportionate number of women in the oldest age group. While the Auschwitz records of those admitted to the camp as slave laborers usually enumerate men and women, they don't enumerate ages. Thus, we cannot assess with the transport data whether the gender differences in survival of the first selection are based on the practice of murdering women with small children or on something else. For that we need individual-level data, shown in figure 11.1.

Overall, the individual Italian data show that women were 10 percent more likely to be murdered after the first selection in Auschwitz, a figure slightly higher than, but similar to, the 9 percent calculated from aggregate transport data. The individual-level data (figure 11.1) indicate that men and women below fifteen and above fifty-four were murdered on arrival at Auschwitz at the same rate, but for individuals from fifteen to fifty-four, significantly more women were murdered.

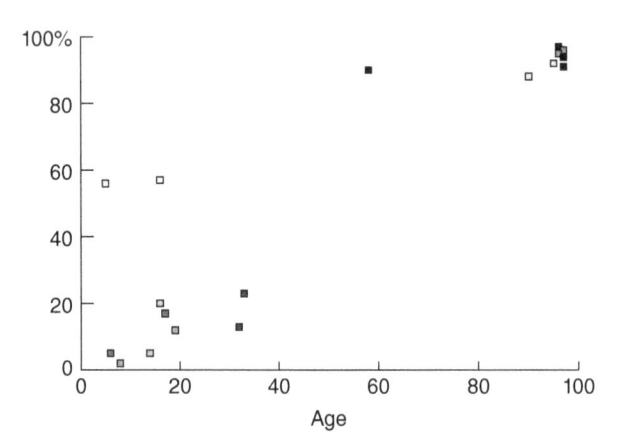

FIGURE 11.1. Age, gender, and the probability of Italian Jews being murdered on arrival at Auschwitz

Note: N = 5,448, those known to be sent to Auschwitz where age data are available. Dark-shaded dots are percent of women murdered and light-shaded dots are percent of men murdered.

The gender gap in the fifteen-to-nineteen-year-old group is somewhat surprising, as it is doubtful that many in this group had young children. Some of the younger ones may have looked childish and been treated like children slightly younger, while the older members of the cohort may have had infants or toddlers or were caring for younger siblings. Overall, though, about 10 percent more men than women in the fifteen-to-fifty-four age group survived the first day, ranging from only a 2 percent difference in the forty-five-to-fifty age cohort to a 15 percent difference in the forty-to-forty-four group.

The data also confirm that those who were sixty or older, men and women alike, were sent to immediate death at much higher rates. Only 8 percent of this group survived their first day at Auschwitz.[27] Given that there is no linear relationship between age cohort and death in this over-sixty group, we can assume that the appearance of physical strength rather than age itself is what mattered. Because women were only a small majority (52 percent) among this older group, this age group does not contribute much to the explanation of the overall gender difference in those sent to be murdered after the first selection. Rather, it was the practice of sending women with children to the gas chambers that creates the gender difference in survival of the first Auschwitz selection.

Survival at Auschwitz

The large advantage men had in surviving the first day at Auschwitz did not carry over to survival at Auschwitz throughout the war. Both our transport data and the individual data indicate that men sent to Auschwitz were slightly more likely to survive the war than comparable women, but the differences were small compared to the differences in survival on the first day.

Looking at those transported to Auschwitz and turning first to our aggregate transport data, 264 of the 290 transports have information on overall survival rates. Of the 228,206 individuals on those transports, 8,762, about 4 percent, survived through the end of the war. There is far less information on the gender distributions of survival rates. Fewer transports, only 143 and 153 (for women and men, respectively), have information on both the number of men and women on the transports and the number of men and women who survived.[28]

Based on these transports, using the total numbers of men on the transports, I calculated an overall survival rate for men, and using the total numbers of women, computed the same figure for women. Based on these partial data, the men's survival rate was significantly higher than the women's: 5 percent to 3 percent (table 11.6). Note that the basis of these figures is different from the overall survival rate, which included twice as many prisoners as the gender-specific survival rates.

TABLE 11.6 Survival rates at Auschwitz

	ALL	ITALY ONLY
Men	.05	.08
Women	.03	.06
Number of men on the transports	63,934	3,755
Number of women on the transports	51,474	3,645

These 2 percent gender differences in overall survival rates at Auschwitz were not nearly as large as those in the 9 percent difference in the initial selection. The women who survived the first selection had higher survival rates in their subsequent time at Auschwitz than did their male counterparts. Overall, however, women were still slightly less likely to survive.

Examining only those for whom we have age information, gender differences are very small. Among those in the fifteen-to-fifty-four age group, women had higher survival rates in three of the five-year cohorts (a 3–4 percent difference), and men in two (2 and 6 percent higher), and the survival rates were within 1 percent in three. Among those over sixty-four, no one survived, male or female. Thus, the gender differences in survival after the first selection dissipated during the rest of the war.

The gender differences in survival rates of Italian Jews sent to Auschwitz are similar to the differences overall in Western Europe. Italian survival rates are higher, however, because Italians were transported in 1943 and 1944, when overall survival rates had improved from earlier years in the war, especially for those transported in 1944 (Welch 2020b, 475).

Because social scientists have only relatively recently rediscovered the Holocaust in their work, it is not surprising that most of what we know about gender and the Holocaust has largely come from scholars in the humanities examining textual material, such as diaries, memoirs, and oral testimony. Their work has shed considerable light on how the Holocaust brought changes in family life and gender roles in the home and outside, sexual violence, and networks of social support in families, ghettos, and camps.

Social science perspectives combined with quantitative data allow us to augment those insights with information on large numbers of people across Europe. Our analysis has shown that the data on transports collected by Yad Vashem can help quantify the differential fate of men and women who were sent east from Western Europe. Data from Eastern Europe will allow a much fuller picture. But meanwhile, we have learned much from these data from the West.

We learned that women were the majority on nearly three-quarters of the transports, reflecting prewar gender proportions and greater "availability" to be rounded up. Women constituted larger proportions on transports from Germany than from the other nations, due to the Nazi regime's treatment of German Jews before the start of the war, which disproportionately reduced the male population.[29] Women's deaths on the first day at Auschwitz were about 13 percent higher, on average, than men's. Striking differences were expected given previous testimonies and studies of individual transports, but the Yad Vashem data allow us to document the magnitude of the differences for a major segment of Europe's Jews. Gender differences in overall survival at Auschwitz, however, were much smaller than the differential murder rates in the first selection. The overall difference was around 2 percent, and there were no meaningful differences in the fifteen-to-fifty-four age group. Though the transport data do not allow the examination of gender differences by age, our individual data from Italian transports do shed light on how age differences shaped survival.

The advent of behavioral social science and the changed political climate stifled social scientists' interest in the Holocaust after the early 1950s, until the 2010s or so. As this volume suggests, new methods, new data, new perspectives, and new questions have revived social scientists' interest. Here, the Yad Vashem data allowed us to ask and answer many questions about transports. Though my focus was on gender, other important questions could be addressed by the data. Detailed information on the place and date of departure will allow researchers to detail the logic of transport flows, looking not just at one country but Europe as a whole. How do the overall magnitude and timing of transports mesh with events in the war or in individual nations, for example?

Learning more about the Holocaust adds to our understanding of genocide and the role of gender in these events. Recently scholars who have studied other genocides have examined women's experiences (Bemporad and Warren 2018; DiGeorgio-Lutz and Gosbee 2016; Sanasarian 1989; Smith 1994). As in the genocides in Armenia, Cambodia, Darfur, Rwanda, and Bosnia, the Holocaust destroyed or dramatically changed family structure and women's role in it. The deportations of Jews during the Holocaust were one part of that, as families were torn apart and both men and women were powerless to protect their children, other family members, and each other.

A key difference between the fate of women in the Holocaust and other genocides is the very policy of deportation of hundreds of thousands of people to their deaths on trains. In Western Europe, almost all murdered Jews had been deported on a transport. In other genocides and in Eastern Europe, mass murder occurred closer to home or after forced marches. These "transports to extinction," as Yad Vashem labels them, are unique in the annals of genocide.

REFERENCES

Adelson, Alan. 1991. *Lodz Ghetto: Inside a Community under Siege*. New York: Penguin Books.
Adler, H. G., Jeremy Adler, and Benton Arnovitz. 2017. *Theresienstadt, 1941–1945: The Face of a Coerced Community*. Edited by Amy Loewenhaar-Blauweiss. New York: Cambridge University Press.
Adorno, Theodor, Else Frenkel-Brunswik, Daniel J. Levinson, and R. Nevitt Sanford. 1950. *The Authoritarian Personality*. New York: Harper and Brothers.
Arad, Yitzhak. 2018. *Belzec, Sobibor, Treblinka: The Operation Reinhard Death Camps*. Rev. and exp. ed. Bloomington: Indiana University Press.
Bemporad, Elissa, and Joyce W. Warren, eds. 2018. *Women and Genocide: Survivors, Victims, Perpetrators*. Bloomington: Indiana University Press.
Bos, Pascale Rachel. 2003. "Women and the Holocaust: Analyzing Gender Differences." In *Experience and Expression: Women, Nazis, and the Holocaust*, edited by Elizabeth R. Baer and Myrna Goldenberg, 23–52. Detroit: Wayne State University Press.
Browning, Christopher R. 2004. *The Origins of the Final Solution: The Evolution of Nazi Jewish Policy, September 1939–March 1942*. Lincoln: University of Nebraska Press.
Cesarani, David. 2016. *Final Solution: The Fate of the Jews, 1933–1949*. New York: St. Martin's.
Cole, Tim. 2016. *Holocaust Landscapes*. London: Bloomsbury.
Czech, Danuta. 1997. *Auschwitz Chronicle: 1939–1945*. New York: Henry Holt.
Desbois, Father Patrick. 2009. *The Holocaust by Bullets: A Priest's Journey to Uncover the Truth behind the Murder of 1.5 Million Jews*. Reprint edition, Basingstoke: St. Martin's Griffin.
DiGeorgio-Lutz, JoAnn, and Donna Gosbee, eds. 2016. *Women and Genocide*. Toronto: Women's Press.
Dwork, Debórah, and Robert Jan van Pelt. 2002. *Auschwitz*. New York: W. W. Norton.
Gerlach, Christian, and Götz Aly. 2004. *Das letzte Kapitel: Mord an den ungarischen Juden; 1944–1945*. Frankfurt: FISCHER Taschenbuch.
Gigliotti, Simone. 2010. *The Train Journey: Transit, Captivity, and Witnessing in the Holocaust*. New York: Berghahn Books.
Goldenberg, Myrna, and Amy Shapiro, eds. 2013. *Different Horrors/Same Hell: Gender and the Holocaust*. Seattle: University of Washington Press.
Gottwaldt, Alfred, and Diana Schulle. 2005. *Die Judendeportationen aus dem Deutschen Reich*. Wiesbaden: Marix Verlag.
Gurvitch, Georges. 1943. "Social Structure of Pre-war France." *American Journal of Sociology* 48 (5): 535–54.
Hilberg, Raul. 1961. *The Destruction of the European Jews*. Chicago: Quadrangle Books.
———. 1992. *Perpetrators, Victims, Bystanders: The Jewish Catastrophe, 1933–1945*. New York: HarperCollins.
"Joods Monument." n.d. https://www.joodsmonument.nl/?lang=en.
Kaplan, Marion. 1998. *Between Dignity and Despair: Jewish Life in Nazi Germany*. Oxford: Oxford University Press.
———. 1999. "Keeping Calm and Weathering the Storm: Jewish Women's Responses to Daily Life in Nazi Germany, 1933–1939." In Ofer and Weitzman, *Women in the Holocaust*, 39–54.
King, Charles. 2012. "Can There Be a Political Science of the Holocaust?" *Perspectives on Politics* 10 (2): 323–41.

Klarsfeld, Serge. 1983. *Memorial to the Jews Deported from France, 1942–1944: Documentation of the Deportation of the Victims of the Final Solution in France.* Paris: Beate Klarsfeld Foundation.
Kogan, Eugene. 1950. *The Theory and Practice of Hell.* New York: Farrar, Straus and Cudahy.
Kwiet, Konrad. 1984. "The Ultimate Refuge: Suicide in the Jewish Community under the Nazis." *Leo Baeck Institute Yearbook* 29:134–67.
Ofer, Dalia, and Lenore J. Weitzman, eds. 1999. *Women in the Holocaust.* New Haven, CT: Yale University Press.
Picciotto, Liliana. 2017. *Il libro della memoria: Gli ebrei deportati dall'Italia.* 2nd ed. Milan: Mursia.
Rajchman, Chil, and Solon Beinfeld. 2012. *The Last Jew of Treblinka: A Survivor's Memory, 1942–1943.* New York: Pegasus Books.
Rees, Laurence. 2017. *The Holocaust: A New History.* New York: PublicAffairs.
Ringelheim, Joan. 1993. "Women and the Holocaust: A Reconsideration of Research." In Rittner and Roth, *Different Voices*, 373–418.
———. 1998. "The Split between Gender and the Holocaust." In Ofer and Weitzman, *Women in the Holocaust*, 340–50.
Rittner, Carol, and John Roth, eds. 1998. *Different Voices: Women and the Holocaust.* New York: Paragon House.
Sanasarian, Eliz. 1989. "Gender Distinction in the Genocidal Process: A Preliminary Study of the Armenian Case." *Holocaust and Genocide Studies* 4 (4): 449–61.
Semelin, Jacques. 2019. *The Survival of the Jews in France, 1940–44.* Translated by Clotilde Meyer. Oxford: Oxford University Press.
Smith, Roger W. 1994. "Women and Genocide: Notes on an Unwritten History." *Holocaust and Genocide Studies* 8 (3): 315–34.
Stone, Lewi. 2019. "Quantifying the Holocaust: Hyperintense Kill Rates during the Nazi Genocide." *Science Advances* 5 (1): eaau7292.
Tec, Nechama. 2003. *Resilience and Courage: Women, Men and the Holocaust.* New Haven, CT: Yale University Press.
Trunk, Isaiah, and Israel Gutman. 2008. *Lodz Ghetto: A History.* Bloomington: Indiana University Press.
Welch, Susan. 2020a. "Gender, Age, and Survival of Italian Jews in the Holocaust." *Genocide Studies and Prevention: An International Journal* 14 (3): 110–28. https://scholarcommons.usf.edu/gsp/vol14/iss3/10.
———. 2020b. "Gender and Selection during the Holocaust: Transports of Western European Jews to the East." *Journal of Genocide Research* 22 (4): 459–78. https://doi.org/10.1080/14623528.2020.1764743.
Yad Vashem. 2016. "Transports to Extinction: Holocaust (Shoah) Deportation Database." http://db.yadvashem.org/deportation/search.html?language=en.

12

ADDRESSING THE MISSING VOICES IN HOLOCAUST TESTIMONY

Rachel L. Einwohner

Sol Liber was fifteen years old when Germany invaded Poland in September 1939.[1] A Warsaw native, he was interned in the Warsaw ghetto along with his parents, sisters, and extended family. Due to his contacts with youth activists, he was recruited for and participated in the Warsaw Ghetto Uprising in April 1943. Sol fought for two weeks, mostly alongside his friend Akiva. As the battles went on, Sol and Akiva hid in a bunker during the day and fought at night. When their bunker was eventually discovered, they were captured by Nazi soldiers and sent to the death camp Treblinka, along with some of Sol's family members. But neither Sol nor Akiva spent much time at Treblinka; instead, they were selected for a work detail and sent away. During an oral testimony videotaped in August 1994, Sol recounted his brief experience at the death camp, beginning with his capture during the uprising and his subsequent transport to Treblinka:

> And they marched us off to the *Umschlagplatz* [loading area for transport trains].... And they put us in the cattle cars [*pauses*] and about 80 people in a car. You couldn't turn. Just like sardines. The windows were wired or boarded up, 3,600 people ... and the minute we went out ... we came to the first station we knew we're going to Treblinka, because we knew the roads. If you go east, you were going to Auschwitz or to another camp. If you went west, you went to Treblinka. We recognized the station that we going the way to Treblinka. Everybody started panicking.... People were getting off their mind. My cousin ... cried to her father, "I want to live." And her father called out "*Shema Yisrael*,"

you know. . . . And the minute we came in, we had the shouts with dogs, "*Raus! Raus! Raus!*" you know. They panicked the people that they didn't know what soon would happen. . . . And when I left the car, my sisters were actually walking like in a daze. They didn't walk a straight line. . . . They picked out 500 young men. We were told we're going to go and clean the Warsaw ghetto. . . . Well, we stayed there about two hours until they cleaned out the cars. You didn't hear a sound anymore. 3100 people . . . it took about two hours. They got rid of them in the gas chamber. [*pauses*] See now I'm getting a little bit . . . it gets to me. And they put us back in the cars. (Liber 1994)

Tens of thousands of Holocaust survivors have, like Sol Liber, given testimony describing their experiences during World War II and its aftermath. As difficult and as painful as accounts like Sol's are to read, they are crucial to the study of the Holocaust. Obviously, survivors bear witness to the atrocities. Not only do they provide eyewitness accounts of those tragic events, but by telling their stories, survivors like Sol Liber provide a fuller picture than what might be learned from official and state records alone (see also Maynes, Pierce, and Laslett 2008; Nyseth Brehm and Fox 2017). Thanks to the work of volunteers and staff at archives and museums around the world, not to mention the dedication of the survivors themselves, Holocaust survivor testimonies have been collected and preserved so that these stories can be told, and retold, indefinitely.[2] Technological advances, such as digitizing videotaped testimonies and transcripts and making them available online, greatly enhance public access to these materials. Such efforts are especially important as the survivor generation grows smaller and the events of World War II become an ever more distant memory.

Yet as important as survivor testimonies are, they present methodological challenges for researchers who work with them. Here I am not referring to disputes about using testimonies that rest on problems with recall or historically inaccurate information (see Finkel 2015; Langer 1991). Instead I focus on potential problems that may arise when studies draw only on testimonies from survivors, without similar data from those who perished. Do such studies introduce systematic biases that preclude an accurate understanding of the Holocaust?

Scholars in many disciplines spanning the arts, humanities, and social sciences study the Holocaust by using survivor testimonies. My inquiry, however, is focused on social scientific studies of the Holocaust that use these data. Social scientists are taught to be thoughtful about their study designs and sampling procedures, with the aim of identifying and minimizing bias in their data. In this chapter I extend these concerns to the use of Holocaust survivor testimonies for social scientific inquiry. Are studies based on survivor testimonies biased, and if so, can these biases be addressed? What research questions can be answered using survivor testimonies, and what questions cannot be answered? Can social scientists properly study the Holocaust by using survivor testimony?

I address these questions by drawing on my own use of Holocaust survivor testimonies in a study of Jewish resistance. I begin by describing my project, the archive from which I gathered testimonies, and how I selected my sample. Then I address the potential for bias in the data, and illustrate my attempts to address those potential biases. In doing so, I argue that an examination of the missing voices contained in the survivor testimonies—that is, accounts of what happened to people who perished, who therefore could not give testimony—helps rule out biases somewhat. I end with a discussion of what this exercise suggests about the use of Holocaust testimonies as social science data.

To be clear, in this chapter my interest lies in ruling out potential biases of survivor testimony data by examining data from Holocaust survivors to learn something about the experiences of those who perished. While I draw on data used for a study of Jewish resistance, my goal here is to make a broader argument about the utility of survivor testimonies for a variety of inquiries, not limited to Jewish resistance. To introduce my argument, though, I begin with a brief discussion of my work on Jewish resistance.

Research Questions and Data

As a social movement scholar, my research interests center on the study of protest and resistance; thus, my work on the Holocaust focuses on Jewish resistance. The study of collective, organized Jewish resistance during the Holocaust presents a challenge to extant theories of social movement emergence, which point to the importance of some kind of political opportunity or "opening," real or perceived, that gives organized actors a chance to mobilize in pursuit of their interests (Meyer 2004). Jewish resistance in the ghettos and concentration camps of Nazi-occupied Eastern Europe, however, occurred despite a clear lack of political opportunity (Einwohner 2003; Maher 2010). From the perspective of social movement theory, then, instances of Jewish resistance are "deviant cases" that are helpful for both identifying scope conditions for extant theories and developing new explanatory concepts.

Some studies use ghettos or camps as units of analysis, and seek to understand why organized resistance emerged in some places but not others (e.g., Einwohner 2003, 2009; Epstein 2008; Finkel 2015). In contrast, the project that I draw on in this chapter is an individual-level study of Jewish resistance, with a focus on participation in organized resistance: why did some Jews participate while others did not? In particular, my interest is in armed resistance, including both armed resistance in the ghettos and partisan activity in the forests. Questions about participation in such resistance can make a contribution to the literature on social movement participation, and especially the work on "high-risk activism" (Loveman 1998; McAdam 1986).

Survivor testimonies would appear to be a useful data source for social scientific studies of participation in organized Jewish resistance. That is because of the variation across survivors in terms of participation in armed resistance. While it was relatively rare, some people (like Sol Liber) did participate in armed resistance. In contrast, many survivors did not. For instance, Pola Israelski was in the Warsaw ghetto at the same time that Liber was, at the time of the Warsaw Ghetto Uprising. The fighting happened to begin on April 19, 1943—the first night of Passover. That night Pola and some friends planned to have a Seder, the Passover ritual meal, but never got the chance:

> And we are prepared for the Seder, then all of a sudden they start to scream, "To the bunkers, to the bunkers, to the bunkers!" then we went up on this . . . how do you call it?, on the attic. And over there was a lot of feathers, feathers. And we all pushed in under the feathers, we didn't make any more Seder. And in the morning we did supposed to go to the bunker, you know, on the ground. . . . We stayed maybe eight days in that bunker. And somebody tell on us. . . . So then they took us out from that bunker. . . . It was already after . . . after the uprising, you know. It was quiet. So they took us out from the bunker and then they took everything, what we possess. I had in my girdle some money. I got to take it off because they said whoever will not give the money, whoever possess something, they will be killed. So we gave. . . . And then we went back that *Umschlagplatz*, like I said, for these few days. And then they took us to Majdanek from there. (Israelski 1995)

Studies that compare testimonies from Holocaust survivors who participated in resistance with testimonies from survivors who did not resist can uncover important factors in the decision to resist. As noted above, Sol Liber had connections to resistance fighters and organizations and was invited to join resistance efforts; in contrast, Pola Israelski lacked these connections. These findings are in line with a robust literature on social movements that points to the importance of networks and organizational memberships that draw people into activism (e.g., McAdam 1986; Morris 1984; Schussman and Soule 2005).

My work on individual participation in armed Jewish resistance during the Holocaust draws on a sample of eighty archived survivor testimonies from the USC Shoah Foundation (https://sfi.usc.edu/), which houses a collection of nearly fifty-two thousand testimonies given by Holocaust survivors and eyewitnesses. The archive includes videotaped testimonies from a wide range of individuals who witnessed the Holocaust, including European Jews, political prisoners, homosexuals, Jehovah's Witnesses, and Roma and Sinti (Gypsy) survivors, as well as liberators. I, however, limit my interest to Jewish survivors.

One of the reasons I chose this archive is its extensive catalogue of testimonies. Using this easily accessible indexing tool, I was able to limit my search to testimonies from survivors of two ghettos: Warsaw and Vilna. I chose these ghettos for two reasons. Notably, youth activists in both of these ghettos planned armed resistance (see Arad 1982; Corni 2002; Gutman 1982; Gutman 1994; Krakowski 1984), so people living in these ghettos had at least some opportunity to join a resistance organization and participate in armed resistance activities. Further, because these were among the largest ghettos in Nazi-occupied Eastern Europe, there is a large research literature (including maps and images) available on each one, which helps contextualize each survivor's testimony. Working with a research assistant, I selected all the English-language testimonies for Jewish survivors who indicated that they had lived in the Warsaw or Vilna ghettos (N = 1,002; 246 testimonies from Vilna and 756 from Warsaw). We then selected a random sample of 40 testimonies for each ghetto, for a total of 80. Because the archive's indexing tool included information about each survivor's resistance activities, we were also able to select testimonies based on whether or not the survivor had participated in resistance. Thus, we created stratified random samples of testimonies from each ghetto, with equal numbers of resisters and nonresisters. These samples included testimonies given in English by survivors who, at the time of their testimony, were living in a variety of countries, including the United States as well as Canada, England, Australia, South Africa, and Israel. According to the archive, all testimonies were given in the language of the survivor's choice, and a majority of the interviews in the archive (54.7 percent of Warsaw survivor interviews and 53.6 percent of Vilna survivor interviews) were conducted in English.

The overall sample consists of forty testimonies from survivors of the Warsaw ghetto and forty from the Vilna ghetto. Although my sampling process was intended to produce equal numbers of testimonies from resisters and nonresisters, upon reviewing the testimonies I realized that a few that were classified as "resisters" in the archive's index were coded erroneously. In some other cases, survivors did resist but did not participate in organized ghetto or partisan resistance; instead they resisted in other ways after leaving their ghetto (e.g., by joining the Polish underground on the "Aryan side" of Warsaw, after the Warsaw ghetto was liquidated and destroyed). Given my interest in ghetto-specific resistance, I recategorized "resisters" as only those individuals who either participated in organized resistance organizations in the Warsaw or Vilna ghetto or fled the

TABLE 12.1 Characteristics of sample of survivor testimonies from the USC Shoah Foundation (frequencies in parentheses)

	WARSAW	VILNA
Survivor's age at the start of World War II[a]		
Born after war started	2.5% (1)	2.6% (1)
0–6	10% (4)	2.6% (1)
7–12	25% (10)	17.9% (7)
13–16	22.5% (9)	33.3% (13)
17–21	30% (12)	35.9% (14)
22–30	10% (4)	5.2% (2)
31 and older	0% (0)	2.6% (1)
Gender		
Male	52.5% (21)	55% (22)
Female	47.5% (19)	45% (18)
Participation in ghetto resistance and/or partisans		
Yes	22.5% (9)	45% (18)
No	77.5% (31)	55% (22)
Total (N = 80)	100% (40)	100% (40)

[a] Birthdate was not included with the testimony of one Vilna survivor, so those frequencies total 39.

Vilna ghetto with the intention of joining partisan groups in the surrounding forests. As a result, my final sample of eighty testimonies had nine resisters from the Warsaw ghetto and eighteen resisters from the Vilna ghetto.

The testimonies followed an interview format, consisting of interviews conducted by trained interviewers who reviewed questionnaires filled out by the survivors prior to the interview. They took place in the survivors' homes and lasted an average of two and a half hours. Each testimony has the feel of a semistructured interview: although the wording of the interview questions varies, they all begin with questions about the survivor's prewar life and then cover personal experiences during the war, including time spent in ghettos and, if applicable, participation in resistance. These testimonies' rich, detailed accounts of life in the Warsaw and Vilna ghettos, and especially of the survivors' assessments of the threats posed by the Nazi regime and their decisions (if any) about taking action to address those threats, are invaluable to an understanding of participation in armed resistance.

Potential Biases of Testimony Data

With my study design and sample, I followed standard social scientific methodology. A sample of testimonies that includes information from both resisters and nonresisters is useful for inquiring about the correlates of participation in resistance, and random sampling is a good practice for minimizing bias. Despite these strengths, all of my data came from survivors; I of course could not include testimonies from people who perished during the Holocaust. Because my data come from survivors only, they have the potential for additional biases that I could not address with my sampling strategy.

The potential for bias in these data is twofold. The first issue is whether the testimony givers are representative of all survivors. Notably, the ages of the survivors in my sample of eighty testimonies are truncated; no one was over the age of thirty-five at the time when organized resistance efforts were taking shape in the ghettos of Warsaw and Vilna. This age distribution is an artifact of the testimony collection efforts themselves. The USC Shoah Foundation collected its testimonies from Jewish Holocaust survivors between 1994 and 1999. To give a testimony, a survivor had to be old enough to remember his or her experiences during the Holocaust but young enough to still be alive fifty years after the end of World War II. In my eighty testimonies, the survivors' ages at the start of World War II ranged from not yet born to thirty-one years old, with an average age of sixteen. Of necessity, there are no testimonies from anyone who was elderly at the time of the ghettos; regardless of their experiences during the war, they could not have lived long enough to give their testimonies in the 1990s.

The second issue is whether there are any systematic differences between Holocaust survivors and those who perished. If so, then a study based only on testimonies from survivors could be missing important perspectives, resulting in a flawed understanding of participation in armed resistance. Some scholarship does point to notable differences in survival among social groups. For instance, in the ghettos, young, able-bodied teens and adults were typically selected by authorities for labor, which sometimes afforded opportunities for survival. In contrast, those who were seemingly "nonproductive" from the Nazi authorities' point of view—namely, children and people who were weak, sick, old, and/or pregnant—were among the first to be deported and killed (Gurewitsch 1998; Ofer and Weitzman 1998). The sociologist and Holocaust survivor Nechama Tec (2003) also argues that there were gender differences in survival in the ghettos, where women were more likely to survive than men: women's traditional homemaking skills, such as knowing how to stretch meager food rations, made them more resilient. Moreover, those who were lucky enough to find work, which often meant the ability to obtain extra food, or to live with a family member or friend were more likely to survive (Ofer and Weitzman 1998).

A "survivor bias"—that is, a systematic bias introduced by having only testimony from survivors, if such a bias exists—potentially complicates my ability to reach conclusions about why people participated in resistance. It is possible that survivors had different reasons for participating in resistance than did people who were faced with the same decision regarding resistance but perished; it is also possible that older respondents may have had distinct reasons for participating in resistance (or deciding not to do so). But without information from the missing voices—those who did not live long enough to be able to give their testimony, either because they were killed during the Holocaust or because their advanced age prevented them from living until the testimonies were collected—how can these biases be identified and addressed?

Addressing Potential Biases

I begin with the first challenge: determining whether my sample is representative of all survivors. Whereas I cannot know if my overall sample is representative of all Jews who survived the Holocaust, by comparing my subsample of resisters with what is known about resistance fighters in the Warsaw and Vilna ghettos in general, the sample seems representative. As table 12.2 shows, the age and gender distribution of the resisters in my sample is similar to the age and gender profile of resisters in the Warsaw and Vilna ghettos, most of whom were young activist men and women in their teens and early twenties (Arad 1982; Gutman 1994). Further, because most resisters were young people, the truncated age distribution of the testimonies as a whole is not problematic, at least as far as the subsample of resisters is concerned.

The second potential source of bias is more difficult to identify and address. Without information about people who perished, it is hard to know how they differed, if at all, from the survivors. I suggest, however, that survivor testimonies can be used not simply as a source of information about the survivors themselves, but also as a source of information about those who did not survive. In fact, one of the many benefits of using survivor testimonies is that they contain traces of others' accounts: the missing voices. Survivors do not simply share their own

TABLE 12.2 Characteristics of survivors in sample who participated in resistance

	WARSAW	VILNA
Resisters' age at the start of World War II		
Age range	11–28	4–31
Average age	16	16
Gender		
Male	88.9% (8)	77.8% (14)
Female	11.1% (1)	22.2% (4)
Total (N = 27)	100% (9)	100% (18)

experiences, but also testify to what happened to others, including both victims and other survivors. While these traces are not the same thing as full testimonies from those who perished, they may still help amplify the missing voices, even if only briefly, and only loudly enough to help rule out bias.

Thus, if these sources and traces can show that there is no systematic difference between resisters who survived and resisters who perished, and between nonresisters who survived and nonresisters who perished, then a researcher can be more confident that findings based on survivor testimony are representative of all resisters and nonresisters (including those who did not live long enough to provide their testimony to the Shoah Foundation). Following this logic, I coded my testimonies, searching for the testimony givers' mentions of people who did not survive. Where possible, I supplemented these mentions with other, published information about the individuals behind the missing voices. Doing so was generally possible only when the testimonies mentioned well-known individuals, such as members of the ghetto administration (Judenrat) and prominent resistance fighters who did not survive their resistance activities. Throughout, my goal was to see if there was any evidence of systematic differences in the decision-making of survivors and victims that would indicate that a sample of survivors would be a biased or incomplete data source for a study of participation in armed resistance. More specifically, I sought evidence that would (1) indicate whether the decision-making of those who resisted and perished was different from the decision-making of those who resisted and survived, and (2) present some account for why fallen resisters fell and/or why surviving resisters survived. Below, I present what I learned from the missing voices.

Learning from Missing Voices

Missing voices are illustrated by Sol Liber's quote at the beginning of this chapter. His testimony mentions the reactions of his cousin, uncle, and sisters in the hours and moments before they were murdered at Treblinka. Not surprisingly, missing voices like these are present throughout the testimonies. Nearly all survivors lost family and friends during the Holocaust, so it makes sense that these missing loved ones would be mentioned in the testimonies. For my data, the structure of testimonies also facilitated the inclusion of the missing voices. The testimonies followed a fairly standard format: at the beginning of each testimony the survivor was asked for the names of family members and invited to say something about his or her family life as a child, while at the end, the survivor was asked to share and describe photos of loved ones. Finally, given the age distribution of the survivors in my sample, many were young enough to be living with or near family members when the war broke out. As they told their stories, these survivors understandably gave accounts of what happened to those family members—and sadly, most did not survive.

Survivors who participated in armed resistance also tended to mention missing voices, both of their families and of their comrades in arms. For instance, elsewhere in Sol Liber's testimony, he described a failed mission to help Jews escape the Warsaw ghetto through the city sewers during the uprising. Liber was shot and wounded during the attempt, and mentioned that ten other resistance fighters died. Other surviving resisters in Warsaw mentioned the age and gender of resistance fighters who died during the fighting, typically by referring to people as "boys" or "girls"; though not terribly specific, such language suggests that the fighters were youths, as opposed to middle-aged people or older. For instance, Sol Rosenberg's testimony included the missing voices of two resistance fighters, a young man and a young woman, with whom he was captured from the city sewers during the Warsaw Ghetto Uprising:

> We were between Nalewki and Miła Street. We got out, he told us, "To keep your hands up," SS, young SS, mean bastards. Tell us to sit down, you know, with your feets crossed us, with the hands up. I must have been fifteen, I was. Was one young lady. And she was wearing, I'll forget, a big long leather coat, and a young man too. And the SS turned around and say, "You must be . . . You must be the leader" to that girl. He shot her on the spot. And . . . and they shot that young man on the spot, "You must be the leader." Two of them, right on the spot. (Rosenberg 1996)

Though it was rare to find references to the missing voices of children or of older people in the context of resistance, Sol Liber's testimony did mention a little girl and an elderly religious man, both of whom had managed to survive in the Warsaw ghetto until the uprising. Although they did not take up arms themselves, they did hide in the same bunker as Liber and his friend Akiva during the fighting:

> We had a square like . . . It covered up the hole . . . you went under the foundation, covered up the hole, they you shook it a little bit and the sand covered it that you couldn't see anything that's something there. The lid, actually . . . and he [the soldier] opened the lid and he said, "If you don't come out we'll throw in a few hand grenades and you'll be buried right here." So everybody figures as long as we alive we have a chance. If he throws a few hand grenades that's all gone. So we all came out. They put us against the wall, with a half-track with a machine gun, and we figured that's it. They didn't kill us inside, they'll give us . . . and

> stood about a half an hour against the wall and they looked all over for others. There was one old man ... there was a couple in the bunker. They came Israel from a visit, from Palestine then, and they got trapped in the war. With a beautiful little girl about 7, 8 years old. She came to visit this old man, the father. And this ... the head of the SS in the ghetto. I think it was Stroop the name. I'm not sure. He took out a ... a big gun, told him to walk in the backyard and he shot him. He had a beard, you know, he looks like a religious man. And those two people also with their child went to Treblinka with us. (Liber 1994)

These traces of missing voices are useful for demonstrating some of the demographic characteristics of the resisters and nonresisters. That is, despite the truncated age structure of the individual testimony givers in my sample, their testimonies provide information about a broader range of individuals, both young and old. Across the testimonies, when making reference to people who participated in armed resistance—whether they survived or not—the survivors tended to describe them as teenagers and young adults, while nonresisters (that is, people who did not participate in armed resistance) ranged from babies to elderly people. These missing voices therefore lend more support to my claim that the truncated age distribution of my sample of testimonies does not necessarily present any bias. In other words, based on the missing voices, I feel more confident that the resisters in my sample of testimonies are representative of all resisters, including those who perished—at least as far as age and gender are concerned.

Beyond assessing representativeness in terms of age and gender, I was also interested in missing voices that described decision-making about resistance, so that I could draw on these voices to determine whether survivors made different decisions about resistance than those who perished. Simon Trakinski's testimony provides a good example. Trakinski, who fought in a partisan unit after fleeing the Vilna ghetto with his brother and some friends, mentioned the missing voices of his father, mother, and grandmother. Describing the last time he saw them, he said,

> I had conversation with my father about going away to . . . into the woods, the partisans. And my father was, you know, a sentimental man and he says, "Well it's a little ... it's too dangerous. Maybe we will outlive the Germans this way." But the only one that said it was a good idea was my grandmother. She said it seems to be the only way to try to survive. She gave ... she gave me the blessing. And my mother ... my mother also was a little hesitant. At the last moment my mother would have liked to join us, but unfortunately, I was powerless about it to take her, because we were organized and the organization forbade it and so on. And so

> we decided we will ... after a few weeks we would get established in the woods we would come back to try and ... and retrieve her. And a few weeks later, on September the 23rd, the Vilna ghetto was totally emptied. Liquidated. And my mother, my grandmother, my aunt, and her little girl were taken away. And, to this day I'm not sure where they wound up.... On the other hand, my father died, I was told, in 1944, about a month before the Russians liberated this part of Estonia, out of exhaustion and ... and malnutrition. And so did my uncle. In Estonia. (Trakinski 1995)

Again, this testimony provides only a trace of the missing voices, but it illustrates some of the differences in decision-making between resisters and nonresisters. Simon's father opposed resistance as too risky, believing that life under German occupation might be survivable; conversely, his grandmother encouraged Simon to join the partisans because that would be the only way to survive. I found this same pattern across the survivors in my sample: people who felt that the ghettos might be survivable were less likely to resist than were those who felt that the threat posed by the Nazi regime was too great *not* to resist. These views corroborate other analyses finding that expectations of survival and assessment of threat drove decisions about resistance in ghettos and death camps (Einwohner and Maher 2011; Maher 2010). Importantly, Simon Trakinski's testimony captures a trace of his father's and grandmother's decision-making with respect to resistance, even though they did not survive.

Finally, the missing voices from these survivor testimonies provide at least some hints as to whether there were systematic reasons why some resisters perished during their resistance activities while other resisters survived. While Sol Rosenberg's account of the young man and young woman who were shot and killed after being caught in the sewers under Nalewki and Miła Streets suggests that (purported) resistance leaders were more likely to be killed than were younger, rank-and-file activists like fifteen-year-old Rosenberg, later on in his testimony he indicated that he fully expected to be shot himself:

> He [a soldier] came to me and said, "What you've been doing in the sewer? How many Germans did you kill?" I said, "I don't know how to shoot, officer.... I never had a gun." ... And he hold that machine gun ... I thought he was going to shoot me. He hold that machine gun and sprayed that bullets right by our feet, you know. I thought he really ... he really ... I seen that's it, he's going to shoot us all up. Young SS, young fellow. A couple more goons, every one of them starting to shoot, trigger happy.... And then came ... they brought in a couple more Jews from somewhere. And they put us on a truck and took us to Umschlagplatz. That's when I went to Treblinka. (Rosenberg 1996)

Rosenberg's story suggests something echoed by many survivor testimonies: survival, especially in the context of risky resistance activities, such as fighting, smuggling weapons and other materials, and fleeing for the forests, was largely based on luck. Many surviving resisters mentioned other resisters who perished, and indicated that they themselves survived because Nazis inexplicably chose not to shoot them, or because they were lucky enough to heal from their wounds during the fighting or to find good hiding places and abandoned caches of food.

Boris Klor's testimony, which includes the missing voice of his sister, provides another example. Klor escaped the Vilna ghetto and fought as a partisan in the forest, and his sister escaped from the Vilna ghetto a week after he did. While some members of her group were caught and killed by Lithuanian police, she and another person managed to evade capture and were able to hide in the woods until Vilna's liberation. Tragically, though, she was later murdered, along with her cousin and another man:

> After the liberation . . . somebody told me that, "You know, your sister and your cousin survived." So I came right away home and I found my sister and my cousin, Shlomo. . . . My sister was a school teacher, so she was ordered by the Russian authorities to go back to teaching where she worked before the war. . . . So she taught in the school and she used to come home in . . . there was a house left . . . our town was destroyed during the war. But a couple of houses were left, so she came for the weekend, she used to come home. So they came, the Polacks, and they said we have to finish what the . . . Hitler didn't finish. And they killed my sister, it was January 20, 1945. They killed my sister, Devora. They killed Shlomo Kaplanowitz, my cousin, and they killed a third man, Isaac Katz. (Klor 1995)

Discussion

The descriptions of the missing voices in my sample of testimonies are of course limited. The voices of the missing were clearly important enough to the survivors to be mentioned in their testimonies. Still, these mentions were, for the most part, relatively brief, and can hardly stand in for full testimonies. So what can we learn from them?

Although the traces of information on the missing voices are simply that—traces—this exercise introduces some broader points for discussion. Missing data can be an issue for social scientific studies. Whereas quantitative researchers in the social sciences have several methods for addressing missing data (e.g., imputation), missing data in qualitative studies is more challenging. What should social scientists do when they need to collect qualitative data from a population or community that no longer exists—such as those who perished during the Holocaust? One option may be to return to the eyewitnesses to collect more extensive information about the missing voices. Whereas archival data, such as testimonies and diaries, cannot be altered for scholarly purposes, researchers can collect new testimonies from survivors—to the extent that this is possible, given a shrinking survivor population—to ask more in-depth questions about the actions and perspectives of those who did not survive.

In addition, while an examination of the missing voices in my sample of survivor testimonies cannot conclusively rule out systematic differences between survivors and those who did not survive the Holocaust, it suggests something that is especially relevant to studies of participation in Jewish resistance. Jews living under Nazi occupation had precious little ability to control their circumstances. Still, the decision to participate in resistance is a separate matter from whether someone survived. While Jews reached different decisions about participation in resistance—based largely on factors that have been identified by extant social movement research, such as networks and threat assessments—whether or not an individual survived resistance, not to mention the rest of the war, appears to have been based on chance. If so, then studies of participation in Jewish resistance that make use of survivor testimonies can proceed without too much concern about "survivor bias" in the data.

Ethics and Social Science Approaches to the Holocaust

In this chapter I have discussed some of the methodological challenges of using survivor testimonies for social scientific studies of the Holocaust—in particular, issues of survivor bias in the data. While discussions of bias are typically relevant to the social sciences, scholars in the humanities who also use testimony data can be similarly concerned with potential differences between the experiences of survivors who can give such testimony and those of the victims who cannot.

The missing voices in my data are necessarily limited. Nonetheless, I conclude that at least for a study of participation in armed resistance, Holocaust survivor testimonies do not appear to be a biased data source. From what I can tell, there is no difference in terms of age or gender between resisters who survived and resisters who perished. Further, the difference between dying and surviving as a resister may well have been based on luck, and was therefore random.

Holocaust survivor testimonies are not the only source of data that can be used to find traces of missing voices. Missing voices are also present in other archival data, such as diaries (including diaries of survivors as well as those who perished) and other documents preserved from the ghettos, such as underground newspapers and community reports (e.g., the famous Oneg Shabbat archives in the Warsaw ghetto—see Kermish [1986]). Without knowing more about the documents that did not survive the destruction of European cities and towns during World War II, it is harder to determine how representative these surviving sources are. Nonetheless, such sources, especially diaries, can give fuller voice to the missing.

Although my discussion suggests that survivor testimony can be a sound source of data for studies of individual decision-making during the Holocaust, such as decisions about participation in resistance, a broader issue remains: the ethical concerns about treating a human tragedy as a setting for scientific inquiry (see Einwohner 2011). I conclude on this point, and do so by returning to the very beginning of this chapter—not its opening quote, but its title. There, and throughout this chapter, I purposely use the term "missing voices" more often than "missing data." This word choice may seem like a small detail, but it is a crucial one. As Boris Klor's last quote above indicates, entering the names of murder victims into a record, such as a testimony, is a powerful memorial device. Each person who was murdered during the Holocaust is a voice, not simply a data point by which one can rule out bias in a sample. In fact, an objective, social scientific discussion of a search for systematic differences between survivors and their missing counterparts in some ways looks past the very reason why those six million voices are missing in the first place.

People are much more than the data that social scientists collect from them, and the study of the Holocaust makes that point especially clear. Yet one need not study genocide in order to appreciate the fact that our data come from real people. The work of social scientists is often focused on social problems: poverty, racism, crime, homelessness, disease, and so on. While we should strive to address biases in our data, we should also be reflexive and respectful of the circumstances that produced those data. Thinking about missing voices may help achieve that goal.

REFERENCES

Arad, Yitzhak. 1982. *Ghetto in Flames*. Jerusalem: Yad Vashem Martyrs and Heroes' Remembrance Authority.

Corni, Gustavo. 2002. *Hitler's Ghettos: Voices from a Beleaguered Society, 1939–1944.* London: Arnold.
Einwohner, Rachel L. 2003. "Opportunity, Honor, and Action in the Warsaw Ghetto Uprising of 1943." *American Journal of Sociology* 109 (3): 650–75.
———. 2009. "The Need to Know: Cultured Ignorance and Jewish Resistance in the Ghettos of Warsaw, Vilna, and Łódź." *Sociological Quarterly* 50 (3): 407–30.
———. 2011. "Ethical Considerations on the Use of Archived Testimonies in Holocaust Research: Beyond the IRB Exemption." *Qualitative Sociology* 34 (3): 415–30.
Einwohner, Rachel L., and Thomas V. Maher. 2011. "Threat Assessments and Collective-Action Emergence: Death Camp and Ghetto Resistance during the Holocaust." *Mobilization* 16 (2): 127–46.
Epstein, Barbara. 2008. *The Minsk Ghetto, 1941–1943: Jewish Resistance and Soviet Internationalism.* Berkeley: University of California Press.
Finkel, Evgeny. 2015. "The Phoenix Effect of State Repression: Jewish Resistance during the Holocaust." *American Political Science Review* 109 (2): 339–53.
Gurewitsch, Brana, ed. 1998. *Mothers, Sisters, Resisters: Oral Histories of Women Who Survived the Holocaust.* Tuscaloosa: University of Alabama Press.
Gutman, Israel. 1994. *Resistance: The Warsaw Ghetto Uprising.* Boston: Houghton Mifflin.
Gutman, Yisrael. 1982. *The Jews of Warsaw, 1939–1943.* Bloomington: Indiana University Press.
Israelski, Pola. 1995. "Interview 5498." Visual History Archive, USC Shoah Foundation. Accessed February 25, 2009.
Kermish, Joseph, ed. 1986. *To Live with Honor and Die with Honor: Selected Documents from the Warsaw Ghetto Underground Archives "O.S." (Oneg Shabbath).* Jerusalem: Yad Vashem.
Klor, Boris. 1995. "Interview 10135." Visual History Archive, USC Shoah Foundation. Accessed February 25, 2009.
Krakowski, Shmuel. 1984. *The War of the Doomed: Jewish Armed Resistance in Poland, 1942–1944.* New York: Holmes and Meier.
Langer, Lawrence L. 1991. *Holocaust Testimonies: The Ruins of Memory.* New Haven, CT: Yale University Press.
Liber, Sol. 1994. "Interview 58." Visual History Archive, USC Shoah Foundation. Accessed February 25, 2009.
Loveman, Mara. 1998. "High-Risk Collective Action: Defending Human Rights in Chile, Uruguay, and Argentina." *American Journal of Sociology* 104 (2): 477–525.
Maher, Thomas V. 2010. "Threat, Resistance, and Collective Action: The Cases of Sobibór, Treblinka, and Auschwitz." *American Sociological Review* 75 (2): 252–72.
Maynes, Mary Jo, Jennifer L. Pierce, and Barbara Laslett. 2008. *Telling Stories: The Use of Personal Narratives in the Social Sciences and History.* Ithaca, NY: Cornell University Press.
McAdam, Doug. 1986. "Recruitment to High-Risk Activism: The Case of Freedom Summer." *American Journal of Sociology* 92 (1): 64–90.
Meyer, David S. 2004. "Protest and Political Opportunities." *Annual Review of Sociology* 30:125–45.
Morris, Aldon D. 1984. *The Origins of the Civil Rights Movement.* New York: Free Press.
Nyseth Brehm, Hollie, and Nicole Fox. 2017. "Narrating Genocide: Time, Memory, and Blame." *Sociological Forum* 32 (1): 116–37.

Ofer, Dalia, and Lenore J. Weitzman, eds. 1998. *Women in the Holocaust*. New Haven, CT: Yale University Press.
Rosenberg, Sol. 1996. "Interview 10098." Visual History Archive, USC Shoah Foundation. Accessed February 25, 2009.
Schussman, Alan, and Sarah A. Soule. 2005. "Process and Protest: Accounting for Individual Protest Participation." *Social Forces* 84 (2): 1083–106.
Tec, Nechama. 2003. *Resilience and Courage: Women, Men, and the Holocaust*. New Haven, CT: Yale University Press.
Trakinski, Simon. 1995. "Interview 612." Visual History Archive, USC Shoah Foundation. Accessed February 25, 2009.

Part III
LEGACIES OF THE HOLOCAUST

13

REMEMBERING PAST ATROCITIES
Good or Bad for Attitudes toward Minorities?

Volha Charnysh

Commemorating past atrocities is often viewed as a means to promote reconciliation, improve the treatment of ethnic and religious minorities, and prevent future violence (Nino 1998; van Iterson and Nenadović 2013; Subotić 2019). Memorialization and commemoration activities are particularly salient in regard to the Holocaust, the paradigmatic trauma of the twentieth century. The explicit aim of International Holocaust Remembrance Day is to discredit political extremism and racial hatred, so that genocide never happens again.

It is unclear, however, whether commemoration actually achieves these beneficial effects. Attempts to memorialize past atrocities produce outcomes that range from formal apologies and financial compensation to vehement denials and intergroup tensions (Art 2010; Mendeloff 2004). Perpetrators and their compatriots have reacted to revelations of a violent past with defiance and anger (Rotella and Richeson 2013; Imhoff and Banse 2009), though they can also experience guilt and shame, become willing to rectify past wrongs, and perceive ethnic others more favorably (Rees, Allpress, and Brown 2013; Wohl, Branscombe, and Klar 2006). Victims reminded of past traumas may feel threatened or experience the old traumas anew, which can increase their hostility and prejudice—against the original perpetrator group as well as against other groups (Canetti et al. 2018; Brounéus 2010).

One explanation for these divergent consequences of remembrance is that the past invites multiple interpretations. As Art (2006, 5) notes, "Even in the prototypical case of 'radical evil'—the Holocaust—the 'lessons of history' are far from self-evident." The extent to which commemorating past atrocities can achieve beneficial effects depends on discursive strategies adopted by domestic political actors. Not surprisingly, political entrepreneurs use history to accomplish more immediate political goals (Subotić 2009; Art 2006). The Far Right, in particular, denies guilt for historical transgressions and emphasizes national victimhood, to distinguish itself from political opponents and win electoral support (Art 2010). The Austrian Freedom Party (FPÖ), Germany's REP, the Movement for a Better Hungary, the National Front in France, the Slovak far-right party Kotleba-People's Party Our Slovakia, and the League of Polish Families (LPR) have all questioned the Holocaust and sought to deny their nations' wrongdoings in World War II. Center-right parties in many East European states have adopted similar tactics by reframing the Holocaust and World War II to portray their nations in a more favorable light and to marginalize their political opponents as unpatriotic (Subotić 2019; Charnysh and Finkel 2018).

What are the implications of these conflicting narratives about past violence? Does challenging the perpetrator narrative with reminders of in-group victimhood affect the lessons people draw from history?

Experimental design is well suited for addressing these questions. In an experiment, specific elements of the narrative can be altered in a controlled setting. No matter how dissimilar the actual historical events are from the social science perspective, information about them can be presented in a similar way, replicating the rhetorical strategies adopted by political entrepreneurs. At the same time, randomization alleviates the concern that the narrative reflects rather than shapes public opinion and that individuals select into different narratives about the past based on preexisting beliefs and political preferences.

Poland is a fitting setting for such an experiment because it both experienced and witnessed genocide during World War II. Poland's Jewish community of 3.3 million was all but eliminated in the Holocaust. The local Christian population sometimes took advantage of the Jews' plight or even turned against their Jewish neighbors, initiating pogroms and stealing Jewish property (Grabowski 2013; Kopstein and Wittenberg 2018; Charnysh and Finkel 2017). Perhaps the best-known incident is a 1941 pogrom in the town of Jedwabne (Gross 2001). Yet Christian Poles also experienced the horrors of the Soviet and German occupations, ethnic cleansing, and forced expulsions. In 1943–45, eighty thousand to one hundred thousand Polish civilians were brutally murdered by Ukrainian nationalists in Volhynia (Wołyń) and Eastern Galicia.

Both antisemitic pogroms and atrocities against Poles are commemorated today. Yet the debates about what these massacres mean for the Polish nation and how to best remember them continue. Many politicians acknowledged Polish participation in the Jedwabne pogrom and adopted a reconciliatory stance toward Volhynia, but the nationalist Right blames the pogrom on the

Germans and overemphasizes Volhynia atrocities to emphasize Polish victimhood in World War II. In 2016, the Polish Parliament declared July 11 a National Day of Remembrance of Victims of Genocide perpetrated by Ukrainian nationalists, provoking tensions with Kyiv. Two years later, President Andrzej Duda signed a law criminalizing statements that attribute responsibility for the Holocaust and other Nazi atrocities to "the Polish nation." The Polish government also renewed calls for reparations from Germany. World War II and the Holocaust remain at the center of political discourse seventy-five years after they took place.

This chapter presents results from an online survey experiment on the effects of competing historical narratives on political attitudes in Poland. Respondents were randomly assigned to stories about well-known episodes of violence and then answered questions about their attachment to nation, attitudes toward ethnic out-groups, and minority protections. The control group read about the 1995 massacre in Bosnia and Herzegovina. The two treated groups were reminded about the Jedwabne pogrom. One of the treated groups also read about the 1943 massacre in Volhynia, with a note that the Polish suffering at the hands of Ukrainian nationalists received less publicity than the Jewish suffering in Jedwabne. This second treatment was designed to mirror the discursive strategies of the Polish Right, which elevates national victimhood to counter criticisms of Polish behavior during the Holocaust.

Approaching the Holocaust from a social science perspective clarifies its current role in domestic politics in Central and Eastern Europe. Reframing the Holocaust is an attempt by political elites to construct a more "usable past" that will legitimize their ethnonationalist vision and appeal to the illiberal and conservative segments of the population. I find that such narratives are indeed capable of increasing ethnocentrism and reducing support for minority rights.

Scholars typically quantify exposure to mass violence ("treatment") using death counts, the duration of the violent regime, or distance to the site where the violence took place (e.g., Rozenas and Zhukov 2019; Charnysh and Finkel 2017). They investigate whether more destructive, long-lasting, or proximate episodes of violence have a higher impact. Yet the long-run political effects of mass violence are also shaped by how specific historical events are interpreted and reinterpreted. The Jedwabne pogrom is a case in point: it was one of many pogroms against Jews in the summer of 1941 (Kopstein and Wittenberg 2018) and peripheral to the elimination of Poland's Jewish minority in the Holocaust, yet it provoked greater soul searching and shaped views on Polish-Jewish relations during World War II to a greater extent than most other, no less horrific incidents. The significance of Jedwabne comes from the contemporary debates about the pogrom, not from the particulars of the pogrom itself. Thus, studying the impacts of specific narratives about the Holocaust is essential for understanding its multifaceted consequences.

This study contributes to work on the legacies of mass violence by investigating an alternative channel of remembrance and (re)interpretation, which likely operates side by side with the intergenerational transmission channel emphasized in existing research (e.g., Lupu and Peisakhin 2017; Rozenas and Zhukov 2019). While the immediate victims are long gone, the Holocaust has become institutionalized in formal institutions and structures across Europe. Its effects are no longer limited to perpetrator, bystander, and victim communities, but are experienced by national and international audiences. In this context, narratives offered by political actors and the media are particularly significant. My approach is most consistent with a recent survey experiment by Antoniou, Dinas, and Kosmidis (2020) in Greece, which finds that upward comparisons between the victimized Greek in-group and the victimized out-group (Jews) increases antisemitism.

I also contribute to the literature on out-group discrimination, which identifies intergroup contact as a particularly effective strategy for reducing prejudice (Scacco and Warren 2018). In postgenocide settings, opportunities for intergroup interaction are extremely limited. Indeed, the reconstruction of World War II memory in a way that unambiguously favors ethnic majorities might not have been possible had Jews remained present in post-Holocaust Eastern Europe (Charnysh 2015). Educating the population about the past in a way that is both historically accurate and conducive to reconciliation is all the more important in these circumstances.

Understanding Reactions to the Difficult Past

I build on research in social psychology to understand how reminders of violence perpetrated by the in-group—alone or countered by reminders of in-group victimhood—shape in-group and out-group attitudes among the population that was not directly involved in the massacre but shares identity with the perpetrator and/or victim of the historical incident.

People derive status from their in-group attachment and are motivated to view the in-group in positive terms (Tajfel and Turner 1986). Reminders of in-group wrongdoing threaten the positive view of the in-group, triggering cognitive dissonance (Festinger 1957; Aronson 1992). Cognitive dissonance is defined as a negative affect that arises when individuals either do something or are induced to think differently about something such that they are confronted with a cognitive inconsistency. Dissonance is "psychologically uncomfortable" (Festinger 1957, 3).

To reduce dissonance, individuals may change their beliefs and behaviors in accordance with the new information about the in-group or, instead, rationalize away the dissonance and avoid change (Steele and Liu 1983; Gubler 2013). These divergent implications of cognitive dissonance can help explain why scholars disagree about the benefits of remembering past traumas.

The first approach to reducing cognitive dissonance is what the advocates of Holocaust education hope for. Reminders of in-group transgressions may produce collective guilt or shame, motivating positive attitudinal and behavioral changes. In particular, people may seek to atone for the harm done by apologizing to the out-group or even providing financial compensation (Doosje et al. 1998; Doosje et al. 2006; Wohl, Branscombe, and Klar 2006). German foreign policy after World War II and the South African Truth and Reconciliation Commission are perhaps the best-known examples of the positive consequences of collective guilt. Reminders of past transgressions may also improve perpetrator attitudes toward third groups: Rees, Allpress, and Brown (2013) find that feelings of moral shame for the Nazi past improve attitudes toward Turkish immigrants among Germans.

The opposite outcome, however, has been documented as well. Upon learning about past transgressions by their in-group, individuals may seek to minimize, deny, or justify in-group transgressions to reduce cognitive dissonance (Branscombe and Doosje 2004, chap. 1; Branscombe, Schmitt, and Schiffhauer 2007). Even in Germany, often portrayed as a paragon of repentance, reminders about in-group-perpetrated atrocities has been linked to "secondary antisemitism," a belief that the Jews abuse other nations' feelings of guilt and are responsible for antisemitic prejudice (Imhoff and Banse 2009). Such reactions may be particularly likely when the perpetrator narrative is contested by invoking in-group suffering. Victimhood narratives impart a degree of moral entitlement on the in-group and thus legitimize harmful behavior toward out-groups (Bar-Tal et al. 2009; Wohl and Branscombe 2008). For example, Canetti et al. (2018) find that exposing Israeli Jews to messages about the Holocaust increases their support for aggressive policies against Arabs and their identification with Zionism.

This chapter evaluates these conflicting predictions about the effects of perpetrator and victimhood narratives on political attitudes in contemporary Poland.

Historical Background: World War II in Poland

Before World War II, ethnic minorities constituted a third of Poland's population. Ukrainians and Jews were the two largest groups, at 13 percent and 10 percent, respectively. Genocide and forced population transfers at the end of the conflict made Poland one of the most ethnically homogeneous states in Europe. The Jewish population, at 3.3 million on the eve of World War II, was first rounded up into ghettos and then nearly completely eliminated during the Nazi occupation. While some Poles rescued Jews, many others were indifferent to the plight of their Jewish neighbors. Some participated in antisemitic pogroms, collaborated with the German police, or stole Jews' property. Grabowski (2013, 3) estimates that about two hundred thousand Jews died at the hands of the Poles during World War II.

One of the most contentious World War II memories in contemporary Poland pertains to a series of antisemitic pogroms that occurred in the summer of 1941 in eastern territories first occupied by the Soviet Union and then taken over by Germany (Kopstein and Wittenberg 2018). The best-known incident occurred on July 10, 1941, in the town of Jedwabne, where the Polish population herded local Jews into the market square, beating and humiliating them, and eventually burned them alive in a barn.

During the war, Polish Christians were also victimized by their neighbors. Taking advantage of the German occupation, the Organization of Ukrainian Nationalists killed about one hundred thousand Poles in 1943–45 in Volhynia (Wołyń) and Eastern Galicia.[1] One of the most brutal massacres occurred on July 11, 1943, as Ukrainian Insurgent Army (UPA) units attacked 167 villages, killing approximately ten thousand Polish civilians (Polonsky 2004/2005, 290). Polish partisans mobilized against the UPA in response, also retaliating against civilians.

Both tragedies were swept under the rug during the Communist period (1945–89). Since the new Ukrainian state was a fellow socialist republic, the perpetrators of Volhynia atrocities were presented as German collaborators.[2] The Holocaust was also viewed primarily through the lens of the broader suffering of the Polish people. The democratic transition provided an opportunity to revisit the past and to reconstruct Poland's national history. The opening of archives spurred groundbreaking research on previously avoided subjects. Although the crimes of the Communist government received the most attention, researchers also shed new light on Polish relations with ethnic minorities.

The publication of *Neighbors* by the Princeton historian Jan Gross (2001) arguably contributed the most to revisiting Polish behavior toward Jews during World War II. The book, which retold the story of the Jedwabne pogrom, prompted soul searching, a forensic investigation at the site of the massacre, and even an official apology by President Aleksander Kwaśniewski, of the Democratic Left Alliance, in 2001. At least three hundred articles on Gross's publication and the events in Jedwabne had appeared in the Polish press by 2003 (Wasserstein 2001; Stola 2003). Some 48 percent of Poles disapproved of Kwaśniewski's apology in a 2001 poll, and the nationalist Right quickly framed revelations of Polish complicity as attacks on the national "honor" and as a diminution of Poland's victimhood in World War II.

Some accused the Polish president of "stoning the Polish nation" by apologizing for the tragedy (Himka and Michlic 2013, 343). Father Tadeusz Rydzyk's *Radio Maryja*, with a circulation of 250,000 and representatives in the Polish Parliament, launched a campaign against the book. It blamed the atrocities on the Germans and accused Jedwabne Jews of collaboration with the Soviet NKVD during the Soviet occupation (Wolentarska-Ochman 2003). Debates over Jedwabne were sometimes bundled with the discussion of Volhynia (Polonsky 2004/2005, 295–96). Critics claimed that Jedwabne received undue attention because of the Jewish lobby, whereas the powerless Volhynia victims were nearly forgotten.

This claim came into the mainstream with the ascendance of the right-wing Law and Justice (PiS) in 2015. In 2016, the PiS government declared July 11 a National Day of Remembrance of Victims of Genocide perpetrated by Ukrainian nationalists. Next, PiS took over a World War II museum in Gdańsk in an effort to restructure the exhibitions and emphasize Polish suffering and heroism, while marginalizing the victimization of ethnic minorities. The party encouraged the commemoration of the so-called Cursed Soldiers, the anti-Communist underground active in the years after World War II, as well as the Katyn massacre of Polish officers by the NKVD in 1940.

At the same time, PiS has tried to rid Poles of guilt over the Jedwabne pogrom and other immoral actions during the Holocaust. PiS-appointed education minister Anna Zalevska (2015–19) blamed the Jedwabne pogrom for "many misunderstandings and very biased opinions" (quoted in Harper [2018, 204]). In February 2018, President Andrzej Duda of PiS signed a controversial law criminalizing statements that attribute responsibility for the Holocaust and other Nazi atrocities to "the Polish nation." In reaction to international criticism, the criminal penalties were later reduced to civil offenses, but the law has done some real damage, intensifying open antisemitism in public debates (Babińska et al. 2018).

Historical revisionism instigated by PiS conforms to public preferences: in a 2015 poll, just 23 percent of respondents agreed that Poles' crimes against Jews were "still valid and needed to be disclosed and publicized" (CBOS 2015, 12).

How dangerous is PiS's rhetoric about the past? Does challenging the in-group perpetrator narrative by emphasizing in-group victimization actually influence individual political attitudes and behavior, or is PiS simply reflecting preexisting opinions and beliefs?

Survey Experiment

In July 2014, I administered a survey experiment in Poland to address these questions. I sampled respondents using the online platform Ariadna (Ogólnopolski

Panel Badawczy Ariadna, http://panelariadna.pl/userpanel.php). The platform provides access to over eighty thousand Polish internet users who, in return for taking surveys, receive points redeemable for various items through the Ariadna Loyalty Program.[3]

Ariadna uses random stratified sampling of subjects to increase the representativeness of its samples. Even though this approach does not generate a true nationally random sample, the subject pool is geographically representative (see table 13.4). Respondents are comparable to the national sample on age and income.[4] The sample is not representative on gender, education, and rural/urban residence: just 35 percent of respondents are male (the national average is 48.4 percent); respondents with higher education make up 35 percent of the pool (above the 21 percent national average); and only 25 percent of respondents live in rural areas (the national-level share is 40 percent). While these characteristics limit the external validity of the experiment, they are less problematic for the interpretation of the differences in attitudes between respondents who were randomly presented with different narratives. Furthermore, the overrepresentation of educated, urban, and female respondents in the survey sample biases against finding significant effects of the victimization narrative, since these demographic traits correlate with lower ethnocentrism and antisemitism and greater awareness of the Holocaust.

All potential participants received an email from Ariadna inviting them to take a fifteen-minute survey about Polish history. Those who clicked on the link were presented with a consent form, which clarified that the survey was anonymous and focused on "the violent historical past," which could make them uncomfortable.[5]

Treatment

Figure 13.1 presents the sequence of questions and treatments graphically. At the beginning of the survey, respondents were asked about the strength of their attachment to Poland. This question allowed a pretreatment measure of in-group identification and ensured that, when presented with the narratives about past atrocities, respondents thought in group rather than individual terms.

Respondents were then randomized into three groups.[6] Each group received open-ended questions about the victim and the perpetrator group in a given historical incident, to gauge prior knowledge about the event. Next, respondents read a short text about this incident, with facts about the massacre, a graphic eyewitness quote, and a collage with photographs of some of the victims created by the researcher from publicly available images. The two treatment groups were

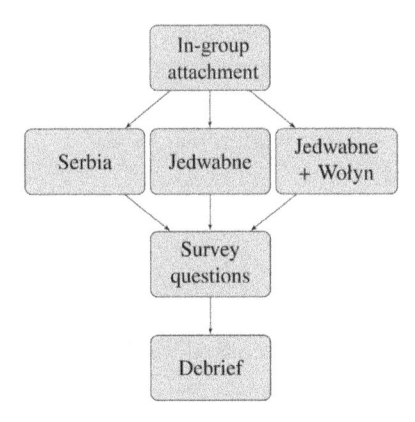

FIGURE 13.1. Schematic representation of the experimental flow

asked about the massacre in Jedwabne. Respondents were reminded that seventy-three years ago, "Poles from Jedwabne burned their Jewish neighbors alive" (see appendix for full text of the treatments). They read a graphic account by an eyewitness, Abraham Śniadowicz, followed by a note that Jedwabne "was not an isolated incident" and that similar pogroms occurred in over twenty localities. After reading the Jedwabne story, the second treatment group also received a message that Poles were also victims in World War II and were murdered in Volhynia, designed to mimic the rhetorical strategies of the Far Right in Poland. The control group instead read about the massacre of Muslim Bosniaks in Višegrad, Bosnia-Herzegovina, in June 1995. They were also told that Višegrad was not an isolated incident and that between 1992 and 1995, an estimated one hundred thousand people were killed, 80 percent of whom were Bosniaks.

As a manipulation check, after reading the narrative, respondents were asked to report *when* the massacre occurred. Those who failed the test likely did not read the story and therefore did not receive treatment. Most were able to correctly identify the year, or even the month, though some responses (33 percent in the control group, 14 percent in the perpetrator treatment group, and 17 percent in the contested perpetrator treatment group) suggested that they did not read or fully understand the text. Below, I present results both for the full sample and for only the respondents who passed the manipulation check.

Random assignment to three groups enabled measuring the effects of contested and uncontested reminders of the in-group wrongdoing, relative to narratives about similar episodes of violence that did not involve the in-group. Because all three groups received information about a massacre, the attitudinal variation across respondents in the three conditions can be attributed to differences in the role of the in-group rather than to exposure to violence as such. Because no group received the victimhood treatment alone, the experiment allows us to measure the effects of contested and uncontested perpetrator narratives, but not the independent effects of the victimization narrative.

Outcomes

The treatments were followed by questions that assessed emotional responses to the survey. Respondents were then asked whether they agreed with statements designed to measure attitudes toward minority rights, antisemitism, ethnocentrism, and pluralism. These statements were modeled on the questions asked in other Polish opinion surveys and presented in randomized order. Responses ranged from 1 (strongly disagree) to 7 (strongly agree) and were averaged to measure underlying concepts.[7]

The minority rights index was based on agreement with four statements: (1) Ethnic and religious minorities should be allowed to express their traditions, such as practicing ritual slaughter; (2) Ethnic and religious minorities should be exempt from the requirement to win at least 5 percent of votes to enter the Sejm (the lower house of Polish Parliament); (3) Ethnic and religious minorities should have an opportunity to use their language for naming localities, side by side with the Polish language on signs; (4) Ethnic and religious minorities should receive financial support from the state in order to maintain their culture and traditions.

Antisemitism was measured based on agreement with the following statements: (1) I get the impression that the Jews use our pangs of conscience over the past; (2) Jews want to get compensation from Poles for the wrongs that were perpetrated by the Germans; (3) Jews often act in secret, behind the scenes; (4) Jews want to have a decisive voice in international financial institutions; (5) Jews seek to expand their influence on the world economy. One concern with using explicit measures of antisemitism is social desirability bias, or the tendency to hide one's true opinions behind more socially acceptable responses. But mean agreement with all five questions was at 4.285, which is high and suggests they are still informative about respondents' true beliefs.

Ethnocentrism, understood as ethnic group self-centeredness and self-importance (Bizumic and Duckitt 2012), was measured as averaged agreement with the following statements: (1) I would rather be a citizen of Poland than of any other country in the world; (2) The world would be a better place if people from other countries were more like the Poles; (3) People should support their country even if the country is in the wrong; (4) There are some things in contemporary

Poland that I am ashamed of as a Pole (reverse order). Correlation of agreement with the first three statements and the fourth statement was low, at 0.13, though results did not change when this statement was excluded from the analysis.

I also measure a related concept of collective narcissism, defined as an unrealistic belief about the greatness of an in-group (de Zavala and Cichocka 2012). In the Polish context, collective narcissism predicts greater antisemitism but not prejudice toward other ethnic groups, "because it increases sensitivity to intergroup threat and support for stereotypical perception of Jews as a particularly threatening outgroup" (de Zavala and Cichocka 2012, 213–14). This concept relates to willingness to reconcile because it predicts retaliatory intergroup hostility. Collective narcissism is measured using agreement with the following statements: (1) My group deserves special treatment; (2) Few people fully understand how important my group is; (3) I get really angry when my group is criticized; (4) The world would be a better place if my group had more say; and (5) I will not rest until my group receives proper recognition. All items were highly correlated with one another ($\rho > 0.63$).

Pluralist views were measured based on agreement with the following statements: (1) No matter what a person's beliefs are, he/she is entitled to the same rights as anyone else; (2) Society should not tolerate political views that are very different from those of the majority (reverse order); (3) Everyone should have the right to express their own political views, even those that are very different from the views of the majority. Agreement with the second statement was only weakly correlated (0.14) with agreement with the other two.

The survey concluded with a number of standard demographic questions about respondents' age, gender, income, religiousness, education, occupation (self-employment), and urban/rural residence (not randomized). All respondents were debriefed at the end.

Results

It is illuminating to first look at the extent of knowledge about the difficult past in the survey sample (see table 13.1). As expected, the majority of respondents were aware of Jedwabne: an average of 36 percent had "heard a lot" about the massacre. For comparison, 20 percent of respondents had "heard a lot" about the massacre in Bosnia-Herzegovina. In the two treatment conditions, which inquired about Jedwabne, 63 percent of respondents reported that Jews were the victims.[8] Some responses to the question about the identity of the victims were quite pointed. One respondent claimed that although Jews were the "direct" victims, the "descendants of the [Polish] perpetrators of this crime" were victimized

TABLE 13.1 Prior knowledge about the events in Jedwabne and Višegrad among survey respondents (the questions were asked before the treatment was administered)

	JEDWABNE MASSACRE	VIŠEGRAD MASSACRE
	Have you heard about the massacre?	
Heard a lot	36%	20%
Heard something	47%	58%
Heard nothing	17%	22%
	Who was the victim?	
	Jews	*Muslims*
Correct response	63%	16%
	Who was the perpetrator?	
	Poles	*Serbs*
Correct response	50%	29%

"indirectly."[9] Another stated that "Jews but also Poles (instigated by the occupier)" were victims of the Jedwabne massacre. Half of the respondents recognized Poles as the perpetrators in Jedwabne, but some clarified that Poles were "encouraged by the Germans." A third of respondents mentioned only non-Polish perpetrators, such as Germans, Russians, and Ukrainians.

Did any of the treatments influence political attitudes? Figure 13.2 graphically presents the coefficients on the main outcome variables for all respondents as well as for only the respondents that passed the manipulation check (and thus definitely read the text). Results across all three experimental conditions are also presented in the regression framework with demographic control variables in table 13.2. The inclusion of demographic controls does not affect the conclusions and even slightly increases treatment effects for some outcomes.

Only the uncontested perpetrator narrative reduced ethnocentric beliefs and collective narcissism in the experiment. Regression analysis of the sample of respondents who passed the manipulation check indicates that relative to the group presented with the uncontested Jedwabne narrative, the control group was more likely to express ethnocentrism by 0.4 points ($p < 0.01$), which is equivalent to a third of standard deviation in this variable. The differences between the control group and the treated group that received the contested perpetrator narrative were half as small in magnitude and insignificant. The results were similar for collective narcissism. Results indicate that although the perpetrator narrative reduces the tendency to aggrandize the in-group and exaggerate out-group threats, challenging it by evoking past victimization offsets this effect.

The two treatment groups also differed in support for minority rights. Contrary to expectations, the reminder of in-group wrongdoing did not increase

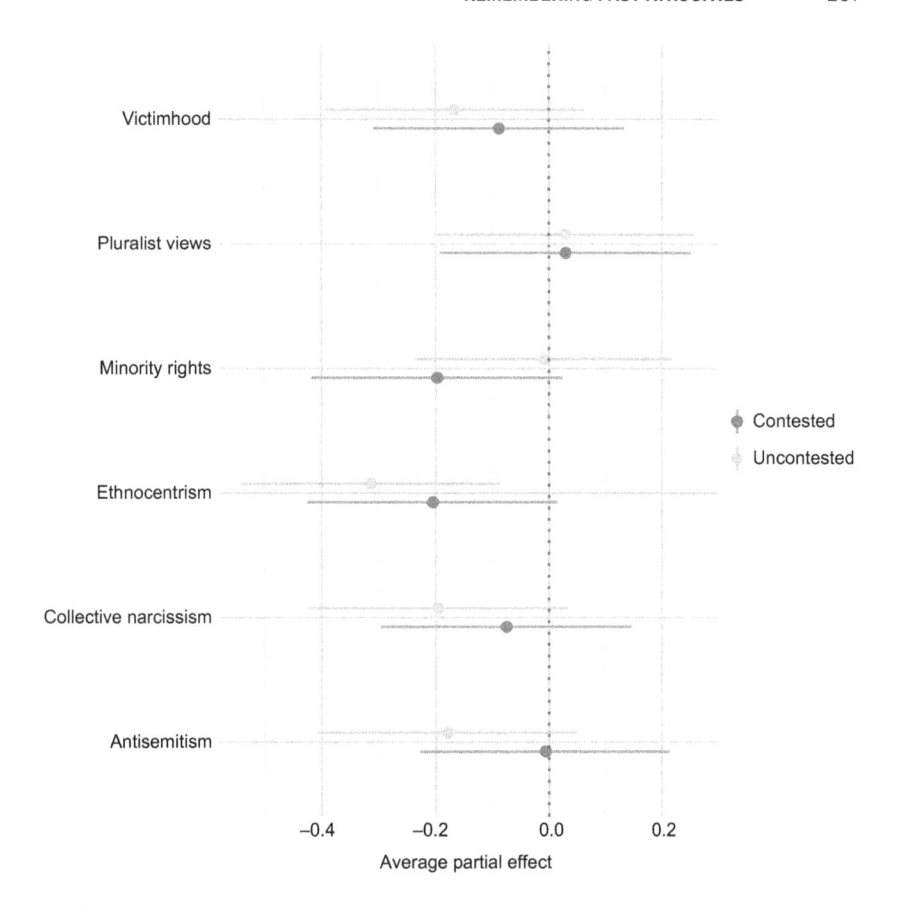

FIGURE 13.2. Effects of perpetrator narrative (full dataset)
Note: The impact of two treatments (contested and uncontested Jedwabne narrative) on selected attitudes. Dots are point estimates of each treatment, relative to the control condition; bars are 95 percent confidence intervals.

support for minority rights, relative to the control group. The contestation of the perpetrator narrative, on the other hand, reduced support for minority rights. The difference is 0.45 ($p < 0.05$). A possible explanation for this counterintuitive result is that bringing up the atrocities in Volhynia by the UPA reminded respondents about the two decades of contradictory policies toward the Ukrainian minority by the interwar Polish governments, which ranged from accommodation to forced assimilation and persecution.

It is important to note that the effect estimates in table 13.2 are conservative, as all three groups were exposed to the narratives about atrocities perpetrated by one ethnic group against another. The effects of commemorating past violence may be larger when the baseline is the lack of discussion.

TABLE 13.2 OLS Regression on treatment groups and demographic covariates as well as a pretreatment measure of knowledge about the historical event in question (subset of respondents who passed manipulation check; standard errors in parentheses)

PANEL A	MINORITY RIGHTS		ANTISEMITISM		ETHNOCENTRISM	
	(1)	(2)	(3)	(4)	(5)	(6)
Perpetrator narrative	−0.12	−0.17	−0.20	−0.20	−0.40**	−0.44**
	(0.20)	(0.20)	(0.22)	(0.21)	(0.19)	(0.19)
Contested perpetrator narrative	−0.45**	−0.50**	−0.08	0.14	−0.21	−0.22
	(0.20)	(0.20)	(0.21)	(0.21)	(0.19)	(0.18)
Male		−0.17		0.47**		0.08
		(0.18)		(0.19)		(0.16)
Higher education		−0.06		−0.11		−0.02
		(0.17)		(0.18)		(0.16)
Age		0.02***		0.02***		0.02***
		(0.01)		(0.01)		(0.01)
Residence: Town		0.06		−0.03		0.46***
		(0.19)		(0.19)		(0.17)
Residence: Village		0.41*		0.17		0.43**
		(0.22)		(0.23)		(0.20)
Observations	349	346	349	346	349	346
Adjusted R^2	0.01	0.03	−0.0005	0.06	0.01	0.04

PANEL B	COLLECTIVE NARCISSISM		PLURALISM		VICTIMHOOD	
	(7)	(8)	(9)	(10)	(11)	(12)
Perpetrator narrative	−0.43**	−0.45**	−0.0003	−0.05	−0.19	−0.22
	(0.20)	(0.20)	(0.16)	(0.15)	(0.19)	(0.18)
Contested perpetrator narrative	−0.13	−0.09	−0.02	−0.06	−0.12	−0.08
	(0.19)	(0.19)	(0.15)	(0.15)	(0.18)	(0.18)
Male		0.06		−0.27**		0.004
		(0.17)		(0.13)		(0.16)
Higher education		−0.32*		0.23*		−0.48***
		(0.17)		(0.13)		(0.15)
Age		0.004		0.03***		0.01**
		(0.01)		(0.01)		(0.01)
Residence: Town		0.12		0.001		0.19
		(0.18)		(0.14)		(0.17)
Residence: Village		0.26		−0.02		0.50**
		(0.21)		(0.16)		(0.20)
Observations	349	346	349	346	349	346
Adjusted R^2	0.01	0.01	−0.01	0.06	−0.003	0.04

Note: *$p < 0.1$; **$p < 0.05$; ***$p < 0.01$

Contrary to expectations, the differences in the averaged antisemitism indicator between the control group and the two treatment conditions were relatively small and did not reach conventional levels of statistical significance. The largest differences in antisemitism were observed between the two treatment groups: respondents in the uncontested perpetrator narrative were less likely to agree with antisemitic statements than respondents in the contested perpetrator narrative, though this difference did not reach statistical significance. Some differences emerged on agreement with separate antisemitic statements. Respondents presented with an uncontested perpetrator narrative were less likely to agree with the statement, "I get the impression that the Jews use our pangs of conscience over the past," significant at the 5 percent level in the full sample.

Finally, pluralist views and perception of in-group victimhood were virtually identical across treatment and control conditions (see table 13.2). Neither of the perpetrator narratives affected support for political pluralism.

I also tested for heterogeneous effects using the strength of national attachment measured prior to treatment assignment (not reported).[10] None of the coefficients on the interaction between treatments and strength of in-group attachment were statistically significant.

Social scientists have typically studied the Holocaust as unique case or, at best, carefully compared it to other, well-established genocidal events (King 2012, 324). By contrast, political actors in Central and Eastern Europe routinely invoke the Holocaust side by side with other traumas of World War II. They make use of the fact that World War II produced "a cascading form of victimhood," where perpetrators in one period were targets in another (King 2012, 332–33). Experimental methods are particularly well suited to investigating how political narratives and historical analogies, accurate or not, shape attitudes and beliefs.

My analysis shows that referencing in-group wrongdoing in the past becomes less effective and may even backfire in combating xenophobia and discrimination in the presence of competing victimhood narratives. The in-group perpetrator narrative (the massacre of Jews by Poles in Jedwabne) reduced ethnocentric beliefs and collective narcissism, yet introducing a competing victimhood narrative (the massacre of Poles by Ukrainians in Volhynia) offset this positive effect. Even more concerning is that the victimhood narrative, routinely used by Polish politicians to deflect attention from in-group wrongdoing, dampened support for minority rights, which was unaffected by the perpetrator narrative in isolation. Respondents were less likely to agree that ethnic and religious minorities deserve special rights and protections in this experimental condition. Furthermore, even the uncontested in-group perpetrator narrative had null effects on antisemitism or pluralist views, which highlights the limitations of Holocaust remembrance in changing deeply held predispositions.

The experiment is not without limitations. As noted above, my respondents sampled are more educated, urban, and female than the Polish population as a whole, which reduces generalizability. In nationally representative surveys, these demographic characteristics predict lower antisemitism and more liberal interpretations of World War II history. Thus, the consequences of competing narratives about the past may be even more pernicious in a more representative sample. Although the survey was anonymous, it is possible that social desirability bias—the tendency to hide one's true opinions behind more socially acceptable responses—prevented respondents from expressing their true views about Jews, minority rights, and their national in-group. The Holocaust is an increasingly sensitive topic in Poland, so future research may benefit from using designs that can mitigate concerns about social desirability, such as list experiments.

This chapter shows the value of experimental methods for understanding the enduring legacies of the Holocaust and intergroup violence more broadly. Most political science and economics studies on these topics have used quantitative and qualitative historical data, developed in isolation from the experimental research on in-group identity and collective guilt done in social psychology. Even though the majority of perpetrators and victims of the Holocaust are no longer alive, experimental designs remain useful and may even be necessary for understanding microlevel mechanisms behind some of the most striking patterns uncovered in this field of inquiry. If we want to understand why living next to a former death camp influences support for the Far Right (Charnysh and Finkel 2017), when exposure to violence will lead individuals to reject the perpetrator's political identity (Lupu and Peisakhin 2017), or why the effects of state-induced famine on political preferences change with shifts in political opportunity structures (Rozenas and Zhukov 2019), we need to investigate how historical traumas are remembered and reinterpreted in contemporary politics. The past is, above all, how we remember it, and its effects on our societies change as new narratives and interpretations emerge.

Appendix

Historical narratives in three experimental conditions

Treatment 1. Poles as perpetrators

On the anniversary of the Jedwabne pogrom: Painful memories of the neighbors

On Thursday (10.07) it was another anniversary of the tragic events from 73 years back, when Poles from Jedwabne burned their Jewish neighbors alive. That day, Jewish townspeople were gathered on the market square, beaten, humiliated, and then driven to a wooden barn on the outskirts of the village and burned alive there. According to Polish historians, no fewer than 340 Jews were killed then.

An eyewitness to this event, Abraham Śniadowicz, described the extermination of Jews from Jedwabne as follows: "Searching for homes, they found old, sick and children, beat them cruelly, chopped off their heads, cut off their tongues, pricked with forks, rushed to the barn. The barn was flooded with gasoline from all sides and set on fire. Terrible smoke appeared, and the screams and crying of burning Jews reached the sky. Who was caught later, thrown with a pitchfork into a burning barn. Gradually the screams grew weaker and a heap of ash remained from the whole mass of Jews . . ."

This was not an isolated incident. While only rough estimates are possible, the number of Jews killed by the local Polish population during the war reaches approximately 175,000 to 210,000 victims—men, women, the elderly, and children. Antisemitic acts by the Polish population of Podlasie were perpetrated in more than twenty localities. The frequency of these events suggests that they were part of a broader phenomenon.

Treatment 2. Poles as perpetrators and victims

Treatment 1 followed by this text:

> Remembering Jedwabne, forgetting Wołyń?

Not everyone agrees with this interpretation of the Jedwabne incident. According to a representative of one of the youth organizations, the ceremonies in Jedwabne serve to make Poles lose their national pride. Others argue that no nation suffered as much as Poles. The issue of Poles' historical memory has become an element of manipulation.

Although the whole world knows about the crime in Jedwabne, hardly anyone knows about the thousands of terrible crimes committed against them in Wołyń. On July 11 and 12, 1943, the Ukrainian Insurgent Army attacked in a coordinated attack on around 150,000 Polish villages and settlements. The situation is abnormal when the young generation of Poles is aware of what the barn in Jedwabne was, and the concept of the Volhynia massacre is some abstract concept, read somewhere by chance on national portals.

> ### Control: Massacre in Bosnia and Herzegovina
>
> On the anniversary of the Višegrad massacre: Painful memories of the neighbors
>
> In June (10.06) passed another anniversary of the tragic events from 22 years back, when Serbs committed crimes against the Muslim population in Višegrad, Bosnia and Herzegovina. Serbian soldiers and police drove Muslims out of their homes, tormented them, and threw dead bodies into the Drina River. According to historians, no less than 130 Bosnians were burned alive in the homes of Bikavac and Pionirska streets.
>
> An eyewitness, Zehra Turjačanin, described the extermination of Bosniaks as follows: "Most people were young women with children, and there were a few old men and women. Serbian soldiers first threw stones at the windows to smash them, and then threw grenades. For some time, they shot the crowd at home and set fire to the house. People were burned alive, everyone cried; what I heard then just can't be described."
>
> This was not an isolated incident. While only rough estimates are possible, between 1992 and 1995, an estimated 100,000 people were killed, 80 percent of whom were Bosniaks. Hundreds of Bosnian towns and villages were eliminated.

TABLE 13.3 Difference in means across the two treatments and control group on main outcomes in full and reduced sample

OUTCOME VARIABLE	ALL SURVEY RESPONDENTS			THOSE WHO PASSED MANIPULATION CHECK		
	MEAN	SD	N	MEAN	SD	N
Minority rights						
Control	3.84	1.55	164	3.98	1.60	110
Jedwabne (Contested)	3.54	1.44	150	3.52	1.46	124
Jedwabne (Noncontested)	3.82	1.56	134	3.85	1.54	115
Antisemitism						
Control	4.38	1.61	164	4.32	1.57	110
Jedwabne (Contested)	4.37	1.69	150	4.40	1.71	124
Jedwabne (Noncontested)	4.09	1.55	134	4.12	1.59	115
Ethnocentrism						
Control	4.27	1.22	164	4.35	1.12	110
Jedwabne (Contested)	4.03	1.12	150	4.09	1.14	124
Jedwabne (Noncontested)	3.90	1.09	134	3.91	1.11	115
Collective narcissism						
Control	3.54	1.49	110	3.62	1.43	110
Jedwabne (Contested)	3.43	1.41	124	3.49	1.48	124
Jedwabne (Noncontested)	3.25	1.49	115	3.19	1.49	115
Pluralist views						

OUTCOME VARIABLE	ALL SURVEY RESPONDENTS			THOSE WHO PASSED MANIPULATION CHECK		
	MEAN	SD	N	MEAN	SD	N
Control	5.64	1.23	110	5.73	1.19	110
Jedwabne (Contested)	5.67	1.20	124	5.71	1.16	124
Jedwabne (Noncontested)	5.67	1.17	115	5.73	1.16	115
Victimization						
Control	4.39	1.45	110	4.35	1.44	110
Jedwabne (Contested)	4.26	1.40	124	4.23	1.39	124
Jedwabne (Noncontested)	4.15	1.36	115	4.17	1.37	115

TABLE 13.4 Distribution of survey respondents at the province level compared to distribution of population in Poland (2014)

PROVINCE (WOJEWÓDZTWO)	POPULATION	% POPULATION	NO. RESPONDENTS	% RESPONDENTS
Dolnośląskie	2,909,997	7.56	27	6.07%
Kujawsko-pomorskie	2,092,564	5.44	30	6.74%
Lubelskie	2,156,150	5.60	18	4.04%
Lubuskie	1,021,470	2.65	13	2.92%
Łódzkie	2,513,093	6.53	26	5.84%
Małopolskie	3,360,581	8.73	33	7.42%
Mazowieckie	5,316,840	13.81	73	16.40%
Opolskie	1,004,416	2.61	7	1.57%
Podkarpackie	2,129,294	5.53	25	5.62%
Podlaskie	1,194,965	3.10	15	3.37%
Pomorskie	2,295,811	5.96	23	5.17%
Sląskie	4,599,447	11.95	65	14.61%
Swiętokrzyskie	1,268,239	3.29	15	3.37%
Warmińsko-Mazurskie	1,446,915	3.76	17	3.82%
Wielkopolskie	3,467,016	9.01	42	9.44%
Zachodniopomorskie	1,718,861	4.47	16	3.60%
Total	38,495,659	100.00	445	100.00%

TABLE 13.5 Balance on demographic variables across treatments

CHARACTERISTICS	TOTAL SAMPLE	TREATMENT 1	TREATMENT 2 (CONTESTED)	CONTROL
Initial group assignment	502	146	171	185
Passed manipulation check	448	134	150	164
Share men	35	32	31	42
Median age	40	42	40	41
Education (share w/ higher education)	34.74	31.11	38.67	34.14
Education mean (levels 1–10)	7.41	7.089	7.52	7.579
Mean income (złoty per month)	3,843	3,748	3,443	4,251
Left-Right ideology median	5.00	5	5	5
Left-Right ideology mean	5.15	4.981	5.306	5.136
Share in village	24.49	26.12	25.85	21.95
Share in city above 100,000 people	38.2	34.33	37.41	42.07

REFERENCES

Anti-defamation League. 2020. "ADL Global 100: Poland 2019 Survey." https:// global100. adl.org/country/poland/2019.

Antoniou, Giorgos, Elias Dinas, and Spyros Kosmidis. 2020. "Collective Victimhood and Social Prejudice: A Post-Holocaust Theory of Anti-Semitism." *Political Psychology* 41 (5): 861–86. https: //doi.org/10.1111/pops.12654.

Aronson, Elliot. 1992. "The Return of the Repressed: Dissonance Theory Makes a Comeback." *Psychological Inquiry* 3 (4): 303–11.

Art, David. 2006. *The Politics of the Nazi Past in Germany and Austria*. Cambridge: Cambridge University Press.

——. 2010. "Memory Politics in Western Europe." EUI Working Paper MWP 2010/01.

Babińska, Maria, Michał Bilewicz, Dominika Bulska, Agnieszka Haska, and Mikołaj Winiewski. 2018. *Stosunek do Żydów i ich historii po wprowadzeniu ustawy o IPN*. Warsaw: Centrum Badań nad Uprzedzeniami. https://www.rpo.gov.pl/sites/default/ files/Analiza_Skutki_ustawy_o_IPN.pdf.

Bar-Tal, Daniel, Lily Chernyak-Hai, Noa Schori, and Ayelet Gundar. 2009. "A Sense of Self-Perceived Collective Victimhood in Intractable Conflicts." *International Review of the Red Cross* 91:229–84.

Bizumic, Boris, and John Duckitt. 2012. "What Is and Is Not Ethnocentrism? A Conceptual Analysis and Political Implications." *Political Psychology* 33 (6): 887–909.

Branscombe, Nyla R., and Bertjan Doosje. 2004. *Collective Guilt: International Perspectives*. New York: Cambridge University Press.

Branscombe, Nyla R., Michael T. Schmitt, and Kristin Schiffhauer. 2007. "Racial Attitudes in Response to Thoughts of White Privilege." *European Journal of Social Psychology* 37 (2): 203–15.

Brounéus, Karen. 2010. "The Trauma of Truth Telling: Effects of Witnessing in the Rwandan Gacaca Courts on Psychological Health." *Journal of Conflict Resolution* 54 (3): 408–37.

Canetti, Daphna, Gilad Hirschberger, Carmit Rapaport, Julia Elad-Strenger, Tsachi Ein-Dor, Shifra Rosenzveig, Tom Pyszczynski, and Stevan E. Hobfoll. 2018. "Collective Trauma from the Lab to the Real World: The Effects of the Holocaust on Contemporary Israeli Political Cognitions." *Political Psychology* 39 (1): 3–21.

CBOS. 2015. "Postrzeganie Żydów i stosunków polsko-żydowskich." Research Report No. 112/2015, September 2015. https://studylibpl.com/doc/1294724/komunikatzbadań---cbos-u.

Charnysh, Volha. 2015. "Historical Legacies of Interethnic Competition: Anti-Semitism and the EU Referendum in Poland." *Comparative Political Studies* 48 (13): 1711–45.

Charnysh, Volha, and Evgeny Finkel. 2017. "The Death Camp Eldorado: Political and Economic Effects of Mass Violence." *American Political Science Review* 111 (4): 801–18.

——. 2018. "Rewriting History in Eastern Europe: Poland's New Holocaust Law and the Politics of the Past." *Foreign Affairs*, February 14, 2018. https://www.foreignaffairs.com/articles/hungary/2018-02-14/rewriting-history-eastern-europe.

de Zavala, Agnieszka Golec, and Aleksandra Cichocka. 2012. "Collective Narcissism and Anti-Semitism in Poland." *Group Processes Intergroup Relations* 15 (2): 213–29.

Doosje, Bertjan, Nyla R. Branscombe, Russell Spears, and Antony S. R. Manstead. 1998. "Guilty by Association: When One's Group Has a Negative History." *Journal of Personality and Social Psychology* 75 (4): 872–86.

———. 2006. "Antecedents and Consequences of Group-Based Guilt: The Effects of Ingroup Identification." *Group Processes and Intergroup Relations* 9 (3): 325–38.

Festinger, Leon. 1957. *A Theory of Cognitive Dissonance*. Stanford, CA: Stanford University Press.

Grabowski, Jan. 2013. *Hunt for the Jews: Betrayal and Murder in German-Occupied Poland*. Bloomington: Indiana University Press.

Gross, Jan Tomasz. 2001. *Neighbors: The Destruction of the Jewish Community in Jedwabne, Poland*. Princeton, NJ: Princeton University Press.

Gubler, Joshua R. 2013. "When Humanizing the Enemy Fails: The Role of Dissonance and Justification in Intergroup Conflict." Paper presented at the NYU-CESS Experimental Political Science Conference, New York, March 2013.

Harper, Joe. 2018. *Poland's Memory Wars: Essays on Illiberalism*. Budapest: CEU Press.

Himka, John-Paul, and Joanna Beata Michlic, eds. 2013. *Bringing the Dark Past to Light: The Reception of the Holocaust in Postcommunist Europe*. Lincoln: University of Nebraska Press.

Imhoff, Roland, and Rainer Banse. 2009. "Ongoing Victim Suffering Increases Prejudice: The Case of Secondary Anti-Semitism." *Journal of the Association for Psychological Science* 20 (12): 1443–47.

King, Charles. 2012. "Can There Be a Political Science of the Holocaust?" *Perspectives on Politics* 10 (2): 323–41.

Kopstein, Jeffrey S., and Jason Wittenberg. 2018. *Intimate Violence: Anti-Jewish Pogroms on the Eve of the Holocaust*. Ithaca, NY: Cornell University Press.

Lupu, Noam, and Leonid Peisakhin. 2017. "The Legacy of Political Violence across Generations." *American Journal of Political Science* 61 (4): 836–51.

Mendeloff, David. 2004. "Truth-Seeking, Truth-Telling, and Postconflict Peacebuilding: Curb the Enthusiasm?" *International Studies Review* 6 (3): 355–80.

Nino, Carlos Santiago. 1998. *Radical Evil on Trial*. New Haven, CT: Yale University Press.

Polonsky, Antony. 2004/2005. "'The Conquest of History?' Towards a Usable Past in Poland Lecture 3: Polish German and Polish-Ukrainian Historical Controversies." *Harvard Ukrainian Studies* 27 (1–4): 271–312.

Rees, Jonas H., Jesse A. Allpress, and Rupert Brown. 2013. "Nie Wieder: Group-Based Emotions for In-Group Wrongdoing Affect Attitudes toward Unrelated Minorities." *Political Psychology* 34 (3): 387–407.

Rotella, Katie N., and Jennifer A. Richeson. 2013. "Motivated to 'Forget': The Effects of In-Group Wrongdoing on Memory and Collective Guilt." *Social Psychological and Personality Science* 4 (6): 730–37.

Rozenas, Arturas, and Yuri M. Zhukov. 2019. "Mass Repression and Political Loyalty: Evidence from Stalin's 'Terror by Hunger.'" *American Political Science Review* 113 (2): 569–83.

Scacco, Alexandra, and Shana S. Warren. 2018. "Can Social Contact Reduce Prejudice and Discrimination? Evidence from a Field Experiment in Nigeria." *American Political Science Review* 112 (3): 654–77.

Steele, Claude M., and Thomas J. Liu. 1983. "Dissonance Processes as Self-Affirmation." *Journal of Personality and Social Psychology* 45:5–19.

Stola, Dariusz. 2003. "Jedwabne: Revisiting the Evidence and Nature of the Crime." *Holocaust and Genocide Studies* 17 (1): 139–52.

Subotić, Jelena. 2009. *Hijacked Justice: Dealing with the Past in the Balkans*. Ithaca, NY: Cornell University Press.

———. 2019. *Yellow Star, Red Star: Holocaust Remembrance after Communism*. Ithaca, NY: Cornell University Press.

Tajfel, Henry, and John C. Turner. 1986. "The Social Identity Theory of Intergroup Conflict." In *Psychology of Intergroup Relations*, edited by Stephen Worchel and William G. Austin, 33–37. Chicago: Nelson-Hall.

van Iterson, Swaan, and Maja Nenadović. 2013. "The Danger of Not Facing History: Exploring the Link between Education about the Past and Present-Day Anti-Semitism and Racism in Hungary." *Intercultural Education* 24 (1–2): 93–102.

Wasserstein, Bernard. 2001. Review of *Neighbors: The Destruction of the Jewish Community in Jedwabne, Poland*, by Jan T. Gross. *English Historical Review* 469:1303–4.

Wohl, Michael J. A., and Nyla R. Branscombe. 2008. "Remembering Historical Victimization: Collective Guilt for Current Ingroup Transgressions." *Journal of Personality and Social Psychology* 94 (6): 988–1006.

Wohl, Michael J. A., Nyla R. Branscombe, and Yechiel Klar. 2006. "Collective Guilt: Emotional Reactions When One's Group Has Done Wrong or Been Wronged." *European Review of Social Psychology* 17 (1): 1–37.

Wolentarska-Ochman, Ewa. 2003. "Jedwabne and the Power Struggle in Poland." *Perspectives on European Politics and Society* 4 (2): 171–89.

14

LEGITIMATING MYTHS AND THE HOLOCAUST IN POSTSOCIALIST STATES

Zvi Gitelman

Henry Ford said derisively, "History is bunk."[1] The Soviet historian M. N. Pokrovsky took history more seriously when he asserted that "history is politics projected into the past."[2] Nowhere was that truer than in Communist countries, where people would say cynically, "The future is easy to predict. It's only the past that is always changing."

Today, history has been politicized in Europe, as nations and states seek to rewrite it to give themselves legitimacy and better reputations (see Subotić, chapter 15 in this volume). States that had been part of the Soviet Union sought to legitimize their existence after the USSR collapsed. In the post-Soviet political landscape, historic states—Russia and the Baltics—could invoke a status quo ante, however short lived the independence of the Baltic states had been. Countries that had not been historic states had a more complicated task. How could they justify their new, post-Communist existence? What could be the "legitimating myth" of these states?

Some—Armenia, Georgia, Moldova—could claim ancient or medieval origins even if they had not enjoyed sovereignty for centuries. Lithuania could hark back to the Grand Duchy of Lithuania. But peoples that had never had statehood—Belarusians especially, but also Ukrainians, only briefly independent—had a weaker historical claim to sovereignty.

Jews, even dead or imaginary ones, are getting in the way of national identity building in some post-Communist nations because they evoke embarrassing memories of the Holocaust (Subotić 2019). The Holocaust is a problem especially for four states that were aligned with Nazi Germany and had participated in the murder of Jews—Croatia, Hungary, Romania, and Slovakia. It also challenges Latvia, Lithuania, Poland, and Ukraine, Nazi-occupied countries where significant numbers of locals participated in the Holocaust. On the other hand, Bulgaria propagates the notion that Bulgarians, like Danes, saved their Jews from the Holocaust, downplaying the Bulgarian deportation of Jews from parts of Greece to Auschwitz and their own forced labor camps for Jews (Sage 2017).

The reluctance of significant segments of the local population to acknowledge the full extent of the crime of the Holocaust and mass complicity in it is the result of a particular logic of competitive victimhood, the foundational block of national mythologies in Eastern Europe and beyond. Adopting a posture of victimization absolves peoples of having been victimizers. Victimization logically leads to demands for redress and compensation. It can be used to justify oppression of others by the victim on two grounds: having been victimized themselves, they could not logically be victimizers; or, having suffered so much themselves, they should be forgiven excesses.

This competitive victimhood is also at the root of extensive effort by post-Communist states to equate the crimes of Nazism with those of Communism, perhaps most explicitly in the Baltic states, which have adopted the narrative of "double genocide," which posits that the Baltics were occupied twice, first by the Soviets and then by the Nazis, and that both occupations were genocidal in nature. We should remember, however, that more people in former Communist states remember their suffering under Communism than remember the horrors of Nazism, since the latter generation has largely passed on. The taboo against comparing the two is gone, but in the West, according to Judt (2005, 826), "this juxtaposition remained controversial" for quite a while. I have argued elsewhere that those who do not live in the former Communist sphere

> should remember that Nazism has passed from memory and experience to history and abstraction for most people in that area. Communism is much more present in the popular memory.... It deprived nations of sovereignty, almost all people of property, many of dignity, and all of freedom.... One cannot expect people to be more moved by the suffering of Jews seventy years ago than by their own sufferings thirty years ago, even if by any objective measure the Jews' suffering, individually and collectively, was far greater.... Those who demand that East Europeans recognize that Jewish suffering was greater *may* be morally right but may also be politically and psychologically obtuse. (Gitelman 2013, 228–29)

National mythologies, however, are central to claims to contemporary political legitimacy, which is why they are so difficult to challenge and debunk. I turn to examining the case of Belarus, which has built its national mythology on claims to have been a victimized but heroic "partisan republic" during the war. This national narrative, not surprisingly, largely ignores the Holocaust.

Myth and Reality in the "Partisan Republic"

While Ukraine is perhaps the most complicated case of grappling with history and its political implications (Wylegała 2016; Fainberg 2013; Himka 2011; Radchenko 2017), neighboring Belarus is rarely mentioned in the contentious discussions of history and its political implications.

Belarus had never been a state when it found itself independent in 1991. How could it justify its newly acquired statehood when even its nationhood was doubtful? The Belarusian national movement was never as strong as the respective national movements in any of its neighbors (Rudling 2015). Belarusian attempts in the early 1990s to create a myth of a medieval Belarusian culture failed to grip anyone's imagination. Some tried to relabel the Polish-Lithuanian Commonwealth (1569–1795) as a Belarusian state. One blurb for a book by Uladzimir and Zmicier (2018) asserts, "The book will demonstrate that the Grand Duchy of Lithuania, or Litva for short, was essentially an old Belarusian state, and the names Litvins/Lithuanians for centuries referred to the inhabitants of ethnic Belarusian lands." But the major theme of Belarusian governments since 1995 is that Belarus deserves sovereignty because it is the "partisan republic," the country that resisted the Nazis ferociously, courageously, making the greatest sacrifices (Rohava 2018). Because one of every four residents of Belarus died during World War II, it deserves statehood and recognition as virtuous and heroic. A contemporary Belarusian estimate is that between June 1941 and July 1944, the partisans injured or killed half a million German soldiers and local collaborators. More than eleven thousand German military trains were blown up, twenty-nine train stations were destroyed, 948 posts and garrisons eliminated. In the course of their operations, some forty-five thousand partisans and "underground fighters" were killed (Schupljak 2008, 35). If these figures are anywhere near accurate, one can understand why, in 1995, Belarusian Independence Day was changed from July 27, the day in 1990 when Belarus declared sovereignty from the Soviet Union, to July 3, the day in 1944 when the Red Army liberated Minsk, the capital. Alongside this version of patriotism and honor, the Jewish history in Belarus, including the Holocaust, is generally ignored (Waligórska 2016).

As David Marples (2014, 116) writes, "The partisans have been adopted as a national state symbol, with veneration for all facets of their activities . . . . The partisan movement has become a legend . . . so frequently perpetuated that it is now impossible . . . to distinguish fact from fiction." In Belarus, the events of a complex multilateral war are presented in exclusively heroic simplified terms in the media, school curricula, history, textbooks, and official commemorations. In a book obviously aimed at an international as well as domestic audience, President Alexander Lukashenko (2019, 21) writes that the memory of World War II "for us . . . is holy. It is believed that Belarusians got independence and sovereignty peacefully, without wars, upheavals—almost for nothing. However, our road to independence was long, difficult and bloody." The book is in Russian and English and has many photographs and a huge amount of data (e.g., how many rifles a unit had), but it makes no mention of nationality, though Soviet Belorussia was inhabited by Belarusians, Jews, Poles and Russians. Only one photograph depicts a Jewish ghetto (Grodno, 19) and there is only a passing reference to the Holocaust: the Germans planned to resettle and "partially exterminate" fifty-one million people in Eastern Europe and totally colonize Belarus. The Einsatzgruppen "were to carry out organized mass killings of Jews, Communists and 'racially inferior' people" (Lukashenko 2019, 21).

In line with this narrative, and as was the case in Soviet times, memoirs published in Russia or Belarus present the partisans as without blemish. In a book published in Lithuania, a Russian author, Sergei Zakharevich (2012, 3), observes that "67 years after the end of the war, the history of the partisan movement on the territory of the USSR . . . remains highly mythologized." He points to the political uses of the partisan experience and the manner in which it is remembered and interpreted. Interestingly, Soviet, Israeli, and post-Soviet Belarusian literature all promote the heroicization of the "*partizanka*" (Feindt et al. 2014).

The differences in the mythologization are that in Soviet literature, the partisans are portrayed as an integral part of the Soviet war effort; in Jewish and Israeli literature, Jewish partisans in Belarus are depicted as resisters to the Holocaust and heroes. Typical is the statement by Shalom Cholavski, himself a former partisan: "In his tragic glory, the Jewish partisan was a shining vision of things to come. In his very existence he bequeathed to the Jewish People the values of a unique Jewish fighting experience" (Yad Vashem 1971, 334).

In *post*-Soviet Belarusian publications, however, partisans are portrayed as heroic fighters for the liberation of Belarus, and perhaps only incidentally of the Soviet Union (Kovalenia 2010). Soviet historians emphasized the role of the Communist Party in organizing partisan resistance, whereas post-Soviet historians and some Jewish partisans see it as more of a grassroots movement.[3] Soviet historians avoided several subjects now being studied outside the former Soviet space: ethnic and gender relations among the partisans, questionable motivations and behaviors among some partisans, Jewish partisans, and collaboration with the Nazis (Botvinnik 2008).[4]

In 1941 and until May 1942, when the Soviet government established a Central Staff of the Partisan Movement, led by first secretary of the Belarusian Communist Party Pantaleimon Ponomarenko, partisan units were directed by their unquestioned commanders to do as the commanders preferred, whether to attack Germans and collaborators, to lie low, to pillage and "requisition," or to help the peasantry. Once the Central Staff was established, the official agenda of the partisans became to attack German infrastructure and units, assassinate German officials and collaborators, provide intelligence to the Red Army, and disseminate anti-Nazi propaganda (Botvinnik 2008, 48).

Thus, during the second half of the war, pro-Soviet partisans became a formal part of the Soviet war effort, subject to central directives and, to a limited extent, to political and military discipline. More than was possible in the regular USSR military, however, partisan conditions and behaviors learned in the first two years of the war allowed for more local decision-making, irregular practices, lack of discipline, local initiative, and the expression of social and ethnic tensions. That may have been especially true of partisans in West Belorussia and West Ukraine.

Late in the war there was a third change among the partisans. When some who had collaborated with the Nazis, as local *polizei* or informers, realized that the tide of war had changed, they went over to the partisans to save themselves. One estimate is that by the end of the war, one of every five partisans had previously collaborated with the Nazis (Bartushka 2011, 71), or had belonged to the Polish Armija Krajowa, the German auxiliary police in Belarus, or the Ukrainian nationalist UPA (Himka 2017, 243).

Partisan Realities

Relying on partisan memoirs poses problems: lapses in memory, the influence of later events, "contamination" by media portrayals—often fictional—of the events the author describes, and so on. This does not make memoirs useless, especially on subjects otherwise not mentioned in Soviet and post-Soviet writings. Bearing the usual cautions in mind, when we examine memoirs and oral testimonies by Jewish partisans we find many testimonies to the capriciousness of partisan commanders, theft, rapes, desertion, betrayal, drunkenness, corruption, and licentiousness. These are described in convincing detail in the Hebrew, Russian, and Yiddish documents.

The partisans "requisitioned" provisions from peasants, sometimes by force. Noach Roitman, a seventeen-year-old partisan at the time, recalls requisitioning salt from villagers "at gunpoint." They would "borrow" a horse from a peasant, load it up with salt, and return to their base. After unloading the salt, they released the horse and, Roitman asserts, it would return to its home (Weitzman and Gitelman 2019, 46).

Sometimes partisans committed robberies that had nothing to do with partisan needs. Many peasants were resentful of the "contributions" and, in retaliation, would inform the Germans of the partisans' location. As one recalled, "We cannot live like this—in daytime we get robbed by Nazis and police, and in the evening you partisans come" (Lapidus 2016, 183). Others cooperated willingly, either out of support for the Soviet regime or the Soviet "motherland," or as a reaction to German atrocities and pillaging.

A second less-than-heroic activity was excessive drinking, justified by cold winters in the woods. According to Moshe Kaganovitch (1948, 64), "Partisan life was chaotic to a certain degree and liquor accompanied it.... Drinking and getting drunk was a matter of 'bon ton' among the partisans. One would often measure the fighting qualities of a partisan by how many glasses of moonshine [*samogon*] ... he could knock down." Alcohol was used to award the partisans (Gogun 2008, 353–54).

Sexual relations were ignored in Soviet and contemporary writings. Most partisan commanders had lovers. They "married" those women, though they had wives and children elsewhere. Those "temporary" or "field wives" enjoyed benefits: they were not sent to combat, they rode in carriages while men were walking, and they were well fed and clothed. Sexually transmitted diseases were widespread. Many women would get pregnant. The fate of the born was "unknown." Ordinary partisans did not have lovers or "temporary wives" like their commanders, which may have led to some tensions and jealousies. Nikolai Ivanovich Martiniuk, a commissar in a detachment, had a wife, Rachil, and a nine-year-old son in a ghetto. After taking a "partisan wife," he ordered a subordinate to rescue the child, but not the mother, from the ghetto. Rachil begged to be taken out too and promised to make no claims on her husband. The child was extracted from the ghetto, but his mother was not. The subordinate tearfully told the story and explained, "I could not disobey our commissar's order. I took the sin upon myself. My God, how much did the boy sob and Rachill [*sic*] would [*sic*] hardly pull him off of her" (Lapidus 2016, 194).

Some partisans raped civilian women, especially those associated with collaborators (Lapidus 2016, 336–83). Jewish women, who often had no proof of identity when they arrived in the partisan groups, were sometimes forced to sleep with officers in exchange for being allowed to stay with the partisans (Bartushka 2011, 83). As a Jewish partisan writes, "The lot of women without a man was doubly bitter. It is impossible to describe the sufferings of those women.... Isolated and imprisoned, exhausted and without hope, [they were] potential victims [*korbn*] of every Gentile [*goy*] and every man" (Gurevich 2006, 231; also see Tec 1998).

Fighters were often summarily executed for violations of orders, on suspicion of espionage, or simply because they were disliked. While fears of spies were sometimes well founded, paranoia was widespread and people were executed based on unconfirmed suspicions. Many commanders were cruel, unyielding, and irrational, often torturing and killing partisans who came under suspicion in front of their comrades in arms (Berk 1992).

Faina Astrometskaya escaped the Minsk ghetto and was in a partisan unit, "Assault" [Shturm], commanded by Leonid Petrovich Shubin. The unit included a Polish couple, Iwinski. According to Astrometskaya, "The two of them were irreproachable people. Iwinskii switched the radio on when the partisans were retreating; he was accused of connection to Germans, of transmitting the partisans' location to them (it was easy to accuse him of treachery because he was a foreigner)." He was shot. Then his wife, Bronislawa, was "shot because they thought that she will avenge her husband."[5] Lunin had his mistress shot because, according to Astrometskaya, he wanted to take another woman in her stead.

The Problematics of Jewish Partisans

Jews did not initially join partisans since they were urban, distrusted the peasantry, did not know how to survive in the forests, and early on did not realize the fate that awaited them (Slepyan 2006, 56–57). Soviet partisans had not organized effectively at the time that the "great wave of exterminations swept over the western areas of White Russia and the Ukraine," and "when the partisan movement had grown into an important factor, there were no longer any Jews in those areas" (Yad Vashem 1971, 324).

People who wanted to join the partisans would not be accepted without bringing arms with them—ghetto escapees, especially women, generally had no weapons. Unarmed people, the old, the very young, and some women were considered just extra mouths to feed. This is why some Jewish partisans, most famously the Bielski brothers, set up "family camps" where noncombatants could hide from the Germans and collaborators while performing tasks, such as shoemaking and repair of clothes and weapons. The Kalinin group in the Baranovich region, led by Tuvia Belskii, included 1,233 people, only 296 of whom were armed (Gerasimova 2005, 4). According to Nechama Tec (1993, 135), "For most of the time about three-quarters of its members were 'older people,' women and children.... The group of its young armed men and those capable of using weapons fluctuated between twenty and thirty percent."[6] A neighboring family camp headed by the Communist Shalom Zorin is estimated to have had 600–700 members (Tec 1993, 195).[7]

According to a Belarusian scholar, Jewish participation in the partisans was limited for three reasons: (1) The Soviet leadership did not want to play into the hands of the Nazi propaganda that claimed that most partisans were Jews, and did not encourage Jews to join up; (2) strange as it may sound, some feared that Jews could be German spies, as every surviving Jew seemed to be alive due to an unlikely event that many believed to be a cover story; (3) traditional antisemitism persisted among Soviet commanders and the rank and file (Kovalenia 2010, 250–51). In any case, by 1944 separate Jewish units were either merged into general partisan groups or absorbed into the Red Army as it moved eastward. This came as a blow to the "Zapadniki" (those who became Soviet citizens in 1939–40), who were fighting more as Jews than as Soviet patriots. "During the entire German occupation I dreamed of fighting the Nazis in a 'purely' Jewish *otriad*, under Jewish command," writes Zalmen Gurevich (2006, 248–49).

When he encountered the Nekomeh [revenge] Jewish otriad, Gurevich recalls, "I enjoyed the distinctly Jewish atmosphere. It became a meeting place for all Jewish partisans from the Russian otriady. . . . Here they spoke Yiddish, Hebrew, Russian. Here one could hear news and get encouragement" (2006, 248–49). But Party Secretary Klimov explained to Gurevich's unit that Jews were not a nation, according to Stalin, and only nations could have national partisan units. Moreover, he added, all-Jewish units would lead to antisemitism and undermine the mobilization of Belarusian peasants to the partisans (250).

Antisemitism

Some Jews who wanted to join partisan units were challenged to carry out a very difficult mission as a condition of acceptance. A Jewish partisan recalled,

> One night, we arrived to a camp . . . of a partisan detachment. . . . The company's commander . . . was willing to accept us . . . provided we . . . derail a train. If we accept the task—we would be equal members in his company, if not—"He would send us on the road that our Jewish brothers took. . . ." We answered him: we will do it. . . . We were able to derail a large freight train—there were forty-three cars in it. . . . We ran back to the base. The commander expressed his gratitude and informed us that from now on we were members of his group.[8]

Jewish partisans who requisitioned goods and animals were even more resented by the peasants than were other partisans. Antisemitism was stronger among the Polish and Belarusian peasants who had been under Polish rule before the war than among the Russian and Belarusian peasants who had been socialized for twenty years to the Soviet idea of "friendship and fraternity of the peoples" (*druzhba i bratstvo narodov*). In November 1942, a report was made to a high-ranking Communist and partisan leader, Comrade "Platon":

> There are a large number of Jews in the partisan brigades. Many are excellent fighters who aim to avenge the cruel murder of Jews by the fascists. The desire by the commanders of some brigades for the creation of separate Jewish brigades is incorrect. Jews are not well loved by the population, and they are referred to as "zhidy" [yids, kikes]. *If the Jews go to a hut and ask for provisions, the peasants will say that the Jews robbed them. If the Jews go together with Russians, though, everything works out smoothly. . . .* [emphasis added]. There were instances when a Jewish group crossed the Neman [River] for provisions; they were disarmed, and the confiscated weapons were given to the peasants who shouted in unison "Beat the Jews; save Russia" while beating up the Jews. (reproduced in Gerasimova 2005, 153)[9]

Barbara Epstein's interviews with survivors of the Minsk ghetto lead her to conclude that there was solidarity between Belarusians and Jews, due to the influence of Communist ideology (Epstein 2008). It should be remembered that it was especially Communists who shared this ideology; the general populace may have been less well socialized.[10] If Belarusians generally had become "internationalists," it would be difficult to explain what seems to have been widespread antisemitism in the Belarusian partisan ranks. Of course, Epstein interviewed only those who were saved and not those betrayed or killed.

Many Jews hid their ethnicity from other partisans, fearing that their own comrades in arms would hound or even kill them. One partisan recalls, "Jewish partisans had to be especially careful, not only around the Germans, but also around their own comrades. Dozens and hundreds of Jews died at the hands of their fellow partisans. The poison of antisemitism filled the air" (Gerasimova 2005, 154). Itke Brown (Lidia Abramson) a woman who escaped the Glebokie (Glubokie) ghetto and joined a partisan unit consisting of "former prisoners of war, all Ukrainians" recalls that when six young Jews joined the group, "these partisans killed all the Jews. They would go on an expedition, and each time another of the Jewish boys would not return. It was obvious that they were murdering them" (quoted in Tec 2003, 293).

An official report stated baldly that in the Vileika region, "the terrorized Jewish population is hiding in the forests. . . .. The partisans do not help them, and are unwilling to accept Jewish youth. The partisan group of N.N. Bogatyrev took the weapons of those who had come to volunteer and then turned them away. *Anti-Semitism among the partisans is quite strong*" (emphasis added). A father and son who served in the partisans observed that the locals in a central Belarusian village near them were friendly, and warned them whenever the Germans or the police were coming. When the partisans moved to western Belarus, however, the population informed the Germans about the arrival of the partisans (Slobin 2009, 216–17).

In March 1944, three partisans, one of whom was likely Jewish, complained to a "special commission":

> The command of the Chapaev brigade is unbelievably antisemitic. The deputy commissar of the Shilov brigade claims that Jews are cowards who join the partisans only out of self-preservation. He also verbally harasses Jewish partisans. These opinions are common to almost all . . . brigade commanders. Those who don't participate are accused of having sold out to the Jews. . .. Antisemitic conversations took place in the presence of the secretary of the regional committee of the Komsomol—Tsezar' Pavliuts. He did nothing to stop these expressions and even encouraged them. When Comrade Leibovich made a remark to Tsezar', Tsezar' replied, "It's none of your business."
>
> In the presence of Jews, people regularly comment that it's a shame the Germans didn't kill all the Jews, since the Jews are pigs and traitors. If a Jewish partisan commits the slightest misstep, the entire Jewish people is blamed. This kind of behavior only plays into the hands of the enemy. It is clearly the result of fascist propaganda. We must take measures to oppose this phenomenon and to enlighten the partisans as to the true national politics of our party. (Quoted in Gerasimova 2005, 155)

Yakov Shepetinskii, a Jewish partisan, recalled that the partisans used to say, "What kind of fighters are you? You are being slaughtered in thousands without resisting."[11] An old Belarusian Communist, Delyatinskii, asked those partisans, "In which POW camp did you rebel?" Nobody answered.[12]

Pavel Vasil'evich Pronyagin was a partisan commander who stood out for his friendliness to Jews. Lilia Bliumenfeld Liker, who had escaped the Slonim ghetto, recalls that Pronyagin organized a special Jewish group, N51, and even accepted Jews who came without weapons. Liker admired Pronyagin for not drinking alcohol, unlike the other partisans, and being well educated. She claims that the Shchors Partisan Detachment planned to attack the Germans in the vicinity of the nearly all-Jewish hamlet, Kosovo (Brest Oblast'), not to rescue the Jews but to inflict damage on the Germans. But Pronyagin attacked a day earlier and brought out three hundred Jews to the forest.[13] Pronyagin established a family camp for the Kosovans. Peasants from nearby villages would come to camp craftsmen—tailors, cobblers, watchmakers—and pay them with potatoes. Some

Jewish families returned to Kosovo in the hope of finding a safe hiding place. All perished.

The complexities of the situations among the partisans are illustrated by the following incident. Pronyagin was ordered to move east and left the family camp to be guarded by a commander, Bobkov, who instead abandoned the families. About two hundred Jews were killed when the Germans discovered them. When Pronyagin returned, Bobkov met him and reported, "Comrade commander! Let me report that by a single blow I got rid of all the Jewish junk! All the Jewish junk has been liquidated!"[14] But, having learned about the annihilation of the Jews, Pronyagin did not report Bobkov's doings to Brigade Commander "Komarov" (the pseudonym of Vasil Zakharovich Korzh, made a major general in 1943 and a Hero of the Soviet Union in 1944 [Marples 2014, 117–22]), perhaps, according to Zachar Zimak, because Komarov liked Bobkov very much. Jewish partisans could never be sure of their standing with their fellow fighters and commanders. Mikhail (Elimelech) Melamed observes that whether antisemitism was expressed and acted on depended on each unit's commander. His brother, Fima, went on a mission with a local Belarusian who called Fima a dirty Jew (*zhidovskaya morda*). "The platoon commander," recalls Melamed, "disarmed this partisan, brought him to Fima, and said: 'He is yours. You can kill him.'"[15]

The need for constant vigilance against infiltration bred distrust, and the lack of a guiding hand, allowed interethnic tensions to fester (Slobin 2009, 358–59). Jewish runaways were sometimes suspected of being fascist spies sent to infiltrate the partisans. Rumors spread about German schools and programs that trained them. Polish Jews were especially distrusted. Arguments and fights were common, especially since most partisan squads lacked military discipline (Gerasimova 2009, 139–40).

Jewish partisans were sometimes suspicious of "their own." Some Jews who attempted to join the partisans were suspected of cooperating with the Germans in the ghettos. Abram Izikson recalls a couple who, according to him, brought gold to his partisan unit, which they had robbed from their fellow ghetto Jews. He personally hung them on horse reins in the partisan camp.[16]

It was dangerous for Jewish partisans to complain about discrimination. One Jewish partisan, Grigory Rivin, was shot by his commander "because of the systematic advancement of Jewish chauvinism, which was expressed in overemphasizing that Jews were not liked in the detachment, were being baited, harassed, etc." There may have been other, more personal motivations at work here. "Rivin did not fulfill the demands of the detachment's command to hand over his excessive personal weapons—two revolvers and a Mauser pistol—to the detachment. He offended the dignity of commanders and leaders of the partisan detachment by calling them naïve and self-promoters, even spoke against the preparation of better food for the leadership, and threatened the commanders to settle things after 'our people,' i.e. the Red Army, move in" (quoted in Musiał 2009, 191).

But the three commanders who signed the order deemed the punishment excessive: "The leadership of the Dzerzhinsky detachment [should be] informed that they acted rashly in the matter of Rivin's shooting. Rivin was not sufficiently guilty of chauvinism nor punished by the partisans at large; additionally, my directive regarding the prohibition to shoot without corresponding permission from the brigade commando was ignored."[17] Platon and others were trying to keep the peace among Jews and others with a careful balancing act, condemning both antisemitism and Jewish nationalism.

Should Myths Be Confronted with History?

Accounts such as these, bringing to light antisemitism, ethnic tensions, and arbitrary behavior among the partisans, do not appear in Soviet or post-Soviet Belarusian literature. Should the "partisan myth" be challenged or complicated by such accounts? The broader question is, should truth (or "truths") be revealed no matter what the consequences? Is the historian always obliged to make public his or her findings, when they might undermine strongly held beliefs that provide social cohesion, political legitimacy, and pride to an entire society?

Some would argue that truth—or as close an approximation to it as humans can make—is an absolute value, and that refraining from telling the truth, even without telling a falsehood in its place, is immoral and dishonest. Knowing the truth but not proclaiming it may not be lying, but it is dissembling.

A *practical* argument for revealing "inconvenient truths" is that challenging sacred state mythologies forces a state that is sure of its virtue and sees no need for self-reflection and critical self-evaluation to reexamine its past behavior. Knowing the truth may encourage the state and its citizens to do better in the future: for instance, Germany dealing with Nazism, Israel confronting aspects of the 1948 war and the post-1967 administration or occupation of "the territories," the United States facing up to its treatment of racial minorities, Poland and the Baltic states reflecting on collaboration with the Nazis and prewar ethnic hatreds, and so on.

A third argument is that people or states who come to believe in their own myths, untroubled by contradictory facts, are likely to be more aggressive, less inclined to self-examination, and less cautious in domestic and foreign policies. Its citizens are more likely to assert "my country right or wrong" and less likely to question state policies, allowing for unthinking support for a demagogue who may actually be acting against their own and others' interests.

Finally, complicating mythology with history could make people more aware that they have not been told the whole truth; cause them to question the propagators of the mythology and thereby make them more alert to being misled; inform schoolbooks, popular books, and media from which people learn; and, most generally, get people used to being skeptical of what they hear, see, and read so that they do more critical thinking.

But would undermining the "partisan myth" change Belarusians' convictions or behavior? Does confronting Hungarians or Romanians with atrocities committed by their predecessors cause them to acknowledge guilt and change their ways, or to resent those who raise troublesome issues, see them as conspiring against "the nation," and blame historians, journalists, and politicians for disseminating "fake news" and besmirching the nation? What would be the consequences of telling new generations of Ukrainians, as some Poles, Russians, and Jews have done, that the UPA fought for Ukrainian independence but murdered thousands of Poles and Jews, among others, in the process (Zięby 2016)? Would that not lead to even more negative attitudes toward Russians, Poles, and Jews, as those who disturb the national myth and betray national honor?

Telling or avoiding the truth is not a binary choice. States handle this issue in different ways. Some permit, encourage, or undertake a thorough, publicly available examination of their founding myths. Others remain passive about the myths but act as if they are aware of the stains on their escutcheons (countries such as Japan, France, or Italy may avoid or delay thorough public reexaminations of their wartime behavior, but they are sufficiently aware of it to avoid repeating it, however much they don't wish to discuss it). And finally, some states proclaim the myth to be absolute truth and condemn any questioning of it as misguided at best, and treasonous at worst. A recent example is Russian president Vladimir Putin's claim in 2022 that Ukraine was created as a state by Russian Bolsheviks (in fact, they opposed Ukrainian independence in 1918–21) and that any Russian citizen who supports Ukrainian independence can be punished by law.

Of course, countries may not fit easily into one of these. Different governments of the same state may have different positions: Ukraine's attitude toward the UPA was much more positive under Victor Yushchenko than under Viktor Yanukovich, and it became more positive again after Yanukovich fled Ukraine in 2014 and settled in Russia.

In the final analysis, national myths and national history are probably not major determinants of thinking and acting in most circumstances—economic calculation and defense are probably more important in guiding individual and collective behavior. But mythology can be manipulated to elevate it in the hierarchy of motivations. At this juncture it is not clear how widely the population of the Russian Federation accepts the myth propagated by its president that independent Ukraine is a "neo-Nazi" state led by a Nazi president (though he is Jewish).

History matters. That is why it is contentious.

REFERENCES

Al'tman, I. A., ed. 2011. *Kholokost na territorii SSSR: Entsiklopediia*. Moscow: Rosspen.
Amacher, Korine. 2018. "Mikhail N. Pokrovsky and Ukraine: A Normative Marxist between History and Politics." *Ab Imperio*, no. 1, 101–32.
Bartushka, Mark. 2011. *Partyzanskaya vayna u Belarusi u 1941–1944 hh*. Białystok: Belaruskaye Histarychne Tavarystva; Instytut Belarusistyki.
Bassin, Yakov, ed. 2009. *Uroki Kholokosta: Istoriia i sovremennost'; Sbornik nauchnykh rabot*. Minsk: Kovcheg.
Berk, Leon. 1992. *Destined to Live: Memoirs of a Doctor with the Russian Partisans*. Melbourne: Paragon.
Boren, Aleksandr, Avraham Biber, and Kopel Kolpanitzkii, eds. 2006. *Partizanim mesaprim*. n.p.: Misrad Habitakhon.
Botvinnik, Marat. 2008. *Holokost v knigah "pamyat" Respubliki Belarus*. Minsk: Kovcheg.
Epstein, Barbara. 2008. *The Minsk Ghetto*. Berkeley: University of California Press.
Fainberg, Sarah. 2013. "Memory at the Margins: The Shoah in Ukraine (1991–2011)." In *History, Memory and Politics in Central and Eastern Europe*, edited by Georges Mink and Laure Neumayer, 86–104. Houndmills, Basingstoke, UK: Palgrave Macmillan.
Feindt, Gregor, Felix Krawatzek, Daniela Mehler, Friedemann Pestel, and Rieke Trimcev. 2014. "Entangled Memory: Toward a Third Wave in Memory Studies." *History and Theory* 53:24–44.
Gerasimova, Inna. 2005. *Vstali my plechom k plechu . . . : Evrei v partizanskom dvizhenii Belorussii, 1941–1944 gg*. Minsk: Asobny Dakh.
———. 2009. *Uroki Kholokosta: Istoriia i sovremennost'; Sbornik nauchnykh rabot*. Minsk: Kovcheg.
Gitelman, Zvi. "Comparative and Competitive Victimization in the Post-Communist Sphere." 2013. In *Resurgent Antisemitism: Global Perspectives*, edited by Alvin H. Rosenfeld, 215–35. Bloomington: Indiana University Press.
Gogun, Aleksandr. 2008. *Stalinskie kommandos. 1941–1945*. Moscow: ZAO Tsentrpoligraf.
Gurevich, Zalmen Uri. 2006. "Kach zeh hitkhil." In *Partizanim mesaprim*, edited by Aleksandr Bogen, Avraham Biber, and Kopel Kolpanitzkii, 231–51. Tel Aviv: Misrad Habitakhon.
Himka, John-Paul. 2011. "Debates in Ukraine over Nationalist Involvement in the Holocaust, 2004–2008." *Nationalities Papers* 39 (3): 353–70.
———. 2017. "Former Ukrainian Policemen in the Ukrainian National Insurgency: Continuing the Holocaust outside German Service." In *Lessons and Legacies*, vol. 12, *New Directions in Holocaust Research and Education*, edited by Wendy Lower and Lauren Faulkner Rossi, 141–63. Evanston, IL: Northwestern University Press.

Judt, Tony. 2005. *Postwar: A History of Europe since 1945*. London: William Heinemann.
Kagan, Jack, and Dov Cohen. 1998. *Surviving the Holocaust with the Russian Jewish Partisans*. London: Vallentine Mitchell.
Kaganovitch, Moshe. 1948. *Der yidisher ontayl in der partizaner-bavegung fun Sovet-Rusland*. Rome: Central Historical Commission at the Union of Partisans "Pachach" in Italy.
Kalcheim, Moshe, ed. 1992. *Mit shtoltsn gang, 1939–1945*. Tel Aviv?: Organization of Partisans, Underground Fighters and Ghetto Rebels in Israel.
Kovalenia, A. A. 2010. *Belarus' 1941–1945: Podvig. Tragediya. Pamiat'*. Vol. 2. Minsk: Belaruskaya Navuka.
Lapidus, Albert. 2016. *Golos pamiatii—the Voice of Memory*. Boston: M-Graphics.
Lukashenko, Aleksander. 2019. *Belarus partizanskaya/Guerilla Belarus*. Minsk: Belaruskaia Entsikklopedia Imia Petrusiia Brouki.
Marples, David. 2014. *Our Glorious Past: Lukashenka's Belarus and the Great Patriotic War*. Stuttgart: Ibidem.
Musiał, Bogdan. 2009. *Sowjetische Partisanen 1941–1944: Mythos und Wirklichkeit*. Paderborn: F. Schöningh.
Overbye, Dennis. 2018. "Stephen Hawking's Beautiful Mind." *New York Times*, March 14, 2018. https://www.nytimes.com/2018/03/14/science/stephen-hawking-timeline.html.
Radchenko, Yuri. 2017. "Ukrainian Historiography of the Holocaust through the Prism of Modern Discourse on Collaboration on the Territory of Ukraine." *Dapim: Studies on the Holocaust* 31 (3): 313–21.
Rohava, Maryia. 2018. "Identity in an Autocratic State: Or What Belarusians Talk about When They Talk about National Identity." *East European Politics and Societies and Cultures* 32 (3): 639–68.
Rudling, Per Anders. 2015. *The Rise and Fall of Belarusian Nationalism, 1906–1931*. Pittsburgh: University of Pittsburgh Press.
Sage, Steven. 2017. "The Holocaust in Bulgaria: Rescuing History from 'Rescue.'" *Dapim: Studies on the Holocaust* 31 (2): 139–45.
Schupljak, Peter. 2008. "Weißrussland als Opfer: Besatzungszeit auf dem Gebiet der heutigen Republik Belarus." In *Täter, Opfer, Helden: Der Zweite Weltkrieg in der weißrussischen und deutschen Erinnerung*, edited by Olga Kurilo and Gerd-Ulrich Herrmann, 28–38. Berlin: Metropol.
Slepyan, Kenneth. 2006. *Stalin's Guerrillas: Soviet Partisans in World War II*. Lawrence: University Press of Kansas.
Slobin, Lev. 2009. *Ostalos' za kadrom i mezhdu strok*. Minsk: Medisont.
Smolar, Hersh. 1984. *Yehudim sovietiyim me-akhorai gidrot ha-geto*. Tel Aviv: Tel Aviv University.
Subotić, Jelena. 2019. *Yellow Star, Red Star: Holocaust Remembrance after Communism*. Ithaca, NY: Cornell University Press.
Tec, Nechama. 1993. *Defiance: The Bielski Partisans*. New York: Oxford University Press.
———. 1998. "Women among the Forest Partisans." in *Women in the Holocaust*, edited by Dalia Ofer and Lenore J. Weitzman, 223–33. New Haven, CT: Yale University Press.
———. 2003. *Resilience and Courage: Women, Men, and the Holocaust*. New Haven, CT: Yale University Press.
Uladzimir, Arlou, and Zmicier Hierasimovic. 2018. *Belarus: The Epoch of the Grand Duchy of Lithuania; An Illustrated History*. Minsk: Technalohija.

Waligórska, Magdalena. 2016. "Jewish Heritage and the New Belarusian National Identity Project." *East European Politics and Societies and Cultures* 30 (2): 332–59.

Weitzman, Lenore, and Zvi Gitelman. 2019. *Noach Roitman: From Baranovich to the Partisans*. Privately published.

Wylegała, Anna. 2017. "Managing the Difficult Past: Ukrainian Collective Memory and Public Debates in History." *Nationalities Papers* 45 (5): 780–97.

Yad Vashem. 1971. "Jewish Partisans—Objective and Subjective Difficulties." In *Jewish Resistance during the Holocaust: Proceedings of the Conference on Manifestations of Jewish Resistance*, 323–42. Jerusalem: Yad Vashem.

Zakharevich, Sergei. 2012. *Partizany SSSR: Ot mifov k real'nosti*. Vilnius: Nasha Buduchynia.

Zięby, Andrzej, ed. 2016. *OUN, UPA i zagłada Żydów*. Kraków: Księgarnia Akademicka.

15

THE INTERNATIONAL RELATIONS OF HOLOCAUST MEMORY

Jelena Subotić

After decades of largely sitting on the sidelines of Holocaust research (King 2012), there has been a recent surge in social science interest in the Holocaust. A number of studies in political science (Charnysh and Finkel 2017; Finkel 2017; Kopstein and Wittenberg 2011, 2018; Monroe 2008; Welch 2014), sociology (Braun 2016; Einwohner 2003, 2006; Einwohner and Maher 2011), political theory (Monroe 2013), geography (Knowles, Cole, and Giordano 2014), and economics (Voigtländer and Voth 2012; Satyanath, Voigtländer, and Voth 2017) have appeared in quick succession, revitalizing a social science focus on the Holocaust.

Yet the discipline of international relations (IR) has remained largely outside this conversation. The purpose of this chapter is to bring IR back into dialogue with other social scientific approaches to the Holocaust and demonstrate how a focus on states' international relations—their relations with other states and actors in the international system—can help illuminate some of the puzzling features of contemporary Holocaust remembrance. Specifically, I discuss the international politics of Holocaust memory in post-Communist Eastern Europe and elucidate ways in which an IR perspective on state memory, identity, international status, and reputation seeking can explain why the Holocaust remains ignored, appropriated, and obfuscated in much of the region that was the central location of the genocide.

IR and the Holocaust

Traditionally, the Holocaust was of almost no interest to mainstream, realist scholars of IR, who—to the extent they paid any attention to World War II at all—focused on Hitler's grand strategy and the interplay of great powers in the run-up to and during the war. IR interest in World War II was therefore as an example of interstate conflict. The Holocaust remained outside IR focus as a primarily "domestic" and inexplicably "irrational" feature of Nazi German policies. This is evident as early as 1962, in the writing of Hans Morgenthau (for a critique of Morgenthau along these lines see Klusmeyer 2009), as well as in the later realist scholarship on World War II (Mearsheimer 2001; Schweller 1998; Copeland 2001, 2012).

Some IR scholars have more systematically analyzed the Holocaust within a broader context of the international politics of genocide. There are analyses that interpret the Holocaust as an example of mass killing of civilians that resulted from the failure of other available policies to produce desirable political goals (Valentino 2004; and for an IR critique, see Desch 2004), or as a consequence of territorial loss and an unmanageable influx of refugees (Midlarsky 2005a), or more broadly the state perception of threat and vulnerability (Midlarsky 2005b).

These advances, while applying more seriously general IR theories to the case of the Holocaust, have still remained within the confines of a state-centric and epistemologically rationalist worldview, which may be ill equipped to fully recognize the multiple dimensions of the Holocaust as a global, political, geographic "international event" rooted less in geostrategic or domestic demographic policies than in a broader international context of racial hierarchy and supremacy.

More recent IR scholarship has begun to look at the Holocaust through the prism of this larger historical context—systemic changes in the international order—such as the crisis of the European imperial system in the twentieth century (Shaw 2013), or even more directly as an "international event" that should be understood through the international context of colonialism and racism (Barder 2021). Germany's war, in this retelling, can be recast as a fundamentally racial war—a war against German racial enemies—and not as an interstate conflict between great powers as traditional IR understood it (Barder 2021). Yet other IR scholars have explored the political and legal implications of the concept of "genocide"—itself created in the aftermath of the Holocaust—and the ways in which the context of the Holocaust informed and shaped the understanding of, and responses to, later genocides in the twentieth and twenty-first centuries (Meiches 2019).

IR and Holocaust Memory

While this turn toward the international context of the origins and dynamics of the Holocaust is in its relative infancy within the field of IR, where IR scholarship has had the most to contribute so far is in its understanding of international Holocaust trauma, memory, and practices of remembrance.

The study of trauma and its international implications and reverberations has long been of core interest to critical, non-state-centric IR scholarship—the strand of IR literature that looks at the international system as an international society with social rules, expectations, identities, and practices that defy a simplistic pursuit of geostrategic interests and benefits. Understanding historical trauma as a core component of state identity, which then in turn explains contemporary state domestic and international behavior, has been of central interest to this scholarship (Edkins 2003; Bell 2006; Resende and Budryte 2014). For example, scholars have analyzed the trauma of the Holocaust as a constitutive element of Israeli as well as German national identities, and as a feature of these identities that explains state alliances and foreign policy decisions (Barnett 1996, 1999; Becker 2013; Nili 2011; Schilling 2014; Pace and Bilgic 2018).

But perhaps the most direct advances that identity approaches to IR have made in relation to Holocaust research are in the growing interest IR scholars are showing in studying international memory politics—ways in which states remember and use the past. While memory studies are their own established field of inquiry (Roediger and Wertsch 2008), over the past decade there has been a surge of interest in how memory informs and shapes state policies and their international relations (Langenbacher and Shain 2010; Fierke 2014; Dixon 2018; Bachleitner 2019), and in how global injustice memories become diffused and institutionalized at the international level (Olesen 2012).

This scholarship begins with the premise that memory is critical to state identity. Just as our own individual memory constitutes our identity, political memory is what constitutes state identities (Olick and Robbins 1998). IR research on political memory has demonstrated how memory helps create and sustain a particular state biographical narrative through the use of historical signposts and careful curating of select events, setbacks and triumphs, myths, and symbols the state uses to construct and maintain its identity (Berenskoetter 2014; Kinnvall 2004; Volkan 1997; Subotić 2016; Khoury 2018). This is what national calendars, days of remembrance, street names, and national holidays are all about (Hom 2017; Omelicheva 2017). A shared sense of political memory orients political community through time, by "providing a sense of where 'we' come from and what 'we' have been through" (Berenskoetter 2014, 270).

Political memory, therefore, is never about the past but is very much about a particular political project in the present that it supports and maintains, which of course was the principal insight of Maurice Halbwachs (1992; also Nora 1989). This shared political memory is then institutionalized through routinized practices of remembrance such as museum exhibits, memorial sites, days of commemoration, and history textbooks, or even inscribed in law (Levy and Sznaider 2006). Historical museums are especially important memory actors, as they are the main sites where historical narratives are being reproduced (Radonić 2017).

Not all political memory, however, is useful for constructing state identity. Securing a "desirable" memory, one that presents the state and the nation as heroes and not villains of some commonly shared and recognizable international story (of a global war, for example), is necessary for a state's continuing sense of stability, but also for its status seeking, for membership in prestigious international clubs (such as the European Union), and for securing all sorts of international reputational benefits. In fact, national memories of a violent past almost exclusively operate within one of three normatively acceptable frames: nation as victorious over evil, nation as resister of evil, or nation as victim of evil (Assmann 2014). A "desirable" memory of the Holocaust is an example of a type of memory that is important for states to maintain and promote in order to belong to the international society of liberal European states.

Working in this framework, IR scholars of memory have identified a particular state political strategy of "mnemonic security," where states defend a specific political memory that constitutes their identity, and do so as a top national priority (Mälksoo 2015; Rumelili 2018; Subotić 2018). The ongoing efforts of the PiS Polish government, for example, to secure a specific and highly favorable memory of Polish behavior during World War II is a prime example of this dynamic (Siddi and Gaweda 2019; Hackmann 2018). Treating seriously state identity construction and maintenance—a core interest of constructivist IR scholarship—can thus provide unique insights into otherwise puzzling state behavior.

State Identity and the End of Communism

A refocus on state identity and its central place in international relations can also offer a different understanding of the end of Communism and the continuing impact of this historical rupture on the international politics of contemporary Eastern Europe. From this vantage point, the stunningly rapid collapse of Communism over only two years (1989–91) created a feeling of profound crisis of identity across Eastern Europe. Since a coherent, stable, and hegemonic system of meaning disappeared overnight, all of the habitual relationships these states had formed and sustained with other states and international organizations became immediately unsettled, and new relationships needed to be developed. Political memory of the old country no longer provided the regime its legitimacy; new histories needed to be created to make sense to the changed societies (Evans 2003).

This period of insecurity was also propelled by internalized feelings of backwardness and inferiority regarding the West (Mostov 1998). This anxiety over being perceived as backward was especially strong during the period of the EU's enlargement to the east, when the EU was surprised at Eastern European candidate states' unwillingness to discuss the Holocaust. One of the EU reports even commented that post-Communist countries were "lagging behind and thus in need of re-education where the remembrance of Shoah is concerned" (Stańczyk 2016, 418). The EU saw this avoidance of dealing with the Holocaust as a "moral failing or as a sign of backwardness" that needed to be remedied (Mark 2010, xvi).

And yet, as part of "rejoining Europe," post-Communist states were asked to join the already established and solidified Western "cosmopolitan" memory of the Holocaust (Levy and Sznaider 2002). They first encountered the European push for this memory of the Holocaust as they tried to join various European organizations after 1991—foremost in their applications for EU membership, but also in their applications for membership in other European institutions, such as, for example, the Council of Europe and NATO (Subotić 2018).

This European narrative of the Holocaust—which understands it as the foundational block of postwar European identity (Assmann 2014)—has, however, created stress and resentment in post-Communist states, which have been asked to accept and contribute to this primarily Western European account as members or candidate states of the European Union. The problem is that the "cosmopolitan Holocaust memory" as developed in the West did not narratively fit with the very different set of Holocaust memories in post-Communist Europe. This lack of fit was evident primarily in the lack of centrality of the Shoah as the defining memory of the twentieth-century experience across the post-Communist space. Instead of the memory of the Holocaust, Eastern European states after Communism constructed their national identities on the memory of Stalinism and Soviet occupation, as well as pre-Communist ethnic conflict with other states. The European centrality of the Holocaust, then, replaced the centrality of Communist and ethnic victimization as the dominant organizing narrative of post-Communist states, and was therefore threatening and destabilizing to these state identities (Subotić 2019, 11).

Further, the centrality of the Holocaust as a *foundational* European narrative was also soundly rejected across post-Communist Europe because of its perceived raising of Jewish victimhood above victimhood of other regional ethnic groups, an effort that is increasingly openly resented (Baer and Sznaider 2017, 106). In the absence of almost any Jews across vast swaths of the East, post-Communist national identities in the region were built on a rejection of Communist pan-national identity (which was built on the loyalty to the socialist and not the ethnic subject) in favor of ethnic majoritarianism. This post-Communist ethnic homogenization left almost no space for narratives of ethnic and other minorities. As Anton Weiss-Wendt (2008) explains in his analysis of Estonia, Holocaust remembrance there was linked exclusively to the Jewish minority and was understood to be a "Jewish issue." Since the Jewish minority in Estonia is tiny, Holocaust remembrance simply does not register for majority Estonians and, when brought up, brings about ethnic resentment and often new waves of antisemitism.

Holocaust memory challenges the identities of post-Communist states in yet another, perhaps more profoundly destabilizing way: it brings about discussions of widespread local complicity in the Holocaust and the social, economic, and political benefits of complete Jewish absence for non-Jewish majorities across the region. Eastern Europe is not only the principal geographic location of the Holocaust, but also the main witness to and—most problematically—the main economic beneficiary of the Holocaust. The annihilation of European Jewry was not only carried out behind the electric wires of concentration camps, hidden from public view. It was also carried out in plain sight of non-Jewish citizens of these countries, on streets, in town squares, and in small villages across Eastern Europe. Non-Jews benefited from this Jewish obliteration, often for generations after the Holocaust (Charnysh and Finkel 2017, 804). Jewish stores, houses, and property have, over decades of pillaging followed by Communist seizures, slowly been dispersed within the general economy, with difficult and sporadic attempts at restitution. This is an issue of great historical importance, and while carefully documented, it is profoundly and persistently resisted by much of the Eastern European public (Himka 2008, 360). It complicates the core national imagination of victimization, suffering, and innocence, and therefore chips away at the foundational blocks of state identity.

From the perspective of post-Communist states, however, while Holocaust memory was not central to their identity, it proved useful for the larger project of bringing East-Central Europe back to "true Europe" (Mälksoo 2009, 655). Without directly challenging the Western memory of the Holocaust, the "new Europeans" instead pursued a form of memory reconciliation by promoting the idea that twentieth-century Europe experienced two totalitarianisms and two genocides—Nazism and Stalinism. As I document in my own research (Subotić 2019), many states across the region attempted to resolve these identity challenges by putting forward a new kind of Holocaust remembrance where the memory, symbols, and imagery of the Holocaust became appropriated to represent crimes of Communism, and in the process influenced the European Union's own memory politics and legislation. The criminal past was not fully denied, but the responsibility for it was misdirected. This accomplished two things—it absolved the nation from acknowledging responsibility for its criminal past and, at the same time, made Communism, as a political project, criminal.

Patterns of Holocaust Remembrance after Communism

Theoretically, an IR approach to Holocaust remembrance can illuminate ways in which states make strategic use of political memory in an effort to resolve their contemporary "ontological insecurities" (Mitzen 2006; Steele 2008; Subotić 2018)—insecurities about their identities, about their status, and about their relationships with other international actors. From this theoretical vantage point, post-Communist states today are dealing with conflicting sources of insecurity. They are anxious to be perceived as fully European by "core" Western European states, a status that remains fleeting, especially in the aftermath of the openly anti–East European rhetoric of the Eurocrisis and Brexit (Spigelman 2013; Favell 2017).

If we understand political memory as constitutive of state identity, and interpret the end of Communism as an external shock that created stress and anxiety in insecure East European states, we can begin to better grasp a series of puzzling and often disturbing patterns of Holocaust remembrance practices across the region.

For example, in October 2017, a commemorative plaque reading "In Memory of the 200,000 Poles Murdered in Warsaw in the German Death Camp KL Warschau" was unveiled in Warsaw. This was a somber ceremony, with the local priest performing Catholic rites and a representative of the Polish army honoring the dead. The only problem: almost none of this was true. There did indeed exist a camp in Warsaw, where a few thousand Polish citizens died during the German occupation. But after the burning of the Warsaw ghetto in 1943, this camp was turned into a concentration and extermination camp for Jews brought in from other parts of Europe, who were used as slave labor to clear the charred remains of the ghetto. A total of some twenty thousand people died in this camp, most of them Jews (Davies 2019). The Polish citizen movement behind this commemorative project was, therefore, not just commemorating victims of their own ethnic group at the expense of other victims—this is an unremarkable and largely ubiquitous feature of commemorative politics everywhere. What is remarkable is that the very clear purpose of this commemoration was to put it in direct competition with the memory of the Holocaust, especially in Poland, the geographic heart of the genocide.

This new historical remembrance in Poland has been going on for quite some time and has attracted much international attention (Charnysh and Finkel 2018). In 2018, the Polish government passed a law that criminalized the use of the phrase "Polish death camps" to designate German Nazi death camps in occupied Poland, such as Auschwitz, Treblinka, and many others, but it also criminalized any insinuation that individual Poles may have committed ant-Jewish crimes during the Holocaust.[1]

Poland is hardly alone. This new historical revisionism has been flourishing across post-Communist Europe and is especially visible in historical museums, monuments and memorials, history textbooks, and rehabilitation and restitution laws. While countries in the region vary considerably in the historical and political circumstances of the Holocaust, the nature of the Communist period, and the post-Communist transition, there is a remarkably strong—but nationally flavored—trend of appropriation of Holocaust memory, especially its narrative and visual repertoire, to instead tell the story of Communist oppression.

For example, in 2014, the Historical Museum of Serbia in Belgrade opened a highly publicized exhibition titled *In the Name of the People: Political Repression in Serbia, 1944–1953*, which was to display new historical documents and evidence of crimes carried out by Communist Yugoslavia in the first postwar years. The most stunning visual artifact displayed, however, was a well-known photograph of emaciated prisoners (one of them Elie Wiesel) in the Nazi Buchenwald concentration camp, taken by a US Army soldier at the time of the camp's liberation in April 1945. In the Belgrade exhibition, this canonic image—one of the most famous photographs of the Holocaust—was displayed in the section devoted to the Yugoslav Communist-era camp for political prisoners on the Adriatic island of Goli Otok, with the caption, "The example of living conditions of Goli Otok prisoners." The visual message of this display was, very clearly, that Communist oppression *looked* like the Holocaust.

Similarly, in Hungary, the House of Terror museum that opened in 2002 in Budapest narrates the story of Hungary's twentieth-century experience as a nation victim of the foreign Communist and, to a much lesser extent, foreign fascist regime. The House of Terror goes out of its way to bring home the message that fascism and Communism were two sides of the same coin. There are multiple visual representations of black totalitarianism and red totalitarianism: the black arrow cross juxtaposed with the red star, the fascist uniform juxtaposed with the Communist uniform. Obviously, equation of the two totalitarian regimes is not new or particularly surprising. What is more interesting is that the blunt message of this state institution is presented through the appropriation of not just Holocaust imagery, but also Holocaust museum visual displays. Most directly, the House of Terror uses the model of the "Tower of Faces"—portraits of Holocaust victims projected onto the entire length of walls in the United States Holocaust Memorial Museum in Washington, DC—to project portraits of Hungarian "victims of Communism," while the "Hall of Tears" in the basement of the Budapest museum is a visual repurposing of the Children's Memorial at Yad Vashem in Jerusalem (Radonić 2017, 283).

Under the government of Viktor Orbán, Hungary has further embarked on a spectacular urban revisioning of its twentieth-century history. The Memorial to the Victims of the German Occupation erected in Budapest in 2014 memorializes Hungary—the country—as the main victim of the German occupation, through a not-very-subtle depiction of Germany's imperial eagle crushing Hungary, which is symbolized by the Archangel Gabriel. The memorial was unveiled overnight and with no accompanying official opening ceremony, in order to avoid any public debate and expected protests (Pető 2019, 472). Indeed, immediately upon its unveiling, Holocaust survivors and their family members placed hundreds of handwritten notes, pictures, and objects outside the memorial that told the story of 430,000 Jews who were deported from Hungary, mostly to Auschwitz. Hungary's was the quickest rate of deportation in the history of the Holocaust, taking less than two months and done with the active participation of Hungarian civil servants (Braham 2016, 6).

In a manner similar to many new public monuments, museums, and memorials across post-Communist Europe, the Budapest memorial uses architecture as a tool to express myths of nationhood, as part of a state strategy of new visual remembrance of the past. Specifically, it narratively replaces the memory of the Holocaust, and the catastrophe of Hungarian Jewish annihilation as the central memory of World War II in Hungary, with the memory of Hungarian victimhood and innocence. It also purposefully removes the responsibility for the murder of Hungarian Jews from Hungary's Axis-allied government and places it firmly with Germany, presenting fascism and its exterminationist policies as alien, foreign intrusions into the Hungarian body politic. This shift therefore completely removes the history of the Holocaust in Hungary before the German occupation in 1944, the period that left sixty thousand Hungarian Jews killed as early as 1942, the genocide carried out not by Germans, but by Hungarian forces under the rule of regent Miklós Horthy (Braham 2016, 5).

This new type of Holocaust remembrance, then, is not exactly denial—Viktor Orbán even declared 2014 a Year of Holocaust Commemoration. However problematic, it does not deny the Holocaust as a historical fact, nor does it challenge its most established narratives. It is also not quite the same as trivialization: while the focus always is on the non-Jewish ethnic majority's suffering, it is relatively rare to hear outright minimizing of Jewish victimization. A more nuanced way of understanding this type of Holocaust remembrance is as *memory appropriation*, where the memory of the Holocaust is used to memorialize a different kind of suffering, such as suffering under Communism, or suffering from ethnic violence carried out by other groups (for a full elaboration of this argument, see Subotić [2019]).

Theoretically, what an IR approach to Holocaust remembrance helps illuminate is that this process is not simply a byproduct of post-Communist transitions; it is in fact an integral part of the political strategy of post-Communist states, which are basing their contemporary legitimacy on a complete rejection of Communism and a renewed connection to the pre-Communist, mythically nationally pure, and, above all, ethnic character of states. It is this rejection of Communist doctrinaire supranationalism and its replacement with old-fashioned ethnic nationalism that colors how the Holocaust is remembered. Holocaust remembrance, then, is no longer about the Holocaust at all, but is about the very acute legitimacy needs of post-Communist states, which are building their identity as fundamentally anti-Communist, which then in turn helps them be perceived as more legitimately European (Mälksoo 2009).

A more systematic focus on state identity and state international status seeking can put these episodes of memory inversion in a contemporary political context and demonstrate that they are not isolated instances of competing memory, but instead critical elements of national strategies of political legitimacy. They serve to reposition national narratives in opposition to those of Communism but also to those historically embraced by Western Europe, and instead reclaim a national identity that rejects multiculturalism and is rebuilt along ethnic majoritarian lines.

Zooming out to the international level helps identify patterns of Holocaust remembrance that would otherwise remain idiosyncratic and inadequately contextualized. An international perspective that places memory politics within the context of the dramatic and rapid demise of East European Communism can demonstrate how post-Communist states have used Holocaust remembrance as a heuristic tool to buttress their international reputation and status. Holocaust remembrance, in this recasting, becomes part of the symbolic international politics of post-Communist states, and not a genuine search for accountability for crimes of the past.

REFERENCES

Assmann, Aleida. 2014. "Transnational Memories." *European Review* 22 (4): 546–56.
Bachleitner, Kathrin. 2019. "Diplomacy with Memory: How the Past Is Employed for Future Foreign Policy." *Foreign Policy Analysis* 15 (4): 492–508.
Baer, Alejandro, and Natan Sznaider. 2017. *Memory and Forgetting in the Post-Holocaust Era: The Ethics of Never Again*. Milton Park, UK: Routledge.

Barder, Alexander D. 2021. *Global Race War: International Politics and Racial Hierarchy*. Oxford: Oxford University Press.
Barnett, Michael N. 1996. "Identity and Alliances in the Middle East." In *The Culture of National Security: Norms and Identity in World Politics*, edited by Peter J. Katzenstein, 400–47. New York: Columbia University Press.
———. 1999. "Culture, Strategy and Foreign Policy Change: Israel's Road to Oslo." *European Journal of International Relations* 5 (1): 5–36.
Becker, Douglas J. 2013. "Memory and Trauma as Elements of Identity in Foreign Policymaking." In *Memory and Trauma in International Relations: Theories, Cases and Debates*, edited by Erica Resende and Dovile Budryte, 73–89. London: Routledge.
Bell, Duncan. 2006. *Memory, Trauma and World Politics: Reflections on the Relationship between Past and Present*. Basingstoke, UK: Palgrave Macmillan.
Berenskoetter, Felix. 2014. "Parameters of a National Biography." *European Journal of International Relations* 20 (1): 262–88.
Braham, Randolph L. 2016. "Hungary: The Assault on the Historical Memory of the Holocaust." In *The Holocaust in Hungary: Seventy Years Later*, edited by Randolph L. Braham and András Kovács, 261–309. Budapest: Central European University Press.
Braun, Robert. 2016. "Religious Minorities and Resistance to Genocide: The Collective Rescue of Jews in the Netherlands during the Holocaust." *American Political Science Review* 110 (1): 127–47.
Charnysh, Volha, and Evgeny Finkel. 2017. "The Death Camp Eldorado: Political and Economic Effects of Mass Violence." *American Political Science Review* 111 (4): 801–18.
———. 2018. "Rewriting History in Eastern Europe: Poland's New Holocaust Law and the Politics of the Past." *Foreign Affairs*, February 14, 2018. https://www.foreignaffairs.com/articles/hungary/2018-02-14/rewriting-history-eastern-europe.
Copeland, Dale C. 2001. *The Origins of Major War*. Ithaca, NY: Cornell University Press.
———. 2012. "Economic Interdependence and the Grand Strategies." In *The Challenge Of Grand Strategy: The Great Powers and the Broken Balance between the World Wars*, edited by Jeffrey W. Taliaferro, Norrin M. Ripsman and Steven E. Lobell, 120–46. Cambridge: Cambridge University Press.
Davies, Christian. 2019. "Under the Railway Line." *London Review of Books*, May 9, 2019.
Desch, Michael C. 2004. "A 'Final Solution' to a Recurrent Tragedy?" *Security Studies* 13 (3): 145–59.
Dixon, Jennifer M. 2018. *Dark Pasts: Changing the State's Story in Turkey and Japan*. Ithaca, NY: Cornell University Press.
Edkins, Jenny. 2003. *Trauma and the Memory of Politics*. Cambridge: Cambridge University Press.
Einwohner, Rachel L. 2003. "Opportunity, Honor, and Action in the Warsaw Ghetto Uprising of 1943." *American Journal of Sociology* 109 (3): 650–75.
———. 2006. "Identity Work and Collective Action in a Repressive Context: Jewish Resistance on the 'Aryan Side' of the Warsaw Ghetto." *Social Problems* 53 (1): 38–56.
Einwohner, Rachel, and Thomas Maher. 2011. "Threat Assessment and Collective-Action Emergence: Death-Camp and Ghetto Resistance during the Holocaust." *Mobilization: An International Quarterly* 16 (2): 127–46.

Evans, Richard J. 2003. "Redesigning the Past: History in Political Transitions." *Journal of Contemporary History* 38 (1): 5–12.
Favell, Adrian. 2017. "European Union versus European Society: Sociologists on 'Brexit' and the 'Failure' of Europeanization." In *Brexit: Sociological Responses*, edited by William Outhwaite, 193–200. London: Anthem.
Fierke, Karin Marie. 2014. "Who Is My Neighbour? Memories of the Holocaust/al Nakba and a Global Ethic of Care." *European Journal of International Relations* 20 (3): 787–809.
Finkel, Evgeny. 2017. *Ordinary Jews: Choice and Survival during the Holocaust*. Princeton, NJ: Princeton University Press.
Hackmann, Jörg. 2018. "Defending the 'Good Name' of the Polish Nation: Politics of History as a Battlefield in Poland, 2015–18." *Journal of Genocide Research* 20 (4): 587–606.
Halbwachs, Maurice. 1992. *On Collective Memory*. Chicago: University of Chicago Press.
Himka, John-Paul. 2008. "Obstacles to the Integration of the Holocaust into Post-Communist East European Historical Narratives." *Canadian Slavonic Papers* 50 (3–4): 359–72.
Hom, Andrew R. 2017. "Patriots All Around: Inter/national Timing, Round Numbers, and the Politics of Commemorative Critique." *Australian Journal of Politics & History* 63 (3): 443–56.
Khoury, Nadim. 2018. "Plotting Stories after War: Toward a Methodology for Negotiating Identity." *European Journal of International Relations* 24 (2): 367–90.
King, Charles. 2012. "Can There Be a Political Science of the Holocaust?" *Perspectives on Politics* 10 (2): 323–41.
Kinnvall, Catarina. 2004. "Globalization and Religious Nationalism: Self, Identity, and the Search for Ontological Security." *Political Psychology* 25 (5): 741–67.
Klusmeyer, Douglas. 2009. "Beyond Tragedy: Hannah Arendt and Hans Morgenthau on Responsibility, Evil and Political Ethics." *International Studies Review* 11 (2): 332–51.
Knowles, Anne Kelly, Tim Cole, and Alberto Giordano. 2014. *Geographies of the Holocaust*. Bloomington: Indiana University Press.
Kopstein, Jeffrey S., and Jason Wittenberg. 2011. "Deadly Communities: Local Political Milieus and the Persecution of Jews in Occupied Poland." *Comparative Political Studies* 44 (3): 259–83.
———. 2018. *Intimate Violence: Anti-Jewish Pogroms on the Eve of the Holocaust*. Ithaca, NY: Cornell University Press.
Langenbacher, Eric, and Yossi Shain. 2010. *Power and the Past: Collective Memory and International Relations*. Washington, DC: Georgetown University Press.
Levy, Daniel, and Natan Sznaider. 2002. "Memory Unbound: The Holocaust and the Formation of Cosmopolitan Memory." *European Journal of Social Theory* 5 (1): 87–106.
———. 2006. "The Politics of Commemoration: The Holocaust, Memory and Trauma." In *Handbook of Contemporary European Social Theory*, edited by Gerard Delanty, 289–97. London: Routledge.
Mälksoo, Maria. 2009. "The Memory Politics of Becoming European: The East European Subalterns and the Collective Memory of Europe." *European Journal of International Relations* 15 (4): 653–80.
———. 2015. "'Memory Must Be Defended': Beyond the Politics of Mnemonical Security." *Security Dialogue* 46 (3): 221–37.

Mark, James. 2010. *The Unfinished Revolution: Making Sense of the Communist Past in Central-Eastern Europe*. New Haven, CT: Yale University Press.

Mearsheimer, John J. 2001. *The Tragedy of Great Power Politics*. New York: W. W. Norton.

Meiches, Benjamin. 2019. *The Politics of Annihilation: A Genealogy of Genocide*. Minneapolis: University of Minnesota Press.

Midlarsky, Manus I. 2005a. "The Demographics of Genocide: Refugees and Territorial Loss in the Mass Murder of European Jewry." *Journal of Peace Research* 42 (4): 375–91.

———. 2005b. *The Killing Trap: Genocide in the Twentieth Century*. New York: Cambridge University Press.

Mitzen, Jennifer. 2006. "Ontological Security in World Politics: State Identity and the Security Dilemma." *European Journal of International Relations* 12 (3): 341–70.

Monroe, Kristen Renwick. 2008. "Cracking the Code of Genocide: The Moral Psychology of Rescuers, Bystanders, and Nazis during the Holocaust." *Political Psychology* 29 (5): 699–736.

———. 2013. *The Hand of Compassion: Portraits of Moral Choice during the Holocaust*. Princeton, NJ: Princeton University Press.

Morgenthau, Hans J. 1962. *Dilemmas of Politics*. Chicago: University of Chicago Press.

Mostov, Julie. 1998. "The Use and Abuse of History in Eastern Europe: A Challenge for the 90s." *Constellations* 4 (3): 376–86.

Nili, Shmuel. 2011. "The Nuclear (and the) Holocaust: Israel, Iran, and the Shadows of Auschwitz." *Journal of Strategic Security* 4 (1): 37–56.

Nora, Pierre. 1989. "Between Memory and History: Les lieux de mémoire." *Representations* 26:7–24.

Olesen, Thomas. 2012. "Global Injustice Memories: The 1994 Rwanda Genocide." *International Political Sociology* 6 (4): 373–89.

Olick, Jeffrey K., and Joyce Robbins. 1998. "Social Memory Studies: From 'Collective Memory' to the Historical Sociology of Mnemonic Practices." *Annual Review of Sociology* 24 (1): 105–40.

Omelicheva, Mariya. 2017. "A New Russian Holiday Has More behind It Than National Unity: The Political Functions of Historical Commemorations." *Australian Journal of Politics & History* 63 (3): 430–42.

Pace, Michelle, and Ali Bilgic. 2018. "Trauma, Emotions, and Memory in World Politics: The Case of the European Union's Foreign Policy in the Middle East Conflict." *Political Psychology* 39 (3): 503–17.

Pető, Andrea. 2019. "'Non-remembering' the Holocaust in Hungary and Poland." *Polin: Studies in Polish Jewry* 31:471–80.

Radonić, Ljiljana. 2017. "Post-Communist Invocation of Europe: Memorial Museums' Narratives and the Europeanization of Memory." *National Identities* 19 (2): 269–88.

Resende, Erica, and Dovile Budryte, eds. 2014. *Memory and Trauma in International Relations: Theories, Cases and Debates*. London: Routledge.

Roediger, Henry L., and James V. Wertsch. 2008. "Creating a New Discipline of Memory Studies." *Memory Studies* 1 (1): 9–22.

Rumelili, Bahar. 2018. "Breaking with Europe's Pasts: Memory, Reconciliation, and Ontological (In)security." *European Security* 27 (3): 280–95.

Satyanath, Shanker, Nico Voigtländer, and Hans-Joachim Voth. 2017. "Bowling for Fascism: Social Capital and the Rise of the Nazi Party." *Journal of Political Economy* 125 (2): 478–526.

Schilling, Christopher L. 2014. *Emotional State Theory: Friendship and Fear in Israeli Foreign Policy*. Lanham, MD: Lexington Books.
Schweller, Randall L. 1998. *Deadly Imbalances: Tripolarity and Hitler's Strategy of World Conquest*. New York: Columbia University Press.
Shaw, Martin. 2013. *Genocide and International Relations: Changing Patterns in the Transitions of the Late Modern World*. New York: Cambridge University Press.
Siddi, Marco, and Barbara Gaweda. 2019. "The National Agents of Transnational Memory and Their Limits: The Case of the Museum of the Second World War in Gdańsk." *Journal of Contemporary European Studies* 27 (2): 258–71.
Spigelman, Ariel. 2013. "The Depiction of Polish Migrants in the United Kingdom by the British Press after Poland's Accession to the European Union." *International Journal of Sociology and Social Policy* 33 (1/2): 98–113.
Stańczyk, Ewa. 2016. "Transnational, Transborder, Antinational? The Memory of the Jewish Past in Poland." *Nationalities Papers* 44 (3): 416–29.
Steele, Brent J. 2008. *Ontological Security in International Relations: Self-Identity and the IR State*. London: Routledge.
Subotić, Jelena. 2016. "Narrative, Ontological Security, and Foreign Policy Change." *Foreign Policy Analysis* 12 (4): 610–27.
———. 2018. "Political Memory, Ontological Security, and Holocaust Remembrance in Post-Communist Europe." *European Security* 27 (3): 296–313.
———. 2019. *Yellow Star, Red Star: Holocaust Remembrance after Communism*. Ithaca, NY: Cornell University Press.
Valentino, Benjamin A. 2004. *Final Solutions: Mass Killing and Genocide in the Twentieth Century*. Ithaca, NY: Cornell University Press.
Voigtländer, Nico, and Hans-Joachim Voth. 2012. "Persecution Perpetuated: The Medieval Origins of Anti-Semitic Violence in Nazi Germany." *Quarterly Journal of Economics* 127 (3): 1339–92.
Volkan, Vamik D. 1997. *Bloodlines: From Ethnic Pride to Ethnic Terrorism*. New York: Farrar, Straus and Giroux.
Weiss-Wendt, Anton. 2008. "Why the Holocaust Does Not Matter to Estonians." *Journal of Baltic Studies* 39 (4): 475–97.
Welch, Susan. 2014. "American Opinion toward Jews during the Nazi Era: Results from Quota Sample Polling during the 1930s and 1940s." *Social Science Quarterly* 95 (3): 615–35.

Conclusion

FROM THE MICRO TO THE MACRO

Daniel Ziblatt

"Big structures, large processes, huge comparisons." This is the title of a 1984 book by the historical sociologist Charles Tilly that also describes one strand at the center of modern social science as it existed in the postwar years. This tradition also characterized the work of the founders of my own field within political science, comparative politics. The central aim of this research tradition was to explain macro differences in the organization of modern and modernizing societies. *National* patterns of political outcomes were usually the topic of interest, including but not limited to big structures and huge processes like state building, violent social revolutions, democratization, economic development, and the emergence of national political party systems.

In this tradition, "big" outcomes were usually also thought to have "big" causes. This macroscopic inclination sought to discern the structural and institutional drivers of different features of modernity. Different rates and patterns of economic development and breakthrough were thought to have been prompted, for example, by the national timing of industrialization (Gerschenkron 1962). The structure of party systems was rooted in underlying patterns of national societal cleavages (Lipset and Rokkan 1967). And paths of democratization were shaped by nationally distinctive historical patterns of revolution and economic change (Moore 1966).

Inspired by this founding generation of scholars, an enduring mode of research has now gone on to analyze an even broader set of topics: why welfare states look different among rich democracies (Esping-Anderson 1990), the sources of different national varieties of capitalism (Hall and Soskice 2001; Iversen and Soskice 2020), different national responses to epidemics (Lieberman 2009), and the robustness of authoritarianism (Slater 2010; Levitsky and Way 2010).

Building on the achievements of this research tradition, however, recent years have been marked by a move in the social sciences away from the "big, large, and huge" to the "small, targeted, and focused." We might dub this a shift in the field from "macro-" to "micro-" comparison. The impetus for this move is theoretical, empirical, *and* methodological. Theoretically, scholars have increasingly argued, the study of the macro may miss what really matters. Scholars argue that macronational outcomes need to be disaggregated into their subnational components because sometimes national units of analysis may conceal important subnational sources of variation. To students of authoritarianism, for example, subnational authoritarian enclaves can persist in what appear to be otherwise democratic national political systems (Gibson 2013; Mickey 2015). Subnational patterns of industrial organization may matter more than national patterns (Herrigel 1996). Local patterns of social ties can give rise to varying patterns of governance capacity that more directly affect the everyday lives of citizens (Tsai 2007). Scholars of violence have moved to the local, pointing to the pitfalls of relying on macrolevel indicators that "may aggregate local cleavages in misleading ways" (Kalyvas 2006, 370). And most recently, even our current populist moment in the West has been understood through this lens: the political resentments that have generated a decade of right-wing populist backlash are most usefully understood in their specific, often rural, geographical milieus (Rodden 2019; Cramer 2016). Substantive outcomes that we care a lot about exist at the local level and fly beneath the radar of Tilly's "huge comparisons."

There are also empirical and methodological reasons for the "micro" turn in the social sciences. The confluence of the "Big Data" revolution and increased emphasis on more rigorous standards of causal inference in the social science has led scholars to seek out treasure troves of disaggregated data with which they can zoom in from the macroscopic to the microscopic in order to analyze how individuals and groups behave. Whether one is analyzing determinants of politicians' behavior in parliaments, combatants in civil wars, or economic entrepreneurs in informal black markets, the disaggregation of "big" processes into "small" ones creates more observations and allows for a more systematic probing of hypotheses with fine-grained data. The result has been a transformation in the practice of social science itself. In fact, a stark generational gap now exists between older scholars who continue to admire the sweeping narratives offered in "big books" and younger scholars who strive above all to craft short but data-intensive articles that meet demanding standards of causal inference in social science journals.

The Study of the Holocaust

The study of the Holocaust, though often isolated from the broader trends of contemporary social science (see the introduction to this volume), has in fact paralleled these broader trends. Early work, as the editors make clear in their introduction, asked big questions, such as, was the Holocaust a logical outgrowth of modernity, or fundamentally opposed to it? And as historians, rather than social scientists, took on the challenge of explaining the Holocaust, an early framing of the study of the Holocaust took hold. It was presumed to be a single event that flowed from Germany's Final Solution designed at the Wannsee Conference in Berlin in January 1942 and implemented by the political center over the course of the Second World War.

Recently, historians have pushed back against this narrative with more fine-grained attention to local and decentered unfolding of events (Gross 2001; Bartov 2018). This volume represents a sustained effort of social scientists to join this conversation. This happens at a moment when not only social scientists but also historians have moved to the micro. At the core of this intellectual convergence is the proposition that the Holocaust is not simply to be thought of as a single "case" or "singular event" that occurred between 1933 and 1945, directed by the hierarchical German Nazi war machine. Instead, King (chapter 1) and the other authors suggest that the Holocaust should be conceived of as a process of (1) *disparate events*—mass killings, pogroms, forced migration, resistance, and survival; in which (2) *multiple types of actors*—perpetrators, victims, and bystanders—participated; all in (3) *multiple locations*—far from Berlin, and outside of German-directed concentration camps, and instead spread across the diverse landscape of both urban and rural communities in Central and Eastern Europe.

Disaggregating and decentering the analysis in this way generates a powerful close-up view that analyzes the Holocaust in its local contexts. Consider Daniel Solomon's analysis, in chapter 3, of the pogrom violence of November 1938's Kristallnacht, which systematically analyzes a dataset of one thousand synagogues across Germany to try to discern which were attacked and which were not. He concludes that attacks were most likely and most severe in cities where the Jewish population was largest and where the Communist Party was strongest, suggesting, in Solomon's view, the symbolic motivation of the attacks—perhaps prompted by an effort to assault Jews where they were most prominent and where the political opponents of pogroms were most electorally successful. In short, characteristics of local milieu and social ties explain the unfolding assault.

Similarly, in his study of three cities in Eastern Europe (Minsk, Kraków, and Białystok), Eugene Finkel (chapter 4) finds substantial cross-city variation in how the Jewish community responded to ghettoization and the Nazi occupations. Whether Jews resisted or adopted other strategies (evasion, coping, or cooperation) vis-à-vis Nazi rule hinged, according to Finkel, on the history of Jewish relations with state authorities and local communities in the pre–World War II regimes. Where a history of social integration with non-Jewish neighbors and authorities was present (Minsk and Kraków, each previously under Soviet or Austro-Hungarian rule, respectively), Jews often "evaded" persecution by assimilating, hiding, or adopting a "fake" identity outside ghetto walls. By contrast, in contexts where the pre–World War II authorities had discouraged or the communities had resisted integration (e.g. Białystok), as happened under pre-Soviet Russian rule and interwar Polish rule, evasion was simply not an option; Jews were more likely to "stay put" or resist. Preexisting structures of authority and social relations shaped how ordinary Jews survived.

When we turn our attention from the victims to the perpetrators, we see similar patterns of local variation in the borderlands of occupied Poland and Western Ukraine, as in Kopstein's analysis, in chapter 5, of the pogroms of the summer of 1941. Here, rather than local ties, it was the structure of political competition that mattered. In these nascent democracies of the interwar years, religious and ethnic cleavages played out in electoral politics in a way that quickly degenerated into more virulent forms of ethnic competition. Converging with Solomon's findings on Kristallnacht, it is where Jewish populations were larger and more mobilized that pogroms were more intense. Kopstein's work (summarized more thoroughly in Kopstein and Wittenberg [2018]) also is suggestive of dynamics in other times and places. Local and communal patterns of political competition tilt some societies more toward ethnically motivated political violence than others.

And finally, even more general cultural tendencies of antisemitism—as reflected in children's stories—are locally rooted, as Robert Braun's analysis (chapter 7) makes clear. Basing his chapter on a new analysis of an old survey conducted in the early 1930s of 50,356 local experts from 19,828 locales on the prevalence of Jewish "bogeyman" stories in local folklore traditions, Braun makes clear that among other factors, it is in Germany's borderlands—regions proximate to territory lost to the post-Versailles redrawing of German boundaries—that these stories had greater circulation. Not only overt violence but even deeper-seated cultural patterns reflected local regional experiences in the lead-up to the Holocaust.

From Disaggregation to Recontextualization

All of the contributions to this volume pursue a similar tack: disaggregation and decentering. Shifting attention away from the "commanding heights" of the Nazi state in Berlin, we uncover the local determinants of violence in Lithuania (Mishkin), Jewish responses to the typhoid epidemic in the Warsaw ghetto (Stone and Lehnstaedt), survival strategies in the Netherlands (Tammes and Simpkin), the relationship between the Catholic hierarchy and the Vichy regime in France (Luft), the gender makeup of victims transported by train to concentration camps (Welch), and what survivors' testimonies can teach us about the resistance to the Holocaust (Einwohner). We also learn about the politics of memory and remembrance outside Germany (Charnysh; Gitelman; and Subotić).

Disaggregation and decentering gives us an "on the ground" picture of the multiple processes and actors that shaped the inner workings of the rupture of the Holocaust in twentieth-century Europe as well as its global aftermath. We learn what happens when societies fall into the chasm of the Holocaust where the rule of law is perverted and small-scale coordination is necessary for human survival. Further, by often operating with systematic data, we can see that these inner workings can be analyzed by applying and testing theory drawn from other contexts—such as theories of "racial threat" (Kopstein, chapter 5) and "symbolic violence" (Solomon, chapter 3).

But understanding the local, proximate determinants inside the Holocaust does not immediately help us answer a broader question: why was it exactly that *this* particular region of Europe experienced the murderous wave of the Holocaust in *this* particular period? After all, that these regions of Europe, long under imperial rule and prone to ethnic rivalries, would suddenly become the sites of massive human destruction when they did is in some respects surprising: by the 1930s, decades of economic progress and the recent democratization of political systems ought to have been liberating, if we are to believe much of the received wisdom of social science (Sen 2001).

To answer a question like this requires, as some of the accounts in this volume suggest, that we step back from the micro to the macro. Relinking the decentered processes within the Holocaust—discovered by projects like this book—to the common antecedent external conditions that activated them nearly simultaneously across Europe is the critical issue for the social scientific study of the Holocaust. In other words, the turn to the micro has to be supplemented by a focus on the macro.

Antecedent Conditions of Human Destructiveness

What triggered the processes identified in this book? One common view is that democracy's belated arrival in Central Europe is directly connected to the wave of human destruction that followed in its wake. The sociologist Michael Mann (2005) has argued that democracy has a "dark side"—a proclivity for ethnic violence. According to this view, democratization destabilizes power relations, unleashes power struggles, and, by prioritizing majority rule, can, at least in the short term, run amok by allowing the majority to tyrannize the minority. Other scholars of contemporary democratization, writing in the wake of the breakup of Yugoslavia and the ethnic conflict of the 1990s (Snyder 2000), have also argued that new democracies with weak institutions are prone to violence because traditional elites encourage ethnic and nationalist violence to maintain power. Political competition amid intense ethnic cleavages can be dangerous. In Kopstein's account (chapter 5), fiercely contested elections in a new democracy coincided with later pogroms in eastern Poland. In Solomon's data (chapter 3), more Communist Party electoral success in Weimar Germany triggered intense synagogue attacks across Germany in 1938.

But focusing solely on the *internal* or domestic antecedent conditions of violence is to presume that democracies develop in relatively closed "natural systems" (Bendix 1967). Implied but never explicitly stated in the accounts in this volume is another perspective: it was *external* constraints and foreign models that triggered the decentered wave of human destruction across Europe in the 1940s. Note, for example, that it was with the arrival of German troops in the summer of 1941 in Lithuania that subaltern paramilitaries engaged in massacres (Mishkin, chapter 6). Or as Kopstein (chapter 5) lays out, it was the presence of German army units, police battalions, and mobile killing units in Western Ukraine in the summer of 1941 that prompted the wave of what Kopstein calls "pogrom rituals" following a common "German script." But a subtle use of power was undoubtedly at work: much of the violence was not done directly with German hands. Nor was the physical presence of Germans in a municipality a predictor of anti-Jewish pogroms (Kopstein, chapter 5). Moreover, as Charnysh, Gitelman, and Subotić note in their contributions, external constraints and models not only structured the Holocaust but also shaped local responses and attempts at *Vergangenheitsbewältigung* outside Germany after the fact. Thus, we need an approach that allows for a more nuanced understanding of the interactions of external and internal drivers of political violence and its aftermath.

Recent political science scholarship on the external drivers of regime change provides one possible approach. Seva Gunitsky's important book *Aftershocks: Great Powers and Domestic Reforms in the Twentieth Century* (2017) has made clear that external drivers of domestic regime change occur not only through direct foreign intervention by hegemonic powers but through two more intricate pathways: inducements and emulation. Gunitsky notes that democratic breakthroughs and breakdowns tend to cluster in time. This fact reflects not internal drivers of regime change but major shifts in the balance of power in international systems. When new rising powers that are governed by democratic institutions (e.g., the United States after 1945 and after 1989) emerge at the apex of the international system, waves of democracy follow. When new hegemons with nondemocratic institutions (e.g., Germany in the midst of the Great Depression) "shock" the international system, then waves of democratic backsliding and breakdown occur. Whether a new hegemon is democratic or not, the historical record of the twentieth century shows that new hegemonic powers take advantage of openings in the international system to impose their own regime type on smaller powers (Gunitsky 2017, 15). Yet great powers' capacity to reshape the world in their image is only partly due to their overt coercive capacity to create replica regimes.

More significant, Gunitsky demonstrates, with echoes of Germany's relations with Eastern Europe, is the power of inducements. A rising power can enlarge its networks of trade and patronage, shifting preferences of coalitions and domestic actors. In post-1933 Germany, Nazi leadership regarded trade policy with Central and Eastern Europe through this mercantilist lens: the open plains of Central Europe were a source of agricultural goods and raw materials for Germany's military buildup. In exchange, these regions would receive credits to buy German industrial goods, creating a German sphere of influence running eastward to the Soviet Union (Kopstein 2021; Hirschman 1945).

A second, equally powerful mechanism is the force of emulation. After Nazi Germany's apparent success in breaking through the Great Depression of the early 1930s, the British home secretary wrote in 1938, "If the Danubian States begin now to put on the Nazi garb, it will be because imitation is the sincerest form of flattery and because they want to ingratiate themselves in time with their future master" (quoted in Gunitsky 2017, 23). Institutional emulation occurs when smaller states voluntarily imitate what they regard as "pioneer" and high-prestige states. The sudden rise of a new hegemon—even a regional hegemon—prompts emulation by reducing uncertainty about the relative success of different models, and so can be driven by both material and ideological motivations. In Eastern and Central Europe, traditional conservatives like Miklós Horthy nurtured rocky governing coalitions with national radicals in the mid-1930s, which passed "Jewish laws" (in 1936 in Poland, 1938 in Romania and Hungary). Though certainly motivated by antisemitism, the ambivalence of Hungary's older political classes was apparent. The Romanian premier Armand Calenescu felt he had to explain that his government's new anti-Jewish law had been passed "pour calmer l'opinion publique," and Polish legislators remarkably described their bill "as an act of necessary cruelty" that they hoped would be carried out without too much "brutality" (Janos 2000, 193).

But these bills set dangerous precedents, and with the rise of Hitler and the growing shadow of Germany's ambitions in the East, beginning in 1939 local fascists were empowered to enthusiastically implement their own agendas with the encouragement of German military forces. The model and encouragement of a high-status power like Nazi Germany was at the very least a "permissive cause," opening the door for the whole destruction of Europe's Jews over the next six years.

When Democracy Dies in a (Global) Hegemon

The Holocaust was not the outgrowth of democratization gone wrong. It was the opposite. It was made possible only when democracy *died*—along with its attendant guarantees, including the rule of law and the civil liberty protections of citizenship. But most importantly, it was when democracy died in 1930s Germany, a (regional) hegemon, that reverberations were felt across Europe and the world. New patterns of inducement and emulation were unleashed. Fascism diffused. And so did the Holocaust.

There is a lesson for our own era. Too often we think of the contemporary challenges to democracy as driven strictly by internal problems. If polarization, demographic challenges, and economic inequality are present, then democracy is at risk; if we are lucky enough to live in a country where such challenges are successfully managed, we can rest easy: democracy is thought to be safe. But we must remember to avoid the myth of the closed natural system.

The failure of democracy in an important power like Russia in the 1990s has had global consequences. Indeed, it is in large part this failure that explains the 2022 Russian invasion of Ukraine—an assault cheered on by nationalists and unfolding in many of the territories analyzed in this book. There is no more vivid contemporary reminder of the malevolent consequences of arbitrary power.

And even more worrisome, if democracy died in a global hegemon like the United States, the reverberations would be even more massive. Not only would America's model of democracy be tarnished, but it would also, the lessons of 1930s Europe suggest, become a source of emulation for would-be autocrats and demagogues around the world.

We have already begun to see the warning signs. In the post-2016 world, as US democracy has decayed, we have begun to witness the resurrection of a fascist international even in established democracies. The rise of radical-right populism in a hegemonic power inspires imitators across the globe using similar rhetoric, similar tactics, and a similar assault on the basic principles of democracy. We have never witnessed democracy die in a global hegemon in the modern era. For this reason, the Holocaust offers an important warning: local processes of political violence, opportunism, and demagoguery that shaped the everyday experiences of the Holocaust were triggered when democracy died in a powerful nation. With this insight in hand, as resilient as some democracies may appear, we must remember that all of our political systems remain vulnerable.

REFERENCES

Bartov, Omer. 2018. *Anatomy of a Genocide: The Life and Death of a Town Called Buczacz*. New York: Simon and Schuster.

Bendix, Reinhard. 1967. "Tradition and Modernity Reconsidered." *Comparative Studies in Society and History* 9 (3): 292–346.

Cramer, Katherine. 2016. *The Politics of Resentment: Rural Consciousness in Wisconsin and the Rise of Scott Walker*. Chicago: University of Chicago Press.

Esping-Andersen, Gosta. 1990. *The Three Worlds of Welfare Capitalism*. Princeton, NJ: Princeton University Press.

Gerschenkron, Alexander. 1962. *Economic Backwardness in Historical Perspective*. Cambridge, MA: Harvard University Press.

Gibson, Edward. 2013. *Boundary Control: Subnational Authoritarianism in Federal Democracies*. Cambridge: Cambridge University Press.

Gross, Jan T. 2001. *Neighbors: The Destruction of the Jewish Community in Jedwabne, Poland*. Princeton, NJ: Princeton University Press.

Gunitsky, Seva. 2017. *Aftershocks: Great Powers and Domestic Reforms in the Twentieth Century*. Princeton, NJ: Princeton University Press.

Hall, Peter A., and David Soskice. 2001. *Varieties of Capitalism: The Institutional Foundations of Comparative Advantage*. Oxford: Oxford University Press.

Herrigel, Gary. 1996. *Industrial Constructions: The Sources of German Industrial Power*. Cambridge: Cambridge University Press.

Hirschmann, Albert O. 1945. *National Power and the Structure of Foreign Trade*. Berkeley: University of California Press.

Iverson, Torben, and David Soskice. 2020. *Democracy and Prosperity: Reinventing Capitalism through a Turbulent Century*. Princeton, NJ: Princeton University Press.

Janos, Andrew C. 2000. *East-Central Europe in the Modern World: The Small States of the Borderlands from Pre- to Postcommunism*. Stanford, CA: Stanford University Press.

Kalyvas, Stathis. 2006. *The Logic of Violence in Civil War*. New York: Cambridge University Press.

Kopstein, Jeffrey S. 2021. "Liberal, Fascist, and Communist Legacies." In *Central & East European Politics: Changes and Challenges*, edited by Zsuzsa Csergő, Daina S. Egletis, and M. Paula Pickering, 39–66. New York: Rowman and Littlefield.

Kopstein, Jeffrey S., and Jason Wittenberg. 2018. *Intimate Violence: Anti-Jewish Pogroms on the Eve of the Holocaust*. Ithaca, NY: Cornell University Press.

Levitsky, Steven, and Lucan Way. 2010. *Competitive Authoritarianism: Hybrid Regimes after the Cold War*. Cambridge: Cambridge University Press.

Lieberman, Evan. 2009. *Boundaries of Contagion: How Ethnic Politics Have Shaped Government Responses to AIDS*. Princeton, NJ: Princeton University Press.

Lipset, Seymour M., and Stein Rokkan. 1967. "Cleavage Structures, Party Systems and Voter Alignments: An Introduction." In *Party Systems and Voter Alignments: Cross National Perspectives*, edited by Seymour M. Lipset and Stein Rokkan, 1–64. New York: New York Free Press.

Mann, Michael. 2005. *The Dark Side of Democracy: Explaining Ethnic Cleansing*. Cambridge: Cambridge University Press.
Mickey, Robert. 2015. *Paths Out of Dixie: The Democratization of Authoritarian Enclaves in America's Deep South, 1944–1972*. Princeton, NJ: Princeton University Press.
Moore, Barrington. 1967. *Social Origins of Dictatorship and Democracy*. Boston: Beacon.
Rodden, Jonathan. 2019. *Why Cities Lose: The Deep Roots of the Urban-Rural Political Divide*. New York: Basic Books.
Sen, Amartya. 2001. *Development as Freedom*. New York: Anchor Books.
Slater, Dan. 2010. *Ordering Power: Contentious Politics and Authoritarian Leviathans in Southeast Asia*. Cambridge: Cambridge University Press.
Snyder, Jack. 2000. *From Voting to Violence: Democratization and Nationalist Conflict*. New York: W. W. Norton.
Tilly, Charles. 1984. *Big Structures, Large Processes, Huge Comparisons*. New York: Russel Sage Foundation.
Tsai, Lily. 2007. *Accountability without Democracy: Solidary Groups and Public Goods Provision in Rural China*. Cambridge: Cambridge University Press.

Notes

INTRODUCTION

1. Some historians explicitly draw on social science concepts and methods, for example Dumitru (2018); Dumitru and Johnson (2011).

2. Wendy Lower (2017, 380) characterized the motivation of conservative historians in the German *Historikerstreit* in the mid-1980s as "an attempt by a few more senior scholars of Nazi Germany to orient the field in directions that would largely resist the shift to a popular and academic interest in the Holocaust as the central legacy of the Third Reich."

3. *Yishuv* refers to the pre-state Jewish community in the Land of Israel.

4. Gerson and Wolf (2007a) briefly review the works by these early sociological theorists, including the Heidelberg University–educated Talcott Parsons (Gerhardt 1993).

5. Of course, historians engaged in debates about the origins of the Holocaust. Especially noteworthy was the dispute between "intentionalists" and "functionalists." Intentionalists maintained that Hitler had long intended to murder the Jews and that one therefore needed to focus on the individual ideological motives (especially antisemitism) of Nazi leaders and followers. Functionalists, by contrast, focused on bureaucratic procedures, rapidly shifting military fortunes, and the "unplanned" unfolding of the Final Solution. A useful summary can be found in Mason (1995).

6. For a review that focuses on recent contributions by psychologists and anthropologists, but includes sociologists and political scientists, see Waller (2013).

7. This Weberian definition of social science has the advantage of being able to demarcate itself from two other ideal typical ways of knowing. The humanities focus less on the "systematic" side and the natural sciences less on the specific dynamics of interaction among interpretive beings.

8. His book was spurned by several prestigious university presses before Quadrangle Books published it in a small print run.

9. A rare exception is Helen Fein's book *Accounting for Genocide*, published in 1984.

10. The most well known of these diaries is *Anne Frank: Diary of a Young Girl* (Frank 1993), first published in the US in 1952, which has now sold thirty million copies. The earliest was *The Diary of Mary Berg*, an autobiography about life in the Warsaw Ghetto that was widely reviewed when it was first published in 1945.

11. The economists Nico Voigtländer and Hans-Joachim Voth (2012) reach back further in time than Goldhagen. Their study of antisemitic violence in Nazi Germany finds spatial continuities over a six-hundred-year period. Black death-era pogroms, they maintain, reliably predict antisemitism and violence against Jews in the 1920s and 1930s in the same locations. This study, a few more by these authors on the Holocaust, and the Acemoglu, Hassan, and Robinson (2011) article we reference later in this chapter remain rare exceptions among economists.

12. No pain was inflicted in the experiments, but subjects thought they were inflicting ever-increasing shocks on Milgram's confederates, who cried out in "pain" and protest when the shocks became stronger.

13. Milgram was the forty-sixth-most-cited psychologist of the twentieth century, and number twelve in mentions in introductory psychology texts (Haggbloom et al. 2002).

14. Hilberg interprets his own understanding of the destruction of Europe's Jews, which perhaps anticipates the limits of the concept of genocide: "The idea that the destruction of the Jews was complex became a fundamental hypothesis that guided my work. The killing, I became convinced, was no atrocity in the conventional sense. It was more, and that 'more' was the work of a far-flung, sophisticated bureaucracy" (Hilberg 1996, 59).

15. A vibrant and sometimes heated debate on this question was spurred by an essay, "The German Catechism," by Dirk Moses, a scholar of comparative genocide, published in 2021 in the online journal *Geschichte der Gegenwart* (https://geschichtedergegenwart.ch/the-german-catechism), followed by a series of responses by a number of scholars on the website The New Fascism Syllabus (https://newfascismsyllabus.com/category/opinions/the-catechism-debate/). For biting criticism, see Saul Friedländer, "Ein fundamentals Verbrechen," *Die Zeit*, July 20, 2021, https://www.zeit.de/autoren/F/Saul_Friedlaender/index.

16. The collection of essays in *Sociology Confronts the Holocaust* (Gerson and Wolf 2007b) focused largely on postwar issues of Holocaust memory and Jewish identity.

17. See https://www.yahadinunum.org/what-is-the-holocaust-by-bullets/. Participants' and onlookers' memories and records and historical and contemporary photographs are included in this database, along with descriptions of the site of each mass murder. Yad Vashem is also building a database of mass killing sites.

18. Psychologists made important contributions to earlier Holocaust research, and some of the classic experiments in psychology, such as the Milgram experiment on obedience to authority, were inspired by Nazi rule, as described earlier. Recently their interest in the event itself has diminished, but several chapters in this book draw significantly on psychological theory and methods.

1. CAN—OR SHOULD—THERE BE A POLITICAL SCIENCE OF THE HOLOCAUST?

1. An earlier version of this chapter was published in 2012 as "Can There Be a Political Science of the Holocaust?," *Perspectives on Politics* 10 (2): 323–41.

2. The reports of the "Extraordinary State Commission for Ascertaining and Investigating Crimes Perpetrated by German-Fascist Invaders and Their Accomplices"—generally known by the Russian initials ChGK—were used at Nuremberg and other postwar trials. The commission's working archive of testimonials and affidavits now forms part of the bedrock literature in Holocaust studies.

2. HISTORIES IN MOTION

1. Many thanks to Max Bergholz, Kate Docking, Amos Goldberg, Karianne Hansen, Dirk Moses, Wolfgang Knöbl, Jeff Kopstein, Derek Penslar, Dan Stone, Jelena Subotić, and Susan Welch for their support, excellent comments on, and encouragements for earlier drafts. All remaining errors are mine.

3. POGROM VIOLENCE AND VISIBILITY DURING THE KRISTALLNACHT POGROM

1. For comments on earlier drafts of this chapter, I thank Michael Bailey, Laia Balcells, Volha Charnysh, Matthew Kocher, Jeffrey Kopstein, Yonatan Lupu, Harris Mylonas, Livia Schubiger, Robert Shapiro, Jelena Subotić, and Susan Welch, and participants in the fall 2018 Civil War and Substate Violence seminar at Georgetown University, the spring 2019 DC Comparative Politics Workshop, the spring 2019 Nationalism and Nation-Building seminar at George Washington University, the 2019 Association for the Study

of Nationalities World Convention, the 2019 Annual Meeting of the American Political Science Association, the December 2019 meeting of the Virtual Holocaust Geographies Seminar, and the January 2020 workshop on Social Science Research and the Holocaust at the University of California, Irvine.

2. An important exception is Voigtländer and Voth's (2012) study of the medieval roots of antisemitic violence, which finds that pogroms in fourteenth-century Germany are associated with the occurrence of synagogue destruction during Kristallnacht, as well as multiple other measures of prewar antisemitism in Nazi Germany. Voigtländer and Voth rely on a separate encyclopedia (Alicke 2008) for their municipal-level measure of synagogue destruction during Kristallnacht.

3. A fuller description of the dataset and research design, including summary statistics for relevant variables, are available upon request in a pre-analysis plan titled "The Logic of Pogrom Violence: Evidence from Kristallnacht" (Solomon 2021).

4. The list excludes or provides incomplete information on sites in the provinces of eastern Silesia, East Prussia, and Pomerania; to enable systematic comparison with Weimar-era political and social data, I exclude synagogues in these provinces from the dataset. The project's 2014 publication, *Pogrom Night 1938* (Synagogue Memorial Beth Ashkenaz 2014), includes additional details about the towns in which synagogues were attacked during Kristallnacht. These details include the dates of first Jewish settlement in the town, pre-1938 changes in Jewish associational life and religious practice, and other violent tactics that pogrom participants employed during Kristallnacht. But that publication includes this information only for towns in which Kristallnacht participants attacked synagogues; it is missing additional information where participants did *not* attack synagogues. In further research, I will combine the information from the 2003 and 2014 publications.

5. The project's 2014 publication (Synagogue Memorial Beth Ashkenaz 2014) indicates that pogrom participants also attacked a subset of *inactive* synagogues that Jewish communities had ceased to use by November 1938. Although attacks on inactive synagogues offer compelling qualitative evidence of another plausible measure of symbolic violence—albeit one that may differ in its observable implications from the visibility hypothesis described above—I will explore this puzzling phenomenon with more systematic data in future research.

6. See Aly and Roth (2004) for further discussion of the 1933 German census, one of the Nazi regime's first efforts to categorize and count Germany's Jewish population. I discuss the ethical and analytic dilemmas associated with using these data in Solomon (2021).

7. The relative ease of mass mobilization in urban centers means that pogroms often occur where populations are large (Tambiah 1997; Varshney 2002). To account for the urban character of pogrom violence, I control for the natural log of each municipality's 1933 population. Organizers of large-scale violence also rely on mass communication technologies to facilitate violence, stoke conspiratorial rumors, and encourage popular resentment against targeted groups (see, e.g., during the Rwandan genocide, Straus 2007; Yanagizawa-Drott 2014). Radio was a critical part of the Nazi communication apparatus and an effective platform for the dissemination of antisemitic propaganda (Welch 2008). To account for the potential influence of radio on the coordination of violence among supporters of Kristallnacht's organizers, I multiply Adena et al.'s (2015) calculation of the predicted strength of German radio signals in 1938 by electoral support for the antisemitic coalition of the Nazi Party and the DNVP.

8. These are tentative results that may change as I revise the data according to the 2014 Beth Ashkenaz publication, estimate new model specifications—such as logit or negative binomial regression models that accommodate the structure of the binary and count data, respectively—or add additional control variables.

4. HISTORICAL LEGACIES AND JEWISH SURVIVAL STRATEGIES DURING THE HOLOCAUST

1. *Halutz* means "pioneer" in Hebrew. The term refers to the early Zionist immigrants to Palestine.

2. According to some sources, December 23.

5. A COMMON HISTORY OF VIOLENCE?

1. Achiwum Żydowskiego Institutu Historycznego (Warsaw).

6. MASS VIOLENCE WITHOUT MASS POLITICS

1. The historiography is replete with references to pamphlets distributed by the paramilitaries, calling Lithuanians to arms against the Jews/Communists/Bolsheviks, the implication being that the pamphlets speak to the effective mobilizing capacity of these groups. But consider the degree to which, in so many other contexts, leaflet drops are considered radically ineffective and likely completely, if not comically, out of touch with their intended recipients. Examples of the use of the pamphlets include Truska (2004) and Levinson (2006).

2. I bracket the differences in how the Germans themselves carried out the killing in each country, but as will become clear, this was not, especially in the Lithuanian case, unrelated to the subalterns' behavior.

3. An objection might be that, for domestic political reasons, the Atlas may have systematically ignored participation by Lithuanian civilians. Given the fraught politics of the Holocaust in Lithuania, this cannot be ruled out. Several facts, however, suggest that these concerns may not be warranted. The first is that the project was organized in cooperation with the Austrian Holocaust Memorial Service, which faces fewer pressures to diminish Lithuanian participation in atrocities. The second is that the project does list Lithuanian partisan or police participation in over 170 killings, facts that might embarrass Lithuanian authorities but that were nevertheless uncovered and published. Finally, the project rigorously documents each recorded event and lists legitimate sources for its information.

4. The country remained highly militarized due to the many outstanding territorial conflicts with its neighbors, such as Germany over Klaipeda and Poland and later the Soviet Union over the territory around Vilnius.

5. The Koniuchowsky Papers have been translated into English and are housed at the YIVO archives. I was unable to access these documents in the course of writing this chapter as the archives have been closed due to the COVID-19 pandemic.

7. TERRITORIAL LOSS AND XENOPHOBIA IN THE WEIMAR REPUBLIC

1. It is important to highlight that some researchers explicitly separate antisemitism from violent mobilization (Kopstein and Wittenberg 2011).

2. In particular, I relied on questions 49, 52, 124, and 125.

3. I will draw only on data collected before the seizure of power by the Nazis in 1933. After the Nazi takeover, the ADV was Nazified and started collecting data in a different fashion using different questionnaires. There is considerable reason to believe that post-1933 data collection was unreliable (Lixfeld 1994).

4. For both measures I experimented with radiuses between .62 miles and 46.06 miles. The main results were identical with the ones presented below. The 31.06-mile radius provided the best model fit.

5. Inspection of figure 7.3a, of course, sheds serious doubt on this possibility, because the northwestern border was hardly touched by the war.

6. Again, I experimented with a wide range of radii to calculate this measure. None of the alternatives provided a better fit or altered the main results.

7. In an additional analysis, I also controlled for the increase in Jewish inhabitants between 1887 and 1925. This did not alter the results but did lead to a reduction in sample size, as data for 1887 are available only for a subset of Prussian counties.

8. I constructed this measure by adding the percentage of votes for Danish, Polish, Czech, French, and Alsace-Lorrainian parties.

9. Nachl. Wilhelm Mannhardt, Staatsbibliothek Berlin Preussischer Kulturbezits DE-611-BF-2979.

8. DEFEATING TYPHUS IN THE WARSAW GHETTO

1. *Warschauer Zeitung*, November 19, 1939, 5.

2. There are several reports by Jewish physicians in the Warsaw ghetto. Cf. Żydowski Instytut Historyczny Warsaw, Archiwum Ringelbluma, I/609, "Denkschrift über eine prophylaktische-sociale Maßnahmen zur Bekämpfung des Fleckfiebers im Jüdischen Wohnbezirk Warschau," n.d. [after June 1941]; Żydowski Instytut Historyczny Warsaw, Archiwum Ringelbluma, I/609, "Denkschrift über die prophylaktischen Massnahmen im Jüdischen Viertel," n.d. [after June 1941]; Żydowski Instytut Historyczny Warsaw, Archiwum Ringelbluma, I/610, memorandum by Komisja Zdrowia, June 28, 1941; Żydowski Instytut Historyczny Warsaw, Archiwum Ringelbluma, I/611, "Walka z tyfusem," March 13, 1942; Żydowski Instytut Historyczny Warsaw, Archiwum Ringelbluma, I/612, "Der kampf mit epidemies, w azoj er iz un wi azoj er darf zayn" [in Yiddish], n.d. [after June 1941].

3. Żydowski Instytut Historyczny Warsaw, ARing I/608, "Uzupełnienia do memoriału w sprawie sytuacji ludności żydowskiej w Warszawie," June 1941, 15.

9. HOLOCAUST SURVIVAL AMONG IMMIGRANT JEWS

1. From the original seven municipalities, Bergen (NH) was excluded, as most Jews from that village were evacuated to Amsterdam in March 1942 (Tammes 2005, 36–40). The Culemborg list can be found at the regional archive Rivierenland, and the Nijmegen list at the municipal archive Nijmegen; scans of these lists were provided by Robert Braun.

2. We used "Namenlijst" (List of names), version dated January 26, 2020, https://www.oorloginnijmegen.nl/index.php/wie-bron/namenlijst-nijmegen-1939-1944. In addition, Carla Rieter-Michelotti, a member of the "werkgroep oorlogsdodennijmegen.nl," was helpful in providing us information on date of arrival and place of migration for a dozen Jewish immigrants who arrived first in another Dutch municipality before moving to Nijmegen.

3. Some Jews tried to escape from the Nazis earlier on during the Nazi occupation; see, for example, Bijsterveld (2016).

4. We accessed copies of these cards via the online archive of the Arolsen Archives (https://collections.arolsen-archives.org/en/search/) between February and June 2020. These copies, however, are black-and-white scans of the colored originals, which may have limited the information gathered from these cards; the original cards were archived at the Dutch Red Cross but from 2018 onward were held at the National Archive with limited access (Schütz 2019).

5. Besides "empty cards," we did not find index cards for some other Jews, which may indicate early escape through hiding, fleeing, or reclassification.

6. According to the Nazi definition, a person was considered a "full" Jew if he or she had at least three grandparents who belonged to an Israelite congregation or had two Jewish grandparents and was married to a "full" Jew or belonged to an Israelite congregation. In the study, they are referred to as Jews. Jews themselves could thus have abandoned Judaism or converted to Christianity.

7. Robert Braun provided us scans of these lists. Archived at the NIOD Institute for War, Holocaust and Genocide Studies, Hauptabteilung Inneres, Abteilung Innere Verwaltung, 123D. This list contains two supplements, one made up in October 1942 and another made up in February 1943.

8. Temporary exemption from deportation for health reasons was very soon limited after an increase in attests (illness statements) during the summer of 1942 (Van den Ende 2015, 161–68).

9. For a complete overview of postwar lists and the matching procedure, see Tammes (2019).

10. NORMALIZING VIOLENCE

1. Ironically, the classic distinction between civic and ethnic nationalism is of France from Germany, as neatly laid out in Brubaker's (1992) analysis of the immigration policies of both countries. Hence, I argue that one of the Vichy regime's main goals through its program of National Revolution was to transform France's political culture for thinking about national belonging.

2. A full discussion of the process by which the French government elected to transfer executive, legislative, and constitutional powers to Marshal Pétain is beyond the scope of this chapter. For a useful analysis, however, see Ermakoff (2008).

3. For a more complete discussion of how the French Catholic Church contributed to Vichy's authoritarian legitimation process and its violence against Jews, see Luft (2020). This chapter summarizes this work with a novel theoretical approach to demonstrate the significance of social science theories and methods for the study of the Holocaust.

4. For a useful overview of the origins of Vichy's Statut des Juifs, see Joly (2013). With reference to the church and why it supported the statute, see Luft (2016, chap. 1).

5. "Loi relative aux ressortissants étrangers de race juive," *Journal officiel de la République française* (or, *de l'État français*), October 18, 1940, 5324; "Abolition du décret Crémieux par Marcel Peyrouton, ministre de l'intérieur," *Journal officiel de la République française* (or, *de l'État français*), October 7, 1940.

6. "Ordonnance allemande définissant le Premier statut allemand des Juifs et dispositions concernant leurs biens; recensement des Juifs avec le fichier Tulard, écriteau 'Juif' sur les devantures des magasins," September 27, 1940 (this law was a part of the second Statut des Juifs); "Loi du 2 juin 1941 remplaçant la loi du 3 octobre 1940 portant statut des juifs," *Journal officiel de la République française* (or, *de l'État français*), June 14, 1941, 2475; "Loi du 22 juillet 1941 relative aux entreprises, biens et valeurs appartenant aux Juifs," *Journal officiel de la République française* (or, *de l'État français*), August 26, 1941.

7. In this sense, we can think of the National Revolution as a classification struggle. As Goldberg (2008, 87–88) explains with reference to the development of the US welfare state, "Conflicts over the citizenship status and rights of welfare state claimants are a particular instance of what Bourdieu calls classification struggles. . . . [T]hey are struggles to class claimants as citizens or paupers." In the case of Vichy France, the struggle was to redefine the nation—who belonged and who didn't—and to classify once-citizens (Jews) as noncitizens or as a particular class of citizens deserving of lesser rights.

8. *Semaine religieuse du diocèse de Lyon*, November 29, 1940. For a detailed analysis of this famous speech, see Georges (2003).

9. Luft (2016, chap. 1).

10. Archives Diocésaines de Cambrai, fonds Chollet, 1B 24, Procès-verbal de l'Assemblée des Cardinaux et Archevêques de France, Paris, January 15, 1941.

11. Archives Diocésaines de Cambrai, fonds Chollet, 1B 24, Conférence Épiscopales de Lyon, February 5–6, 1941.

12. *La Croix d'Auvergne*, May 4, 1941.

13. Archives Diocésaines de Cambrai, fonds Chollet, 1B 26, Procès-verbal de l'Assemblée des Cardinaux et Archevêques de France, Paris, July 24–25, 1941.

14. Quoted in de Pury (1978, 731).

15. Archives de l'Archdiocèse de Lyon, fonds Gerlier, Interventions de Cardinal en Faveur de Divers Juifs, 1940–1943, November 26, 1941.

16. Archives de l'Archdiocèse de Lyon, fonds Gerlier, Interventions de Cardinal en Faveur de Divers Juifs, 1940–1943, November 26, 1941.

17. Archives de l'Archdiocèse de Lyon, fonds Gerlier, Interventions de Cardinal en Faveur de Divers Juifs, 1940–1943, December 5, 1941.

18. Gerlier explains his rationale, as discussed in the previous section, in a letter to Monsignor Henri-Alexandre Chappoulie, the episcopate's delegate to Vichy, contained in Le Centre National des Archives de l'Église de France (hereafter CNAEF), 3CE 23, Relations Cardinal Gerlier/Mgr. Chappoulie (1940–1944), December 14, 1941.

19. As Poznanski (2001, 43) notes, however, a few were able to obtain exemptions at first, and then, with the passing of the second Statut des Juifs in June 1941, all public officials would lose their jobs with no exceptions.

20. Archives de l'Archdiocèse de Lyon, fonds Gerlier, Correspondence Cardinal Gerlier avec La Nonciature, February 4, 1941; February 26, 1941; February 28, 1941.

21. Archives de l'Archdiocèse de Lyon, fonds Gerlier, Correspondence Cardinal Gerlier avec La Nonciature, February 4, 1941; February 26, 1941; February 28, 1941.

22. Suhard, on his decision to decline the nomination, details how he told Pétain that he had "great confidence in him" and would "love" to join the national council, but he worried that doing so would "reduce my influence in religious affairs to 80%" and he would better serve the marshal by staying "on the religious plan." Archives Historiques de l'Archevêché de Paris, fonds Suhard, 1D 14 18, Journal Suhard, January 15–27, 59. (Hereafter, I refer to this source as "Suhard's diary.")

23. Archives Nationales, 3W 347, Télégramme 1496, Abetz à Ribbentrop, December 13, 1941.

24. Suhard's diary, October 1940, 48.

25. Suhard's diary, September 16–19, 1940, 45.

26. Archives de l'Archdiocèse de Lyon, fonds Gerlier, Affaire Helbronner, December 8, 1941.

27. Archives de l'Archdiocèse de Lyon, fonds Gerlier, Affaire Helbronner, December 8, 1941.

28. Archives de l'Archdiocèse de Lyon, fonds Gerlier, Affaire Helbronner, December 8, 1941.

29. Archives de l'Archdiocèse de Lyon, fonds Gerlier, Affaire Helbronner, December 8, 1941.

30. Archives de l'Archdiocèse de Lyon, fonds Gerlier, Affaire Helbronner, December 8, 1941.

31. *Semaine religieuse du diocèse de Lyon*, November 29, 1940.

32. "Dans un vibrant discours, Mgr. Gerlier engage tous les Français à s'unir autour du Maréchal," *Journal des débats*, December 28, 1940.

33. CNAEF, 3 CE 38, Ministère de l'intérieur, sous-direction des cultes et associations, relations avec M. Pierre-Sauret, sous-directeur, Mémoire à Consulter pour une Politique Religieuse de l'État, n.d.

34. *Vie sociale de l'église: Documents et actes officiels; Années 1940–1942* (Paris: Maison de la Bonne Presse, 1942), 51.

35. Suhard's diary, October 1940, 47.
36. *Vie sociale de l'église*, 54.
37. Archives de Consistoire Israélite de France, fonds Moch, bobine 3, correspondence between Jacques Helbronner and Isaïe Schwartz, letter of protest from the Grand Rabbi of France to Maréchal Pétain, October 22, 1940.
38. Archives de Consistoire Israélite de France, fonds Moch, bobine 3, correspondence between Jacques Helbronner and Isaïe Schwartz, letter of protest from the Grand Rabbi of France to Maréchal Pétain, October 22, 1940; letter from the Grand Rabbi of Paris, Julian Weill, to Maréchal Pétain, October 23, 1940.
39. *Semaine religieuse du diocèse de Lyon*, November 29, 1940.
40. CNAEF, 3CE 22, Voyages de Cardinal Suhard archevêque de Paris à Vichy (1941–1943), letter from Suhard to Pétain, November 3, 1941.
41. *Semaine religieuse du Paris*, January 10, 1942.

11. USING THE YAD VASHEM TRANSPORT DATABASE TO EXAMINE GENDER AND SELECTION DURING THE HOLOCAUST

1. The author thanks Emily Kiver, Elyana Adler, and Donna Bahry for their assistance. This chapter draws on earlier work published in Welch (2020a, 2020b).
2. Reinhard Heydrich, for whom Operation Reinhard was named, was the head of the Reich Security Main Office, responsible for the deportations of the Jews.
3. We distinguish between "death camps" or "killing centers"—that is, the Operation Reinhard sites of Belzec, Sobibor, and Treblinka, plus Chełmno and Maly Trostinets, on the one hand—and Auschwitz, on the other. Historians estimate that more than 1.7 million were transported to the Operation Reinhard killing centers, another 150,000 to Chełmno, some 65,000 to Maly Trostinets, and 1.1 million to Auschwitz. On Maly Trostinets, see *Shoah Resource Center*, Yad Vashem, accessed November 22, 2017, http://www.yadvashem.org/odot_pdf/microsoft%20word%20-%206636.pdf. See also Stone (2019).
4. Łódź was the last ghetto to be destroyed, with its remaining residents sent to Auschwitz in August 1944.
5. For a fuller discussion of the research on gender and greater elaboration of the findings described in this chapter, see Welch (2020b).
6. For a period in 1944, men, women, and children from several Terezin transports were sent to a "family camp," but in July 1944 all of them were gassed.
7. In a few cases we do know precisely what happened to those sent to the ghettos. Some transports headed to Kaunas and Riga instead took their prisoners to the nearby killing sites—the Ninth Fort and Rumbula Forest, respectively—and slaughtered them. In that sense, these transports were similar to those to the death camps, where, in most transports, all the prisoners were murdered within a few hours.
8. Yad Vashem (2016). The database is searchable by prisoner name, departure and arrival destination, date, and transport number.
9. These histories include Gottwaldt and Schulle (2005).
10. One important source incorporated into the Yad Vashem data is Czech (1997), a day-by-day record of arrivals, departures, and deaths, including the numbers from each transport sent immediately to be gassed; data on transport schedules, but not the people on the transports, can be found, for example, at "The Holocaust: Lest We Forget," http://www.holocaust-lestweforget.com/westerbork-transport-schedule.html. The German state archives also has a memorial book listing deportations from various Western countries (http://www.bundesarchiv.de/gedenkbuch/chronicles.html.en?page=1), but not with individual listings. Information on transits to and from Terezin are found in Adler, Adler, and Arnovitz (2017). There are excellent sources memorializing each Dutch Jew

who was deported, but there is no link to their specific transport (cf. "Joods Monument," https://www.joodsmonument.nl/en/; and "Akevoth: Genealogical and Historical Research on Dutch Jewry," https://www.dutchjewry.org).

11. Data on transports originating in Eastern Europe are currently being added.

12. Kaplan (1998); Kwiet (1984).

13. For example, many transports to Auschwitz stopped at Cosel (Kozle) ninety miles east of Kraków, where fit men were taken off for hard labor at work camps nearby. For one of hundreds of examples of the imprecision of extant records, see the records of Transport 405 from Frankfort to Raasiku, Estonia, on September 24, 1942, accessed February 17, 2020, https://deportation.yadvashem.org/index.html?language=en&itemId=9439285&ind=1.

14. A few passengers on some transports were Sinti.

15. These include transports to Berlin, Drancy, Gurs, Vittel, and Westerbork.

16. The German name for Terezin was Theresienstadt.

17. Transports also varied by month, a less obvious finding (not shown). There was a remarkable consistency in the seasonal transports in 1943 and 1944, with about one-third each in the first two quarters and twenty percent each in each of the last quarters. In 1942, half the transports were in the summer as the program got underway full scale then.

18. But for 23 percent, we were not. See, for example, Yad Vashem's description of the transport from Westerbork to Auschwitz on October 16, 1942, accessed July 10, 2019, https://deportation.yadvashem.org/index.html?language=en&itemId=6509525&ind=27. Though it is filled with useful information, no gender breakdown on the transport has been retrieved, though Danuta Czech's information on those sent to the labor camp rather than being gassed on arrival is included. In a few cases, the prisoners are classified as men, women, and children. In those cases, we estimated the children to be evenly divided between boys and girls. That estimate conforms with one known data compilation on the sex breakdown of children on transports from the Łódź ghetto (Ringelheim 1993, table 11.2).

19. Gender composition data are unavailable for 22 percent of Auschwitz and concentration camp transports, 15 percent of Terezin transports, and 10 percent of killing camp transports.

20. Gurvitch (1943) describes the overall profile of immigrants to France in the interwar period.

21. While 90 percent of French Jews survived, only about 60 percent of the non-French Jews living in France did (Hilberg 1992, chap. 11).

22. Stone's data source is found in Arad (2018, 68–88).

23. Jewish prisoners revolted at Treblinka in August 1943 and Sobibor in October, hastening the closing of the camps. The camp officials, anticipating the arrival of the Soviet army, had already ordered the bodies dug up and burned. Later they destroyed the buildings and created farmsteads where the camps had been.

24. I have seen no similar data for Poland and other Eastern European transports.

25. For an excellent example of the use of quantitative data to reveal something new and important about the Holocaust, see Stone (2019), which examines transports to Sobibor, Belzec, and Treblinka during three months of 1942 based on railroad records. Stone does not examine gender.

26. The differences in a paired sample test (N = 200) was .13, t = 8.95, sign = .00. If we examine only the larger transports (those with at least one hundred prisoners), the differences were nearly identical, though the proportions were lower for both men and women: 33 percent of women and 49 percent of men were selected to be slave laborers.

27. The small eighty-five-and-over group was an anomaly among the men, because five of twelve survived the first selection, compared to one of twenty-seven women.

28. I was able to document survival rates for only 5 percent of the 1941 transports, jumping to 32 percent in 1942, and then to between 38 percent and 40 percent during the rest of the war. The proportion of transports with survival rates from different countries is much more disparate, ranging from only 18 percent in Germany to 100 percent in Italy. Belgium, France, and Luxembourg also had survival rates by gender for more than half their transports.

29. Though the Reinhard actions were explicitly directed toward elimination of Polish Jews, the Reinhard killing camps were the destination for thousands of Western European Jews too.

12. ADDRESSING THE MISSING VOICES IN HOLOCAUST TESTIMONY

1. I thank Jeff Kopstein, Jelena Subotić, and Susan Welch (z"l) for their comments and guidance on this chapter. I also thank Becka Alper for her research assistance. This work was supported by a grant from the National Science Foundation (#SES-0817659) and a fellowship from the Center for Social Sciences at Purdue University.

2. Well-known archives in the United States include the Shoah Foundation at the University of Southern California, the Fortunoff Archives at Yale University, and the US Holocaust Memorial Museum in Washington, DC.

13. REMEMBERING PAST ATROCITIES

1. These regions are in Western Ukraine today but belonged to the Polish Second Republic before World War II and contained large Jewish and Ukrainian minorities.

2. This was not inaccurate, as some Ukrainian nationalists initially collaborated with the Nazis in murdering local Jews.

3. This research was approved by the Harvard Institutional Review Board, Protocol No. CR14–2380–01.

4. The median age of respondents is forty (identical to the national median of thirty-nine), and the mean income level (3,843 złoty per month) is near the national average (3,740 złoty) in 2014, despite a high nonresponse rate to this survey question.

5. Respondents who did not complete the entire survey received partial compensation for the share of the survey they completed. The questionnaire was completed by 445 (88 percent) of the 503 respondents who started it.

6. Balance tests across treatment conditions are presented in table 13.5. Slightly more respondents assigned to control (N = 164) completed the survey (135 and 150 respondents received the uncontested and contested Jedwabne treatments, respectively). There are significantly more men in the control condition (at 42 percent) than in the two treatment conditions (at 32 and 31 percent). Lower attrition rates in the control group may have been due to the sensitive nature of the Jedwabne treatment. In other surveys of Polish respondents, men exhibit a higher prejudice toward Jews and other minorities and are more likely to agree with statements such as, "Jews still talk too much about what happened to them in the Holocaust" (Anti-defamation League 2020). While attrition at this stage of the experiment is problematic for inference, it would arguably bias the coefficients on both treatments downward by reducing the proportion of male respondents, who are most likely to negatively react to the perpetrator narrative.

7. An alternative empirical strategy would be to use factor analysis to reduce dimensionality, but this would complicate the interpretation of effect sizes.

8. Counted here are also a few responses that claimed that Jews and another group (Poles, Ukrainians, or Gypsies) were victimized.

9. "Bezpozrednio zydowcy mieszkający w tej miejscowozci ale pozrednio takze potomkowie sprawcow tej zbrodni" [sic].

10. In the overall sample, 29 percent and 55 percent of respondents reported a "very strong" or "strong" attachment to Poland, respectively.

14. LEGITIMATING MYTHS AND THE HOLOCAUST IN POST-SOCIALIST STATES

1. "History Is Bunk, Says Henry Ford." *New York Times*, October 29, 1921.

2. Quoted in Amacher (2018), 103.

3. Zakharevich (2012, 58) asserts that the Communist Party had no popular base during the Nazi occupation. The main motive for popular support for the partisans was fear of the consequences of failing to support the Soviets (58–63).

4. Gurevich (2006) tells how Piotr Danilochkin, a Soviet POW whom some Jews liberated from a POW transit camp and who later became a partisan commander, showed him a manuscript chapter about Jewish partisans he had written in a book published in the USSR in 1983, but the chapter had been cut out by the censor.

5. Faina Astrometskaya, interviewed on December 5, 1997, Minsk, Visual History of the Shoah, ID 38724, summary by Julia Bernstein, June 7, 2011.

6. Some memoirs of the Bielskii partisans are Moshe Beirach, *Vezot li-teu'dah* (Kibbutz Lohamei ha-Getaot: Ghetto Fighters House, 1981); Yehoshua Yoffe, *Partizanim* (Tel Aviv: Tversky, 1952); B. Levin, *B'ya'arot ha-nakam* (Tel Aviv: Ha-kibbutz ha-Meuhad, 1968); and Jack Kagan and Dov Cohen, *Surviving the Holocaust with the Russian Jewish Partisans* (London: Vallentine Mitchell, 1998).

7. According to Kagan and Cohen (1998), Zorin was an officer in the Red Army from 1918 to 1924 and was a carpenter by trade. The entry for Zorin in the Russian-language encyclopedia of the Holocaust in the USSR says that in January 1944, Zorin's family camp, known as "Section 106," had 556 members, about 400 of them escapees from Minsk. Of them, 137 formed two combat units. There were about 150 children in the camp, mostly orphans. Seventy of them were in a school, the only one in the Naliboki Forest. The Zorin group was distinguished by its medical services, rendered to partisans from various groups and to the local population, led by Rozalia Livshitz, who had been an instructor at the Minsk Medical Institute (Al'tman 2011, 337).

8. A similar but even more cynical "test" is reported by Grigorii Isers, March 2, 2009, http://iremember.ru/partizani/isers-grigoriy-izrailevich.html, summary by Julia Bernstein, January 17, 2012.

9. Platon's real name was Vasily Yefimovich Chernyshev. See United States Holocaust Memorial Museum, "The Bielski Partisans," Holocaust Encyclopedia, accessed April 17, 2022, http://www.ushmm.org/wlc/en/article.php?ModuleId=10007563. Some former partisans say that Platon's wife was Jewish. See, for example, Abram Izikson, interviewed on December 25, 1997, New Britain, CT, Visual History of the Shoah, ID 37207, summary by Julia Bernstein, September 6, 2011.

10. Compare the works of Hersh (Girsh) Smolar (Smoliar) on the Minsk ghetto and Jewish resistance. Smolar was an activist in the Jewish Sections of the Soviet Communist Party (Evsektsii) before the war and was the editor of the Yiddish newspaper *Folksshtimme* in Warsaw after it, as well as the most important political leader in the Yiddish-speaking groups of the Polish United Workers Party. He writes that in 1944 he was motivated to write about the Minsk ghetto, partly because of the "general refusal of the central authorities of the Communist Party and Soviet government in Belorussia to pay any attention to anything to do with Jews under German occupation. . . . It is obvious that in those conditions I could not tell the whole truth . . . [partly because of] manifestations of anti-Semitism among the partisans" (Smolar 1984, 8).

11. The same accusation was hurled at Gurevich by the Cherkessovtsy unit.

12. Interview with Yakov Shepetinskii, February 12, 2008, http://www.iremember.ru/partizani/shepetinskiy-yakov-isaakovich.html, summary by Julia Bernstein, December 9, 2011.

13. Lilia Liker, interviewed on April 17, 1996, Tel Aviv, Visual History of the Shoah, ID 13684, summary by Julia Bernstein, October 24, 2011. Her story is supported by the reportage of Ella Maksimova, "Zhil li pravednik po pravde," *Izvestiia*, March 1, 1995. I am grateful to Rita Margolina, formerly of Yad Vashem, for bringing this article to my attention.

14. Yakov Shepetinskii claims that Bobkov, commander of the Fifty-Third Partisan Group, shot his father and uncle, Isaak and Samuil Shepetinskii. Interview with Shepetinskii, February 12, 2008.

15. Interview with Mikhail (Elimelech) Melamed, December 7, 2010, http://iremember.ru/partizani/melamed-mikhail-elimelekh-aleksandrovich.html, summary by Julia Bernstein, January 31, 2012.

16. Izikson interview.

17. United Raion Center Ivenets, Order to the Stalin-Partisan Brigade, No. 0048, June 3, 1943, F. 1329, op. 1, d. 35, ll. 8–9, in Musiał (2009), 191.

15. THE INTERNATIONAL RELATIONS OF HOLOCAUST MEMORY

1. The law was amended in June 2018 to make the offense civil and not criminal.

Notes on Contributors

Robert Braun is assistant professor of sociology at the University of California, Berkeley. He received his PhD from Cornell University in 2017. Before joining Berkeley, he taught sociology and political science at Northwestern University. His research focuses on civil society and intergroup relationships in times of social upheaval and has been published in the *American Journal of Sociology* and the *American Political Science Review*. His first book, *Protectors of Pluralism*, explains why some local communities step up to protect victims of mass persecution while others refrain from doing so. His second book, *Blood Lines*, will trace the roots of racial antisemitism by studying the geographical spread of xenophobic themes in children's stories throughout twentieth-century Germany.

Jan Burzlaff is the William A. Ackman Fellow for Holocaust Studies at Harvard University. A graduate of the École Normale Supérieure, Paris, and the 2016–17 Jane Eliza Procter Fellow at Princeton University, Burzlaff's recent publications include "Icons, Trodden Sand, and the Violence of the Gaze: Looking at the Holocaust"; "When the Fires Were Lit: Anti-Jewish Violence in Eastern Europe, 1917–45"; and "Confronting the Communal Grave: A Reassessment of Social Relations during the Holocaust in Eastern Europe." His dissertation is a transnational history of Jewish survival during the Holocaust, with additional interests in visual and spatial histories, comparative genocide, and violence in the modern era and on a global scale.

Volha Charnysh is assistant professor in the Department of Political Science at the Massachusetts Institute of Technology. With a 2017 PhD in government from Harvard University, in 2017–18, she was a fellow at the Niehaus Center for Globalization and Governance at Princeton University's Woodrow Wilson School of Public and International Affairs. Her book, *Uprooted: How Post-WWII Population Transfers Remade Europe*, examines the long-run effects of forced migration in the aftermath of World War II in Poland and West Germany, synthesizing several decades of microlevel data. The project is based on her PhD dissertation and was awarded the 2018 Ernst B. Haas Best Dissertation Prize by the APSA European Politics and Society Section and the Best Dissertation Prize by the APSA Migration and Citizenship Section. Her other ongoing work examines the politics of authoritarian regimes, the effects of wartime property transfers, and generational transmission of political attitudes and behavior. Her articles have appeared in the *American Political Science Review*, the *British Journal of Political Science*, *World Politics*, *Comparative Political Studies*, and other outlets.

Rachel L. Einwohner is professor of sociology at Purdue University. She received her PhD in sociology at the University of Washington in Seattle in 1997. Her research focuses on the dynamics of protest and resistance, and her interests include questions related to protest effectiveness, the role of gender and other identities in protest dynamics, and mobilization under repressive conditions. She has explored these topics within a diverse set of movements and protests, including the US animal rights movement, the college-based antisweatshop movement, and Jewish resistance during the Holocaust. Her published work has appeared in the *American Sociological Review*, the *American Journal of Sociology*, *Social Problems*, *Mobilization*, and other outlets. Her book, *Hope and Honor: Jewish Resistance during the Holocaust*, examines the efforts to create resistance movements in the Jewish ghettos of Nazi-occupied Warsaw, Vilna, and Łódź during World War II. She is also the coeditor (along with Jo Reger and Daniel J. Myers) of *Identity Work in Social Movements*.

Eugene Finkel is associate professor of international affairs at the Johns Hopkins University School of Advanced International Studies (SAIS). He received his PhD at the University of Wisconsin–Madison. His research focuses on how individuals, institutions, and societies respond to extreme situations: violence, state collapse, and rapid change. Finkel's first book, *Ordinary Jews: Choice and Survival during the Holocaust*, analyzes how Soviet and Polish Jews chose their survival strategies under the Nazi occupation. His second book, *Reform and Rebellion in Weak States*, coauthored with Scott Gehlbach, uses economic theory and historical case studies to explain why, in weak states, reforms often provoke rebellion. His articles have appeared in the *American Political Science Review*, the *Journal of Politics*, *Comparative Political Studies*, *Comparative Politics*, *East European Politics and Societies*, the *Slavic Review*, *Democratization*, and several other journals and edited volumes.

Zvi Gitelman is professor emeritus of political science and Preston Tisch Professor Emeritus of Judaic Studies at the University of Michigan. He has written or edited nineteen books and many articles on Soviet, East European, and Israeli politics. They include *Jewish Identities in Postcommunist Russia and Ukraine: An Uncertain Ethnicity*, and *The New Jewish Diaspora: Russian-Speaking Immigrants in the United States, Israel, and Germany*. Gitelman's current research is on World

War II and the Holocaust in the Soviet Union, and on the politics of history in the former socialist states.

Charles King is professor of international affairs and government at Georgetown University. His research has focused on nationalism, ethnic politics, transitions from authoritarianism, urban history, and the relationship between history and the social sciences. He is the author or editor of eight books, including the *New York Times*–bestselling *Gods of the Upper Air: How a Circle of Renegade Anthropologists Reinvented Race, Sex, and Gender in the Twentieth Century*, *Midnight at the Pera Palace: The Birth of Modern Istanbul*, and *Odessa: Genius and Death in a City of Dreams*, which received a National Jewish Book Award. King's articles have appeared in scholarly journals such as *World Politics* and *Slavic Review* and in public outlets including the *New York Times*, the *Washington Post*, and *Foreign Affairs*.

Jeffrey S. Kopstein is professor of political science at the University of California, Irvine. His research focuses on interethnic violence, voting patterns of minority groups, and antiliberal tendencies in civil society, paying special attention to cases within European and Russian Jewish history. These interests are central topics in his latest book (with Jason Wittenberg), *Intimate Violence: Anti-Jewish Pogroms on the Eve of the Holocaust*, which received the 2019 Bronislaw Malinowski Award in the Social Sciences, given by the Polish Institute for Arts and Sciences of America. His articles have appeared in *World Politics*, the *Journal of Politics*, *Political Theory*, *Comparative Political Studies*, *Slavic Review*, and other journals and edited volumes. In 2021–22 he was the Ina Levine Invitational Scholar at the United States Holocaust Memorial Museum.

Stephan Lehnstaedt is professor of Holocaust studies and Jewish studies at Touro College Berlin. He has lectured at LMU Munich, HU Berlin, and the London School of Economics, and was a research associate at the German Historical Institute Warsaw from 2010 to 2016. In 2015 he received the "Powstanie w Getcie Warszawskim" (Uprising in the Warsaw ghetto) medal from the Polish Association of Jewish Fighters during World War II. Among his books are *Der Kern des Holocaust: Bełżec, Sobibór, Treblinka und die Aktion Reinhardt*, and *Occupation in the East: The Daily Lives of German Occupiers in Warsaw and Minsk, 1939–1944*.

Aliza Luft is assistant professor of sociology at the University of California, Los Angeles. Her research and teaching interests include political sociology, war and violence, social boundary processes, and cognition. Her empirical work, based in Rwanda, France, Israel, and the United States, is comparative-historical, qualitative, and quantitative. In various projects, she studies how formal institutions, social affiliations, and individual desires interact and bear on decision-making in times of war.

Benjamin Mishkin is a doctoral candidate in the Department of Government at Georgetown University, where he studies US civil-military relations.

Andrew J. Simpkin is a lecturer in statistics at NUI Galway, where he specializes in applied statistics and data science. His research focuses on longitudinal data analysis, functional data analysis, genomics, and data science. He is involved in many interdisciplinary projects across medicine, engineering, biology, sociology, and sports science, and has spent time researching at the University of Canterbury (New Zealand), the University of Bristol (UK), and Columbia University (US).

Daniel Solomon is a PhD candidate in the Department of Government at Georgetown University. His dissertation research focuses on the determinants of pogrom violence in Nazi Germany, the United States, and the United Kingdom. In addition to his PhD work, he is an associate research fellow at the US Holocaust Memorial Museum's Simon-Skjodt Center for the Prevention of Genocide, where he previously worked as a research assistant, and an affiliated scholar at the International Justice Lab at the College of William & Mary. His research has been published in *Comparative Politics* and *Genocide Studies and Prevention*.

Lewi Stone works at the interface of mathematics, biology, and epidemiology. Having trained in mathematics and physics at Monash University, with a PhD focusing on biological modeling, Stone gained postdoctoral experience at the University of Melbourne and the Weizmann Institute, followed by more than twenty years at Tel Aviv University, as professor and director of a biomathematical unit. His recent work is highly interdisciplinary, and deals with explaining population demography and epidemiology during the Holocaust.

Jelena Subotić is professor in the Department of Political Science at Georgia State University. She received her PhD from the University of Wisconsin–Madison. Her most recent book, *Yellow Star, Red Star: Holocaust Remembrance after Communism*, won the 2020 Joseph Rothschild Prize in Nationalism and Ethnic Studies, the American Political Science Association's 2020 European Politics and Society Book Prize and 2020 Robert L. Jervis and Paul W. Schroeder Award for the best book on international history and politics, and honorable mention for the 2020 Barbara Heldt Prize, for the best book by a woman in any area of Slavic/East European/Eurasian Studies. Her first book, *Hijacked Justice:*

Dealing with the Past in the Balkans, was translated and published in Serbia. Her research has appeared in numerous journals, including *International Studies Quarterly*, the *European Journal of International Relations*, the *Journal of Peace Research*, and *Foreign Policy Analysis*.

Peter Tammes is currently an honorary senior research associate in primary health care in the population health sciences at Bristol Medical School, and a senior research officer at the Office for National Statistics (UK). He received his PhD from the Department of Sociology at the Radboud University Nijmegen, and his dissertation on the Holocaust was awarded the Praemium Erasmianum Foundation's Research Prize. This and follow-up research on the Holocaust focused on differences in survival chances of Jews in the Netherlands related to individual characteristics and contextual factors, using original registration lists of Jewish inhabitants in 1941–42, post–World War II victimization lists and other administrative sources. The findings have been published in several journals, including *Social Science History*, the *Journal of Interdisciplinary History*, the *European Journal of Population*, the *International Journal of Epidemiology*, and the *American Journal of Epidemiology*. He also published a booklet on the Jews of his home village (Bergen, the Netherlands) during World War II. A prestigious Veni grant from the Dutch Research Council allowed him to study assimilation trajectories of Jews in pre–World War II Dutch society.

Susan Welch was professor of political science at Penn State University. The author of seven books and nearly two hundred articles focusing on issues of gender and race, her recent publications examined gender, survival, and the Holocaust, focusing on transports from Western Europe to the East. She also wrote on Americans' attitudes toward Nazis and Jews during the Nazi era and Americans' knowledge of the Holocaust during World War II and subsequently. Her unfinished book was titled *The Hunted: World War II through the Experiences of 20 European Jews*.

Daniel Ziblatt is the Eaton Professor of the Science of Government at Harvard University and director of the Transformations of Democracy research unit at the WZB Berlin (Social Science Center Berlin). He earned a PhD in political science from the University of California, Berkeley, in 2003. He is a specialist on challenges to democracy, and his 2018 book, *How Democracies Die* (coauthored with Steven Levitsky), has won substantial acclaim and several prizes. His previous book, *Conservative Parties and the Birth of Democracy*, won the American Political Science Association's 2018 Woodrow Wilson Prize for the best book in government and international relations and the American Sociological Association's 2018 Barrington Moore Prize.

Index

Abramson, Lidia (Itke Brown), 275
Adler, Stanisław, 172–73, 196
Adorno, Theodoro, *The Authoritarian Personality*, 4
Aftershocks (Gunitsky), 302–3
age, as survivorship factor, 188–89, 220–23, 232–33, 234–35, 236
Agrippa (Jewish king), 116, 117
Akiba (Zionist movement), 96–97
Aktionen (actions), 27–28, 91, 92, 93, 94–95
Alexandria (Egypt), violence in, 106, 116–17
Algemeen politieblad, 183
alliances, 40–41, 45, 200–221
American Political Science Association, 6, 7
antisemitism
    and Catholic officials, 197–98
    comparisons of, 111–15, 118, 119
    disease encouraging, 161–63, 307n11
    as field of study, 3–8, 307n11
    memory affecting, 246–47, 248, 249–50, 288
    and mythology, 274–78
    and pogroms, 72–73, 74, 77, 80, 309n7
    in political science research, 21–22, 30, 33, 38–39
    radio communication affecting, 309n7
    in social science research, 56, 60
    study methods for, 141–48, 254–55
    study results for, 148–55, 256–63
    xenophobia encouraging, 139–40
Arendt, Hannah, 25
Ariadna (online platform), 251–52
armbands, symbolism of, 113, 127–28, 134
Astrometskaya, Faina, 273
Atlas Der Deutschen Volkskunde (Mannhardt), 142–43, 310n3
atrocities, commemorating
    effects of, 245–48
    study methods for, 251–54
    study results for, 254–63
Auerswald, Heinz, 171
Auschwitz, 27, 212, 213–14, 217, 219–23
Austro-Hungarian Empire, 90, 99
authoritarianism
    in Germany, 155
    of individuals, 4
    legitimation of, 201
    in Lithuanian politics, 125, 130
    micro-level study of, 298
    in Polish politics, 130–31
    rise of, 208
    as root of violence, 133–34
    of Vichy regime, 196, 198
The Authoritarian Personality (Adorno, et. al.), 4

Babi Yar massacre, 35–36
Barasz, Ephraim, 94
Bauminger, Heszek, 96
Beaussart, Roger, 204
Belarus and Belarusians, 269–71, 274–77, 279
Bérard, Léon, 203
Berg, Mary, 173
    The Diary of Mary Berg, 307n10
Berger, Ronald, 181
Beth Ashkenaz Synagogue Memorial Project, 75
Białystok, 89, 90
Białystok ghetto, 88, 91–92, 94–95, 97–98, 99–100, 101–2
bias, in research, 227–28, 239–40
Bieberstein, Mark, 93
Bielski brothers, 43, 273
bishops, Catholic, 197–98, 201–8
Bloodlands (Snyder), 59
Bobelis, Kazys, 129
Bobkov, Commander, 277, 318n14
bogeymen, Jewish, 60, 140, 142–45, 148–54, 155, 300
border regions, 144, 146–48, 151, 152, 155
Bosnia and Herzegovina massacre (1995), 247, 253, 255, 262
Bourdieu, Pierre, 199–201, 208, 312n7
Boyarski, Khone, 127–28
Brown, Itke (Lidia Abramson), 275
Browning, Christopher, 26, 30
    Ordinary Men, 7

Calenescu, Armand, 303
camp system, 27, 58, 180, 191–93, 218, 314n3.
    See also family camps

325

capital
  political, 198, 199–201, 208
  social, 200
  symbolic, 198, 199–201, 206, 208
Catholic Church
  conversions to, 183
  and Jews, 142, 146, 202–8
  study methods for actions of, 201–2
  study results for actions of, 202–8
  and Vichy government, 197–98
causality, 32–33, 36, 74, 180, 298
children
  in camps, 219–21, 272, 273, 317n7
  and disciplinary folktales, 140, 142–43
  and disease, 173
  in memory, 235–36, 261, 262
  at transport destinations, 213, 315n18
Cholavski, Shalom, 270
Chollet, Jean, 203
Christians and Christianity, 118–19, 183, 246, 250. *See also* Catholic Church
chronology, in social research, 33–34
Claudius, 117
cognitive dissonance, 248–49
Cole, Tim, *Geographies of the Holocaust*, 12
collaboration and collaborators
  consequences of, 14
  encouragement of, 196–97, 204
  political aspects of, 125–26, 132–33
  representations of, 270–71
  as survival strategy, 88–89, 92–96, 98
  as understudied area, 38
commemoration, 245–46, 251, 257, 289
Communists
  German, 76
  inaction by, 317n10
  Jewish, 92
  and Kristallnacht, 78
  misrepresentation by, 275
  in post-Communist era, 286–92
  resistance by, 95–98
  in study data, 146–47
  as target, 107
Comparative Studies in Society and History, 53
contingency, in social research, 32
conversions, religious, 118, 119, 183
cooperation, 37–40, 88–89, 92–96, 98, 179, 203–5
coping, as Jewish strategy, 89, 98–102, 179
Council of the Association of French Rabbis, 203
COVID-19, 173–74

Cyganeria bombing (1942), 97
Czerniaków, Adam, 166

Danilochkin, Piotr, 317n4
decision-making, 234, 236–37, 240
democracy, 16–17, 301–5
denial theories, 56–57, 267–69
deportation
  and health policies, 162–63, 170–71
  from the Netherlands, 177–81, 182–92
  rates of, 198
  remembrance of, 291
  transport for, 211–19, 223
  to Treblinka, 174
Desbois, Patrick, 27
The Destruction of the European Jews (Hilberg), 4, 25–26
destructiveness, human, 301–4
The Diary of Mary Berg, 307n10
disaggregation, 26–28, 298, 300–301
diseases, 161–64, 173–74, 272, 307n11. *See also* typhus
DNVP (German National Peoples' Party), 77, 309n7
Duda, Andrzej, 247, 251

Eastern Galicia, 109, 111, 112–13, 246, 250
Einsatzgruppen, 29–30, 105, 107, 114, 270. *See also* SS
Epstein, Barbara, 275
ethnocentrism, 247, 254–55, 256
ethnonationalism, 73, 77, 247
European Union, 28, 287, 288
evasion, as survival strategy, 36, 88–89, 98–102, 178, 180–83, 188

family camps, 274, 276–77, 317n7
farm (Kopaliny), 97
fascism, 112, 131–32, 290, 304
Fighting Organization of the Jewish Halutz Youth, 96–97
Final Solution, 26, 27, 33, 40–42
Finkel, Eugene, 43, 56
  Ordinary Jews, 61
Flaccus, Governor, 116
folklore, 140, 142–43, 148
France, 28, 196. *See also* Vichy regime
Frank, Anne, 25
Frenkel-Brunswik, Else, *The Authoritarian Personality*, 4
functionalists, 32, 307n5

Gaius, 116
Galdikauskas, Adolfas, 132–33
gender, as survivorship factor, 188–89, 211, 213–14, 217–24, 232–33, 235–36
genocide. *See also* mass killing; mass violence
  in foreign relations, 41
  and Holocaust, 1, 8–10, 87–88, 308n14
  as international concern, 283–84
  as state policy, 34
  as study area, 22, 58, 60–61
  women in, 223
Geographies of the Holocaust (Knowles, Cole, and Giordano), 12
Gerlach, Christian, 41
Gerlier, Cardinal, 202–5, 206
German Communist Party (KPD), 76
German National Peoples' Party (DNVP), 77, 309n7
Germany. *See also* Weimar Republic
  in historical studies, 11, 25–26, 155, 299, 303–4
  memory in, 249, 284
  in World War I, 162
  in World War II, 33–34, 39–41
ghettos, 162–63, 212–14, 218. *See also* Białystok ghetto; Kraków ghetto; Minsk ghetto; Vilna ghetto; Warsaw ghetto
Giordano, Alberto, *Geographies of the Holocaust*, 12
Goebbels, Joseph, 69
Goldhagen, Daniel Jonah, 56
  Hitler's Willing Executioners, 6, 33
Goldstein, Bernard, 170, 173
Göring, Hermann, 162
Grosman, Chajka, 97–98
Gross, Jan, 55, 56
  Neighbors, 6, 29, 250
Gunitsky, Seva, *Aftershocks*, 302–3
Gurevich, Zalmen, 274
Gypsies, 26, 30, 31

Hagen, Wilhelm, 165
hatred, 73, 154–55
Health Council, Jewish, 167–68, 169, 171, 174, 175
Hehalutz Halochem (HH), 96–97, 98
Helbronner, Jacques, 202, 204–5
Heydrich, Reinhard, 107, 162, 314n2
HH (Hehalutz Halochem), 96–97, 98
Hilberg, Raul, 5–6, 7–8, 32–33, 55, 211, 308n14
  The Destruction of the European Jews, 4, 25–26

Himmler, Heinrich, 126–27
Hirszfeld, Ludwik, 163, 167–70
Historikerstreit, 55
History & Memory, 55
History as Social Science, 57
Hitler, Adolph, *Mein Kampf*, 161–62
Hitler's Willing Executioners (Goldhagen), 6, 33
Holocaust (miniseries), 4
Holocaust, significance of, 1, 44–47, 119–20, 299–300
Horthy, Miklós, 291, 303
hospitals, 164–65, 167
House of Terror museum, 290–91
Hungary, 28, 30, 40, 290–91

identity, 39, 44–45, 99–100, 260, 281–86, 292
immigrants
  survival of, about, 177–78
  survival of, study methods for, 178–88
  survival of, study results for, 188–93
In Flaccum (Philo), 116
in-group, 248–49, 259
intentionalists, 32, 307n5
international relations, 40, 154, 283–86, 289–92
In the Name of the People (museum exhibit), 290
IR (international relations). *See* international relations
Iron Wolf, 129, 131–32
Iskra, 96, 97, 98
Israelski, Pola, 229
Italy, 37
Iwinski family, 273

Jedwabne Pogrom, 6, 29, 105, 246–48, 250–51
Jewish Council. *See* Judenrat (Jewish Council)
Jewish Police (Ordnungsdienst), 92–95
Jewry in Eastern European Space (Seraphim), 162
Jews
  attitudes toward, 140–42, 146–49, 151–56
  in historical perspective, 56, 58–62
  in memory, 246–51, 254–61, 287–92
  misrepresentation of, 267–68, 270, 273–78
  pogrom violence against, early, 114–20
  pogrom violence against, recent, 104–14, 124–25, 126–30, 132–33
  post-Holocaust, 2, 5–6
  survival, study methods for, 177–88, 216–17
  survival, study results for, 188–93, 217–22
  survival strategies of, 89–93, 95–102
  transport of, 211–14

Jews (continued)
    treatment of varying, 12–13, 27–28, 36–37, 196–99, 202–8
    and typhus, 161–63, 167–68, 172, 174–75
Joan of Arc, 206–7
Joods Monument documents, 216
Journal des debats, 206
Judenrat (Jewish Council)
    as collaborators, 92–94
    data sources from, 181, 182, 183–84, 185
    and deportations, 180–81
    representation on, 90
    and typhus, 165–68, 170–71, 173

Kalinin group, 273
Kaplan, Chaim, 164, 173
Kinderschreck, 140, 142–44, 152
King, Charles, 14, 54, 120, 299
Klarsfeld, Serge, 216
Klor, Boris, 238, 240
Knowles, Anne Kelly, *Geographies of the Holocaust*, 12
Kogan, Eugene, *The Theory and Practice of Hell*, 3–4
Kopstein, Jeffrey S., 72, 90, 106, 300, 302
Korzh, Vasil Zakharovich "Komarov," 277
Kovno ghetto, 167
KPD (German Communist Party), 76
Kraków, 89, 90
Kraków ghetto, 88, 91, 93, 96, 98, 99–100, 101
Kristallnacht
    about, 69–70
    factors leading to, 180, 309n2
    study methods for, 74–78, 309n4
    study results for, 78–84
Kühl, Stefan, *Ordinary Organizations*, 55–56
Kutorgiene, Helena Buivodaite, 127

LAF (Lithuanian Activists' Front), 124, 132–33
The Last Days of Hitler (Trevor-Roper), 25
Law and Justice (PiS) party, 251, 286
Lenski, Mordechai, 165, 169
Le Roy Ladurie, Emmanuel, 53
Levi, Israël, 203
Levinson, Daniel, *The Authoritarian Personality*, 4
Liber, Sol, 226–27, 229, 234–36
lice, 160, 173
Lietukis Garage massacre, 128
life course approach, 177–81, 192–93
Liker, Lilia Bliumenfeld, 276
Lithuania
    misrepresentations of, 269
    political situation in, 125, 130–35
    violence in, 104–5, 124–25, 126–30, 310n4
Lithuanian Activists' Front (LAF), 124, 132–33
Lithuanian Nationalists Union (LNU), 125, 130
Łódź, Poland, 31
Łódź ghetto, 213–14
Lukashenko, Alexander, 270

Mannhardt, Wilhelm, *Atlas Der Deutschen Volkskunde*, 142–43, 310n3
marriages, mixed, 183
Martiniuk, Nikolai Ivanovich, 272
mass killing, 8, 27–28, 34–42, 42–47, 134, 284. *See also* genocide
mass violence, 24–25, 37–40, 44–47, 125, 128–30, 132–35, 247–48. *See also* genocide
Mein Kampf (Hitler), 161–62
Melamed, Fima, 277
Melamed, Mikhail, 277
memorialization, 245, 291–92
memory
    appropriation of, 56–57
    and international relations studies, 283–86
    in post-Communist era, 286–92
    study methods for, 251–55
    study results for, 255–60
men, at transport destinations, 213, 219–22, 315n18
men, in memory, 261–62
migration and migrants, 72, 218. *See also* immigrants
Milgram, Stanley, 6–7
minorities, attitudes toward
    study methods for, 251–55
    study results for, 255–60
Minsk, 89, 90
Minsk ghetto, 88, 91, 92–93, 95–96, 98, 99–101, 317n10
Mire, Gola, 96
misrecognition, 200, 201
Mushkin, Il'ia, 92
myths, and antisemitism, 274–78
myths, and history, 278–80
myths, of nationhood, 267–71, 291

narcissism, collective, 255, 256, 259
narrative, 181, 246, 247–48, 249, 252–60, 287–88
National Day of Remembrance of Victims of Genocide, 247, 251
nationalism. *See also* ethnonationalism
    and antisemitism, 111
    causes of, 140, 154–55
    civic, 312n1

ethnic, 312n1
exclusive, 139
in Lithuanian politics, 125, 131–32
in memory, 246–47, 250–51, 292
in pogroms, 111–14
pre-World War II, 38–39
National Revolution, 196, 198, 199, 207, 312n1, 312n7
Nazis
cooperation with, 92–93, 196–97, 204
Dutch response to, 177–81, 183–84, 188
misrepresentation of, 268, 288
New Order of, 13–14, 40
political alliances of, 132, 267–68
in political science research, 32–34
resistance to, 95–97
in social science research, 2–4, 6, 10
during typhus epidemic, 167, 174
violence encouraged by, 80, 81, 107, 126
Neighbors (Gross), 6, 29, 250
Netherlands, Jews in
study methods for, 178–88
study results for, 188–93
Neumann, Franz, 5–6
Nicolle, Charles, 161
NKVD (People's Commissariat for Internal Affairs), 105–6, 110–11, 114, 251
non-Jews, 31, 59, 116, 126–30, 288
nonresisters, 230, 231–32, 234, 236–37
non-survival, of Holocaust
about, 227–28
study methods for, 228–34
study results for, 234–40
normalized violence
about, 197–201
study methods for, 201–2
study results for, 202–8

occupation, military, 24, 28, 31, 35–37, 43–44, 54
Operation Reinhard, 212, 219, 314n3
Orbán, Viktor, 291
Ordinary Jews (Finkel), 61
Ordinary Men (Browning), 7
Ordinary Organizations (Kühl), 55–56
Ordnungsdienst (Jewish Police), 92–95
OUN (Organization of Ukrainian Nationalists), 30, 106, 112–14, 116, 250
out-group, 248–49

partisans
in Belarus, about, 271–80
in Belarus, misrepresented, 269–71
violence by, 126–28

Penson, Jakub, 164–65
People's Commissariat for Internal Affairs (NKVD), 105–6, 110–11, 114, 251
perpetrators
about, 300
identity of, 127–28
in memory, 245, 248–51, 255–61
mind of, 25
overemphasis on, 87–88
and victims, 28–31
Pétain, Phillipe, 196–97, 198, 202, 204–7, 313n22
Philo, *In Flaccum*, 116–17
Picciotto, Liliana, 216
Piguet, Bishop, 202, 207
Piłsudski, Józef, 130–31
PiS (Law and Justice) party, 251, 286
Platon, Comrade, 275, 278, 317n9
pluralism, 74, 77, 147, 255, 259
pogrom (Alexandria, 38 CE), 106, 116–17
pogrom (Valencia, 1391), 106, 118–19
pogrom (word), 9, 70, 114, 116, 134
pogroms. *See also* Kristallnacht
about, 69–70
civilian participation in, 124, 126, 128–30, 132–33, 310n3
in memory, 246, 250
pogroms (Western Ukraine, 1941)
about, 8–9, 104–7
participants in, 106–14
political aspects of, 114–15
pogrom violence
about, 69–74
external forces, 106–11
local forces, 111–16
political aspects of, 114–20
study methods for, 74–78, 309n7
study results for, 78–82
Poland
Holocaust memories in, 246–48, 251–56, 259–61
interwar, 90, 92–93, 97–102, 130–35
misrepresentation by, 289–90
Soviet occupation of, 108–10
and Ukraine, 111–12
violence against Jews in, 105
and World War II, 29, 124, 249–51
Pronyagin, Pavel Vasil'evich, 276–77

racism, 24, 26, 39, 72, 161, 284
radio and radio signals, 77, 309n7
Radio Maryja, 251
Redlich, Shimon, 108

Reivytis, Vladas, 129
religion, 101, 108. *See also* Catholic Church; Christians and Christianity
remembrance, 245–48, 259, 285–86, 292
resistance and resisters
  as Jewish strategy, 88–89, 90, 95–99, 300
  and rescue, 42–47
  testimony from, about, 228–34
  testimony from, of nonsurvivors, 235–40
  testimony from, of survivors, 235–40
Ricerca della Fondazione Centro di Documentazione Ebraica Contemporanea, 216
Ringelblum, Emmanuel, 165, 169
The Rise and Fall of the Third Reich (Shirer), 25
Rivin, Grigory, 277–78
Romania, 30, 38, 40, 42, 303
Rosenberg, Sol, 236, 237–38
Rosenmann, Gedaliah, 94
Rosenzweig, Artur, 93
Russia, 13, 267, 304
Russian Empire, 90, 100

Sanford, Nevitt, *The Authoritarian Personality*, 4
Sauret, Pierre, 205
Schindler's List (film), 5
Schwartz, Isaïe, 203, 205–6
Secret Union of Officers (SUO), 131–32
Seraphim, Peter-Heinz, *Jewry in Eastern European Space*, 162
Shepetinskii, Yakov, 276, 318n14
Shirer, William, *The Rise and Fall of the Third Reich*, 25
Shoah (film), 5, 25
slave labor, 212, 219–20, 289
Šlepetys, Jonas, 129
Smetona, Antanas, 125, 129, 130–32, 133
Smolar, Hersh, 95, 317n10
Snyder, Timothy, 27, 109
  Bloodlands, 59
social science research
  and ethics, 239–40
  and history, 53–62
  Holocaust overlooked by, 2–8
  Holocaust unique to, 9–11
  importance of, 11–14, 17
Sophie's Choice (film), 5
Soviet Union
  Jewish integration in, 90
  and Jewish resistance, 43–44, 92–93, 96–98
  in Lithuania, 132
  misrepresentation by, 268, 270–71
  Nazism and, 119
  and violence, 26–27, 35–36, 38–39, 60, 105–6, 107–11, 246
  in World War II, 29–30, 31
Spain, Jews in, 118
Special Operations Unit, 92
Sperre (deportation exemption), 180–81, 183–84, 185, 186, 189
Spira, Symche, 93
SS, 27, 30, 36, 129, 162, 219. *See also* Einsatzgruppen
state identity, 281–86, 292
Statut des Juifs, 196, 198–99, 204, 205–6, 313n19
Stets'ko, Iaroslav, 112–13
Suhard, Emmanuel, 204, 205, 206, 313n22
SUO (Secret Union of Officers), 131–32
survival, of Holocaust. *See also* non-survival, of Holocaust; survival strategies
  study methods for, 178–88
  study results for, 188–93
  transport records of, 214–15, 221–23
survival strategies
  about, 88–89
  cooperation as, 92–95
  coping as, 98–102
  evasion as, 98–102
  geographical variation in, 90–92
  resistance as, 95–98
  study methods for, 89–90
symbolism, in violence, 69–70, 71, 199–200, 201, 206–7, 208
synagogues, actions against, 69–70, 75–79, 309n2, 309n5
Szyper, Henryk, 109–10

Tec, Nechama, 6, 213, 232, 273
Tenenbaum, Mordechai, 98
territorial loss
  about, 139–41
  study methods for, 141–48
  study results for, 148–55
testimony, about Holocaust
  about, 226–28
  study methods for, 228–34
  study results for, 234–40
The Theory and Practice of Hell (Kogan), 3–4
threat, economic, 139, 146
threat, geopolitical, 140, 154–55
threat, in-group, 256
threat, out-group, 255, 256
threat, political, 72, 117, 139, 146–47, 151–52, 154

threat, power, 72, 78, 106, 146
Tilly, Charles, 297
Trakinski, Simon, 236–37
transport, of victims
  about, 211–14, 314n7, 315n14
  data sources for, 214–15
  study methods for, 215–17
  study results for, 217–23, 315n18, 315n27, 316nn28–29
trauma, 245, 260, 284–85
Treaty of Versailles, 140
Treblinka (death camp), 13, 174, 212, 226, 315n23
Trevor-Roper, Hugh, *The Last Days of Hitler*, 25
truth(s), 278–79
typhus
  about, 58, 159–68
  study methods for, 168–71
  study results for, 171–75

Ukraine, 35–36, 42, 105–15, 279–80, 304
Ukrainian Insurgent Army (UPA), 250, 271, 279
Ukrainian Military Organization, 112
Ukrainian National Democratic Organization (UNDO), 111–12
Ukrainians, 29–30, 105–6, 108–15, 246–47, 249–50
USSR. *See* Soviet Union

Valencia, Spain, violence in, 106, 118–19
Valeri, Valerio, 202, 203–4
Vichy regime
  about, 196–98
  in research, 58
  study methods for, 201–2
  study results for, 202–8
victimhood, 29, 30–31, 247–50, 254, 259, 268, 287
victims
  ethnicity of, 39
  life course affecting, 177–78, 180–81, 184–85
  and memory, 245–49, 251–54, 255–56
  misrepresentations of, 290–92
  and perpetrators, 28–31
  stereotypes about, 87
  study methods for selection of, 215–17
  study results for selection of, 217–23
Vilna ghetto, 230–32, 233, 236–37, 238
Vilnius, 97–98

violence. *See* mass violence; normalized violence; pogrom violence
violence, in social science research
  and Holocaust, 17, 23, 54, 56
  need for, 1, 14–15, 58, 59–60, 300–302
visibility, attracting violence, 71, 76, 80–82
Voldemaras, Augustinas, 129, 132
Volhynia, 246–47, 250–51
Volksdeutsche, 39–40
vom Rath, Ernst, 74

Waffen-SS, 30
War and Remembrance (miniseries), 5
Warsaw, Poland, 29, 289
Warsaw ghetto
  about, 159
  formation of, 162–63
  survivor testimony from, 229–32, 234, 236–37
  typhus in, extent of, 163–66
  typhus in, fighting against, 166–75
Warsaw Ghetto Uprising, 226, 229
Warschauer Zeitung, 162
Weber, Max, 199
Weill, Julien, 204, 206
Weimar Republic, 76–78, 140, 145–47, 150–51, 161, 302
Westerbork (transit camp), 181, 182–83
Western Ukraine, 105–15
women
  in memory, 235–36, 261, 262
  misrepresentations of, 272
  in partisan camps, 273
  at transport destinations, 213, 219–23, 315n18
World War I, 147–48, 151–52, 161
World War II
  Catholic Church during, 197
  disease during, 163–64, 174
  in memory, 246–48, 249–51, 259–60
  reframing of, 269–70
  research ended by, 143
  survivor testimony from, 227, 232
  victimhood caused by, 29, 259

xenophobia
  about, 15, 16, 139–40
  study methods for, 141–48
  study results for, 151–55

Yad Vashem, 15–26, 31, 88, 214–15, 219, 222–23
Yad Vashem Transport Database, 214–15, 222–23
Yoffe, Moshe, 92
Young Lithuania, 125, 130

Zabłotniak, Ryszard, 165, 175
Zakharevich, Sergei, 270, 317n3
Zionism, 115, 249
Zionist groups, 43, 96–98, 111
Zorin, Shalom, 96, 317n7

Lightning Source UK Ltd.
Milton Keynes UK
UKHW011816141222
413936UK00004B/68